D1766046

WITHDRAWN

C 02 0419039

Angus Macdonald - last known photo

King Robert the Bruce inspired Scottish tradition
of bravery and commitment to a code of honor.

The Macdonalds of Largie

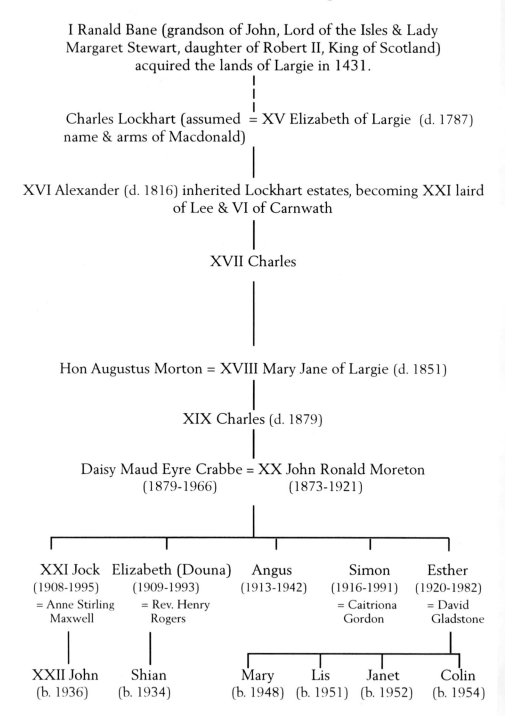

I Ranald Bane (grandson of John, Lord of the Isles & Lady Margaret Stewart, daughter of Robert II, King of Scotland) acquired the lands of Largie in 1431.

Charles Lockhart (assumed = XV Elizabeth of Largie (d. 1787) name & arms of Macdonald)

XVI Alexander (d. 1816) inherited Lockhart estates, becoming XXI laird of Lee & VI of Carnwath

XVII Charles

Hon Augustus Morton = XVIII Mary Jane of Largie (d. 1851)

XIX Charles (d. 1879)

Daisy Maud Eyre Crabbe = XX John Ronald Moreton
(1879-1966)   (1873-1921)

XXI Jock   Elizabeth (Douna)   Angus   Simon   Esther
(1908-1995)   (1909-1993)   (1913-1942)   (1916-1991)   (1920-1982)
= Anne Stirling   = Rev. Henry   = Caitriona   = David
Maxwell   Rogers   Gordon   Gladstone

XXII John   Shian   Mary   Lis   Janet   Colin
(b. 1936)   (b. 1934)   (b. 1948)   (b. 1951)   (b. 1952)   (b. 1954)

The Gladstones

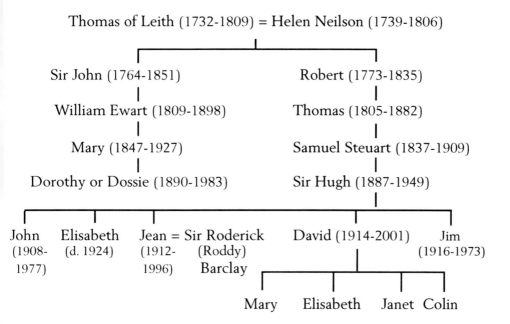

Thomas of Leith (1732-1809) = Helen Neilson (1739-1806)

Sir John (1764-1851)

William Ewart (1809-1898)

Mary (1847-1927)

Dorothy or Dossie (1890-1983)

Robert (1773-1835)

Thomas (1805-1882)

Samuel Steuart (1837-1909)

Sir Hugh (1887-1949)

John (1908-1977)   Elisabeth (d. 1924)   Jean (1912-1996) = Sir Roderick (Roddy) Barclay   David (1914-2001)   Jim (1916-1973)

Mary   Elisabeth   Janet   Colin

The Crabbes

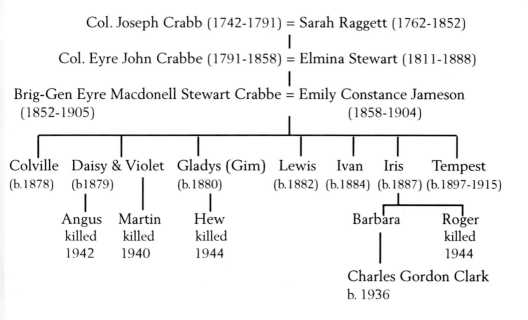

Col. Joseph Crabb (1742-1791) = Sarah Raggett (1762-1852)

Col. Eyre John Crabbe (1791-1858) = Elmina Stewart (1811-1888)

Brig-Gen Eyre Macdonell Stewart Crabbe = Emily Constance Jameson
(1852-1905)   (1858-1904)

Colville (b.1878)   Daisy & Violet (b1879)   Gladys (Gim) (b.1880)   Lewis (b.1882)   Ivan (b.1884)   Iris (b.1887)   Tempest (b.1897-1915)

Angus killed 1942   Martin killed 1940   Hew killed 1944   Barbara   Roger killed 1944

Charles Gordon Clark
b. 1936

San Francisco, Paris, Southerness, Washington, Santa Fe

LARGIE CASTLE

A RIFLED NEST

MARY GLADSTONE

firefall ᵗᵐ

For Julia

who accompanied me on my travels to South-East Asia
in search of her great-uncle, Angus. Adding humour and
determination to the quest, she put up with mild food
poisoning, heat stroke, mosquito bites and even the
fear of being captured by pirates in the Indian Ocean!

WEST
DUNBARTONSHIRE
LIBRARIES

PRICE	SUPPLIER
£12,08	A2
LOCATION	CLASS
DP	728.81
INVOICE DATE	
28/4/17	
CESSION NUMBER	

First Edition: March 2017

hardcover: 9781939434302
paper: 9781939434821
ebook: 9781939434708

© 2017 Mary Gladstone, all rights reserved.
No part of this book may be used or reproduced
in any manner whatsoever without specific written
permission, except in the case of brief quotations
embodied in critical articles and reviews.

Cover: Largie Castle, painter unknown;
 in the possession of Sir John Maxwell Macdonald Bt

Design & Editorial
Elihu Blotnick

FIREFALL EDITIONS
literary@att.net
Canyon, California 94516-0001
Galloway, Scotland DG9 9PU

www.firefallmedia.com

THE HIGHLAND SEA [tm]

A FIREFALL ORIGINAL SERIES

Non-fiction Narratives
by Mary Gladstone

Largie Castle, a rifled nest
a search for self and family
1 (2017)

Glengarry Dragons
2 (2017)

Inheritance
The Moss of Cree
growing up in Scotland
3 (2018)

British spelling, punctuation and grammar, plus author
idiosyncracies are maintained throughout the series.

Introduction

Angus Macdonald (Argylls Museum)

MY PARENTS' FAMILIES were surprisingly similar: both grandfathers were Scots, one from the Highlands, the other from the Lowlands. Born in the 1870s, each man owned a country estate and lived in a Scottish baronial mansion or castle, built in the mid nineteenth century. After leaving Eton, grandfathers John Moreton Macdonald matriculated at Magdalen College, Oxford and Hugh Gladstone at Trinity College, Cambridge. Marrying within twelve months of each other (April 1906 and January 1907), they chose brides from south-east England's Home Counties; John's Daisy came from Hampshire and Cecil from Hertfordshire.

The firstborns of each family arrived in January 1908, the Highland family naming their boy Jock and the Gladstone baby, John. Each couple added two more boys and a pair of girls to their brood. My father was the Gladstone's second son and fourth child; my mother was the Macdonald's fifth and youngest. Sadly, both sets of grandparents lost one of their children: when Elisabeth Gladstone was fifteen she fell ill from meningitis and died.

Although the Macdonald fledglings survived childhood, their luck ran out after they came of age. When war was declared in 1939 all six boys (now young men) from the two families entered the armed services to fight for their King and country against Hitler and the Axis countries. Angus, the Macdonalds' second son was the only member of either family to become a professional soldier, serving as a commissioned officer in the regular army. He joined the Argyll & Sutherland Highlanders, and travelled with his battalion to Malaya. In December 1941 when the Japanese invaded, he took part in the peninsula's defence. Two days before the Fall of Singapore (15 February 1942), my uncle was ordered to escape to Sumatra where he boarded a ship bound for Ceylon. Two days into the voyage, a Japanese submarine torpedoed the liner, and all, except a handful of passengers and crew, perished.

While I was growing up, I knew little about Uncle Angus, who suffered from exposure and drowned in the Indian Ocean on 2nd March 1942. He was the absent one, his youthful image trapped in a black and white photo on Mummy's dressing-table in her bedroom. Standing by her jewellery box, hair brush, Kirby grips and powder compact, Angus' picture served as a shrine to her own lost youth. Because he lived longer, his name held more significance than the memory of my father's older sister. More importantly, out of her three older brothers, Angus was Mummy's favourite. He was also destined for a high social position and would inherit an ancient title, and become the 25th Lockhart laird, owner of the Lee and Carnwath property west of Edinburgh.

When I was young, I vaguely registered I was deprived of an uncle. Since Mummy told me Angus was 'lost' and not 'dead', I imagined him marooned on a desert island and one day he would find his way home. I was so convinced he was still alive that I hid in our loft and wrote him letters that began, "dere Unkel Annges..."

I may have lost Angus but I had plenty more uncles. There were six in total. Jock, my mother's oldest brother was perpetually remote, still troubled by the amputation of his right leg after stepping on a land mine in northern France in 1940. Simon was my mother's least favoured sibling so we seldom saw him. On the Gladstone side was Jim, my father's younger brother. Dad zealously guarded their close relationship from his children, so this uncle also became a distant figure. John, the eldest Gladstone, lofty in height and in attitude, was overbearing to the young. Of the uncles 'by marriage', Henry, spouse of Mummy's sister was, if not avuncular, a conscientious, advisory figure. Perhaps his role as a clergyman encouraged it. The other was Roddy who was very posh. He drove a Jag and, as British ambassador to Copenhagen, then Brussels, he even rode around in a Rolls. During his second ambassadorial posting, he had a chauffeur called Poot, who looked like Odd Job, the bodyguard of 'Goldfinger' in the James Bond film. Uncle Roddy seldom talked to anyone, least of all children.

Uncles, supposedly genial and indulgent, are different from fathers. I pictured Angus, had he been alive, as attentive, affectionate and generous. What my father failed to give, he would provide: pens, crayons, books, bicycles, skates, skis, even boats, ponies and when older, a shiny, new car. This abundance was merely a dream. Angus was permanently absent, his photo encased in a light tan leather frame and the only way I could get at it was by climbing on to a chair and peering into his image on Mummy's dressing table. He shared the frame with my grandfather, John Ronald Moreton Macdonald, both men lost to her. I liked to compare the two. Angus on the left, smiling into the camera, proud of his bushy moustache and looking far more mature than his quarter century and John, clean-shaven, Edwardian in flavour, with a stiff, round, shirt collar. I accepted these men died before their allotted span: Angus at 28 and John, 48.

Angus interested me most. He was an unknown, a tabula rasa or clean slate and, like the picture of the proverbial donkey at a fairground, I could pin a tail on to him wherever I wished. All kinds of feats, qualities and kindnesses belonged to him, as he would never have to measure up to them. Yet, surrounding his memory was hesitancy, a lack of clarity and rawness. Something connected with his death hurt my mother and even made her feel ashamed. When families keep children in the dark, they imagine the worst. What, then, was it about Angus? Was he hero, coward, monster or victim when he drowned on the night of March 2nd 1942?

My mother died in 1982, 40 years after Angus lost his life, and my father 19 years later in 2001. Following both parents' deaths I wished to know more, and it was the discovery of Angus's letters to my mother that prompted me to find out. These short documents were the nearest I could get to finding my lost uncle: one written from India in April, 1939 and the other in August 1941 from Malaya, the first in ink and the second type-written. I had to discover what actually happened to him and took up the quest.

I knew what my uncle looked like ever since I was big enough to reach up and examine his photo. I'm sure the portrait helped keep his memory alive, but Angus was out of bounds, the story of his death a no-go area. For years I thought his picture was taken somewhere on a chilly day in Scotland because he was wrapped in a hat, scarf and jacket. I now appreciate how young and hopeful he appeared standing in the shade outside a white colonnaded building in the Cameron Highlands, one of Malaya's hill-stations. There, away from the heat and crowds of his Singapore barracks he snatched a long-awaited fortnight's leave. Only recently do I realise, the felt hat protected his head from the sun, and the silk scarf helped him feel cool as did his light, linen jacket.

I look again at his snapshot, at the tree in the background, an archway on one side and balustrade on the other and realise Angus is a complete stranger. For me the picture is as distant from my own experience as the Middle ages or the court of Henry VIII might have been. Yet only seven years separate the day of my birth from that Malayan morning in August 1941 when the shutter clicked. Within that period, and especially after the end of the War, when an iron curtain descended from Stettin to Trieste, another form of partitioning occurred: a barrier between my uncle's generation and my own.

Positioning themselves behind this demarcation line, my parents seldom talked about the Second World War, but when they did it was of ration books and petrol coupons, humorous anecdotes about Italian POWs and reminiscences on war-time courage during the blitz. Those tales only partially satisfied me because they were sanitised abridgments intended for youthful palates.

Once when I was young, I attended a smart county dance where my mother's female friends arrived in swirling silk and satin while their men came in tails sporting war-time medals. Each man's lapel confirmed the generational divide: they were men and women while we, the younger generation, were boys and girls; they had fought in the War and we had not. They took centre stage to our supporting roles. Knowing a grittier, nastier world than we, they guarded their wartime secrets against our curiosity.

I was raised in an old family (part landed gentry, in part military) whose members were trained to cope with war so that when tragedy hit, they responded with dignity and understatement. They weren't good at expressing warmth or empathy but excelled at perfunctory ceremony, followed by appropriate silence. Into that silence I arrived to a family scarred by death and maiming.

And there the matter of Angus might have rested, had my sisters and I not discovered in September 2001 two of his letters in the top of my long deceased mother's desk. They were wrapped round a photograph of her three kilted brothers each looking like a gawky schoolboy. Peculiarly, the picture was folded vertically. I can only guess, that as a young female officer in the Auxiliary Territorial Service, she wished to fit the bundle into a narrow pocket of her army jacket so that, after her brother went missing, she could snatch a glimpse of his last written words. I find it hard to imagine my twenty-one year old mother's anguish, as she kept vigil for her lost brother, hoping that he was still alive. She surely found comfort in those letters as she turned over each phrase, smiling at the quiet humour, noticing a touch of pedantry here and a hint of irony there. She sieved through the substance until she gleaned all that she could and read them not in the public glare of the Mess, parade-ground or canteen but in her room or while on leave at Largie, their home in Argyll on the Kintyre peninsula.

My sister, Lis, found the letters shelved between old school reports, a membership for the local alpine plant society and a pedigree certificate for one of my mother's spaniels (long since dead). A hush descended as Lis unfolded the top letter. When she saw Angus's signature, she handed the letters to me. "Mary, you have them!" she whispered. Though something sacred had fallen into our hands, I didn't pore over them then, but put them away in a file.

Six months later in February 2002 came the sixtieth anniversary of Singapore's fall to Japan. Books were published about "the worst defeat in British history"; the newspaper reviews followed; in Singapore itself they held conferences and remembrance services.

People from Britain and the Commonwealth whose relatives were caught up in the debacle made pilgrimages there, but from my home in Edinburgh the anniversary hardly touched me. I read a couple of book reviews on the subject and listened to BBC Radio 4's "Archive Hour", that explored the fate of Singapore's civilians after the Fall. At that point I was still unaware how this cataclysmic event had shaped my life.

A few years later it dawned on me that each time the year's shortest month approached a pall of gloom enveloped me until I was swamped by depression. Our Edinburgh Februaries are never cheerful. Short days and harsh winds sweeping in from the Forth make many of its citizens feel sombre. But it wasn't just the poor weather, the after-effects of seasonal indulgence or even an un-healthy bank balance that affected me. Painful memories from my past began to attack; that iron curtain raised by my parents to protect me from their grief was porous and their pain still filtered through.

It had been most virulent when I was a child and sensitive to the absence of fun in our house.

We seldom laughed, never sang and were raised in silence with no baby bed-time lullabies or humming of catchy tunes. My father never whistled while he worked on his farm: he mowed the lawn, counted his livestock and mended fences in surly silence. Our only music came from his record-player that blared out Italian opera awash with theatricality and tragic passion. My mother listened to Jimmy Shand on the radio but preferred the sound of a bag-pipe lament.

There were occasions of forced jollity when at local dances and ceilidhs my parents clasped one another in a stilted fox-trot or came together awkwardly to shuffle through an eightsome reel. Generally, my mother tamped down her grief and avoided a head-on confrontation with her sorrow, though sometimes she was caught unawares. A recording of a war-time siren set her off down the road of horrible memories, the receipt of a telegram (even a highly-decorated greetings one) made her tremble. At church dur-ing Remembrance Sunday, she was overcome by emotion, partic-ularly when the congregation sang hymns about the perilous sea.

My gloom persisted. I looked out of my window and gazed at sheets of sleet, diagonal projectiles shot from the sky. I decided I must find out what happened to Angus. My unconscious urged me to investigate, but my rational mind advised me to forget as I was afraid of discovering a skeleton in the cupboard. When I was young I broached the subject with my father. Never very articulate when it came to emotional matters he stuttered a few words: "Awful!" "You mustn't talk about it!" "For Heaven's sake, don't ask your mother!" and like a battery-spent machine, his voice then dwindled to a halt.

I returned again to the file containing Angus's letters. The first was hand-written, in small print that belied a far from modest signature. (Angus had underlined his name and punctuated it with a full stop.) It was Easter Day, 1939 and the letter came from India in the Deccan where he was stationed. My uncle was no introvert, but a young soldier of twenty-five wanting adventure. This, he hoped shortly to get by travelling to Kashmir on a shooting expedition. But before he detailed his plans, he congratulated his eighteen year old sister on gaining a place at Somerville College, Oxford. "Enjoy Oxford!" he advised. "I did!"

This terseness was followed by an enquiry as to her whereabouts; as she and their mother were at that moment on a cruise in the Mediterranean, he feared their itinerary might have been interrupted by Mussolini's invasion of Albania on April 7th of that year.

In his second letter, dated August 1941, typed and sent from the Cameron Highlands in Malaya where he was on leave, Angus apologises for being a poor correspondent. After a brief description of his hotel (mock Tudor with olde-worlde beams and a wishing-well in the garden) Angus arrives at the important news. He had bought a new 6 h.p. Fiat. "I must say it is a grand wee car and has done me very well indeed," he wrote. As the smallest vehicle on the market, it was an odd choice for a man of six feet four. "As you may imagine," he continued, "I look a bit of a sight driving about in this tiny little car with my head sticking out several inches through the sunshine roof."

The letter ends with cryptic remarks about the state of the world. Would Japan invade, he wondered? If they did the Allies would smash them. This gung-ho approach might have been, if not for his sister's benefit, then for the censor's.

Both of these communications display a breezy optimism with a glaze of humour.

There was no doubt he was a loyal servant of the Crown, but still frank enough to gripe about the heat and his homesickness. "I'd give anything to be back home for a week or two at Largie," he wrote.

There is only so much you can eke from a brother/sister correspondence. My mother was hardly likely to be a confidante to her brother's drinking exploits or sexual adventures in the fleshpots of Singapore city. That's if he, a promising young officer, indulged in such activities. Angus and Esther's relationship was not especially intimate; their social background, where brothers and sisters attended different boarding schools, prevented it. He was seven years her senior and, in the absence of their father who died when they were very young, he might well have served as a father substitute.

I folded the letters and replaced them in the file. They were all I had to help me bridge the gap of sixty years and grasp the nature of my mother's relationship with her brother. It wasn't much but it was something. Whereas once my uncle was just a man in a photograph, now he had a voice, distinctive in idiom, quirk and form.

I realised then, now that she and my father were dead, who was to stop me from discovering what happened? I grabbed the telephone directory, looked up "army" and found the number of Edinburgh Castle museum. That was military, wasn't it?

"If he was in the Argyll & Sutherland Highlanders, it's Stirling Museum you want," said a polite woman on the other end and she gave me the number. I rang it, and when another female voice answered I faltered.

"Was he Major Charles Angus Macdonald?" she asked.

"I don't know!" I couldn't confirm his rank.

"I think he was. He was brigade major…of the 12th Indian Infantry."

If I was honest, I had little idea of the difference between a brigade, battalion or regiment.

"Here it is!" she said, "He was killed at sea…."

It was a shock to hear the manner of my uncle's death described by a stranger. I wanted to correct the lady and tell her he wasn't killed but lost. The distinction was important.

"...on 2nd March, 1942." the voice explained. "He left Singapore on the 14th February, two days before the surrender."

"How do you know he died on that date?" I asked.

"Aitken's book states it was on the 2nd of March."

"Who was Aitken?" I was frustrated by the woman's reluctance to explain.

"Aitken kept a record of all soldiers' deaths and hid it while he was in captivity. Major Macdonald is in it."

It puzzled me how Aitken came by the news but this detail was not what I wanted to concentrate on just then.

"And his next of kin was his mother."

I felt a weight pressing on my chest, and a prickling sensation attacked my throat. I wanted to scream at the disinterested woman privy to my family tragedy. They say that experiences can last from one generation to the next. If that is so my tears then joined those of my mother and grandmother.

"The reason I'm ringing," I mumbled, "is I want to know what happened after his ship went down."

I heard the woman speak to somebody else in the background.

"Can I help?" the voice belonged to a man.

"I don't know but...I just...." I told him that something happened after his ship was torpedoed, when many of the crew and passengers were in the water, either clinging to flotsam or perched on rafts, while a lucky few managed to board the only launched lifeboat. I didn't know what it was but it was dreadful, and nobody in my family would talk about it. Someone (I wasn't able to say whom) wrote about the event in an article or a pamphlet or even a book. I had wanted to know about it for over thirty years, but nobody in my family would breath a word.

"You have to understand there was such confusion at that time," the man's voice was consoling. "It was all so chaotic and reports back were often inaccurate."

"But something awful happened," I insisted. "A bad, maybe even shameful thing. Do you know?" I asked.

"I can't think…you know, this is my subject…the Fall of Singapore. It's been written about over and over again but it still fascinates people. These men were incredibly brave…Brigadier Paris, Captain Mike Blackwood were remarkable men. So was your uncle. He was a real hero in his wee car."

"But something awful was written about him…."

"I can't think what, except maybe it's Walter Gibson's book, "The Boat" that you're referring to. It's impossible to verify what he wrote as nobody survived except two Javanese sailors, a Chinese woman called Doris Lim, who was murdered by her husband in Sumatra, and Gibson. So, we'll never know what happened. I'm sorry, but this is far too complex a subject to discuss over the phone. Come in sometime. We'll try to help."

I explored many other avenues and points of view first, however, at the beginning of his life, to better understand his death.

Esther Macdonald Gladstone - Mum

GOING BACK

— 1961 —

IN SUMMER Mummy was a homing pigeon. You just had to point her in the right direction, and she drove all the way from our farm house in SW Scotland on the Solway Firth to Kintyre, her birth-place, where she grew up with her brother. This long finger of Scotland, once described by the Vikings as "almost an island", juts out from the heart of Argyll towards Northern Ireland. The channel separating each country is only a distance of fourteen miles. In those days, the Fifties and early Sixties, the car journey was a marathon with at least one ferry crossing, sometimes two, and a trek involving tail-to-tail crawling up the west bank of Loch Lomond and along further loch-sides, before we reached our final lap. If that was not difficult enough, our Morris Oxford lacked power steering and had no seat belts or child-proof door-locks. Colin, our young brother sat in the front beside Mummy, while we three, Elisabeth, Janet and myself, perched on the back seat. We got used to the car's violent motion; hurled first to the right, then the left, our small stomachs lurched at every bend.

Mummy liked to stop on Loch Lomond-side for a picnic lunch. So, keeping the water on our right as we drove past bays and pine trees growing by the road-side, she pulled in at Luss away from the stuttering ribbon of cars and caravans.

"What's that?" one of us pointed to a figure on a plinth stand-ing in the water a few feet from the bank.

"It's a statue of a boy!" Mummy said.

"Why is it there?"

"Not sure," Mummy poured diluted Kia-ora orange juice into a small beaker. "I think it's to remember a child who drowned!" she said, reluctant to explain further. We stopped reaching for potato crisps and ham sandwiches and tried to understand. Draw-ing in our breaths, we turned our young minds towards the sub-ject of death.

"Why did he drown?" one of us asked.

"I don't know. Perhaps he fell into the water, found himself out of his depth and didn't know how to swim, so he drowned." I could hear Mummy's voice tremble, but she recovered her equilibrium before casting an eye over the food lying on the rug. "Anyone want a chocolate biscuit?" she asked picking up a packet of Viennese whirls.

"What's it like to drown?" Being her oldest and the most inquisitive, I often troubled her with awkward questions.

"You are so demanding, Mary!" Mummy turned from me to watch a duck preening its feathers by the water's edge; fumbling in her bag for a packet of cigarettes, she extracted one and lit it. The sharp intake of breath as she inhaled made me think of a person touching something hot. Only when plumes of smoke began to waft from each of her nostrils did Mummy relax.

"It's better not to think about these things."

"Why?"

"Believe me it's best not to," she insisted. "You're far too young to understand."

"Am I?"

Mummy parted her lips, not to take another draw from her cigarette but to speak. However no words came, only a sigh. She raised the cigarette again to her mouth and sucked in another quota of nicotine and found her voice, soft with smoke. "It's no use talking about the past."

I stared at her, at the white stick growing a head of ash, and sensed her irritation. She threw me an apologetic smile, then hummed a tune. I knew it. We all did. It was Andy Stewart's *A Scottish Soldier*. Colin had a 45 rpm record of the hit. "There was a soldier, a Scottish soldier." My mother's frown turned into a smile as she began to sing. Listening was painful; she was out of tune and had no sense of rhythm. "Who wandered far away and soldiered far away." She looked again at the duck now grooming its bill. "There was none bolder with good broad shoulder." Why had we children liked that song? Stewart's voice, vital and virile, often reverberated through our passageway at home from sitting room to kitchen, even upstairs in our bedrooms. Over and over again Colin would reach for the sleeve, draw out the disc, sling it on the turn-table, drop the needle on the vinyl, and off it went. I had never seen Mummy's reaction and wondered if she had one at all.

On this occasion, she straightened her back and looked out towards the statue. Her delivery was sharp and stark with each word belched from the depths of her diaphragm: "And now the soldier, the Scottish soldier, who wandered far away and soldiered far away, sees leaves are falling and death is calling, and he will fade away in that far land."

Mummy stubbed out her cigarette on a pebble and gathered up the debris from our picnic. "It's time to go!" Back in the car she slammed her foot on the accelerator and asked if we wanted to play I-Spy.

"Why did he drown?" I wouldn't let go of the subject.

"I'm not talking about it, Mary!"

At the head of the loch was Tarbet, not to be confused with the Tarbert we were aiming for farther away. Following the twisting road we reached the Rest and be Thankful, whereupon Mummy burst into chatter. She was like that. We could drive from one county to another in silence and then without apparent cause, she plunged into telling us a story, sharing a joke or just reminiscing. "In the old days", she said, "when people travelled by horse and carriage they got tired climbing this hill, so at the top they took a rest and were thankful!"

Farther up the A83 we crossed a hump-back bridge outside Inveraray. "Look to your right, children!"

I peered out of the window and saw a bleak castle of grey stone with pointed turrets. "That's where the Duke of Argyll lives. And he's a Campbell!" My mother's lip curled in disgust. "Macdonalds before me have always fought the Campbells."

"Do you still?" asked Elisabeth.

"Don't be silly!" Mummy chuckled. "That was ages ago."

Clan lore and loyalty were alien concepts for us four born and brought up south of the Scottish geographical divide.

From my seat in the back I saw Mummy slacken her grip on

the steering wheel. She was coming back to the west coast of Kintyre, bound by the Atlantic. But to what? All she had was a grieving mother, an uninterested older brother badly wounded during the War, and a ruined castle once her home.

The corkscrew bends stopped; we were now on a straight stretch of road sweeping south towards Campbeltown; my mother gazed out of the car window to slithers of land surrounded by sea. "There's Jura and that's Islay in the distance! See?" I could hear the excitement in her voice. That was the difference between her childhood and ours. Whereas she had salt in her veins we had mud, our young lives spent by an estuary, next to sluggish, half-caste water belonging neither to river or sea.

"Down there is Gigha! And the little one is Cara where the Broonie lives!"

"The Broonie?" I chimed.

"I'll tell you about him and if the sea is calm I'll take you there."

"I want out!" moaned Janet who wriggling in her seat made a lunge for the door handle.

Mummy swivelled her head round to see what my sister was up to and rammed her foot on the brake. "How dare you!" she spat. "I told you never, I repeat never to touch the door handle. I've a good mind to smack you!"

For a moment I thought Mummy might carry out her threat, but she revved up the engine urging the car down the road. "There it is!" she waved towards a slope overlooking the sea. Half-hidden by a swathe of rhododendron was Ballure, Granny's house now that Largie was in ruins.

She was there standing on the front door-step as we drew up on the gravel, her white hair in a net at the nape of her neck. She had strung a rope of pearls around her throat, whose loose skin hung in swags like snow drifts against a fence. Granny never wore black; to do so was to admit that her lost son would never return. She preferred brown and wore as many different shades of it as she could muster. On this day she had on a tweed skirt the colour of beech leaves in autumn and a twin set of donkey brown. As I clambered out of the car, I came face to face with her feet enveloped in flat, brown shoes, that looked like boats from which emerged stick-thin legs wrapped in beige silk stockings.

"Esther, darling!" she purred opening her arms to Mummy. "How lovely you've come! We must eat! Straight away!" Her eyes, shielded by spectacles with dark brown circular frames, had a dewy appearance. They fixed on Mummy, following her as she walked through the Ballure public rooms and up the elegant staircase.

Granny ate at six. Never later. This was for Robert's benefit because he liked his evenings off. He was her cook but had once been the butler at Largie castle. Then when its roof was removed after the last War, Robert took charge of the cart with all Granny's furniture and possessions and helped her move into her new nearby home. There they both remained, she in the front part of the house with its proportioned windows and portico entrance and he in the back with its plain windows and door that led to the scullery and laundry at a lower-lying level. Up the back stairs was his sitting room, bedroom and bathroom. The distinction between front and back was striking, Granny's quarters were embellished with rows of books in cases: Fielding, Scott, Stevenson and Dickens, collections in calf with gold tooled lettering. Her furniture was Jacobean mixed with eighteenth century Sheraton tables, sideboards and consoles. The staircase had a mahogany rail and brass rods at each tread, that helped keep the carpet strip in place.

Robert's domain was functional and poky with no carpet on the stairs. His rooms were out of bounds, so we could only imagine what they were like. We knew he listened to the radio because in the garden we heard the nine o'clock news blaring from his window. He smoked a pipe; we sniffed its fumes as we passed him on the drive. To us he spoke little, and if he did it was usually to scold. "Don't touch!" "Mind that kettle!" "Keep out of there!" "Away from the larder!" Robert was always the same; he wore a blue apron over his trousers and shirt and served food better than he cooked it. He carried hot dishes with a solemnity only seen in well-trained butlers, and it pained him not to do the honours by serving personally each diner, as he had done at the castle. In his demoted position as cook, all that was required after preparing and cooking the food was to carry it into the dining room and lay it on the sideboard.

I had forgotten how her home smelled different to our own with its whiffs and pongs of the farm. Hers had a suggestion of the past, of old country houses where camphor, lavender and lemon verbena fragrances reigned. They wafted from old mahogany canisters whose lids when opened revealed dried flowers and pomander. I heard a sound like a rifle shot as Granny sat down. It was her knee joints. When we were all seated and eating our lamb chop, I detected another. It was the rattle of Granny's dentures as she chewed, and by the end of the meal these chimed in unison with the tinkling of her pills, as she lifted them in their mother of pearl container from the table's dumb waiter.

"Go and play in the hall, children!" Granny said.

In this drafty precinct were portraits of a young boy and girl. These were of Jock and Douna, my mother's eldest siblings. The boy's face was handsome and thick-set, his hazel eyes twinkling in the evening light, while his sister, with pointed features offset by a white lace collar, looked elfin and other-worldly. But where were the portraits of the other children, of Simon, our mother and Angus, the uncle nobody talked about? If my grandparents, Daisy and John had commissioned portraits of their eldest two, why weren't the rest of their offspring painted? Had money been tight? Perhaps the First World War had intervened and all the available portraitists, instead of having children to sit for them, painted servicemen instead. Were Jock and Douna more important than the other three and if so, why? Birth order was significant in our family, which kept property intact by leaving the lion's share to its oldest son. So, as the eldest it made sense to have Jock's portrait done but didn't they also want one of Angus, their second son, himself the future inheritor of a large estate in central Scotland? If one existed was it removed. after he failed to return home from the Far East after the war? But a child has little desire to think more about someone she has never met, and I was no exception. Angus was gone and I'd little idea what he was like.

The following morning we drove farther into Mummy's past, to Largie castle itself. The steading and old coach house are empty. So too is the gardener's cottage nestling by the big iron gate into the walled garden. Only a couple of semi-detached houses standing apart from the others are lived in. Washing hangs on the line of the nearest dwelling, and I notice a pair of overalls next to a floral apron. Mummy drives us past the houses, up a slope with fields on our right until we reach a wood with chestnut and beech trees. There in the clearing is the ruin of Largie Castle. Mummy leaps out of her seat, slams the car door shut, thrusts both hands deep in her jacket pocket, and strides from us. The song of a bird is incongruously mellifluous in such a setting. The eeriness of the ruin commands a bat's shriek or at the very least a rook or crow's cry. "A blackbird!" Mummy's smile overlays a sigh.

The sound of the wind in the trees ebbs and flows much like the rhythmic swell of waves at the sea.

Running towards an open space un-obscured by trees and looking towards the islands, I can see the line of the shore below. The sea is all around us, playing a part in our lives as it has done for generations, first as a barrier, then an artery to Gigha, Cara, Jura, other parts of the mainland, to Ulster and Ireland itself. It has transported traders, fishermen, pirates, pilgrims and saints. Its disasters are etched in men, women and children's memories: fishermen who went off and never returned, yachtsmen drowned in a squall, swimmers caught in treacherous cross-currents. The last war brought a spate of maritime calamities like the Aska, a British steamer, which in 1940 after being bombed in Belfast fetched up on the north coast of Cara.

The paved ground by the castle's south elevation gives way to a large hole in the ground; this was the pond where Angus and Simon floated toy boats that dodged water lilies and skimmed over fish that swam in the water's lower reaches. There's nothing left but a tangle of briar and bramble. Looking up at the tower's smooth walls, its skin of harling missing, we notice a thatch of creeper around the doorway: Russian vine or ivy, dark and luxuriant like a pubic fuzz. Largie's rooflessness frightens me. The castle has no chimney pots, rafters, slates or tiles; its guttering has gone and the drainpipes are missing.

"Don't go inside!" Mummy warns.

"Why?"

"A stone might fall on you!"

But I want to see where Mummy spent her childhood, where she learned to walk and talk, to discover where she hung her coat after going outside, where her boots stood and what kind of floors she trod: tiles, floorboards, stone, or parquet. I long to see the colour of the walls, the mouldings encircling each ceiling, the size of the window panes. I'd like to shove my weight against each door, hear the echo of feet on the drawing room floor. Which passageways she ran through and if the staircase banisters were low enough for her to slide down? Where did she escape to when brother Simon bullied her, and when they had guests which rooms they used. Was there a special .one, a secret place where she could compose her dreams and aspirations. What fragrances rose from the flower displays, and how pungent were the kitchen aromas? Where did they celebrate Christmas, hold parties or arrange trysts; above all I want to see, smell and feel inside the rooms in which she had slept, dreamed, laughed and wept? There stands Largie Castle, cast off like an abandoned coat, forlorn and despoiled.

"Why did they take the roof off?"

"It was too expensive and also quite uncomfortable to live in," Mummy explains in a throw-away voice.

Pursing her lips, she leads us to the wood and halts at a stream edged on both sides by bamboo thicket. Lis runs fast up a path wedged between long, tall shoots that shiver in the wind, before moving to a wet hollow below the castle, where rhododendron bushes grow with olive green leaves and stems of peeling bark.

"Granny wants a cutting," Mummy aims a pair of secateurs at a branch growing parallel to the ground. The castle might be gone but Granny still comes to tend the garden, pruning a boisterous shrub, propping up another whose branches are damaged by wind, clearing the weeds from a third, propagating here and planting there. It is her way of perpetuating what remains and continuing the fight against the invasion of rabbits, deer and bad weather.

Out through the tall iron gate and into the courtyard we reach the doorstep of the nearest semi-detached house, with residents at the door waiting. Katie in green overalls, is pink-skinned with a face framed by short, wiry hair swept from her brow. Somewhere at the back of the house is sister Bella feeding the hens. Katie invites us into the kitchen with its high sills, brass door knobs, smell of furniture polish, and loud sound of a ticking clock. I listen to her conversation. People up here speak differently: with care and deliberation as if they're translating from another tongue. Katie is chatty and Bella monosyllabic mostly, but there is a distance between them and us; we are like foreigners in a place my mother calls home. Katie lifts from a shelf a biscuit barrel. Off comes the lid as she removes three chocolate wafer biscuits.

"Will you take a Blue Riband?"

We sisters accept and Mummy declines. As I bite into the biscuit I forget the decapitated castle, crumbling crow-step gables and smashed turrets and taste the sweet stickiness of the chocolate wafer. Bella opens the kitchen door. A small brown feather lies on her lapel. It remains there, her insignia only descending to the gleaming linoleum when a draft surges in. "How is Mrs Macdonald?" she asks.

Mummy's reply is bland. She never mentions Granny's sharp tongue, her insomnia, the pain in her wrists, her inexplicable phobias like her hatred of cats, and her silences when she stands at the front door gazing out to sea.

They talk about the Macdonalds, their neighbours and the men on the estate like Ronald Reid, the gamekeeper and Sandy Rowan, the odd job man. Dozens of names are metioned except for one. Their chatter skirts around anything that connects with my mother's brother, Angus.

They circle the wound, retreating from that area of my mother that still suffers. Living on in the shadow of her now ruined home, raising hens, growing potatoes, picking currants and growing old uneventfully, Katie and Bella are balm to her.

"Where are we going?" Janet is cross when the car turns left at the foot of the Largie drive. "We are going to the beach. I'm wearing my swimming costume under my trousers and blouse, so we are going. We must!"

"Stop whining!" Mummy is resentful. We motor past Killean and Cleit church before climbing a steep hill and stopping at the summit. "Stay in the car!" Mummy opens the door and walks beyond the verge towards a monument looking like a wedding cake squatting on the crest of the hill. Because it's raining our view is poor, so we press our noses against the car window and watch her climb the steps, un-snib the gate, and tread along the gravel path.

When she reaches the stone she raises her head to read the letters on the monument, and I can just detect what they are: the names, John, James, William, Robert and Callum; the top batch is big and the bottom, with Angus's name, quite small.

"What's she doing?" asks Lis.

"I don't know!"

Mummy's world is inadmissible. Repelled by silence we subsist on a gruel of unfinished sentences, incomplete explanations, and elliptical replies. Shut out from the truth our world contracts, so that when adults discourage us from letting our minds and imaginations roam and explore, we stop expressing ourselves and retreat into a timid conventionality. Someone told me that silence is golden, but I could never understand why. For me it is frightening and represents not the most precious of metals but the most base.

"You said we could go for a swim," Janet complains. "I told you I put on my costume under my trousers. See!" She rolls down the waistband of her cords to reveal a strip of crushed poplin underneath.

"Don't be impatient! We're going now!"

We swim at a beach below Low Dunashry, a farm near Ballure. The weather is dull and overcast, and a strong wind whips the waves by the shore into a frenzy of spray and froth. Colin begins to cry. "Too noisy!" he wails and turns his back to the din of the Atlantic rollers.

"Think of a boat out on this!" whispers my mother. She is

talking to herself, not us. "You know," she points out to sea, "next stop out there is America!" and bends down to collect her basket and rug (of Macdonald tartan). She sets up a windscreen of towels and jackets draped over a walking stick and the handle of a spade, but it's no use. Sand blows everywhere: on the rug as soon as we lay it down, in cups, beakers, and most annoyingly on to our food, a thin layer over the biscuits, apples and sandwiches.

— April, 2009 —

I'm going back to Kintyre, but this time I approach it from Edinburgh. If I were making the journey from the south, as we did with Mummy, I would cross the Erskine Bridge, but I motor to Stirling instead. Once through the muddle of directions and diversions, I find Loch Lomond-side a doddle. Where are the bends that swung our little bodies to and fro? Instead, the road leaves the loch and slices through open terrain. I fly past the Luss statue and, as for the Rest and be Thankful, it's hardly a climb at all. I cruise up it in fifth, no bother, and wonder what there is to be thankful about. Maybe the weather; it's an okay spring afternoon, neither sunny nor cloudy. Everything has been ironed out. Somewhat sanitised too with seat belts, sat navs, and canned music through the glens. It is anodyne and safe cruising up re-sculpted hills and over streamlined bridges. Stopping at a village, I stand in a queue for a bag of chips and weak tea in a polystyrene cup. At Inveraray I cross the river, leaving the old humped-back bridge on my right. Lochgilphead looks bleak and empty but rhododendrons are in bloom, not the common purple ponticum that runs riot everywhere, but the more recherché sort with crimson, cream and yellow flowers. I roll down my car window and sniff. Wood smoke. There's little wind, just a dampness in the air. A sea bird sings. It's an oyster-catcher, I think.

The last lap is long as I swirl past people-less hamlets. At the isthmus's head is Tarbert followed by a chain of by-passed villages. Where have all the people and their homes gone? I drive past the entrance to Ballure, the lodge house still standing but tidied up and kept now, I guess, for holiday lets.

The road to Largie, the place where Mummy was born, is blocked by a dilapidated hen-run belonging to a resident at the steading. Stopping my car in the courtyard, I make for the old walled garden. It's water-logged. Rain teems down and I hear a clap of thunder. Hens scatter for cover and I curse myself for not having worn my wellingtons. Trying to keep my feet dry I dodge the puddles and scramble out of the garden through briar and bracken.

There's no obvious path but plenty of fallen trees, toppled beeches, and rhododendron, some still flowering. I look for the site where the castle once stood. Where though? Even the pile of rubble, all that's left of Largie, is concealed. And the pond? Surely something remains of that. I am disoriented. Once a huge chestnut tree grew by the drive. Has that fallen too?

Somewhere, in amongst the vegetation, I find a mound of moss and realise it is a pile of stones. That's it. Largie. I climb to the top of the rubble and try to gain a view of the islands out west, but a galvanised steel shed and some ash trees conceal it. A tractor has scoured tracks on the ground, and where it is boggy someone has laid sheets of corrugated iron to prevent vehicles from sinking into the soil.

It begins to pour again.

"They shouldn't have done it!" my father protested. "It was a fine example of Scottish Baronial." As an architect he was particularly vocal against the razing of historic buildings. "It wasn't a real castle!" argued my mother. "It was just pretend."

"It was a very good pretend."

This was true. My grandfather's grandfather had it built for him after his wife, Mary Jane, died in 1851. While she was alive, I like to think she was a restraining influence on her mate, the Hon. Augustus Moreton, Conservative MP for a Gloucestershire constituency and the second son of a newly-created English earl. She was confident in her ancestry (the Largie Macdonalds traced their line directly back to Somerled and Ranald Bane) and was happy to live in the old Largie, which was little more than a fortified farmhouse. Augustus had other ideas. With Prince Albert heading the trend at Balmoral, he was one of the many Victorians who fell for the charms of the Highlands, wishing to scottify himself. Why not upgrade the ancient family he had married into by building a proper ancestral pile, one that looked old even if it was not? Glasgow-based Charles Wilson won the commission and drew up plans with a distinct antiquarian approach. The only remit received from the impractical Augustus, whose intentions for the new building were for sport and entertainment rather than serious living, was to forget about convenience and concentrate on aesthetics. This Wilson managed.

Bay windows were out. If any visitor to the new Largie wished for a panoramic view of the Gigha, Cara, Jura, or Islay ribbon of islands, he was to be disappointed. Wilson installed small, sash windows in keeping with the French chateau style of the sixteenth and seventeenth centuries and sacrificed large rooms and sprawling wings for vertical dimensions with a tower at the centre, its rooms accessed by a spiral staircase. Even the exterior walls covered in pebble dash or harling were intended to look ancient and hoary.

"It was bloody uncomfortable!" was my mother's defence.

This was also true. The glass entrance leaked when it rained, and the stairs were a nightmare to climb especially for Jock, my mother's brother who inherited Largie. While in France at St. Valery with the British Expeditionary Force in June 1940 my uncle (Angus's oldest brother) stepped on a land mine which severely injured his leg, and shortly after his evacuation back to England it had to be amputated. "The tower only had one room to a floor so it was all stairs," my mother explained.

"It was a good building, and it shouldn't have been pulled down!" With his honours diploma from The Architectural Association, my father felt entitled to have the last word on the matter.

It was bucketing down now, and I stopped trying to keep dry, my only recourse being to shelter under a tree, one that had not fallen like a soldier on a battlefield. I felt miserable. Seeing all this neglect depressed me, but I wasn't sure why. Nobody in the family particularly regretted Largie's demise. "If it was still standing," said my cousin John who inherited the estate "we could never afford to keep it up." Built on the ill-gotten gains of an Englishman married to a Highland heiress, Largie had been toppled after only four generations. I realised I didn't mind that Mummy's childhood home had vanished, but the ground on which I stood was still there, and that was where my roots lay; even though the tree was ravaged they were still strong and deep. I looked beyond the wood and saw a deer bounding across the grass. My spirits lifted as I watched the animal sprint for cover. Hope, I reasoned, is never far from despair. The deer's grace and agility were a symbol against all this decay and I applauded Jock, my uncle, for tearing down the castle, elegant sham that it had been.

Tucked up in bed that night in my cousin's house, I could not sleep. My mind darted from one subject to another, resting first on Angus, my uncle, then on Mummy and her Largie childhood. Finally, the Luss statue came to mind. I had missed it on my drive to Kintyre, because the road by-passed the place where the figure stood. A few days previously in preparation for the journey, I had investigated its history on the internet and discovered my mother was incorrect in assuming the statue was a monument to a drowned boy. A London builder had erected it to remind him of the happy holidays he had spent as a child playing there by the water. Tragedy had attacked my mother and her family so forcibly, that it was natural for her to put the worst complexion on what she saw in the water.

It was many years before I learned that her brother had died twice.

BUT MUMMY was proud and resilient. Doubtless her strength came from the knowledge that she was born into a long line of Macdonalds. Although our branch can trace its roots back to 1164, it was almost three hundred years later that Ranald Bane, grandson of John Macdonald, Lord of the Isles, struck lucky. He was an excellent soldier, like many of his descendants and, after serving his chieftain in 1431 at the Battle of Inverlochy, he became Largie's first laird (lord), on receiving a large area of land on the Kintyre peninsula in the south-west Highlands. The family still owns some of the original property.

This sense of belonging and stability gave my mother confidence. Freighted by generations of Macdonald ancestry, she knew who she was, and, similar to the giant Californian redwood or old English oak, her roots were deep. Sad-eyed, dark and Celtic in appearance, she possessed an instinctive knowledge of the land around her. Her older sister, Elizabeth (or Douna as she was usually called) adopted many traditional Highland habits and country pursuits. She span Cheviot wool, collecting lichens from rocks on the shore to make natural dyes. She also bred spaniels and, when she became engaged to Henry Rogers, a young clergyman, she rushed to a neighbour and held out her bloody left hand (she had just skinned a rabbit) to show off her expensive emerald and diamond engagement ring.

Like native Americans or Australian Aborigines, Mummy and Douna communed with native spirits and were conversant with local legend. Living among the heather, hills and tides of the sea, they tracked animals, caught herring and, by sniffing the air, could tell when the rain, mist or storms were approaching. They tasted young nettle-tips and sorrel growing by the ditches, chewed rosehips and haws, and popped between their fingers fuschia buds. They swore they had second sight and could see fairies and the little men of soil, moor, tree and glade. However, all Highlanders could lay that claim: from John, their well-educated father to Rob, the butler who was convinced a fairy had snaffled his butter knives with mother of pearl handles, that he stored in a leather covered box lined in maroon velvet. 'The Broonie' was the offender; he had a room, 'seomar bhrunaidh' in Gaelic, at the top of the Largie tower. This Highland fairy was the Macdonald's familiar spirit or aide.

The Broonie or 'uruisg' was popular in folklore and every large house or castle in Scotland had one. In appearance he was small with a wrinkled face; he had short, brown, curly hair and wore a brown tunic and hood. He was partial to dairy products but the family was tactful in the way they presented them. He would not openly receive any offering. So servants left him bowls of cream and chunks of cheese in discreet places beside the dairy door or in a kitchen corner.

The Macdonalds' protector was temperamental. Once he was in such a temper that he hurled from his home on Cara a huge stone that landed on the mainland at Beachara, near Largie. But if the Macdonalds played their cards well and 'got on the Broonie's right side,' he was obliging. When a nursemaid fell asleep while she was in charge of an infant, the Broonie pinched her sharply on her earlobe. Being shy, the Highland fairy liked to perform tasks at night while everyone was in bed. He would mop the scullery floor and even wring out the washing. He was quick to take offence and if the cream was sour, the cheese mouldy, or someone tried to trap him into speaking to them, he would threaten to desert the family. During most seasons the Broonie vanished, but, come harvest-time soon after hay-making, he was very helpful. Unlike other harvesters, he never bound his sheaves with rope. Yet, the greatest storm failed to blow the straw away.

The Largie Broonie knew all about the sea. More than domestic duties, work in the byre, or in the fields, he was a maritime aide. All West Highland chieftains were good sailors and to prove it the Macdonald coat of arms has four symbols; one is a boat. The Broonie helped these sailors by changing the wind in their favour especially if a Macdonald was being chased by the enemy, a Campbell. He guarded the water between the mainland and Cara, the Macdonald's island situated one kilometre south of Gigha. The only Scottish island still in the possession of descendants of the 'Lord of the Isles,' Cara, meaning 'dearest' or 'dear one,' is the Broonie's domain. A mere three-quarters of a mile long and half a mile wide, Cara has a house built in 1730 of two storeys with a slate roof and an attic. Formerly, it was let to a junior member of the family who paid rent to the laird. Latterly, until 1930 when it was abandoned, a shepherd lived there. Forty years later, an enterprising Glasgow architect bought the building and renovated it. Because of Cara's strategic position between Scotland and Ireland, the house in the late 18th and early 19th centuries was used to survey the sea for smugglers. At the island's south end is a large rock formation, the Broonie's chair. If a visitor sits on it and makes a secret wish, it is granted.

For several centuries the Broonie's sole companions were a herd of feral goats, descendents of castaways from the Spanish Armada. In 1588 after Francis Drake routed the Spanish fleet off the southern English coast, several galleys were blown off course, some fetching up in north-westerly waters off Scotland's Kintyre coast. Did the Broonie help to run the ships aground? We know he intervened with the wind, becalmed waters, and even commanded full force gales, in order to dash enemy ships against the rocks or sink them.

Many ask when the Broonie became the Macdonalds' familiar spirit. By all accounts, he was only a figment of their imaginations, a projection of their hopes and fears: when the weather failed, a horse became sick or an enemy attacked, the family believed it had displeased the fairy. But if the sun shone, a healthy baby was born, and the harvest was good, the Broonie obviously approved of them or so they thought. This elf had always existed and served the family ever since Bane took possession of Largie. After the first Largie laird's death, his sons, grandsons, and great grandsons were far from civilised in their behaviour: they fought each other and the neighbouring clans; they stole cattle and consequently they were imprisoned, outlawed, and some were exiled to Ireland.

For several centuries organised warfare replaced clan raiding.

In 1644, Angus, the 10th Largie laird, fought against the Covenanters of the Commonwealth, to put King Charles back on to the throne. When he took part in the Battle of Rhunaharoine Moss, which lies below the old Largie Castle, his land was confiscated. After the accession of the monarchy in 1660, they were restored and Angus, no doubt, expressed a note of thanks to the Broonie for his intervention! Angus's son, John was a friend of a Campbell of Kilberry. In 1715 the Duke of Argyle ordered Kilberry to arrest his chum. Knowing the strengths and weaknesses of all Campbells, the Broonie made sure that, on that particular winter morning, the woodcock flew in from Scandinavia and Kilberry would want a day's sport. When the time came for him to arrest John of Largie, the latter suggested they go out shooting. His friend complied, and no arrest was made.

John's eldest son, also called John, owned the estate at the time of the last attempt to restore the Stuarts in 1745. This was the time when the Broonie excelled himself. John Macdonald summoned his clansmen to join the forces of Prince Charles Edward Stuart at the Battle of Culloden. On their way there they stopped at Clachan, a small village north of Largie, for refreshment with the Minister. Was it the Broonie or the Minister, who spilled a kettleful of boiling water over Macdonald's foot, causing him to return home and take no farther part in the Jacobite Rising? Might the Presbyterian Minister have wished to strike a blow to the Episcopalian Stuarts, or perhaps he hoped to save a friend from being involved with 'the rebel Highland army' and consequently risking his family being dispossessed? I like to think that the Macdonalds' impish Highland spirit played a part in this incident!

Undoubtedly, the Broonie liked to exert his supernatural powers, even playing Cupid if necessary. His most successful matchmaking was in finding a spouse for Elizabeth Macdonald, the female Largie laird who succeeded her father in 1768. Seven years previously she married a younger son, Charles Lockhart from an old Scottish aristocratic family. This alliance provided a buttress and cushion for the two families, not least the Macdonalds whose fortunes were often more uncertain than those of the Lockharts.

Perhaps the Broonie began to tire of his charges after the new Largie Castle was built in 1859. Even though Augustus Moreton acknowledged the Macdonald's resident fairy, by allowing him a room at the top of the castle, he may have already lost interest in them. Did they displease him by committing a heinous crime?

At that period many Highland lairds betrayed their tenants by introducing sheep to the hillsides and raising rents, so that the crofters were unable to subsist as they had before, and many left their homes and emigrated to America. Dozens of Largie families boarded un-seaworthy ships for the State of Carolina in the USA. As for the Macdonalds, several Largie lairds were short-lived. After giving birth to six children, Mary Jane died in her early thirties, her eldest son Charles, aged 39, and John Ronald, my grandfather, at the age of 48. During World War Two, disasters abounded. Was it a case of nemesis resulting from hubris, or did the Largie elf flee after World War Two when the castle was razed and his room destroyed?

Friends, family and neighbours shake their heads and ask where was the Broonie when John Ronald died, Jock was injured, and Angus lost his life in S.E. Asia. It's hard to understand what was in the mind of the fairy, if he existed at all. Over the past two hundred years, life has been far from easy for the Macdonalds. But like a tree whose roots have fastened deep in the soil, the family has survived. When a nest is rifled, the bird mourns, but by the following spring it returns and the nest is filled again.

PATIENCE

THE MACDONALD NEST-BUILDERS, important to me, were John and Daisy, my grandparents. I knew Daisy, of course but John was an unknown as he was to Mummy. Like her brother Angus, her father was lost to her, as he died when she was still a baby. By all accounts, John was rational, scholarly and business-like. But he lived in the Highlands where the people's first language was Gaelic and their beliefs and customs were ancient and often fanciful. Similarly, my Lowland-born father, in listening to the language spoken by his nursemaids, nanny, and gamekeeper, found the Lowland Scots tongue rich, evocative and colourful. He developed a particular love for the poetry of Robert Burns, who lived near Dad's childhood home in Dumfriess-shire, and drank with his great, great, grandfather, Samuel Clark.

Mummy told me that John had once seen the Broonie standing under the chestnut tree at Largie. Maybe that was the last time the Macdonalds spied him, before a more sinister entity entered their world. Not at Largie Castle, but at Ballure, the house we visited each summer. Reputed to have a ghost called Janet, Ballure's occupants suffered from doors banging and the stomping of feet up and down the stairs. Fearing the villagers might refuse to cook or clean for her, if they heard that there was a ghost at Ballure, Granny kept mum about it. The story was that John had promised Ballure to Janet but reneged on the vow. Was she John's mistress? A youthful indiscretion that turned sour?

The most fanciful story of my grandfather is when he saw The Bird. In Gaelic culture, this meant he, the Largie laird, was about to die. Mummy said it was large and white but could not tell if it was a swan, goose, gull, gannet, or albatross. I picture it as a snowy owl with a penetrating gaze. After Jock, the 21st Largie laird, was severely injured in France, Granny asked if he had seen The Bird. He confessed that none of any description had come into his vision, while he lay on death's door in his hospital bed. At that critical time, the Macdonalds took the absence of The Bird as an indication that Jock wouldn't die. In the end, he outlived all his siblings.

Apart from his second sight and a belief in the super-natural, John was successful, adventurous, and bold. Like his predecessors and father, he was an expert yachtsman, who could judge the tides and treacherous currents off the Kintyre coast and in the Irish Sea. He was familiar with the West Highland weather, the Atlantic storms, the rain breaking over the islands, and the balmy peninsula's climate with its frost-free, temperate winters. My grandfather often sailed to Northern Ireland to stay with his sister. John had a profound interest in France, its culture, literature, customs, and cuisine. He was a keen farmer and kept Highland cattle that won prizes at agricultural shows all over Scotland. The Largie laird looked after his property, cultivating many species of trees. Interested in the spoils of the late Victorian plant-hunters who brought back shrubs and other exotic plants from the Himalayas, Asia, South America, and Australia, he planted at Largie rhododendrons, azaleas, bamboo, and monkey puzzle trees.

But like Achilles, the ancient Greek hero, John suffered from a physical defect which set him apart from others. Had he not been very deaf, he would have entered politics and taken a more active part in public life. His disability suggests that my grandfather, although well-born, intelligent, courageous, and expert in several fields, was flawed. His scholarship (he was to publish in 1915 a three tome History of France) was good but not great. He was no match for the social historian, G. M. Trevelyan, John's contemporary from a similar social background, or the earlier British historians, like Edward Gibbon or Thomas Babington Macaulay. It's unfair to label him an also-ran, but nobody could claim his work was up there at the top. Another contemporary was Winston Churchill, the eldest son of a duke's younger son. Because Churchill inherited no castle or country estate, he pushed his talent farther than John and, of course he lived longer.

If we want to find out what my grandfather looked like as a boy, I have his photo, taken at Mr John Moffat's Edinburgh studio at 125 Princes Street. Can you imagine it? John Ronald and his mother trotting up in a cab with no cars or concrete but plenty soot and horse dung. There he is, Mummy's father, my grandfather standing in a bare room as if on stage with a painted backdrop of panelled dado and large gothic window, to suggest an ancestral pile, as Moffat knew Mummy's papa was gentry, the thirteen year old 20th laird of Largie (his father, Charles, having died in 1879 when John was only six).

He is a proper little Lord Fauntleroy, dressed in velvet breeches and jacket, satin waistcoat, fine lawn cravat, stockings, and buckled shoes. His short dark hair closely cropped (ready I presume for his first half at Eton) and his brown eyes, watchful and wary. He looks intelligent, not rumbustious but quiet and self-contained, as is evident in the books he owned. I have a few: Bacon's *Essays* and the poetry of Shelley, Francis Thompson, Keats and Coventry Patmore.

However, there's one slim volume, a navy-blue, cloth-bound, manual on card games that intrigues me more. It was a present to John for Christmas, 1884 when he was eleven, and his widowed mother (if it was she who gave him the book) chose a manual on games of Patience. All 29 of them. Can you believe it? Not a water pistol (if they existed then), or a bow and arrow. Mind you, under the guidance of the Largie gamekeeper, I'm sure he had the chance to shoot, and his father, a keen sportsman, who kept a pack of otter hounds, would have left him a set of Purdeys or the like.

Elizabeth needed her only son in the drawing room, for him to be seen and not heard, able to amuse himself, and while away those wet, Kintyre afternoons playing Patience, just as today his great, great grandchildren peer into a screen and play solitaire, only no cards are flipped, but a mouse is clicked.

I said there were 29 games, each diagrammed with cards whose primary colours, the reds, blues and greens are indistinct at best and smudged at worst. But there's one — I only discovered it the other day — like a door into a secret world, hidden on the end cover after the author's advertisements. Someone (who I don't know) has added game number 30. It is clock patience with a pen and ink diagram, circular of course, and the instructions on six

42

lines at the foot of the page. The hand-writing is small and well-formed, obviously not a child's, with Roman numerals for the hours. It most likely belongs to the same person who inserted John's name at the front of the book but whether it was him, who added it, or his mother, or even a fond aunt, I will never know.

I also have a copy of a portrait of my grandmother, Daisy, as a five year old with twin sister, Violet, painted by Ethel Mortlock and exhibited at the Royal Academy in 1885. Dressed in red coats and hoods, they stand in a wintry Hampshire field. The connection is that Daisy played Patience. She also read books, practised, not petit point, but gros point embroidery in thick vibrant coloured wools. But later in life she loved Patience. It was quaint the way Granny referred to the jack of the pack as the knave, the word capturing another world, a Victorian era of hansom carriages, top hats, music halls, and cavalry charges. When she played cards and discovered a knave, she announced it with her oh, so confident, brigadier-general's daughter's aplomb. I can imagine her well-ordered world. How innocent-sounding was a knave then, once a term for a male servant, but even in Granny's day it had the ring of someone undesirable. He was a rogue, a tricky customer but never, as it is now, associated with the openly unsavoury, the name of a pornographic magazine; or futuristic as the knave of hearts is used to name the informal area being explored by the Phoenix spacecraft on planet Mars.

Why a book on Patience? The author, W. H. Cremer Jun, with those post-nominal letters suggest his American origins, as the Brits give their names handles for social ballast, so that mister or esquire suffice, but never junior. Firstly, Cremer Jun was known as a toy-seller to "little folk," the word 'children' was not then coined as he never includes it in his advertisements. To supply the best for his "little patrons," who are encouraged to "learn from their amusements," he searches the workshops of France and Germany for the best he can find.

Cremer Jun also sold children's books, especially instructional manuals. John's one on Patience has an exhortatory title worthy of Robert Baden-Powell of the scouting movement: *Patience by*

Perseverance. As a late Victorian's answer to today's stocking-filler, the book provides on its front cover a wily instruction for a child of the Empire, the biggest the world ever saw: "if at first you don't succeed, try, try and try again." I remember Mummy repeating the phrase when I knitted a ribbing in moss stitch or darned a hole in my gym slip, schooled my pony to turn on the forehand, or practised my French verbs. I wondered how many times I should try before I was entitled to give up. I weighed up the advice and couldn't agree with the stoical dictum. Just as I couldn't agree with turning my cheek, the usual advice from the pulpit. How many era have been saddled with this advice? And did it stem from my grandfather's generation? I have modified this epithet so that my daughter is regaled with the Churchillian dictat, 'never, never, never give up,' which is more contemporary.

Cremer Jun's little book aims at more than diversion. It has an imperial motif, giving the nod to hierarchy. Each game has a name: King, Queen, General, Admiral, Sultan, Duchess, Emperor, Engineer, and Rifle Corps. I admit it includes less status-loaded themes like Garcon, Windmill, Baby, Fox, Lion, and even the Rejected. It's the word, 'Patience' that intrigues. Wasn't there a Gilbert & Sullivan opera called *Patience?* Cremer Jun gives no date for his publication but the opera, opening in 1881, was a satire on the aesthetic movement and was the first show in London to employ electric light. I can well believe that middle class Gilbert & Sullivan devotees would have come down hard on anything purporting to the beautiful or useless, the aesthete in other words. When John was at Magdalen College, Oxford, a hard core of undergraduates berated anyone displaying the least trace of the pansy within their cloisters. W. H. Cremer Jun catered for those anti-aestheties, his card games a call for robust imperialism. I'm sure my grandfather followed those strict codes of manliness, courage and reserve. Or did he?

Daisy and Violet: twin-daughters of Captain Eyre Crabbe, Grenadier Guards, painted by Ethel Mortlock, exhibited at the Royal Academy in 1885, now in the possession of Richard Willan.

ROBERT, THE BUTLER

IF JOHN WAS MANLY, courageous and upright, he owed these attributes to a fleet of men and women downstairs in the castle, behind the green baize door, who saw to it that his food was cooked and served, the cutlery and china washed and stacked. They also laundered his clothes, cleaned his boots and rooms, and tended his wife and children; his animals, both domestic and wild too. These were his staff or servants. In literature, there are well-known alliances between the high and low-born, the most celebrated being Cervantes' Don Quixote and Sancho Panza. The French playwright, Moliere demonstrates in his drama this upstairs/downstairs mindset of idealistic, impractical masters and their down-to-earth, knowing retainers. The cerebral, religious John had one such manservant who even served as ersatz father to Mummy, Douna, and her three brothers after John's death. He was Robert, the butler, who was never known by his surname, McKinven, unlike Whetton, the butler at Capenoch, Dad's childhood home. We called him Robert, but he was Rob to his peers. Highland society was less formal and more intimate than that of the Lowlands or England.

Robert was sensitive to The Other World, the domain of elves, fairies, and broonies. He was wary of the Largie Broonie and never visited his room at the top of the tower, especially after dark. Everyone at Largie listened to what my grandfather said but he could not easily hear them, or his wife and children. While the Broonie was neither seen nor heard in the castle, although his deeds were noted, Robert was always visible but seldom spoke. That was his job: to serve silently. A butler is the soul of discretion and enablement. Presiding over the dining table he moves noiselessly from one person to the next, hearing what they say but never admitting to listening; far less, repeating what he hears, in the basement in the servants' hall where cook, housekeeper, kitchen maids, footmen, and others reside.

As senior member of staff, Robert took his job seriously. Others chuckled at his solemnity. A West Highland boy from the islands (born on Islay) with an Englishman's airs and graces. When Lachlan, the footman from Perthshire where houses were bigger and posher, asked his superior if he had come across a butler's revenge, Robert blushed, nervously adjusting the right corner of his bow tie. He knew but wasn't going to admit that it was a silent, smelly fart made by the butler beside a dislikeable guest as he served a row of people at the dining table.

Too bad that Robert never spoke up, turning the voiceless stink into words. We knew him as a monosyllabic old nag, sitting at Ballure on the step dividing the kitchen from the pantry, reading *The Herald*. We never met his twin, Sam the shepherd, and I guess that when they got together on the hill, they spoke in Gaelic, a language outlawed by the authorities and spoken by herdsmen, shepherds, and gamekeepers to the cattle, sheep, and dogs, and to the Broonie, of course.

But I can hear Robert's thoughts. I absorbed his history bit by bit. He speaks through me, to me when I encourage him:

> My teacher couldn't tell us apart. Unlike us, he wasn't from the Islands. Someone said he came from Aberdeen, the Granite City. He called us his Gaelic twins or Celtic Castor and Pollux. We were Sam and Rob to everyone else. Sam liked the outdoors and the sheep: the gathering, dipping, clipping, and lambing. Then, he'd be up all night when the ewes dropped their lambs. I preferred being inside. I even arranged flowers in vases, stacked crockery, laid the table, served soup, and saw that all was fine. That's what I liked. When we left school there was no work on the island so we went to the mainland to Mr Moreton Macdonald, laird of Largie. Sam minded his sheep and I was hall-boy first, then footman in the castle. Serving in the pantry, I washed silver after the meals and polished it. I wiped bread crumbs off the dining table and saw that no smears were left on the glasses. Then the laird died in 1921, and I was promoted to butler. At first, Sam wouldn't speak to me. He thought I'd

47

got above myself. Being the butler meant I was head of the household and had a right to respect. But the Largie staff still saw me as one of them, an island boy made good, but not that good. Not like other McKinvens from Islay who went to America. They made incredible good over there, they say.

I'd already served in the War, but I don't talk about it. Nobody does. Why should we? We lost our friends and relatives, and there's no honour in that even if I received a medal. What good did that do? It was just a piece of hard, cold metal, not warm like the touch of healthy, young skin. That's what we all wanted. Friendship, romance and a good life. Not guns, bullets, mud and death. All love was destroyed in that war to end all wars. Then there was another and every Macdonald was in it: Mrs Macdonald's three sons, a son-in-law, and even Esther, her youngest. She drove trucks in convoy and tried to shoot down German aircraft.

I just polish those knives, the ones with the mother-of-pearl handles. I found them in their leather box lined in maroon velvet, and blamed the Broonie for taking them. I check all the spoons, not confusing teaspoons with the ones they use for drinking coffee. I separate the dessert spoons from the soup spoons. This is important. I cannot abide a diner using an incorrect implement. There's a time and place for everything. There's a time to laugh and a time to cry, a time to act and a time to desist. You see, I listen to the readings of the scriptures in the Kirk. I listen to the voice of the Lord. And I know how to clean silver with the proper cream, to put my elbow into it and not slacken at my job.

The old days are gone. I was not only in charge of the dining room and the pantry but also the wine cellar. As footman under the previous butler I learned how to recognise a good claret and what temperature to serve it. Then there were the white wines, the Chablis, Chardonnay, Riesling, and Moselle, generally preferred by the ladies. The laird liked his burgundy blood-red and potent. To a boy who had only tasted uisge bheatha (whisky), Mr Macdonald's wine cellar was very foreign. He told me that Scots loved French wine and for centuries it had been shipped to the port of Leith near Edinburgh. The Auld Alliance between France and Scotland against England, our common enemy, encouraged us to drink it. After the Jacobite Rising failed, clandestine followers of the Stuarts drank toasts to Bonnie Prince Charlie, exiled on the Continent, by passing their wine glass over a jug of water, indicating that they still championed 'the king over the water.'

Largie wasn't a grand household like the Duke's castle at Inverary. Servants doubled up. Pantry maids helped in the kitchen and cook performed the duties of the housekeeper. I served as valet to the laird. That's how I learned how gentlemen dress: in high quality, understated tweeds when they were at home. I read his books and discussed with him matters far from the scope of my island childhood.

I take pride in the way I serve. When the young footman, Lachlan, a thorn in my flesh, questioned my methods, I told him straight. I open the door to guests, and he takes their hat and coat. It's my job to announce their arrival. For a first visit I am obliged to call out their full title. This would be simple for an ordinary guest but some of the Largie visitors were very grand. There was The Earl of Sandwich, descendant of the man who invented the sandwich. Addressing and introducing high-ranking clergymen was my hardest task. The Laird's friend, the Archbishop of Canterbury, was a mere clergyman when I first came to work at Largie, but he soon climbed the ecclesiastical ladder until he reached the top. My instructions were to refer to him as 'The Most Reverend and Right Honourable the Lord Archbishop of Canterbury.' Quite a mouthful for a Gaelic- speaking boy from the islands.

After Mr Macdonald died I tried to help Jock, Angus, and that scallywag, Simon. They're good-looking, mind, but you have to watch them, otherwise, when I serve them, they take more than their fair share. I give them a warning glance, which says, "there's three more to serve!" I can't tell them direct as I would with my own family, "Two spoonfuls of that stew or else I'll clip you round the ear!" You have to be polite and never say it straight. That's what a butler is, quiet, observant and, above all, polite.

When Mrs Macdonald decided to leave the castle, Jock said he would pull off its roof to avoid paying taxes. With his leg shot off, he can't manage the stairs up to the tower. Sam says it's wrong to destroy the castle. So do the others like Sandy, Mary, and Johnny. It's their home too. Everyone has a part to play and where do they go now? When Mrs Macdonald received that telegram, in the buff envelope that we all fear, she caved in. I could see how it was. She gave up. Angus was lost, the telegram said. Lost at sea. I knew what that meant; lost meant they found no body to prove he was killed. Lost meant he was either blown to pieces or he was laid out cold in the jungle, exposed on desert sand, lying on a mountainside, or bobbing on the ocean waves. Mrs Macdonald wanted to leave the castle and go up the road to Ballure and asked me to come. I agreed even though I'd be a cook and not the butler. Now I prepare cod pie, shepherd's pie, beef stew, and herrings in oatmeal. I know that dish. We went out as boys with the boat to catch herring in the bay. I cook mutton also. There's plenty of that, although Mrs Macdonald doesn't like it. She prefers cauliflower and macaroni cheese. Her appetite is poor and she drinks little. She's restless having suffered all those tragic events. She once received dozens of visitors, and her sisters were her mainstay, especially Violet, her twin. But Violet has died. I liked to serve these ladies in the castle. It's not the same here although I carry the main dish into the dining room with as much ceremony as I did at Largie. I present the food with dignity no matter who the guests are, even when Esther and her children visit. I could do without them. What an un-

50

ruly lot! Three spoiled, cheeky girls. Big girls who don't know how to hold their tongues. I pity their teachers. If they'd had mine, they'd know about it. I serve them properly, but Mrs Macdonald insists I place the dish on the sideboard so they may serve themselves. To save me work, she's bought a dumb waiter, that sits in the centre of her dining table. Times have changed. You wouldn't believe that they now serve themselves, when I remember the laird had a valet and Mrs Macdonald a lady's maid. Now she washes her dishes herself, cooks breakfast on my days off, although I prepare the vegetables for her lunch, before I go out. I know my place. I stay in the other part of the house, the servants' quarters, but she still worries about me. "What'll happen to Robert after I die?" she asked her daughters. She knows that Sam has gone; so have all my family and I seldom visit the islands now. "I must find a place for him to live," she said. She worries about me just as I worry about her. Twins of a sort, we're like peas in a pod but not the same one. Our pods are different.

Robert McKinven

51

NOT ONLY THE TWENTY-ONE year old McKinven twins, but the whole neighbourhood were present at Largie on 22nd June 1911 to celebrate George V's coronation. It was a balmy day, and the Macdonalds' friends, neighbours, and estate workers were determined to enjoy themselves. Sam directed the traffic, many guests arriving by foot, but the rich came by pony and trap, while the richest sailed in by car.

The shy Broonie kept away from the crowd. It's my guess he sulked on Cara and refrained from chucking stones over the water. The Largie garden party was a good social mix: landowners' wives rubbed shoulders with the partners of shepherds, carpenters, and gamekeepers. Farm-hands tossed the caber; mothers chivvied their children to run a three-legged race or the egg and spoon. Refreshments were restricted to tea for the women, beer for the men, and the children drank lemonade. Each child received a present of a Coronation mug, heralding a new era from the peaceful, fat Edwardian years. Most Kintyre people were una- ware of what was about to happen in the world at large.

In a spirit of noblesse oblige, John and Daisy wafted through the throng, welcoming each guest both the titled and the most humble. Their two children, three and a half year old Jock and Douna, who was almost two, were tidily dressed, their collars and cuffs starched and sandals polished to a high shine. For that afternoon Nanny Dempsey was in charge of the Macdonald children, ensuring they steered clear of the courtyard pond.

Exactly two years later on 22nd June 1913, Daisy gave birth to her second son. Arriving in what is now seen as a lull before the storm, Angus entered a far from stable world as nobody denied that clouds were forming over Europe and that war with Germany was a possibility.

However, life in Kintyre was a world apart, and all at Largie appeared peaceful. John may have been only the third owner and occupant of the castle but his land had belonged to the family for generations. This rootedness and sense of belonging was a decided advantage for Angus. In having lived in one place for so long, the family took on a mythic pallor, that had the effect of subordinating all those born into it. The Largie Macdonalds' ancestral line served as ballast for each generation in turn. As the second son of Largie's twentieth laird, Angus lacked for nothing: a home delivery with a midwife in attendance, nursemaids, a relaxed mother, interested father, regular feeds, fresh air, a spacious room, and, above all, silence. Jock and Douna's voices may have occasionally interrupted the infant's sleep but generally an air of calm surrounded baby Angus. In June 1913 John was busy working on his magnum opus. Gone were those rumbustious days of Angus's grandfather, Charles.

On July 25th, a month after his birth, two clergymen arrived at Largie to baptise him.

Considering the men's senior positions in the Anglican church, you would have thought that Angus was the most important infant in the country. The first, Byrd Spence Burton from Boston, Massachusetts, ended his career in the 1940s as Bishop of Nassau (and towards the end of the decade he also baptised me). The other, Cosmo Gordon Lang, Archbishop of York, had only one more rung of the ecclesiastical ladder to climb before he landed a bulls' eye.

Some thought it overkill to bring in an archbishop for the occasion. However, Lang and John were close and had met when the former was a simple clergyman, decades before he was to become, in 1936, the chief obstacle to Edward VIII retaining his throne if he married the twice divorced Wallis Simpson. Unlike Winston Churchill who championed Edward's cause, Lang was strongly opposed to it. In his view the king was flawed, his lifestyle decadent, and his friends frivolous. He was unstable and had undergone treatment for alcohol abuse.

The high Anglican priest met my grandfather in 1893 at Magdalen College, Oxford when he was Dean of Divinity and John a freshman. They became friends and when Lang visited Largie two years later he fell in love with the place. He wanted to be close to the sea and to look over to the islands, to walk in the woods, and stride over the heather on the hillside. This part of Kintyre, halfway down the peninsula's western sea-board, was where he wished to come for rest and peace, away from the mayhem of the southern cities where he worked. John chose a site on a hill to the north-west of the castle and, with the help of some men on the estate, built his friend a simple house of wood and stone. "The Tave" (short for Tavantaggart, which means in Gaelic The Priest's Rest) is still lived in although, after a fire during World War Two, it had to be extensively renovated.

During Angus's short life and because he lost his father when he was so young, substitute fathers were important for him. Although distant and preoccupied, Lang served as one. In fact, he played a vital and prolonged role in the lives of all the Macdonalds. He returned each summer (and sometimes at Easter) to Largie so that, as his biographer notes, all Macdonald children "as they appeared, were his, by christening, confirmation, and general adoption."

I picture him in the Largie chapel with dark, thinning hair wearing a white lawn surplice over a black cassock holding the baby dressed in his christening robe. Leaning over the font and assisted by Burton, who hands him a bowl of water, he draws the sign of the cross on the infant's forehead and names him Charles Angus. The baby's mother and father stand to the right while, on the left, George Hutchinson, John's Oxford friend, pledges his duties as godfather.

Charles was Angus's official name and it held a special significance. It gave the nod to the Macdonalds' Jacobite sympathies and therefore a salute to the Largie branch's kinswoman, Flora Macdonald, who, after the Rising of 1745 and having done her duty by Prince Charles Edward, stayed with her Largie cousins for a year before she set sail for Carolina in the United States.

The name also acknowledged the baby's bon viveur, sports-loving grandfather. Most importantly, he was named after Charles Lockhart, who on marrying in 1762 Elizabeth Macdonald of Largie, joined his property to hers. Later, the two families fell out, but in 1913 the Lockhart estate belonged to an old man with no heir. Someone had to inherit and there was a strong possibility that Angus was in the running. So, his parents pragmatically named their boy after the man who had initiated the original Lockhart union with the Macdonalds. However, from the start of his short life, the boy was known to family and friends by his second name, Angus.

Largie Castle stood secluded on a hill, so that the young boy and his siblings were separated from other families on the estate and neighbouring farms. Their home had rooms for all purposes from boot-hole, pantry, larder, study, and library to gun room. It even had a small precinct for Christian worship (the chapel of the Holy Spirit, consecrated in 1890).

And, of course at the top of the tower was the Broonie's room. As young children, Angus and his sisters and brothers learned that if they misbehaved the family spirit was not to be trifled with; it might even carry them away into the hills and they would never be seen again. On the other hand, if Angus fell and hurt himself his nurse-maid would gather him in her arms and tell him the Broonie would soothe his troubles away. The Broonie could do anything, if he put his mind to it. He made hens lay, urged cows to give milk, and made the sun shine. The Macdonald children learned that the Broonie was far more ancient than their ancestors or Largie itself, even older than the names of the local farms and villages. He pre-dated Christianity and the arrival of saints like Columba. It was as if each Macdonald child was born with a foothold in two spiritual camps: Christian and pagan. Perhaps that was why Daisy and John promptly arranged the baptism of their babies so that the Highland elf, far more ancient than Christ, made no claim on them. It amuses me that John, a devout Christian, believed in the uruisg. However, bi-spirituality and bi-lingualism had persisted for aeons in these parts, and, although Christianity adopted many native pagan festivals and sacred places, the old religion was never wholly extirpated, not even from the minds of the most sophisticated like my grandfather. Never-theless, these two strands of other-worldliness were a given for the Largie children. Possibly the future prelate raised an eyebrow at the Macdonalds' beliefs. One can only smile at the thought of a capricious Broonie, who chucked stones and pinched sleeping nursemaids, rubbing shoulders with a prince of the church. But I'm sure the moody fairy had little effect on Lang's enjoyment of his Highland retreat.

It is difficult to imagine Kintyre before the Great War, but Kit (Margaret) McNeil draws a fascinating picture of the community in the MacAlister Chronicles. At the time of Angus's birth there were only two cars in the district, and they belonged to the Mackinnons of Balinakill and the Kennedys of Glencreggan. If a vehicle passed the house (you could hear the car engine from a long way off), people rushed to the window with binoculars to identify it. Until 1913 the common mode of public transport was the stage coach, drawn by two or three horses that travelled from Campbeltown to Tarbert, carrying the mail and changing horses at Bellochantuy, Tayinloan and Clachan. Adults and children grabbed a box-seat beside Willie Young, the driver. Nobody sat inside, as it was reserved for calves tied in sacks, hens, or goats. Soon after Angus's birth, a bus replaced the Kintyre stage-coach although by that time the family owned a car and used a governess cart for visits to the village and to neighbours' homes.

Family photographs tell a story, not only in their content, but by the frequency with which one or other child is photographed. John and Daisy spared no expense in taking snap-shots of Jock, their firstborn. As a baby, bonneted and swirled in fine cotton, he is either wheeled in a chariot pram around the Largie garden, propped on his father's arm, or with his parents helping him build a sandcastle on the shore. Of Angus there is little.

John was affectionate and also loved his eldest daughter, Douna. When very young, she suffered from a temporary blindness. Nobody knows what caused it and, in spite of being comforted by Margaret Dempsey, their Ulster nanny, John insisted on cradling Douna in his arms until she recovered. But John's principal affection went to Jock, his firstborn and heir. Birth order or the practice of primogeniture, was too important. It made John Largie's 20th laird and Jock the 21st.

This procedure, where the first son takes all, is an arrangement whereby families follow the ancient strategy, of maintaining a family line where younger siblings are left to fend for themselves, as the family's influence and power depend upon it. Unfair though this is, it is how ancient British landed families survive, off-setting or minimising the effects of gambling debts, death duties, or in-heritance tax, failed business ventures, and spendthrift children.

Division into caste is rife. In traditional schools, brothers are distinguished by labelling the eldest 'major', the second 'minor' and the third 'minimus'. However, the second son ('minor'), Angus might inherit greater wealth than his older brother and therefore overtake him and become 'major'. Thus equality be-tween the Macdonald brothers was possible, something unthink-able with the Gladstones where my father was never allowed to forget that he was only a second son, a 'minor', without wealth.

Still, by the time Angus appeared in 1913, the camera at Largie played a more sporadic role. A dark-haired days' old infant sleeps in Daisy's arms, but the image fails to explain who it is. "DMM and one of us" is written on the photograph's reverse. Roses climb around the door-frame and since they bloom in mid-summer, the time when Angus was born, perhaps this is the first picture of him.

The dwindling photos of Largie newborns may have been due to events far from home also. As Angus moved from breastfeeds to solids, there were murmurs above and below stairs during those sabre-rattling, pre-war months of 1914. In the laird's dining room and the servants' quarters, men discussed if they would volunteer. On 4th August, 1914, war was declared.

During those anxious weeks, eyes turned westward towards nearby Ireland, a country in turmoil. But a month previously an Austrian archduke visiting Sarajevo, was shot. That clinched it.

As the Largie visitors' book testifies, a stream of guests stayed that summer: men dressed in civilian clothes, others in dark blue, and a number clad from head to toe in the colour of dust. Some-times Angus entered the drawing room after tea to meet them.

Once or twice he saw a man in black trousers and jacket with a white collar and a crucifix around his neck. This was Lang or Taggart, as the family called him, who enjoyed the company of the Largie children. With their regular features, well-laundered clothes, and a nanny to wipe their noses and straighten their hems and cuffs, it was easy to find them attractive. Doubtless, the archbishop suffered the Macdonald children more readily than the ones he had come across when he was (what is now patronisingly termed) a slum priest. Nevertheless, contact with Daisy and John's offspring became less frequent, when in 1914 not only the war impinged but the cleric abandoned the Tave for Ballure, situated three miles farther north. At the end of the year Angus, who was unaware of the gravity of world events, saw that the hair of the man with white collar and crucifix had turned white. Had he been old enough to understand, the young boy would have learned that Lang, in making a plea to the British public not to demonise Germany, was ridiculed and excoriated by the press.

If, at this time, the men in the young boy's life were in a state of flux, the women remained constant. In the afternoons, if it was fine, as it was that summer, his mother pushed Angus in his pram. Sometimes another lady came and no, the infant was not seeing double, although she was of a similar height to his mother and had the same eyes, pitch of voice, and hair colour. This was Violet, Daisy's identical twin sister. As she had done for his older sister and brother, Daisy treated Angus to rides in the donkey cart. But where was Dochie Darroch, who put the animal between the shafts? Where were Rob and Sam? Even John departed Largie in January, 1915, soon after Angus's second Christmas.

While their father was gone, a favourite place for the older children to play was in the woods around the castle. Jock and Douna paddled in the burn, surrounded by bamboo and rhododendron. Beyond, was a hill and on its brow perched the kennels. The keeper's spaniels barked, howled, and pounded the wire of their runs, when visitors called. The two eldest Macdonald children often made a trip there, not just to stroke the dogs but to see what the keeper had caught. Sometimes they saw dead rabbits, moles, and foxes. But lately things had changed. The pheasant coops were empty, and, because so many young men, including a keeper, had gone to the Front, sport on the estate was neglected. In peace-time, Largie earned more from its game rents and letting the castle, than from renting the fields. During the war all shooting for sport ceased.

Too young to follow his older siblings, Angus accompanied his mother to the walled garden where, at the end of a cinder path edged with slate slabs, they reached a border of michaelmas daisies, hollyhock, spiraea, and Canterbury bells. A keen gardener, Daisy realised how neglected the space had become. At the greenhouse on the north wall, further horticultural chaos met them. Trailing vines obstructed their entry. In the garden's centre, a half dozen bottle-shaped yews surrounded a fountain. I've no idea if the fountain played during those blood-soaked years, for Angus to watch its drops of water glisten in the sun. When unable to go outdoors, he stayed in the nursery with meals sent up from the kitchen. Food, served on thick, white china, was plentiful but bland: eggs, beef, mutton and fish with milk puddings for dessert. Adults and guests dined downstairs on crested bone china, while the cook, maids and butler ate in the servants' hall from willow-patterned plates.

In summer, 1915 John returned. Sometimes father and children visited the steading where other children lived. However, they spoke in a tongue the Macdonald children were unable to understand, and to add to their feelings of separateness, they learned their three "r's" in splendid isolation from Maude Harding, the Largie governess, while these local boys attended the school at Rhunahaorine. It's a wonder that John and Daisy's children picked up so few words in Gaelic, as even the herdsman used it to talk to his cows and the highland bull, one of which in John's youth was called David Dubh and won prizes at the Perth show.

Although the war played no direct role on civilians in Kintyre, Germany's U boats, present in the water off Scotland's west coast, threatened British shipping. However, no zeppelins invaded the air space and, unlike World War Two, there was an absence of blitzkriegs or area bombings. The government brought in rationing of sugar, tea, coffee, but Largie had plenty of vegetables, soft fruit and fresh meat. Was it confusing for Angus to see his father leave home? John first left when Angus was eighteen months and did not return until after his second birthday. Yet, deaths and casualties affected all corners of the country. Not one village or town escaped the arrival of the War Office buff telegram. The sight of the postmistress on her bicycle grew familiar; as her knuckles rapped on the front door, a curtain inside twitched at the window. Whistling stopped, children became mute, dogs whimpered, and the curtains were drawn. Angus hardly understood what had happened, but the dead men's ghosts lingered in courtyard, stable, barn, passageway, and drive, their personalities permeating their old haunts.

Then it all came much closer. Fortunately John was back from France at the time. On a morning in the first week of October, 1915, the postmistress's bicycle climbed Largie hill to deliver a letter from Violet, who was heavily pregnant (she was to give birth to her first child, Andrew on December 21st). She had offered her name as next of kin for her youngest brother Tempest, serving in France with 3rd Battalion Grenadier Guards, in case he was wounded, captured, or killed. The letter communicated news of the young officer's death on 27th September near Hill 70 at Puits during the battle of Loos. Since Tempest was orphaned at the age of eight, the older Daisy and Violet had become his substitute parents. At the time of his death their young brother was barely eighteen years and had joined the Guards on 17th April of that year, after he finished his training at the Royal Military College, Sandhurst.

It was a terrible shock. Cosmo Lang was not there as a source of comfort. He had stayed at Largie earlier that month but had returned to York two weeks previously. However, Daisy's brother, Lewis, a naval officer on HMS Hardy of the Grand Fleet, paid a visit on 14th October and stayed for a week. Born in 1897, Tempest was the baby of the family, but his was a sad, short life. After losing his mother when he was seven and his father a year later, he was sent to Summerfields preparatory school and then Winchester College from which he was expelled at the age of fifteen. He then entered Dulwich College and from there was admitted to RMC, Sandhurst. Tempest was to Angus what Angus was to me: an absent uncle, a name, an image in a photograph and for us both (Angus and me) merely a signature in a book given to our mothers.

John left home again in early 1916, and the months slipped slowly by before he returned, by which time Angus was almost three. Other men came back, some robbed of a limb or with disturbed minds. Worst of all were the young men who never returned and at the steading, in the village, and on the farms and crofts, silence descended. When, at last peace came in 1918, Angus was five and a half. Few were jubilant when victory was built on so much sorrow. Schoolmaster reports from Kintyre villages gave little mention of the war, in a collective desire to draw a veil over the trauma. The memoir of a Largie neighbour skims over these years, listing the names of the fallen but little else.

The country was in debt and farming prices were at an all-time low. The landowners had had their heyday, but for Angus and his siblings, life was only beginning. There had been other wars and they too had ended. Nevertheless, the adults knew that the recent cataclysmic events had sounded the death knell for the old way of life.

Most poignant were the absences, particularly of Tempest, whose signature in the Largie visitors' book is seen, first in a childish hand as a schoolboy, then at various addresses in and around London, and finally at RMC, Sandhurst. Another absence was Thomas Nelson, an Argyll friend who lived at Achnacloich and was killed in 1917. A year later his widow, Margaret met the French minor Impressionist artist, Paul Maze, from Paris and introduced him to the Macdonalds, before she married and had two children (Pauline and Etienne) by him. The community talked of erecting a memorial to the dead. John was determined to commemorate locally the Largie and Killean fallen and not have their names subsumed on an impersonal Campbeltown memorial stone. In the end they built one on a hill at Glenbarr looking out on to Cara to chastise the Broonie. From his seat on the island's southern shore, the Largie spirit could look over the sea to the monument and regret the deaths. The war took its toll; many looked older than their years. A photograph of my grandfather seated on a deck chair outside the castle taken shortly after the armistice shows him beginning to go bald.

Magdalen photo with John Ronald
Moreton Macdonald and Cosmo Lang

FLORA MACDONALD

I'VE EXPLAINED WHY Angus's first name was Charles. The Macdonalds supported the Jacobite cause, which meant they were loyal to Prince Charles Edward Stuart, the Young Pretender who tried to gain a victory in 1745 over the House of Hanover, the ruling British monarch of the time. The most famous name associated with Charles or Bonnie Prince Charlie is Flora Macdonald whose reputation has not worn well.

Scotland, a tough country in its religion and climate, has never been easy on women. Worn by men, the kilt signifies an androgynous garment but the nation itself has always been predominantly masculine. As I write, the Scottish Parliament is now dominated by three strong women: Nicola Sturgeon, First Minister, Ruth Davidson (Conservative) and Kezia Dugdale (Labour), but not that long ago, women were no more than appendages of father, uncle, brother, husband, or son. Only the chosen few, counted on the fingers of one hand, stood out from the crowd. They were 11th century Margaret, Queen of Scotland, saintly and anodyne, and Mary Queen of Scots, to some an idiot for choosing bad men and not heeding her advisors' warning to avoid sailing to England for asylum. There were others but possibly the most trivialised and commercialised is Flora Macdonald who, on her mum's side was related to the Macdonalds of Largie. To fess up to being related to Flora, is to invite mirth. No, you're NOT! Not HER, is the usual comment. That schmaltzy, tartan-clad woman depicted on the lids of shortbread tins! You're having me on! You can't be! Well, yes, I am.

Born in 1722, Flora was the daughter of Ranald Macdonald of Milton, South Uist in the Outer Hebrides and Marion, daughter of Angus Macdonald. Flora's father died when she was a child and the clan chief, Macdonald of Clanranald, her father's cousin, brought her up. She was partly educated in Edinburgh. In June 1746, when she was 24 and living on Benbecula, another island in the Outer Hebrides, Bonnie Prince Charlie, after the Battle of Culloden, took refuge there. The Prince's companion, Captain Con O'Neill from County Antrim in Ireland and Flora's cousin, asked her for help. The Hanoverians controlled the island although they used the local militia to keep order. The situation was not unlike Nazi-occupied France or Holland during World War Two with an active underground organisation and collaborators working for the occupiers. The Macdonalds were secretly sympathetic towards the Jacobites but Flora hesitated and then agreed to help. The commander of the local militia was her step-father, Hugh Macdonald, who gave a pass to the mainland for herself, a man-servant, and an Irish spinning maid (Betty Burke), who was the disguised Prince, and a boat crew of six. They departed for Skye on 28th June. Their voyage is described in the celebrated *Skye Boat Song*:

> Speed bonny boat, like a bird on the wing
> Onward the sailors cry.
> Carry the lad that's born to be king
> Over the sea to Skye.
>
> Loud the winds howl, loud the waves roar,
> Thundercloud rend the air,
> Baffled our foes stand by the shore
> Follow they will not dare.
>
> Though the waves leap, soft shall ye sleep,
> Ocean's a royal bed,
> Rocked in the deep, Flora will keep
> Watch by your weary head.
>
> Many's the lad fought on that day,
> Well the Claymore could wield,
> When the night came, silently lay
> Dead on Culloden's field.

Burned are their homes, exile and death
Scatter the loyal men,
Yet ere the sword cool in the sheath
Charlie will come again.

When they arrived on Skye, Flora hid the Prince among the rocks by the shore, while she searched for help. They proceeded to Portree, the main town of the island and then to the isle of Raasay. But the crewmen gossiped about Flora's passenger and she was arrested, taken to London, imprisoned in the Tower but released the following year. Charles had better luck and departed Scotland from Lochaber on L'Heureux, a French frigate, and arrived in France that September. On 6th November, 1750, aged 28, Flora married Allan Macdonald, an army captain. Settling on Skye they became parents to five sons and two daughters, and in 1772 they moved to the Macdonald family estate at Kingsburgh, Skye.

While the 18th century lexicographer, Samuel Johnson and his diarist sidekick, James Boswell, were conducting their well-documented Highland tour, they met in 1773 the Macdonalds. "She is a woman of soft features, gentle manners, kind soul and elegant presence," wrote Johnson of Flora. He also paid her the tribute, immortalised on her memorial at Kilmuir: "Hers is a name that will be mentioned in history and if courage and fidelity be virtues, mentioned with honour."

Shortly after this meeting, Flora stayed at Largie at the old castle, no more than a fortified house situated at the village of Rhunahaorine, a mile or two north of the present Largie. Today, only one wall of the old building stands. It was modest and had no crow-step gables, turrets or tower like the new castle. Flora had two brothers, Angus and Ranald who liked shooting, possibly the woodcock that flew into Kintyre from Norway at the beginning of winter. One day they went to Cara for a day's sport, and Ranald was shot. By all accounts it was an accident, but the Broonie can be accused here, if not of malevolence, then of gross negligence.

In 1774 Allan and Flora emigrated to North Carolina (many Jacobites settled there, as the state was named in honor of King

Charles I). Captain Macdonald served the British Government in 84th Regiment of Foot (Royal Highland Emigrants). Legend has it that in February 1776 Flora rallied the Loyalists, supported by her husband, to advance to Moore's Creek Bridge, where they met with defeat. Macdonald was captured and imprisoned for two years until 1777. Thereafter he moved to Fort Edward in Windsor, Nova Scotia and took command of 84th Regiment of Foot, 2nd Battalion. After her husband was jailed, Flora went into hiding while the American Patriots ravaged her plantation and grabbed her possessions. She re-united with her husband in the Fall of 1778 at Fort Edward. The following year Flora returned to Scotland. During the passage over, pirates attacked the ship. Refusing to leave the deck, she received a wound in her arm. On reaching Skye she stayed with relatives. Allan returned in 1784 and regained his estate in Kingsburgh. Flora died there in 1790 aged 68.

The Stuarts, both Old and Young Pretender, particularly the latter, have not gone down well in history. Quintessentially, Prince Charles Edward Stuart was a romantic figure and a heroic failure. With a Polish mother, Maria Sobieska, and having spent all of his childhood and early youth in Italy (in Rome and Bologna), he was virtually a foreigner and not a suitable leader for the Scottish Highlanders. Failing to take the Crown of Scotland (and England), he slunk back to the Continent and lived a dissolute life. The memory of the unprepossessing Charlie, who was largely unconcerned about the terrible fate that met his followers after his defeat, has cast a shadow over Flora's reputation. She's not taken seriously. People snigger at her feat in making Bonnie Prince Charlie cross-dress as her Irish maid. It's pure pantomime, they joke. But she was brave, Alan Ramsay's portrait of the Jacobite heroine testifies to her strength. When she was arrested, the authorities could have paraded her through the streets of London and even imposed on her a public execution, a fate suffered by hundreds of other Jacobites. Instead they locked Flora in the Tower of London. When she and her husband emigrated to America, her life was not easy; she lost everything. Finally, on her voyage over the

Atlantic, she was more than gutsy when confronted by pirates.

Was Flora another example of the Macdonalds' fatal flaw or, in a broader context, of Scotland's tendency to see itself as a failure? In having struggled for centuries to hold its own against England, its larger neighbour, Scotland has now achieved a strong identity. As for Flora she, along with her Highland compatriots, was pitted in a desperate, but doomed, fight for freedom against an invading force. Was she outstanding? Yes! Courageous? Yes! But, in the end her judgement was as poor as that of Mary Queen of Scots. She backed two losing sides. First, the Jacobites, then the British in the American War of Independence. She championed the 'rebels' first, then the 'Crown.' Are the Macdonalds beleaguered by their ambivalence between the Establishment and the non-conformist? This dilemma runs like a thread through each generation. From the days of the Scottish freedom-fighters of the 13th and 14th centuries, to the Jacobite period when Flora played her part in the Highlanders' bid for its own Government, to the present day, Scotland has struggled to assert itself as a nation.

Flora Macdonald by Allan Ramsay,
in Ashmolean Museum, Oxford

I'M SURE JOHN, my grandfather, was filled with ambivalence too. All Highland lairds were. After the failure of 1745, when many were dispossessed for their Jacobite sympathies, much that distinguished the Highland way of life was banned. Speaking Gaelic was forbidden, and the kilt and bagpipes were outlawed. Many chieftains, themselves targeted by the Hanoverian Government, raised rents or cleared their tenants off the land and introduced sheep instead. Little by little these lairds became less concerned with their followers. Actually the rot began as far back as the early 17th century, when James VI (1 of England) insisted the clan chief's eldest son (or daughter) be educated away from the Highlands. In this way the Crown started to anglicise the area, thus taming and eventually subjugating it. Although Scottish lairds often attended English schools, in John's case Eton, they still felt a visceral loyalty towards Scotland, but in my grandfather's day, making the nation a region and calling it North Britain, became a trend. When war was declared in August 1914, England, Wales, Scotland, and most of Ireland pulled together against the common enemy, and John was the first to want to participate.

The Great War took its toll on our grandfather. Late Victorian studio portraits of the young laird show him very much at ease striking a Harry Lauderesq pose in kilt, sporran, and tammy. These photographs suggest a relaxed, somewhat vain youth. As he reached early middle age, John is captured cuddling his firstborn, ambling by the Largie pond, or scything grass in his policies. A few years later, however, everything has changed, and a further picture reveals a sombre moment in northern France. In officer's uniform, he stands on a step outside a chateau, behind a French private leaning on crutches and an elderly, decorated Gallic soldier. Here John's effervescence is replaced by exhaustion.

What happened? At the outset of hostilities John was 41 years of age, too old for joining up. Although eighteen months later in 1916 under The Military Act of 27th January, the army accepted men as old as he. However, it was not his age that disqualified him from active military service, but his health. His deafness counted against him although earlier in his life he had joined the Argyll & Sutherland Highlanders' 3rd battalion of Volunteers.

Greatly disappointed, John watched his contemporaries dust their epaulettes and prepare to defend their country. Thomas Nelson of Achnacloich near Connel was one, while James Howard Lindsay of Lunga, of 14th Battalion of the London Scottish, County of London Regiment, was another. Younger men also were in a fever to join up, like the sons of May Tarrat. The two brothers, born twelve months apart, lived on the Knapdale peninsula at Ellary.

To add insult to injury, John had a fleet of brothers-in-law eligible to serve. His wife Daisy, one of eight children, came from a long line of professional soldiers, her father a hero of the Boer War. She had four brothers too: among them, Colville a professional soldier, Lewis a naval man, and the baby of the family, Campbell Tempest at the Royal Military College, Sandhurst. To make matters harder, Daisy's twin sister Violet had just married a 60th Rifles officer, Hugh Willan, shortly to go to the Western Front.

From his West Highland lair, John followed the news of the struggle besetting a country he admired. As a man who loved France's history, countryside, people, language, and customs, the prospect of this nation's defeat was intolerable. News arrived of the battle of Mons, where the British held out against the enemy but had to retreat when the Germans attacked from the south. Belgium was quickly over-run and its allies retreated. When the Kaiser's troops advanced towards Paris, reaching twenty miles from its outskirts, the French general, Joffre, launched a counter-strike transporting troops by any means possible: in lorries, buses and even taxis. This was the first battle of the Marne which saved the French from defeat but exhausted them, as they failed to gain any strategic advantages.

Following the news of these events, John read in *The Times* the notices of the wounded and dead. He also learned about the damaged cities and towns he had visited before the war: the unconscionable destruction of Reims Cathedral, France's West-minster Abbey, where French kings had been crowned. Germany bombed the cathedral on 20th September. The scaffolding around the north tower caught fire and the lead on the roof melted and poured from the rivuleted mouths of the stone gargoyles. Fierce battles raged in Ypres a fortnight later, and on October 3rd the cathedral and the Cloth Hall burned down.

Ineligible for active service, John could do little. He tried to enlist as a medical orderly for the British but the Royal Army Medical Corps turned him down. By this stage British volunteers were rushing to France: men unsuitable for active service either because of their age or disability, and women who wished to dress wounds but had little training in nursing. Determined to halt the outflow of hopefuls, the British Red Cross stepped in and the War Office gave instructions to limit the number of volunteers.

One pre-war guest at Largie was Granville Bromley-Martin who visited in autumn of 1906, the year of John and Daisy's marriage. During the first months of the war the Macdonalds, still in touch with Granville, learned that his older sisters, Madeline and Susan, were trying to establish a hospital for wounded servicemen. While stopping at Vichy in France, a relative noticed a train-load of wounded French soldiers with nobody to care for them. This gave the sisters the idea of setting up a small nursing unit. Madeline Bromley-Martin was well-connected and one of her contacts was Kathleen Scott, widow of Captain Robert Falcon Scott, whose doomed expedition to the Antarctic two years previously was still fresh in the public's memory. Lady Scott, who studied sculpture under Auguste Rodin, lent her name to the enterprise. Winning publicity, contacts, and money she organised a motor ambulance corps for the hospital. Once she gained permission for her venture, the redoubtable Madeline Bromley-Martin, raised in Worcestershire where she took piano lessons with Edward Elgar, began to search for suitable staff. She recruited Emma Maud Banfield, who, as matron, was put in charge of twelve trained nurses. Although many offered their services free, the professional staff had to be paid. Since initially they received no financial help from the French authorities, money had to come from private donors. One of them was the author, painter and explorer, Emily Georgiana Kemp, who paid for the nurse's salaries. Dr. Graham Aspland was chief surgeon, while the painter and Slade Art School professor, Henry Tonks, who had trained as a physician, was the hospital anaesthetist. Providing unpaid support to the staff were twenty volunteers: probationary nurses and medical orderlies.

For the hospital building, the French government offered the Bromley-Martins a remote chateau in Haute-Marne in the village of Arc-en-Barrois, some sixty miles behind the fighting line. Originally the hunting retreat of the Duc de Penthievre, (a grandson of Louis-Philippe) the chateau was situated in a wooded valley. The river Anjou flowed through this peaceful area. With the premises established, the staff were answerable to the French army's Service de Santé and could only admit French patients. Additionally, all hospital personnel had to arrive in France with a personal guarantee signed by the Hon. Arthur Stanley, MP, co-chairman of Britain's Joint-War Committee. With its sizable rooms, high ceilings, large windows and roomy corridors, the chateau was admirably suited for its new purpose. In early January, 1915, after gaining access, the Bromley-Martin sisters cleared all the main rooms of furniture and brought in beds to create the wards.

Converting a royal residence into a functional hospital presented a challenge, as the chateau had neither gas nor electric lighting, an adequate lift, hot running water, proper drainage, or efficient heating. However, it boasted a lovely park with three acres set aside for cultivating food for the patients and staff; timber from the woods was used as fuel for the hospital.

On 27th January, 1915 with a staff of sixty, the hospital opened with 110 beds. It served the wounded from the French 3rd Army Corps who fought in the Argonne, a large forested region north of Arc-en-Barrois. Very quickly men needing treatment inundated the hospital so while the chateau handled severe cases (like septic wounds), a convalescent unit in the village, headed by Miss

Kemp (later Susan Bromley-Martin) dealt with less serious complaints.

When John heard from Granville Bromley-Martin about Madeline's nursing unit, he acted quickly. Hopital Temporaire was too good an opportunity to miss, as it was the only one in France taking voluntary orderlies. He was a perfect candidate: well enough off to finance his passage and work for nothing, a Franco-phile, as proved by his exhaustive oeuvre on the country's history which was about to go to press in 1915. He also spoke French.

He not only persuaded Madeline Bromley-Martin to take him on but also won an all-important guarantee from the British Government. When John arrived at Arc-en-Barrois to act as a medical orderly, stretcher-bearer, and ambulance driver, he worked with John Masefield, future poet laureate, who described my grandfather as "very tall, a public school type, stone deaf, who follows me like a faithful dog." Another orderly was the Impressionist artist, Wilfrid de Glehn, who arrived at the chateau in early 1915 with Jane, his American artist wife. She drew pastel portraits of the patients to raise money for an artificial limb fund. I have her drawing, dated 20th December 1915, of John: a sensitive study of a middle-aged man in army uniform. Judging from photographs of my grandfather, de Glehn made his neck too thick and chin too dimpled; when I first saw the sketch, I failed to recognise him.

Hopital Temporaire attracted other men and women from the arts. Some were living in France, and their response to men mobilising on the Front was to help the country in crisis. Many had few family ties and were perfect candidates for work at the hospital. The poet and art scholar, Laurence Binyon, part of whose poem *For the Fallen* has become an integral feature of Remembrance Sunday services, lent a hand at Arc. Some of his most famous poems like *An Orderly's Day* and *Fetching the Wounded* were inspired by his time there. Artists served in nearly all departments of the hospital: Susan Strong, a Wagnerian opera singer, who ran a shop in Paris selling luxury lingerie, volunteered to cook at the chateau.

The hospital relied on both professional and amateur; John's orderly colleagues also included an architect, an Oxford don. and R.C. Phillimore, son of Lord Justice Phillimore, who supplied two ambulances, one driven by himself and the other with his chauffeur behind the wheel.

Madeline Bromley-Martin accepted a bevy of well-connected probationers (unqualified nurses), like Miss Prideaux Brune, the Hon. Gertrude Forbes-Sempill, Lady Elizabeth Keppel, Lady Lillian Robertson, and the Hon. Dorothy Emmott.

In an environment dominated by women, the orderlies were invaluable for heavy lifting, stretcher-bearing, and driving vehicles. John might have found work hard at the hospital, as he was unused to manual labour or assuming a subordinate role. After a life of leisure with a full complement of staff to wait on him, he now had to lift patients, wash floors, mend broken furniture, and take orders. Initially he fetched the wounded, as at home he was used to driving vehicles along winding, country roads.

The hospital had two ambulances and eventually five, driven by orderlies who doubled as stretcher-bearers. They collected the wounded at Latrecy station seven kilometres from the chateau. Setting off by rail early in the morning from Clermont, the injured soldiers travelled in closed carriages with no windows, just slits. Each truck contained four iron frames that held three stretchers, one over the other. When the train reached its destination helpers dragged the frame into the middle of the carriage, the vibration causing great pain to the occupant. "The men were very done up and exhausted after their long train and motor journey, especially as our roads were very rough and stony," wrote a hospital orderly on reaching the chateau with the wounded. John describes "a take-in night" in an article written in 1916 for *The Cornhill Magazine*:

> "A little crowd of French peasants at a wayside station some forty miles behind the fighting line is awaiting the arrival of the nightly train de santé with offerings of soup, wine, coffee, and fruit for the wounded. The great engine headlight draws slowly nearer, and the heavy train clinks and

bumps to a standstill with its load of four or five hundred wounded. It is a 'take-in night' at the Hospital of Arc-en-Barrois, not far from Verdun."

My grandfather describes graphically how "the Englishmen in khaki" (orderlies like himself) find the severely wounded:

"The glistening eyes tell of fever: almost all are so weary that it is an effort for them to answer questions, some are rambling in their talk; often we get poor fellows who have lain out for days in the thick forest of the Argonne before they have been found; these men are terribly emaciated. Recently there have been several shocking cases of burns, most of which have ended fatally, but there seems to have been no asphyxiating gases; the character of the ground probably forbids it."

John's glowing report of entente cordiale and unstinting admiration of the French, particularly their willingness to accept an English-run unit, continues. The patients are not just naturally polite but excel in "their blitheness, playfulness and unfailing sense of fun. Their sense of humour has been more valuable to the French in the present crisis than legions of doctors and nurses."

Food came from all quarters: trout from the river, asparagus from the meadows, truffles from the woods, and even venison sometimes, gifts from the local peasants and farmers. It's unsurprising that John wrote of the hospital at Arc in such terms. He was putting a positive spin on their activities. The situation was critical; France and the Allies were in crisis. He wrote to gain publicity (and money), as the hospital relied on donations to continue.

The truth revealed much in-fighting and battles of egos. Wilfrid de Glehn, a charismatic figure, was often at loggerheads with the strong-minded Madeline Bromley-Martin. John was caught between the two factions, and because of his deafness, de Glehn often manipulated him into signing papers that their director would never have sanctioned. Other reports showed more struggles; Eva Smith, a nurse who joined the staff when the hospital opened, indicates that it was hard for diverse personalities to work together. John Masefield took a swipe at the probationers too, whom he regarded as over-privileged dilettantes.

My grandfather returned to Largie in July 1915 but received letters from patients asking him to return. Leaving his family (Daisy was in the early stages of pregnancy), he returned to Arc-en-Barrois five months later. Life at the hospital was even more hectic than before. A stream of seriously wounded French soldiers swept into the wards. This time John had responsibility over Wilfrid de Glehn, a decision that caused bad feeling. Madeline Bromley-Martin liked to surround herself with men and women from her own social background and wished to use John as a bulwark against de Glehn, whose socialist, agnostic leanings made her uneasy. Although excellent at organisation and marshalling staff, Miss Bromley-Martin was no book-keeper. She got in a muddle with her bills as she wrote most of her accounts on scraps of paper. Rob Martin-Holland, her brother-in-law and John's Eton contemporary, coerced her to put her affairs in order. From London, where he was a banker at Martin's in Lombard Street, Rob played a vital role in the hospital's organisation. He and Nell, with other volunteers like Daisy, helped raise funds and interview staff for the hospital.

John was the obvious candidate to straighten out the hospital's book-keeping. Not only was he a stalwart with none of de Glehn's caprice, he was better suited to this job than working as a medical orderly because his deafness stood in the way of satisfactory social interaction. Now his disability would no longer be an embarrassment to him.

Most funds came from 800 private subscriptions. At the beginning, Susan Bromley-Martin managed these, while Rob Martin-Holland oversaw the finances. To cover all expenses the hospital needed £400 a month, and this was achieved if one hundred individuals or organisations pledged £4.00. Much of the money came from English donors, but the town of Wilmington in America donated an X-ray machine and a dental ambulance. One

American family supported a ward of ten beds while countries as various as Norway, Ireland, the Portuguee British, and the USA maintained over thirty. Hospital staff frequently wrote appeal letters and newspaper articles, like Laurence Binyon's *An English Hospital for French Soldiers*, in which he quotes the enthusiasm of a patient, "I shall tell the people that the English are 'les braves gens' and that country is my second home."

The year 1916 saw the longest, most devastating armed conflict known to man. The battle of Verdun began towards the end of February and lasted until mid December. Some claim it was France's Stalingrad, when a quarter of a million were killed and half a million wounded. The hospital at Arc-en-Barrois was filled to the gunnels. At the height of the Verdun battle, John wrote to Nell Martin-Holland in London to ask if she would recruit a clergyman for the hospital. Although the local curé paid regular visits to the wards and patients and staff attended Mass in the village, many English personnel who were Anglican were forbidden to celebrate communion in a Roman Catholic church. Unfortunately, the Martin-Hollands could find no one for Hopital Temporaire.

It wasn't easy for Daisy at Largie either but she had assistance from Margaret Dempsey and Maude Harding. My grandmother spent most of her pregnancy without her husband but she had him back in time for the birth of Simon. The next year the indefatigable pair discussed the possibility of working at the hospital together. Fortunately they never put their plan into operation, as the Macdonald children had suffered, not only from their father's absence but also from Daisy's visits to London to help raise hospital funds.

After the armistice in 1918, the family was to enjoy a few years of calm. Sadly, this unity was not to last. The last publicised event at Largie before John's death was the conference of Scottish bishops in April 1921. Barely six months later, in early September, he was taken ill with a duodenal ulcer that had troubled him for some time.

Lang was at Ballure when John became ill. The archbishop

summoned Daisy, who was away from Largie, and called a Glasgow specialist. The doctor failed to arrive in time to help (the journey involved a train ride to Gourock, a ferry to Tarbert, and a drive of twenty miles to Ballure). On September 7th, after a blood transfusion John collapsed and three days later he died. His body was laid in a coffin made of timber from the Largie woods and piped to the family burial-ground.

John Moreton Macdonald, by Jane de Glehn

NOTWITHSTANDING THE EARLY DEATH of their father, the Largie children learned early to entertain themselves and were good at games like Solitaire, which consists of a circular board with rows of marbles. It works on the principle of drafts, where the player hops one marble over another and at each move the vaulted piece is eliminated. The aim is to finish with one marble on the board. This game, a favourite of Daisy's, was shoved on to the laps of fidgety children, before and after lunch, and they were expected to play quietly.

The Macdonalds enjoyed solitude, so they favoured card and board games for one player. However, the Largie visitors' book proves the family was sociable but frowned upon gambling; few of them played Bridge. Nevertheless, they indulged in unsophisticated card games, that demanded speed more than intellectual ability, like Racing Demon; hard on the family's pocket, the game required one pack per player. Given the boisterous way it was played, many cards were destroyed.

The Macdonalds read keenly. I have the remnants of Daisy's book collection: George Meredith, Thackeray, R.W. Emerson, Charles Lamb and collections of poetry and essays given to her by Gertrude Leverton-Harris, whose husband, Frederick, was a British politician and art-collector.

Unlike her husband, my grandmother lacked a room of her own. John worked in his large library on a three volume history of France. I've little idea when he began this magnum opus of 1,316 pages, which opens at the time of the Romans and ends with the Franco-Prussian war (1870-71). The Largie visitors' book shows my grandparents stayed in Oxford at 7 Cross Road for the winter of 1910, which suggests that John was working on the book at that time and seeking help from his old Magdalen tutor, Charles Fletcher. By 1914 the work was complete. "This book," wrote John from northern France in May 1915, "was in the press before anyone dreamt that we should be standing beside our traditional enemy on the very battlefields, where we have so often confronted her." The timing was unfortunate; John worried that in the light of France's recent trials, he had overstated "the temperamental weaknesses of the French," but he could not alter the work as it "would be so biased as to lose its value".

A largely unfavourable American review (the book was published on both sides of the Atlantic) appeared in April 1916. Charles Downer Hazen, shortly to bring out his own work on the French Revolution and Napoleon, admired John's first two volumes, but found his treatment of the Revolution owed too much to the conservatism of Edmund Burke.

Conversely Dr Walford D Green, a biographer of Voltaire, claimed in the English History Review of July 1916, that John was at his best when covering the Revolution and Napoleonic Wars. He excelled with his interpretation of contemporary authorities and modern times.

My grandfather's enthusiasm was not limited to "the country over the water." He was also interested in local history and in 1921 (the year of his death) was elected the first president of the Kintyre antiquarian society.

I'm sure John never allowed his children to touch his books. Like the gun room, his library was out of bounds. Had Angus ventured into the airless space, soundproofed by rows of books, he might have noticed how his father numbered them. On the inside front cover he wrote a letter in capitals followed by a lower case roman numeral, then one in Arabic. For example: A iv 12. Important volumes carried a book-plate with the Macdonald motto, "semper paratus pugnare", which means "always ready to fight," and a coat of arms of a man in armour, his face concealed by a helmet and visor. His shield, divided in four parts, had a lion rampant on the top left hand and a crusader's gloved hand holding a crucifix on the right. A boat occupied the bottom left side while a fish took up the right. The lion signifies the Macdonalds' affiliation with Scotland and the crucifix the defence of the faith; the fish demonstrates that they were followers of Christ and the sailing boat: nautical skills. A boat for the West

Highland chieftain of yesterday was as much a status symbol as a smart car is for today's company executive.

The children's reading-matter included Lewis Carroll's *Alice in Wonderland*, an Edwardian anthology of children's short stories written by John Buchan, Hilaire Belloc, and Cynthia Asquith, and an illustrated children's encyclopedia of dogs.

Most of the children's books have disappeared, but I have a good idea what else the young Macdonalds read as Mummy tried to influence my reading with her preferences. With three older brothers, her tastes were muscular rather than feminine. Neither Susan Coolidge's *What Katy Did*, nor Louise May Alcott's *Little Women*, ever graced her collection.

She enjoyed adventure stories like Arthur Ransome's *Swallows and Amazons*, *Kidnapped* by Robert Louis Stevenson, and John Buchan's *Greenmantle*. Forbidding me Enid Blyton's *The Famous Five*, she sent me to boarding school with a copy of Rudyard Kipling's *Stalky & Co*. I have to smile at its unsuitability as the opening paragraph has Stalky and pals puffing cigarettes outside the school gate.

Although ungrateful at the time, I realise Mummy was correct. In spite of his schoolboys indulging in nicotine hits, Kipling's fiction was good, if not great, while the vastly popular Blyton was pulp.

Mummy introduced me to books about animals too: Anna Sewell's *Black Beauty*, Henry Williamson's *Tarka, the Otter* and J.W. Fortescue's *The Story of a Red Deer*. She and her brothers had read dozens of animal stories. It was hardly surprising. All beasts, domestic and wild, were crucial to the family as their livelihood depended upon them. They employed shepherds, herdsmen and keepers to manage these creatures. It made perfect sense for the Largie children to read this kind of book. The more heart-breaking, the better. *Black Beauty*, an equine *Oliver Twist*, is a plea for the plight of the Victorian carriage horse, while Tarka and the deer tale are stories that question the slaughter of animals for sport. It was confusing for Angus and Esther to read these books when all around them, at Largie and on the neighbouring estates, shooting birds and small animals, was not only accepted but regarded as a must.

How the Largie children amused themselves during long, winter evenings, as there was no television and little radio, is hard to picture. Doubtless, each child had toys: a miniature train, lead soldiers, a magic lantern, a pouch of marbles, or a kaleidoscope. I suspect that John's affliction, while he was alive, dictated what they did and assume that my grandfather's deafness encouraged him and his family towards silent pursuits like playing Patience, Solitaire and reading. For most of his life John was "stone deaf," which suggests his disability was severe. When thinking of a stone, a barrier, unyielding and cold, comes to mind. This "obstruction" affected his relations with his children, who perhaps found him distant and unresponsive. It's hard for a child to be patient with the deaf. I picture Angus shouting to be heard and feeling frustrated with his father's inability to respond. Because he could not hear his own voice, John might have spoken stridently, which would have made his children blush or feel rejected by him.

"Father, can you hear me?" Angus touches John's sleeve.

"What?" his father looks up from his desk while writing a letter.

"I saw a squirrel today!"

"What?"

"I saw a squirrel!"

"You saw a skittle?"

"A SQUIRREL!"

"Don't shout!"

I've dozens of questions about John's problem. When did he become deaf and how did he handle it? Could he lip-read? Possibly people laughed at him if he tried out an ear trumpet; it made him look so old. Doubtless he wore a hearing aid but in those days they were enormous. The apparatus tended to break and had to be sent away to be mended. It's unsurprising, then, that John expressed his thoughts and feelings on paper and that this form of communication also became the norm for his children.

With limited exposure to the spoken word, as is often the case with children of deaf parents, Angus grew up quiet and reserved. It's taken me some time to piece together the effect impaired hearing has had, not only on Angus's generation, but my own. When I was a child, activities requiring few words were preferable to those employing verbal communication. Garrulousness was unnecessary, even ostentatious or vulgar. It was better to be an individual of few words. Absorbing these dicta, I confused taciturnity with wisdom.

Still waters did not necessarily run deep and a babbling brook wasn't always an indicator of superficiality. For an inquisitive, verbal child, my family's credo that "silence is golden" and "children should be seen and not heard," was perplexing. Perhaps this was my deaf grandfather's legacy.

Evidently, John brought reflection and quietness to Largie (although I cannot think his children were silent all the time).

When Jock went to West Downs in 1916, aged 8½, Angus learned to read with Miss Harding. After instruction on the alphabet and guiding him through simple texts about cats on mats, she introduced him to Latin: simple verbs like amo, amas, amat. "Where do they speak this?" he asked.

"Nowhere!" she admitted. "They spoke it a long time ago in ancient Rome."

"Where's that?"

"Italy!"

"They don't speak it today?"

"No. That's why people call it a dead language."

"What's the point in learning a dead language?"

"Latin trains the mind." In learning Latin, a boy absorbed knowledge of the Roman belief system, seen as a splendid foundation for joining the British establishment.

Angus had heard of training animals, puppies mainly. House training, they called it, so they didn't wet the carpet or chew slippers. But training the mind, by learning words that meant nothing, and in what they called a dead language, was strange.

Miss Harding persisted. "Come along, Angus. Repeat after me, amo, which means?"

"I love!" he spat. "But I don't love…It's wet to love. Big boys don't love. They…."

How could he admit to loving when he had to leave home, adapt to a new regime with strange boys and even stranger masters who beat you when you played rough games or if you were bad. Jock had often scared him about the prospect; so what had love to do with it?

Warning him not to interrupt, Miss Harding then introduced him to declensions (even harder than conjugations) like mensa, mensae, etc.

"This means a table," she explained. "The first word is a table as the subject, the second is if you want to address one, and the third…."

"What do you mean?" he asked.

"If you are talking to one, you say mensae!"

Angus burst into fits of laughter. First it was love, then it was talking to tables. He had heard of people talking to themselves, which was, they said, the first sign of madness but….

After mensa, mensae, mensam he learned dominus, domine, dominum. He understood that word. It meant a master, and before his childhood was over, he would come across a variety of them, some good and others dismal.

Then his governess produced a better one. Bellum, meaning a war. He liked the sound of that and began to march around the schoolroom chanting bellum, bellum, bellum, belli, bello, bello, bella, bella, bella….

On visiting Largie, Angus's Aunt Violet extended his knowledge of Latin by lending him a book of stories about ancient Rome. Its author knew how to entertain uninterested boys. He asked them to lay aside their dictionaries and forget about Caesar and Livy and just listen.

In simple English, Arthur O. Cooke, tells the story of how Rome began. Most young children would be enthralled by an opening chapter of a she-wolf suckling two baby boys. In the accompanying illustration she looks like a shaggy German sheepdog as she gives twins, Romulus and Remus a motherly lick on their cheeks. After a boring chapter about the Romans snatching their enemy's women, the real meat appears.

For Cooke, clearly Rome is a blueprint for young, twentieth century, British patricians. He doesn't stint on heroes like Coriolanus, Cincinnatus and Spartacus, the slave, but the man with the most resounding courage is Publius Horatius, who held Rome's Sublician bridge over the river Tiber against the invading Etruscans. Here was a real hero, a man who, against the odds, drove back the enemy hordes. Firing the imagination of innumerable children, it is about the struggle to keep a bridge at all costs (the Romans had already lost one of the city's seven hills and if they let the others fall, all would be lost). Horatius realised that it would be better to destroy the Sublician bridge than let the enemy cross it. While his soldiers hacked it down at one end, Horatius, helped by Spurius Latrius and Herminius, confronted the Etruscans at the other and stood firm until the bridge fell, whereupon Horatius plunged, fully armed, into the Tiber below and swam ashore to the Roman side.

I like to think that the Horatius story was Angus's favourite and, when he went to bed and failed to fall asleep, he thought of him and dreamed he'd be as brave as that Roman one day.

Jock, Angus, and Simon

IN 1919 WHILE ANGUS learned his Latin conjugations and declensions in the Largie schoolroom, a distant cousin, Sir Norman
Lockhart from Lanarkshire, died. My grandparents attended his
funeral and the reading of the will. Wishing to heal the rift between the Macdonalds and Lockharts, the deceased decided to
leave the estate of Lee and Carnwath to John and Daisy's second
son. On coming of age, therefore, Angus would be the head of a
distinguished, Scottish family, its roots going back to the 14th
century or earlier. Old records reveal that a William Loccard
was granted the lands of Lee in 1272 but the name, Lockhart
(originally Loccard) is mostly associated with King Robert the
Bruce, Scotland's greatest freedom-fighter.

During the late 13th and early 14th centuries Scotland fought
like a tiger to maintain its independence from England. On the
death in 1290 of seven year old Margaret, grand-daughter of
Alexander III, there were 13 rivals for the Scottish throne. Fearing a civil war, important members of the nation asked Edward I
of England to arbitrate. Under his influence, John Balliol, Lord of
Galloway, was crowned king of Scotland. Within two years,
Edward had turned the country into a vassal state and demanded
Scottish troops and funds for an invasion of France. Balliol refused
and informed the French king of Edward's plans.

After the English invaded Scotland in 1296, a succession of
leaders including William Wallace (remember Mel Gibson in
Braveheart), won several victories over the English.

By 1306 there were two claimants for the Scottish crown:
Robert the Bruce and John Comyn, who agreed that each, in
renouncing his claim to the throne, would support the winner,
who would grant his rival substantial land in return. But Comyn
broke the agreement by informing Edward of Bruce's intention
to be king. Comyn wished to gain both throne and land, in be-
traying his rival. In a fit of rage, Bruce murdered John Comyn at
Greyfriars' Kirk in Dumfries.

Within five weeks of the killing, Bruce was crowned king of Scotland at Scone. Thereafter, he won several battles against the English, the most famous at Bannockburn in 1314.

Bruce died in 1329. During the following year, Sir James Douglas, a noble from a prominent Scottish Lowland family commonly known as the Black Douglas's, set off with a party of knights and squires for the Holy Land. Their aim was to carry Bruce's embalmed heart to Jerusalem and deposit it in the Church of the Holy Sepulchre, where Christ's putative tomb is located. For the medieval mindset, Jerusalem was the centre of the universe. Both Douglas and Bruce before him, possessed maps showing this city at the heart of the globe and poised strategically between the continents of Asia, Europe and Africa. According to the patriarch Abraham, Jerusalem was 'the place where God was seen.' It's important to note that these medieval knights and squires had not set out for Paris, the city of lovers or Rome, famed for its power, both temporal and religious, but Jerusalem, the city that all Jews, Christians and Moslems regarded as their spiritual centre. This was the reason for Douglas's pilgrimage, their purpose to expiate their late leader's guilt. Ever since he had killed John Comyn, Bruce's conscience had pricked him. Yes, the man had tricked him but that was no excuse for his murder. Bruce was aware of another killing, also committed in a place of worship, this time in the south of England. In wishing rid of Thomas Becket, Archbishop of Canterbury, Henry II had encouraged four of his knights to commit the terrible deed in a cathedral. The Becket story made Bruce catch his breath and his cheeks burn; no amount of priestly absolution could expunge his crime. Although Bruce's victim was neither priest nor martyr, he was a man nonetheless, whose life he had destroyed. Unlike Henry's followers, Bruce's Scottish knights, in undertaking this journey, were making amends for their leader's wrongdoing. The word, heart in French, 'le coeur,' gives rise to the adjective 'courageous.' Bruce, undoubtedly, possessed that quality but it would take more than a little courage for these knights to carry his heart to the Holy Land. Nevertheless it had to be done; it was their late king's dying wish.

Douglas's party included seven knights, comprising Sir Symon Loccard, who had fought for Bruce in the Scottish War of Independence, Sir William St. Clair of Rosslyn, Sir Robert Logan of Restalrig, Sir William Keith of Galston, Sir Kenneth Moir, Sir Alan Cathcart, and Sir Robert de Glen, and 26 squires including Walter Logan, John St. Clair, the younger brother of Sir William and William Borthwick. Douglas took charge of the heart, placing it in 'ane cas of silver fyn, enamilit throu subtilite' and hung it around his neck. Sir Symon was the leader's right hand man and carried the casket's key. As custodian of Bruce's heart, Loccard guarded access to the object that embodied Scotland, its identity, existence, and heritage.

They set off from Montrose on the East coast of Scotland. Imagine the scene: the crew's oaths and laughter as they unfurled the ship's sails, the fond farewells of wives and children as they wished their men bon voyage, the clatter of well-shod horses' hoofs, and the sight of their colourful trappings. Remember, it's 1330, less than a decade before the outbreak of The Hundred Years War (1337-1453), when England's Plantagenets grabbed France from the house of Valois.

For over 800 years ever since the end of the Roman Empire, the cavalry ruled in battle and Europe still used heavily armed, mounted warriors or knights on horses. But the winds of change were approaching. Decking out a knight for battle wasn't cheap. A farm horse cost pennies while a war horse was valued in guineas. This concentration of wealth could be felled by a peasant in cheap, leather armour, armed with a yew-tree bow and ash arrow. Only sixteen years after Douglas's pilgrimage, at Crecy in France, this point was proved when Welsh troops with their longbows destroyed the French cavalry.

If not entirely ignorant of the future, Douglas, Loccard, St Clair and the other knights were men of principle, their conduct owing more to the age of chivalry, than to the voice of the common man.

Inspired by Sir Symon, the Lockharts' belief in service and loyalty to the Crown would continue through the centuries until the present day.

Consider again what's happening on the Arbroath harbour front. Nervy horses, afraid of the sea, the clamour of the crowds curious to watch the knights and squires' departure, and music: blasting horns, shrill pipes, crashing cymbals and banging drums. Like a shepherd sending his dog to round up the flock, the music commands Douglas's party to board ship. Bands of stevedores have already mounted barrels of salted beef, biscuits unblemished by weavils, and oatmeal into the ships' hold. More men load wine, armour and weaponry. Fodder for the horses has its place as has the squires' bedding. Medicines are locked in the captain's quarters.

The ship's highway is the sea and it heads for the coast of Flanders, to Sluys. To while away the hours, the knights tell stories; home-grown fables like Thomas the Rhymer and the Queen of Elfland. Some knew sagas from the north, terrible Viking tales of rape and pillage. Others enjoyed the lives of saints, sinners, and Charlemagne and his court. One (was it St Clair or Sir Robert Logan?) told the tale of a foreign princess who set sail from a snowy land to marry a Scottish prince, but pirates kidnapped her. Or was her fate more humdrum, and she fell sick at sea and wasted away? A more fanciful version was that a sea monster swallowed her whole. The well-read Douglas and Loccard enjoyed Chretien de Troyes and Robert de Boron's scenes of Camelot in which they described how, in the late 5th and early 6th centuries, King Arthur led Britain against the Saxon invaders. Douglas loved telling his audience about Merlin, the magician and Excalibur, the magic sword, and especially Lancelot, the prize swordsman and jouster, the king's great friend, until he seduced Queen Guinevere, Arthur's wife. Sir Symon drew strength from the story of the Holy Grail. With its special powers, this bowl that held Christ's blood, was supposedly resting in Britain protected by sacred guardians. As their ship rode the waves of the North Sea, did the less reverent of the party compose rhymes about Loccard's key?

Loccard was 30 years old and married. Did the others give the key a more earthy emphasis? But Loccard was 'a parfit gentil knight,' full of noble sentiments.

After docking at Sluys, the knights rested for twelve days and discovered that King Alfonso XI of Castile planned an attack on the fortress of Teba in southern Spain in his campaign (1327-1333) against Muhammed IV, Sultan. Alfonso had declared war on the Moorish Emirate of Granada and invited other Christian kings to join him in his crusade.

By 1327, Alfonso had captured the castles of Olvera, Pruna and Torre Alhaquime. His second expedition in 1330 was to attack Teba, 25 miles east of Olvera and a key fortification in the defence of Malaga.

On learning of Alfonso's plan, Douglas seized the chance to honour another desire of his late king. Robert the Bruce had always wished to join a crusade to fight 'God's foes,' so by carrying the dead monarch's heart with them into battle against the Moors, Douglas could fulfil Bruce's other wish. While the knights waited in Sluys, Douglas held court on board 'as if the late king was present,' commented a contemporary source. He was trying to promote his mission and attract others to his cause.

They set sail on a stormy sea, voyaging south past the Normandy coast and into the Bay of Biscay. Many had misgivings about their decision but it was no use. The dice was cast. They must cross not the Rubicon but a wide, blustery sea. Many passengers wished they could travel by land in spite of the risk of a horse shedding its shoe, a saddle breaking, or grazing their knees after a fall. But Douglas had made his decision, and they had agreed to follow. A few horses were on board; their leader's favourites: his grey mare and bay gelding and those owned by Loccard, Logan and St. Clair. You might ask why. Were Spanish nags no good?

Having known the animals since they were fillies and colts, watched them mature and initiated them into battle in many a Border skirmish, these warriors would ride on no other. But the animals suffered badly. Cats do well on board; dogs and horses do not. Hoofs are made for dry land, not tilting floors and creaking timbers.

The slate and pewter grey skies of Biscay were accompanied by plunging rain. Along with his equines, Douglas brought his fool, an irreverent, witty midget. Today he is your alter ego but yesterday, your conscience. To those knights he was an elevated Sancho Panza to their purposeful Don Quixote. To possess a fool was a royal prerogative. This one belonged to Bruce and when he died, Douglas took him on. Holding his rosary, the fool inspected each bead: "slate grey, pewter grey, primrose yellow, buttercup yellow, ruby red, blood red," chanted the midget, as he sat cross-legged in the ante-room close to the deck. He never suffered from sea sickness. The sailors retched, Douglas's skin turned the colour of mould on a Stilton, while Loccard shut himself up in his cabin, but the fool fingered his rosary, each bead a different shade until he had counted them all on their string. Then he confused his adjectives, "brown earth, red earth, red heart, black heart, white deed, black deed." It was a black deed that drove them here in the direction of...who knew where? Spain? Malta? Jerusalem? "A black deed," he repeated as he thrust a bead forward to meet its companions. "As black as King Henry when..." The fool mumbled, realising his words were treasonous, although Henry had not been his king but he was a king nonetheless. "A very black act but it's turning white with a red heart." There it was, his late master's heart in his present master's casket, and Sir Symon held the key to the heart of Scotland, its existence, identity and soul. The fool continued reciting his array of colours, "red heart, black heart, but the black, if we travel long and hard enough, becomes white. Our deeds are many colours but few are white."

Leaving Biscay their ship ploughed southward passing Santiago de Compostela, on the north-west tip of the Iberian peninsula, and hugged the coast until it reached the south. In late June they arrived at the mouth of the Guadalquivir river and proceeded upstream, disembarking at Seville. Douglas presented his credentials to Alfonso XI who offered him horses, armour and money. But the Scottish noble refused. He and his knights were humble pilgrims who sought 'absolution for their sins' and only wished to fight for him.

After their voyage, the Scots rested and while they relaxed, foreign knights paid their respects, including a handful of English nobles who had previously fought them in battle.

Alfonso's task was to lay siege and capture the fortress of Teba, which stood on a high hill.

To breach its walls was hard but unlike the Portuguese, who acted like mercenaries, Douglas's party was fuelled with a passionate righteousness. Wearing white and carrying white shields with blue borders, studded with white stars, the Scottish knights called upon St. Andrew to come to their aid. Unlike the Moors, their helmets had no visors while Douglas and the Islamic leader, clad in chain mail and heavy armour, were mounted on hooded horses wrapped in thick cladding.

The Castilian king appointed Douglas in lead his army's foreign contingent. However, drinking water was scarce and troops had to march two miles south of the castle to fetch it.

The Moslem leader, Uthman bi Abi-l-Ula, a Berber noble, discovered the Castilian's weakness and sent raiding parties to intercept them, but Alfonso responded by setting up defensive patrols. Some contemporary reports claim that Douglas was killed in one of these forays. The Gran Cronica de Alfonso XI refers to 'the death of a foreign count through his own error.'

Realising that he was unable to defeat the Christians in an open battle, Uthman tried to force Alfonso to abandon the siege by setting up a diversion. Under cover of darkness, while the Islamic cavalry introduced a diversionary attack across the river at Teba, another section attacked Alfonso's west flank. Having received advanced warning, Alfonso kept the bulk of his army in his camp and sent troops to check on the river assault (it is argued that Douglas was part of this reinforcement). The story goes that as Douglas rode well in front of his followers, he turned back to rejoin them, but the Islamic cavalry made a counter-attack. On seeing the enemy surround William St. Clair, his leader charged to the rescue but Douglas, St Clair, his brother Robert, and Sir

Walter Logan were all killed.

Where was Sir Symon Loccard? Perhaps he was taken ill and was unable to join the fray or Douglas urged him not to accompany him as he galloped to St Clair's rescue. Whatever the reason, Loccard survived while most of the party perished. It's possible that he replaced Douglas as leader of the foreign knights in Alfonso's army, thus gaining access to the Moslem prisoners. One was an emir, and when his mother arrived with money to plead for his release, a curious triangular coin dropped from her purse. Noticing the speed with which she recovered it, Sir Symon guessed it was valuable and insisted he have it. As the woman gave it up she told Loccard that the coin was more valuable than gold or silver. Blood red in colour, it was an amulet with magical powers and was kept as protection against the evil eye.

Not confined to coinage, Islamic amulets were often woven into oriental carpets such as kilims, to offer protection for their owners. The coin had properties that cured fevers, staunched bleeding, healed the bites of rabid dogs, and quelled sickness in horses and cattle.

Sir Symon tested its medicinal properties in Spain, and back in Scotland its healing powers became well known. This amulet was called The Lee Penny after the family seat, Lee Castle, and its story and how Sir Symon came to own it formed the basis of Sir Walter Scott's 1825 novel, 'The Talisman'. The Lee Penny is mounted on a silver coin that hangs from a silver chain and is still in my family's possession.

Although the Castilians won the Battle of Teba against Uthman it was a Pyrrhic victory for the Scots, who lost their leader and many other brave knights. On managing to recover Douglas's body with the casket holding Bruce's heart, the remaining knights and squires decided to return home. Before Douglas's body could be repatriated, the party had it boiled in water to separate the flesh from the bones as only the latter, with Bruce's heart, could be transported on the long sea voyage back home. Loccard and Sir William Keith of Galston undertook that task. Back in Scotland, the heart was buried at Melrose Abbey and Douglas's remains at St. Bride's Kirk, in South Lanarkshire. Sir Symon changed his name to Lockheart, later Lockhart, as he was the sole holder of the key to the locked casket. He added the image of a heart and fetterlock to his family coat of arms and introduced the motto, 'corda serrata pando' ('I open locked hearts'). Sir Symon died at the ripe age of 71. As with survivors of war, particularly the conflict of 1914-18, he had to live with regret and possibly guilt in having escaped death in battle when many of his friends perished.

Angus, therefore would inherit the curious amulet, supposed to protect him from all perils, as he too, like his older brother, stood in line to become the owner of a castle, Lee Castle or The Lee. He would gain also the land surrounding it, farms, silver, jewellery, and a painting by Sir Joshua Reynolds. Situated at Auchenglen in the Clyde Valley in South Lanarkshire, the original castle, (extensively rebuilt in the 19th century) had been the seat of the Lockharts of Lee from the 13th century until 1919, when Sir Norman Macdonald Lockhart died. When Angus's younger brother, Simon became the owner of the estate 30 years later, he sold the castle. In 2004 it was put on the market and there were rumours that film star John Travolta, a wealthy French duchess, and a website entrepreneur were interested in buying it. It sold for $8.5 million, much less than the asking price. For this figure the new owner became the 35th baron of Lee and acquired 261 acres, a castle, where Bruce signed a charter under the Pease Tree in its garden, and where Oliver Cromwell had once dined. The Lee has two lodge houses, a banqueting room, ballroom, 14 bedrooms, a heated swimming pool, and a 25 member band: the pipes and drums of the Barony of Lee.

At six years of age, Angus was unaware of what was meant to fall into his lap when he came of age.

On a hot June morning I stepped on to the platform of Winchester railway station. Making my way through the barrier, I followed instructions — downloaded from the internet — to the building that once housed West Downs preparatory school, where the Macdonald boys had been educated. I trudged uphill from the town-centre, past the police station and prison on my right and the county hospital on my left, until I reached what is now the West Downs campus of Winchester University.

West Downs as a school fell short by nine years of reaching its century, when it closed in 1988. The forbidding building seen in a photograph of 1897 when Lionel Helbert, the school's founder bought it, had changed beyond recognition. A gravel sweep frilled with cars had replaced the lawn. The sash dormer windows were swopped for modern ones. A privet hedge grew close to the ground floor windows, and pyracantha climbed the walls, adding a touch of greenery where it had once been dingy and bare. Students sat cross-legged on the grass by the east end of the building. Some smoked and others drank beer from a can. It was hot and sticky, yet I felt a chill rising from the base of my spine, until it reached my chest. This was where he was sent, as were his brothers, Jock and Simon.

I had heard about the ordeal, not from my uncle of course, but from my father, who entered West Downs in 1922, the same year as Angus. "I was always cold," he said, "and hungry." He demonstrated how he made the yoke of his boiled egg go further by cutting toast into soldiers and dipping each piece into it. No amount of sun could displace my father's chill.

Evidently it wasn't enough for the Macdonald brothers to stay at home and go to the local school at Rhunahaorine, a mile from the castle. I'm sure they would have liked to sit on benches at rough, ink-stained desks with the other children and play tig with them in the school yard. But, like their father before them, Angus and his brothers were sent away to school. As early as the 1820s, most upper class boys from all over Britain went to private boarding schools. I'm sure Angus's parents never questioned the practice although John hated being sent to Eton, which tended to savage boys from the fringes of the British Isles. Daisy was accustomed to the tradition; while her four brothers attended boarding school, she and her sisters stayed at home, where they received their schooling from carefully-selected governesses. In 1895 when the Crabbes lived at Guildford House, Farnham. Daisy's parents, anxious to appoint a Protestant, employed 'a North German finishing governess with advanced English skills, Parisian French, and fluent Italian (acquired in Italy)'. Two years later the family found a Swiss Protestant governess with no knowledge of Italian.

I wondered how Angus had felt about his new school. Destined to enter West Downs in 1921, he was reprieved on account of John's sudden death. Jock was less fortunate and set off hotfoot from his father's funeral for his first term at Winchester College. When the following year Angus made the long journey to his new prep school in the south of England, he must have felt he was travelling to a different planet. Kintyre, its traditions and way of life, was and still is worlds away from the English home counties. For the nine year old, probably accompanied by his mother or Jock, it was an exciting, arduous expedition. Taking the boat from Tarbert they sailed to Gourock on the Clyde, then caught a train for Glasgow, whereupon they boarded a night train to London's Euston station.

Happily, West Downs had forsaken their Eton suit of black trousers and short jacket for a dark, grey one, but Angus still had to wear a shirt with a separate collar attached with a front and back stud; also a pin and clip to keep his tie in place. He also wore braces, which not only supported his trousers but his underpants too by means of loops. He was unfamiliar with the noises: the sound of a guard's whistle, porters wheeling trolleys, a newspaper seller's cry and the chatter of travellers while a voice from the loud-speaker announced strange place names. People brushed past as he clutched a Gladstone bag (his trunk was sent ahead as Passenger's Luggage in Advance) and grasped his ticket to show it at the barrier. A taxi conveyed him across London to Waterloo where he boarded a train for Winchester. To reassure the boys, especially the new ones, the head-master, Kenneth Tindall, accompanied them then.

Tindall's predecessor was Lionel Helbert, 'a most enlightened man. He made a genuine effort to understand his pupils'. On his father's side, he was of Jewish descent — an ancestor having settled in England at the time of Oliver Cromwell. After attending Winchester College and Oxford University, Helbert became a clerk in the House of Commons, but soon realised that his talents lay elsewhere and in 1897 founded a private school for boys. The man's empathy with the young is shown by his approach towards Peter Scott, son of Lady Scott and Captain Scott, the doomed Antarctic explorer. When Helbert discovered that Scott was bullying another boy, instead of punishing him, he asked Peter, already fascinated by natural history, to give a talk on his favourite reptile.

For the first ten years, West Downs had a superb headmaster. But, as early as 1907 there were signs that Helbert now suffered from nervous strain. By 1914, when war broke out, his health deteriorated. New boy Antony Knebworth wrote that his head-master "always looks cold and dull and stern." Helbert became increasingly unwell, as he learned of the deaths of Old West Downs' boys. In 1917, whether from exhaustion, depression, or grief, Helbert suffered a mental breakdown and two years later, in November, 1919, he died.

This exceptional headmaster went to great lengths in attracting boys from the 'very best families' of the gentry and aristocracy. During the first ten years of the school, Helbert paid visits to the boys in their own homes to become acquainted with them before they entered his school. Helbert made no visit to Kintyre (his name is absent from the Largie visitors' book) to meet Jock before he entered West Downs in 1916. During the Great War, civilians were subject to travel restrictions. The War years brought other strictures too. Food was in short supply. Duncan Sandys, future colonial secretary and son-in-law of Winston Churchill, wrote on 23rd May, 1919, that he ate sausages and toast for breakfast, the first since the start of the War.

If conditions at West Downs were a bit Spartan after the armistice, little had changed when Angus arrived three years later: the dormitories had no carpets or curtains; a box lay by each bed for the boys' possessions and a stool was supplied for clothes when the occupant went to bed. Boys also had a wash-hand basin with a jug of water and a foricas under their bed. Borrowed from Winchester College, this word meant a chamber pot. Young boys learned that West Downs used Latin words not only for objects but for family members like mater (mother), pater (father), soror (sister) and frater (brother).

British preparatory or private schools are the fee-paying equivalent of state-sponsored primary (junior) schools. A boy attended his prep school between the ages of seven or eight until he was twelve or thirteen. Prep schools were hot-houses for public (secondary) schools, which were anything BUT public, as they charged a lot to attend. To enter a public school, a boy sat an exam (Common Entrance). Some, like Winchester College, were very rigorous. For anyone wishing to make it to the top in politics, the diplomatic or colonial services, the army, church or in business, it was essential to attend a sound preparatory school and a good public school. From there, the individual entered university: either Oxford, Cambridge or Trinity College, Dublin. For example, when in the early nineteenth century, rough diamond John Gladstone, a socially aspiring Liverpool entrepreneur asked his friend, the Tory politician, George Canning, how he could best launch his sons' careers, Canning told him to send them to Eton. Gladstone followed his friend's advice. His first son, however, was bullied and abused at the famous school but when his youngest, William Ewart, attended, Eton served him well enabling him to gain a place at Christ Church, Oxford, from which he graduated with a double first. These institutions' ritualistic practices helped a boy to enter an arcane, exclusive domain, and it was social suicide not to attend them. In Angus's day, these schools, both prep and public, were as keen on character-building (instilling a sense of leadership, self-confidence, inner discipline and a team spirit) as on academic prowess.

The custom of educating children away from home stems from classical times. "Plato," writes Philip Mason in *The Men Who Ruled India*, "taught that the guardians of State should not know their parents." The author concedes "the English did not go as far as that, but when they were eight years old, children from whom rulers were to be chosen, were taken away from home for three-quarters of every year, taught not to mention their mother or their own Christian names and were brought up in the tradition of Sparta, which Plato admired."

The practise of expelling a child, particularly a boy, from the parental home, in order to raise him as a leader, is not confined to the British. At nine years of age, former African National Congress leader and first black South African president, Nelson Mandela, was schooled at the home of a local ruler of a neighbouring village. Mandela was lucky; his host became his guardian, while at West Downs, Angus was one of a crowd, a mere cog in an educational machine. My guess is that during those first few days, he missed his mother and Largie, as he tried to come to terms with the new regime of rules, strange rituals, and a lack of privacy. He had no wet-nosed dogs to stroke, no West Highland lilting accents to listen to and no soft Argyll rain to feel. The Broonie, whose impish presence at Largie was often sensed even if never seen, felt very far away. Different to those at Largie, the smells at West Downs were of boiled cabbage, a metallic tang of cutlery, the sound of an occasional car or lorry changing gear, as it climbed the hill outside the school, and possibly a din in the distance of tin plates being beaten against window frames by prisoners of the local jail. Surrounding the boy were the voices of others, shouts from the more confident, and suppressed sobbing of some in their first term. The best he could do was remain silent, maintain a stiff upper lip, and not cry because blubbing was sissy.

After a brief tour of the building and simple meal, the boys attended a short service (Christianity was the corner-stone of West Downs) in the chapel to sing hymns, listen to verses from the

Gospels, and intone prayers by the school's founder.

The sad nine year old wondered how to get through the next twelve weeks, which lay before him like an eternity. The school discouraged parents from visiting except during the summer term when, for Paters' Day, families arrived to watch performances of the school play (usually a Shakespeare comedy) and the boys play cricket. Because their home was so far away, the Macdonald boys received few visits from Daisy.

What Angus certainly endured at the start of the term was a thorough health inspection. Like his predecessor, Kenneth Tindall was a health fanatic. In his defence, there was every reason to be concerned about his charges as in the days before the discovery of penicillin, anti-viral drugs, and antibiotics, it was wise to be cautious. However, both Helbert and Tindall cosseted the boys to such an extent that the school earned the sobriquet of "Wet Downs." From the day the school opened in 1897, Lionel Helbert advertised its health-giving aspects: at 350 feet above sea level the air was bracing; the building was well-ventilated; qualified nurses were employed. and a doctor visited daily. When boys returned after the holidays. they handed in a doctor's certificate confirming they were free from any infectious disease. They also experienced "Puffing Billy" (the nearest modern equivalent is a sauna); 12 to 15 boys crammed into a tiny, enclosed space infused with antiseptic and filled with steam. Its purpose was to ward off colds. After this ordeal, Angus had his hair examined for head lice. Additionally, a close eye was kept on his bowel movements: constipation in boys was taken seriously and they had to sit on a commode so their efforts could be inspected by the matron. If nothing was produced, she threatened the boy with an enema. Like everyone else, Angus's temperature was taken twice daily in sickness and in health. Fortunately my uncle missed the West Downs' 'Ice Age,' a period when Kenneth Tindall's wife threw open in all weathers the school windows and added vitamins to the boys' diet. Mrs Tindall was influenced by Captain Scott's widow, who brought up Peter in rigorous conditions. Lady Scott's theory was that a cold atmosphere (akin to the Antarctic where her husband perished) hindered the spread of infectious diseases like measles, mumps, whooping cough, and flu. It is a wonder that Angus survived. One minute he was fretted over, the next hurled into sub-zero conditions.

To enquire about Angus I approached Nick Hodson, the Old West Downs Society secretary who, after investigating school records came up with nothing. "I have been unable to find anything of interest about Charles Angus Macdonald," he wrote. "He was not capped for either football or cricket. I am sorry to be so short of information about him; the one thing I can guess being that he was no great games player." This was of interest. If a private school boy demonstrated sporting abilities, he earned an exalted position in the hierarchy. In these schools, sport was an obsession passed from fathers to sons. In sum, sportsmen and athletes were favoured over scholars. It is unfair to surmise that Angus was poor at sport. If he didn't excel in football or cricket, at Winchester and Magdalen College, he was good at rowing.

I debated why Angus had a low profile at West Downs. He may have found it hard to adapt in so many ways, but as a middle sibling, he did learn to 'fit in.' While the oldest is fussed over and the youngest encouraged, the child in the middle may feel overlooked. Angus found Jock a hard act to follow: in looks, sport, and even in the choice of a marriage partner.

My next move was to write to Angus's few remaining contemporaries, men in their nineties. "What a delight to be drawn into thinking about West Downs," wrote one of my uncle's contemporaries. "It was such a very good school. I'm sorry I can't help you. I have searched, cudgelled, scraped my memory for Macdonald — Christian names were taboo — without any success at all. Oddly, there was a Gladstone, whom I remember clearly!" he added. My correspondent was certain Angus had been "no buffalo", the patrol to which he was assigned at West Downs. Since boys of each patrol slept in the same dormitory, the gentleman would have known Angus if he had been in his patrol.

As early as 1914 Lionel Helbert championed the scout movement, founded by Lt-Col Robert Baden-Powell, the hero of the South African war. Both the founder of West Downs and Kenneth Tindall had much in common with this remarkable man, who was fond of music and drama. Unlike Baden-Powell, Helbert and Tindall were educators rather than soldiers but they were patriotic and upheld such qualities as virtue, honesty, service and, most significantly, a healthy body in a healthy mind. Scouting fitted their beliefs and Helbert (possibly the outbreak of war influenced his decision) adopted scouting to the exclusion of all else. Marches and parades replaced sport, and a scout band was established for boys to learn to play the bugle and the drum. They studied flag reading and signalling by semaphore; scout-masters taught them to shoot with an air rifle, conduct bicycle drills and route marches. Each boy learned to salute and take the scout oath. Critics believed the scout movement smacked of the armed forces but Helbert felt it instilled independence in the young and many welcomed lessons in tent pitching, fire-making, and outdoor cooking.

As a scout, Angus worked towards gaining a stalker's badge: instead of shooting a bird or small animal with a gun (the Largie gamekeeper would've taught him that), he shot photographs. Another challenge was the naturalists' badge, which required a contestant to identify birds, flora and fauna.

Scouting supplied the bedrock for Angus's eventual career as a soldier; wearing uniform, practicing self-defence, using his initiative, and being of service to the community were all valuable steps towards becoming an army officer. Favouring the outdoors, scouting expected the young to be resourceful and part of a team; these activities had a profound effect on the reserved but independent Angus. Baden-Powell considered that scouts were descended from medieval knights, gifted with manliness, bravery and heroism. It would be nice to think that these figures resonated with Angus as he was in line to inherit land once held by Sir Symon Loccard, the renowned Scottish medieval knight. As for Baden-Powell, the hero of Mafeking, he was well aware of another brave soldier from the South African War: Angus's maternal grandfather, Eyre Macdonell Crabbe.

The West Downs regime forbade boys to read comics or eat sweets. At the start of each term staff vetted the boys' reading matter: John Buchan, Robert Louis Stevenson and Rider Haggard were permitted, but Edgar Wallace and the Saint were not. Even letters home with their shaky grammar, erratic spelling, and traces of suppressed emotion (we "read between the lines", my mother once told me on receiving my letters from boarding school) were censored. West Downs was not all Latin conjugations, cold dormitories, and outdoor walks with each boy carrying a Burberry over his arm, but boys had to be formal.

Good table manners were expected. If anyone transgressed he was sent to the pigs' table. Oscillating between rigour (ink was known to freeze in desk wells) and pampering, was the practise of instilling moral values in the boys that made them exercise a conscientiousness far beyond their years. The school worked hard under Tindall. He and his staff were expert in helping pupils pass into the public school of their choice.

In 1926 Angus passed successfully into Winchester College. From West Downs on Romsey Road, Angus's public school was only a few streets away. Hidden behind the cathedral in College Street the college is situated in the oldest part of the city. There Angus was shocked to find himself, not at the top of the school ladder as he was at West Downs, but on the bottom rung. The thirteen year old was unable even to rely on the support of Jock who, on leaving Winchester that summer, went up to Magdalen College, Oxford, but his older brother's reputation helped Angus make a smooth entry into his assigned house, Moberly's (Toye's in Wykehamical jargon). Nevertheless, Angus had to handle not only a new regime, but also the prospect of fagging, bullying and various initiation rites; if he was very unlucky he might even receive a flogging from his housemaster.

Maybe Jock gave Angus the low-down and warned him that older boys would impose tests on the school's arcane vocabulary and other odd customs like eating off a wooden plate, one side for the first course and the other for the second. Mum told me about this but lately I've discovered that only scholars did it.

Angus and his brothers entered Winchester College as Commoners, which meant their families paid school fees; scholars went for free.

If Jock was sparing on advice, Kenneth Tindall was not. Like Lionel Helbert, he was an old Wykehamist. Both knew what awaited a boy fresh from his prep school. (Winchester had improved immeasurably since the previous century when at one point in the early 1800s discipline was so bad that troops with fixed bayonets were called in to restore order.)

As a parting gift, West Downs' headmasters gave each boy a gold cross, inscribed with the letters HBP, which stood for the school motto: Honest. Brave. Pure.

I've a photograph of Angus in Winchester College uniform with his family outside Largie. The way Daisy lays a protective hand on his shoulder suggests she's apprehensive. The Winchester career of her younger brother Tempest ended in expulsion.

Midway down College Street at the school entrance, stood an ink-stained desk. Winchester College now hawks its antiquity and, as the oldest public school in England, is entitled. I visited at the behest of Suzanne Foster, Winchester College's archivist, who led me to a building nearby, up a narrow staircase to the oak-panelled Warden Harmar's room, now the Fellows' library and Reading Room for archives, renovated and re-opened on 3rd September, 2006 by, appropriately, the bishop of Winchester. The school was founded by William of Wykeham, bishop of Winchester in 1382. I ran an eye across the crowded bookshelves, one section dominated by the Oxford English Dictionary, another filled with leather-bound volumes and yet another, which was locked, with medieval manuscripts. I was quite prepared for a host of schoolmasters like Dumbledore of Hogwarts in J K Rowling's *Harry Potter* novels to enter and dust down their cloaks and chalk-grimed mortar-boards, before they adopted their seats.

At Win Coll, pupils are known for their slang and abbreviated words; lavatory (foricas) is 'fo', the dons' common room notice board is 'do co ro no bo' and a senior commoner prefect is 'sen co prae.' It is as if verbal dexterity, the speed with which a boy expresses himself, is paramount or a form of public school blazé-ness and the ultimate in cool. Harrow has its songs, Eton its own arcane language, but nothing beats the Win Coll argot.

"Here's *The Wykehamist*," Ms. Foster said, pointing to a stack of old journals, "which has news on cricket matches, football, steeple-chasing, shooting, rowing, cultural trips abroad, debating, natural history, and archaeology. You're bound to find something about him in those! And since he was keen on rowing I've set aside these." She handed me the boat club log books bound in black. "Perhaps your best bet is to look at his house-master, H. A. Jackson's reports." I glanced to my left and saw a few sheets of paper in neat hand-writing. "He was known as The Jacker," she explained. "Strangely," she added handing me a copy of an extract from the War Service Record and Roll of Honour, in which Angus's obituary appears, "we sometimes get to know more about the dead than the living." Indeed, the Win Coll obituary revealed more about Angus than their records on Jock and Simon.

I was thrilled. At last, I was on Angus's trail. Daisy may have destroyed his school letters, those cursory missives in which he scrawled requests for cash, intimations that he had won at Fives, or complaints about his housemaster. Although West Downs had closed down and with it many of its records, Winchester had come up trumps. I turned to the Jacker and like an artist who reveals more of himself than his sitter, the character of Angus's house-master in his reports is communicated as clearly as his subject. The man's style is individualistic, wacky, and imbued with the public school ethos of the time.

Lionel Helbert, Kenneth Tindall and The Jacker were dedicated, principled men with first class minds, in effect, ersatz fathers to the Macdonald boys, and played a vital role in their young lives. These school-masters' main job, then, was to produce men who would serve the empire.

Most Win Coll housemasters had wives, but some were unmarried. Out of 19 housemasters during this period, only five were bachelors; the Jacker was one. In Jackson's time, housemasters had more autonomy than his counterpart today. Each man encouraged his boys to be fiercely competitive with those from other houses. While absolute loyalty was expected, the Jacker rewarded a boy's allegiance by showing a firm, if not total, commitment to him. Jackson was concerned with the instruction of 'new men,' as the 13 and 14 year olds were termed. House photographs from 1929 to 1932 show him seated among his 38 charges outside Moberly's. Wearing a bushy moustache, he looks alert and avuncular. On a rug at his feet is a line of silver trophies that house members have won during the school year. You can detect how pleased he is; the greater volume of pots, the wider the grin.

When it came to the schoolboys' reports, Jackson held in equal importance academic work, sport (In this, Jock was especially gifted), health, and the boy's attitude towards the house community. The housemaster expected boys to behave in a way that demonstrated a nascent manliness, in which pluck, energy, perseverance, good temper, self-control, discipline, co-operation, and esprit de corps were present. Being referred to as "an excellent type" fifteen year old Simon evidently passed muster. The Jacker, therefore, prized Simon's character as much, even more possibly, than his sporting talent or scholarly abilities (in this he struggled more than his brothers). While Angus was "quiet and sensible," his brothers were "excellent and capital." When Jock and Simon departed Moberly's, the Jacker was "very sad" to see them go, but at Angus's exit he wrote that he "will be very welcome here".

A clue to his less fervent enthusiasm is in Angus's health record. During the spring term of his second year he "went off to an operation," a cause for concern for Jackson. Would Angus be able to row or swim during the following half (term)? A few years later the adolescent boy faced a more serious physical problem, a "strained heart". Fortunately, the doctors found "nothing much wrong" and the following summer as Angus prepared to leave Winchester, the Jacker noted he was "delightful after last summer's scare".

Out of the three brothers, Angus fared the best academically. Undoubtedly he benefited from A. T. P. Williams' regime. On this man's appointment as headmaster in 1924 he updated the school curriculum, so that modern languages and history enjoyed parity with Latin and Greek. From the early 1900s, history at Winchester began to replace the classics. This trend accelerated under Williams' watch. History was Angus's subject and, as he matured, the Jacker hoped that he would do well in it, if the subject continued to interest him.

Angus's extreme height (he was 6 feet 3 or 4 inches) was a disadvantage. School-masters quickly blamed him for lack of judgement and for acting immaturely. They had to remind themselves that the boy was "a year younger than he looked." Nevertheless, my uncle became a competent house prefect, but he never displayed the casual brilliance of Jock, nor the convivial charm of Simon. The writer of Angus's Win Coll obituary alleges Angus was "reserved and not easy to know." Angus received none of the cachet awarded Jock. Nor was he able to relax and "play the fool" like Simon.

Win Coll was not overtly sporty and Angus not outstanding in any case. He still was expected to chase a ball over a muddy field and row down the Itchen. Not even Winchester escaped the prevailing games cult, where Angus could gain courage, endurance, assertion, and self-control. Public school sportsmanship also helped a boy to develop high moral qualities and be willing to sacrifice himself for others.

Jackson makes no mention of Angus in the school cadet force. Winchester wasn't military. Even in 1914, when patriotic fervour was at its height, Montague Rendall, the headmaster announced "I am not at all afraid of any spirit of militarism at Winchester College; other influences are too strong." These were implied in Eleanor Fortescue-Brickdale's 1926 triptych, a commemoration to the headmaster, now hanging in the school Chantry, depicting a mounted knight accompanied by his squire. The words beneath the image are didactic and exhortatory, if not archaic and romantic: "Look unto the rock whence thou art hewn. Serve as thy brethren served and in peace or in war, bear thyself ever as Christ's soldier, gentle in all things, valiant in action, steadfast in adversity."

It's doubtful if Angus took these words seriously and whether, on entering Win Coll, he knew he wanted to become a soldier. The best he could do was join the school cadets. The Officers' Training Corps was unconcerned with serious warfare although previous members like Archibald Wavell, commander of the British Army in the Middle East, and Commander-in-Chief of ABDA (American British Dutch Australian) Command, Hugh Dowding, Air Chief Marshal and Commander of RAF Fighter Command, and Charles Portal, Marshal of the Royal Air Force and British Chief of the Air Staff, were to win the top jobs in the British armed forces during World War Two. However, these men's exalted status owed nothing to their careers in the school Corps. For one of these three, his sole memory of Winchester College Corps was watching a colleague eat worms to while away the boredom of manning a defensive position. The Corps' purpose was not so much military but educational. It gave Angus an opportunity to pass "A Certificate," the first test he faced in becoming an army officer.

I folded my uncle's school reports by their house-master and tidied up the books and documents. With the clatter of feet and the rolling of trolley wheels in the rooms below, Suzanne Foster re-appeared. "I'll take you to see Patrick Herring at Moberly's." She had kindly arranged a meeting with the house-master. "He's set aside some time for you to look around."

Winchester's ten boarding houses are scattered in the old part of the city but within easy walking distance of the main school. As we arrived at the house's front door I expected to meet a master with hooked nose and a dew-drop hanging from the end of it, brandishing a cane in one hand and a Latin primer in the other. But when it opened, it revealed a genial man dressed in smart blazer and flannels who looked more like a country lawyer than a Win Coll housemaster. Originally an Elizabethan farmhouse with Georgian and Victorian additions, Moberly's principal rooms are oak panelled. In the best sense of the word the rambling building resembles a private house. Mr Herring led us to his study in which the south-west facing window permitted streaks of sunlight to stream in to the room. "Here are some house photographs!" He handed me a bundle. "Do you see him there?" I peered at the first with its group of boys, both old and young, many looking solemn, while others appeared belligerent or individualistic, their attitudes reminding me of the saying "You can always tell a Wykehamist but you can never tell him much."

The main reason for my visit was to view Moberly's memorial, a wooden board attached to a wall in the dining room, inscribed with the names of all men from the house killed in both world wars. As boys tuck into helpings of meat and two veg, jam roly-poly or prunes and custard they can peer at the names of Toye-ites who fell. Most poignantly, the memorial board shows the names of three brothers, all killed during the Great War. Angus's name is there as part of the toll of Second World War deaths.

After leaving Moberly's, we followed a wall of brick, chalk, and flint back to the college's main entrance and strode towards the old cloister with its ancient graffiti, illicit carvings worthy of a fifteenth century ASBO (Anti Social Behaviour Order) but now a historical curio.

War Cloister is a traditional, sandstone structure, designed by Sir Herbert Baker, assistant to Edwin Lutyens in laying out the plans for New Delhi. After World War One the school required a fitting memorial for all 500 Wykehamists killed. It made sense to erect a covered walk so that the names could be viewed in comfort, and a cloister corresponded well with an enclosed community like Winchester College.

"Five hundred!" I tried to grasp what effect these deaths had had on those left behind and multiplied the figure by two for the grieving parents, then added more for sisters, brothers, sons, daughters, spouses, and grandparents. The grief mushroomed. When we stepped down one walkway towards a pillar carved with Angus's name I noticed on another the name of Tempest, Daisy's youngest brother. Although I had only discovered very recently that my great-uncle Tempest was killed in World War One, I knew little else as any mention of his name caused such sadness in the family. When Suzanne Foster showed me a photo album of

Wykehamists killed in the Great War, I saw for the first time what he looked like and it was clear that his nephews, particularly Jock, bore a striking resemblance to him. In late September, 1915 Tempest (second lieutenant, 3rd Battalion Grenadier Guards) was reported missing on the Western Front. Early in the afternoon of September 27th Brigadier-General J. Ponsonby informed his officers that they were to attack Puits 14 (near Loos) that evening. Unaware that the rest of their company had retired, Tempest, a fellow officer and his men were surrounded by the enemy. They tried to drive them back but were outnumbered. Most of the party retreated to safety but Tempest 'was last seen standing on a wall throwing bombs at the enemy when he was killed.' It is unclear why my great-uncle made himself a target and whether this act was one of extreme bravery or utter madness. Tempest's end resembled that of John Kipling (Rudyard's son), who joined the Irish Guards as a 2nd lieutenant. He was also killed, at the age of 18, in September 1915 near Loos. Like half a million other "lost boys" John Kipling and Tempest Crabbe have no known grave, the shellfire being so great that their bodies were blown to pieces. Their names are on a memorial that lists them as missing but 'Known unto God.' I wanted to linger at War Cloister so that I could admire the stonework, the vaulted roof, and the carved lettering by Laurence Turner. But it was all for the dead, for lives unable to have been led, and I wished I could have waved a wand to make these boys come back to life.

Approaching the river Itchen I saw a boy rowing and, half-closing my eyes, imagined him as Angus. It wasn't hard. Little here had changed and it made me see how tradition, although stulti-fying at times, also sustains. The boy's boat was no different to the ones Angus had rowed, only it was plastic and not wood. If the school had not quite won me over to the virtues of tradition, one of its songs succeeded in bringing a tear to my eye. On the evening before my expedition, I visited Win Coll's website and listened to a recording of *Domum*, a song sung in chapel at the end of the the summer term. 'Domum dulce Domum' is the re-frain (Latin for 'home, sweet home'), delightful words to sing at the end of a school year. However, the irony of the word 'dulce' struck me when I strolled through War Cloister and remembered Wilfred Owen's bitter poem on the Great War, 'Dulce et decorum est pro patria mori.'

Wykehamist on the Itchen

FROM WINCHESTER I bussed to Oxford, where Angus attended university. I wanted to take a look at Magdalen, his old college and whatever else was relevant to his Oxford days. I drove from the outskirts over Magdalen bridge to the historic part of the city. Here was the enclave of the élite; in my uncle's day they belonged to a hereditary social elect, whereas today their status is due to a meritocracy.

Amid these biscuit-coloured, buildings, Britain's future winners cavort. Oxford is not for also-rans. Only the best jostle here. As a Scot, used to plainer structures, I marvelled at the spires that appeared to leap, vault, and dance in the sky. At the end of the High Street the bus turned left past colleges, each hiding its beauty behind a dignified street façade. At the terminus on the less prepossessing side of the city, I set off for Falklands House on Oxpens Road, the home of the Oxford University Air Squadron. I would leave the treat of Magdalen, its chapel, quad, and river walk for later.

Like my father who was an undergraduate at Cambridge University, my uncle learned to fly because it was the 'in thing'. Privileged young men and women flew. There were records to break and mountains to soar over (the Marquess of Clydesdale in an open cockpit bi-plane was to fly over Everest in 1933 achieving similar accolades to astronauts a generation later). Flying was glamorous, daring, fast and sexy. In the same year that Angus joined the Oxford University Air Squadron, Sir Alan Cobham, one-time member of the Royal Flying Corps in World War One, staged air displays with trained pilots in a variety of aircraft. Cobham's aerobatic stunts, when he and his colleagues put their aeroplanes into vertical, lateral rolls and spins, were known as Cobham's Flying Circus and they toured the country until the end of 1935, visiting airfields and any patch of ground that could be landed on.

Sir Hugh Trenchard, Marshal of the RAF, had the idea of starting air squadrons in universities. Founded on 1st October, 1925, Cambridge was the first, followed by Oxford eleven days later. The idea was to promote an interest, not only in flying but to forge an affiliation with the universities on aviation technology. Angus joined on 14th October, 1932 at the beginning of his second year. On a more pragmatic note, university air squadrons offered training at government expense. It was an attractive proposition learning to fly for free as, unlike most Magdalen men who dined well, drank to excess, and owned a car, Angus was on a modest allowance. After John's death, Daisy sold most of the family heirlooms and the north part of the Largie estate to pay for death duties. Thereafter, money for the family was tight.

In Avro 504K aircraft, members of the Air Squadron flew, both in vacation and term-time, from an airfield near Bicester at Upper Heyford, a picturesque village of Cotswold stone cottages, surrounded by arable and grazing farmland. Used since the 1920s as an RAF base with a runway, once the second longest in Europe, the airbase is now abandoned.

Falklands House is a functional structure with security gates, where visitors announce their arrival through an intercom. I hankered after punting students, dons on dilapidated bikes, honeyed stone archways, in fact anything philosophical and forgetful, but I was in Falklands House now, the name plunging me back to the time when Margaret Thatcher ruled the waves, at least in the South Atlantic. "I only have the essentials like your uncle's entry date, his attendance at a summer camp in 1933, his address and that he was killed during World War Two." Dick Stanton, the adjutant was apologetic. I already knew from his army service records that Angus had a pilot's licence (category "A") with 90 hours flying, including 35 hours solo. "We have a photograph of him at the 1933 summer camp!" I peered at the picture and quickly found him in the back row, instantly recognisable because of his superior height.

Behind a front line of seated instructors in RAF uniform, was a group of students in casual wear: blazers, flannel trousers, shirts, and ties, assembled beneath the wing of an aeroplane. This was the first image I'd seen of Angus as an Oxford undergraduate and I felt a similar thrill to the day before when Suzanne Foster showed me his schoolboy photos. At sixteen, he was quite tall and struck a pose. The following year (possibly because of his illness) he appeared startled and ill-at-ease. At eighteen years and about to leave for Magdalen, he was a prefect and, although not looking entirely easy within himself, he still displayed a sense of accomplishment. Most intriguing, was the length of Angus's hair: at Win Coll, it was short with a side parting, but at Magdalen he let it grow. Having shed his schoolboy diffidence, Angus looked happier at Oxford. Evidently, he had no wish to fly professionally. Aeroplanes and long hair were one thing, but when it came to a job he had to be 'down to earth' and shorn.

One perk of joining the university Air Squadron and gaining a pilot's licence was flying solo. As soon as Angus acquired his certificate he took off in a plane from Upper Heyford and flew to Largie, landing at Killean, situated a few miles south of the castle. The late Ian Macdonald, a young neighbour at Largie, and Winnie Bird (daughter of Ronald Reid, the game-keeper), remember the occasion and how Reid added a touch of humour by writing in the estate game book that 'a large bird flew over; an aeroplane!'

At that period, private flights in small aeroplanes were the vogue. People paid to view their homes from the air. Just as tea flights offered for a couple of pounds a view of London, Angus flew Kintyre residents up the coast from Killean to Rhunahaorine for five shillings (25 pence). Ian Macdonald watched from the ground. "I would have gone up like a shot if I had had the money!" he said. "But the well-off farmers went instead!"

Affluent neighbours were not the only passengers. One figure with a high profile also ventured up, Cosmo Lang who, by that time, was Archbishop of Canterbury. J.G. Lockhart writes that "Lang had an exhilarating experience" when a friend of the young Macdonalds took him up in an aeroplane. My hunch is that it was Angus who piloted Lang. Perhaps Lockhart, whose book was published in September, 1949 (three months after Simon presented a petition in an Edinburgh civil court to presume that Angus was dead) preferred not to refer to him by name out of fear of distressing Daisy. Some warned against the archbishop's decision claiming the plane was unsafe, but Lang's main concern was that the press might get wind of his spree and write a story about it in the papers. To throw the hacks off the scent, eighteen year old Simon impersonated Lang by wearing his cloak, something the fun-loving prankster welcomed. "I very soon got over the first inevitable sense of dizziness," wrote the seventy year old prelate of his flight, "and was greatly excited to see the islands and Arran and the moors, with Largie and Ballure, from a great height. Indeed the experience seemed to anticipate a little what death might be like — old familiar objects becoming fainter and fainter as one rose into another world."

After finishing with Falklands House I retraced my steps to Magdalen College for an appointment with archivist, Dr Robin Darwall Smith. Lost in what was once a male haven, I felt the stones themselves harboured a cloistered misogyny. Magdalen displayed a ghostly silence as it was exam-time. A group of giggling students ran into the quadrangle and grouped together for a photo. Amongst the old architecture, the young women in modern dress struck a startling note, as I expected them to wear mortar-boards and gowns, not open neck shirts, jeans, long blonde hair, and high heels. I stepped into Hall, traditionally the social nucleus for undergraduates, then drifted into the chapel; small, ornate, and decorated, only its shell remains unchanged since the fifteenth century. Both Win Coll and Magdalen were founded by bishops of Winchester, William of Wykeham and William of Waynflete respectively, and each chapel is surprisingly similar in design, so it was an easy progression (in architecture, at least) for Angus to make from his school to university college.

However, the atmosphere at Magdalen in the early Thirties was different to the silliness of the Twenties. Angus's period here was part of a darker, harsher decade.

In the year that he went up to Oxford, when extreme right-wing Germans formed the Harzburger Front, Bishop Schreiber warned against the advance of National Socialism. Oswald Mosley was removed from the British Labour party and farther away, but significantly for Angus, the Japanese attacked the Chinese province of Jehol in the final month of 1931. Yet Lord Cecil, a member of the British government, claimed war was never so improbable.

Little is known about Angus's Magdalen days. However, in his letter to Esther written from India on Easter Day, 1939, five years after he down down, he states that he enjoyed it. My uncle followed his father and Jock to Magdalen, the seedbed for John's lifelong friendships. When my grandfather came up in 1891 Lang was Dean of Divinity, Alan Don, who became Dean of Westminster, was an undergraduate, and the ultra-Tory Charles Fletcher was first full-time Magdalen don in modern history.

Herbert Warren, President of Magdalen from 1885, had retired only three years before Angus's matriculation and, although the man's influence had diminished over the years, his attitudes still prevailed. Young men, he believed, must be physically fit and possess un-enquiring minds, which should be directed towards service before scholarship. Christian morality and virtue were preferable to a sharp intellect.

Warren believed in preparing sons of the well-to-do to run the empire for the general good. However, by the time Angus went up to Magdalen, the college had already embarked on the long road towards egalitarianism.

Nevertheless, the trend persisted of accepting Commoners into the college, either because they were the sons or grandsons of old members or for their rowing prowess and not because they were outstanding academically. So, Magdalen was still renowned for its indolent Commoner. "A lack of academic seriousness invaded the whole undergraduate body," wrote Vice-President Driver in 1933. Almost half the college's intake was from public schools like Eton, Harrow, and Winchester College and the subjects studied were mainly the humanities although physics, zoology, economics, French, and politics, were beginning to be taken seriously. At Magdalen, Angus read modern history, the subject his father chose forty years previously. Modern history was more popular now, since interest in the classics had begun to fade. Science as zoology and chemistry were not prioritised yet, and Angus's ambition was to be a 'good all-rounder.' Like other men from the main public schools, he was able to saunter through Oxford and still gain a second class degree.

Dr. Darwall-Smith's office was off the Cloister Quadrangle up a narrow, winding stair. He had invited me to view a photo of Angus when Magdalen went head of the river in the 1933 Torpids (in plainer language, he was part of a winning crew in a college rowing contest for oarsmen of second rank).

"Jock Fletcher-Campbell gave it to us," said Dr Darwall-Smith. The surname sounded familiar so I checked it out on my return home. Sure enough, Jock Fletcher-Campbell was a first cousin of Anne (nee Stirling Maxwell), Angus's sister-in-law, brother Jock's wife. "He came to watch the Torpids a few years before he died."

It was a commemorative photograph of the college's eight oarsmen seated in the quad. Dressed in cord trousers and V-necked sweater in a Fair Isle pattern, my uncle had a schoolboyish, startled look. Dr Darwall-Smith wished to help in my research but, unlike Win Coll, Magdalen kept few records of undergraduates from Angus's time. "Please let me reassure you on something," he had written a few months earlier "it is not so much a case of my not allowing you to see existing records here at Magdalen, as that, sadly, they just do not exist at all in any form or manner of any kind. Charles (he meant Angus) came up to Magdalen just before we began to keep files on individual students. Again and again it seems to me that, at this period, public schools were so much better than Colleges at keeping records of their members, both during and after their time there. I'm therefore glad that Winchester came up trumps on this for you."

In sport, especially on the river, Angus came a poor second to Jock, who reached his pinnacle when he rowed for Oxford against Cambridge in 1929. In spite of being an Oxford Blue, Jock's Magdalen years were lean in rowing triumphs. It may have been due to the beginnings of antagonism towards oarsmen. Nonetheless, money was showered on the boat club in the Twenties and

Thirties and, in 1927 they introduced a new barge, which was used as a changing room and for oar storage.

Because Magdalen was a small college, its boat club was introduced quite late (1859) but it made up for lost time and by the late 1800s and early 1900s the majority of the Oxford boat crew were from this college. Top oarsmen were usually ex-public school boys but when Angus arrived in 1931, this exclusivity was being challenged (American Rhodes scholars helped break down the class barrier and two, Roger Black and William Whipple rowed with Angus). As Magdalen ceased recruiting undergraduates for their rowing expertise, the college lost its pre-eminent position on the river. However, under George Gordon (Magdalen's President from 1928 to 1942), the downhill slide halted. During the Thirties, as a result of systematic training, Magdalen went head of the river in the Torpids and Summer Eights (a rowing inter-college contest for oarsmen of first rank) and remained triumphant throughout that decade. Angus benefited from this rise in rowing standards and by the end of his second year in 1933 was in the winning crew. The Torpids, a bumps race, where boats are rowed single file, each trying to catch (bump) the one in front, is suited to long, narrow waters and offers a sharper feeling than a timed race. As the name suggests, the Torpids, for less expert oarsmen are held in the seventh week (the beginning of March) of Hilary (the spring term) for four days. Although Angus never made it into the first eight of the Summer Eights (a fashionable event in Oxford University's calendar), he rowed for the second eight in 1933, when they were bumped by Oriel and New College, and the following year by Balliol.

In each race, Angus rowed with a Rhodes scholar from the United States Military Academy of West Point. Roger Black coincidentally died in a car crash in America the same year Angus was lost at sea in South East Asia. Jock Fletcher-Campbell, who became a clergyman, was in the bow seat; next was William Whipple (also from West Point), and F M McFisher. At stroke six was Wykehamist, Lionel Sackville-West who, after the war, settled at the family estate of Knole in Kent and each time his wife gave birth to a daughter (they had five), Sackville-West's literary cousin, Vita, wrote a poem bemoaning their failure to produce a male heir. At seven came Thurston (Tut) Irvine, the younger brother of Andrew, himself an oarsman but a member of Oxford's Merton College. In 1922 he rowed for Oxford in the boat race against Cambridge and two years later, aged 22, accompanied George Mallory on an expedition to climb Mount Everest where they both lost their lives, and finally the stroke, William Hughes. The boat was coxed by John Haldane.

Undoubtedly Angus's lesser rowing skills still helped him gain a place at Magdalen. Although he never competed with Jock, Magdalen's captain of boats from 1928 to 1929 who rowed in the Oxford University Fours in 1927, Angus's contribution was considerable. He was strong, athletic, and large and because of his size (12 stone 2 lbs), took a middle position in the boat (positions 3, 4 and 5 being 'the engine-room' of a crew with both height and weight an advantage).

Not much has changed in college rowing since Angus's day: boats are plastic and the oar blades resemble a paddle more than the pre-war slim pencil shape. The hearty amateur ex-public school ethos has vanished; colleges recruit undergraduates for their academic ability and not for sporting skills so that today rowing is seen, not as a competitive sport, but a pleasant form of exercise. Only the blue boat crew who compete in the famous boat race is highly competitive; these men are 25 year old postgraduates of Olympic standard.

In Angus's day, oars had no white lily embellished on their blades. Today each boat is named. In Angus's era they merely had the college coat of arms on the bow. There was no lycra either; any garb went for practice-rowing but for Eights week and the Torpids, crews wore a white singlet with black trimming, baggy towelling shorts, and a white sweater with a black line along the V.

I realised how much Angus must have liked Oxford. Signifying sport and leisure rivers, particularly those in south-east England where he went to university, had treated him kindly.

The sea was different. As a means of travel, it served a more serious purpose, its thoroughfares prone to disruption by both man and nature.

With an absent father (who was no oarsman) and a reserved mother, rowing supplied Angus with an acceptable form of intimacy and comradeship. In the end, this redoubtable pastime may have helped determine his future career in the army. Flying was too solitary and individualistic an activity for a man raised to be part of a team.

I intended to end my Oxford visit in the place where I had begun: at Falklands House. It not only housed the air squadron but also the university's Officers' Training Corps. I learned here that instead of entering the Royal Military College, Sandhurst (the usual destination for a young man wishing to become an army officer), Angus gained at the Oxford University Officers' Training Corps (OUOTC) his Certificate B, which entitled him to a commission in the special reserve of officers or in modern terms, the Territorial Army. To be certain, I wrote to the Royal Military Academy, Sandhurst asking if he held records on Angus. "Your uncle," came the reply, "would not have attended RMC, Sandhurst as he was commissioned directly into the army via the OTC. The absence of an entry for him in the RMC Gentleman Cadet Register confirms this."

During World War One, branches of the Officers Training Corps at UK universities trained some 30,000 officers. After the armistice the Corps reverted to basic military training but by the 1930s, when Angus joined the OUOTC, recruitment increased, peaking in 1938 as a response to the Munich crisis. Angus was attracted to the idea of joining. Instead of applying for the Royal Military College, Sandhurst, he could become an undergraduate and, while studying for an honours degree in modern history, join the Corps which provided his kit, awarded a small salary, and offered him the chance to be in an independent regiment with its own cap badge and insignia. So long as Angus played his cards carefully, he'd be eligible for the special reserve of officers. The University Delegacy for Military Instruction (a body that superintended candidates for army commissions), demanded he take a course in military history. He did. He also received instruction and pratical experience in being part of a regular army unit, learning military drill, field-craft, map-reading, camouflage, first aid, weapons training, radio procedure, how to set up an overnight patrol base, and fire and manoeuvre as part of a team. After this initial stage he acquired skills in leadership, although officer cadets within the unit were appointed to NCO roles after moving into the Senior Division. For example, Angus served as an officer cadet before being promoted to the post of Company Quarter Master Sergeant. Cadets received instruction on how to manage a minor unit, planning and decision making, giving orders and ensuring they were carried out, debriefing after an exercise and assuring the welfare of those under their command. The knowledge and experience gained were valuable alternatives to Sandhurst. On a more theoretical note, he learned about indirect firing, the use of directors, slide rules, range tables, distant aiming points, parallel lines, angles of sight, angles of deflection, and predictions. It was all complicated maths and probably not a subject in which any Macdonald was especially gifted. However, my uncle passed with flying colours.

A few months before taking his final exams in 1934, Angus completed a nomination form for entry into the British army. Extolling his performance, the adjutant of the OUOTC, wrote that Angus had reached "a very high standard of efficiency and was always willing to take charge and was a useful instructor." Neither was the colonel of the Military Delegacy disappointed and recommended that Angus be "third in order of merit for a scholarship on his first appointment." All he needed now was to be accepted by the first regiment of his choice: the Argyll & Sutherland Higlanders.

Going back to the very beginning into the mists of time, the Macdonalds were warriors. Living in the Highlands, the clans fought each other regularly. They also struggled against foreign invaders: Vikings and later soldiers from the Continent. They remembered how ships from Philip of Spain's armada in the 16th century, blown off course, ended up off the Kintyre coast.

Then there was the Lockhart branch whose distant ancestor Sir Symon was the quintessential soldier, a crusading knight no less. More recently, after the failure of the Stewarts in the 1745 Jacobite rising, the Macdonalds played a lesser role in fighting, but on Daisy's side of the family soldiering was in the blood. Although her forebears included businessmen, Dublin whiskey distillers, Edinburgh hoteliers, men of the cloth and (ignominiously) individuals who owned Jamaican sugar plantations worked by slaves, the Crabbes (her father, grandfather and great-grandfather) were all army officers.

Angus's great-great grandfather, Joseph Crabb (the family had not yet added an 'e' to their surname), born in 1742, was nineteen when he was commissioned as a lieutenant in the 84th Regiment of Foot and sailed to India, then called "the East Indies," but the troops returned to England in 1765 and were disbanded. Three years later, after languishing at home on half pay, young Joe seized his chance and joined the forces of the East India Company. The Company by then was not only a commercial organization but employed an army to govern large areas of India. Undoubtedly Joseph went for the money; any young man with ambition at that time headed east, as the subcontinent was seen as a honey-pot, a Dubhai of the mid-eighteenth century. Joseph became a major in 1773. The following year, he served in the Rohilla War when Warren Hastings, now governor-general of British India, joined forces with a tribe of Afghans who had entered India. Together they fought the Marattas with the purpose of strengthening the state of Oudh. In 1781, during his final year with the Company,

Joseph received orders to take the Fort of Lutterfpoor. Leading his troops "by secret and almost impracticable ways," he arrived at the village of Lora where he routed the Rajah of Benares, who grabbed his diamonds and fled on a camel to the mountains. The following day the intrepid Joe marched through the Pass of Sukroot and seized Lutterfpoor. Hastings was delighted. He thanked Major Crabb, promoted him to the rank of colonel, and commissioned artist, William Hodges, once employed by Captain Cook, who discovered New Zealand on his second voyage, to compose a picture of the fort.

Back in England, the public was not so happy. Many saw the 'nabobs' (the top British officials in India) as no more respect-worthy than today's bankers who claim large bonuses. Warren Hastings came under suspicion and in 1788 was put on trial for corruption. During his impeachment, the former governor-general was questioned about his treatment of the Raja of Benares, and Lieutenant-Colonel Crabb was called to give an account of the incident. It's unsurprising that his report vindicated his former boss: "reports were circulated one half-hour, and contradicted the next, and no one can trace the origin," alleged Crabb.

At least four successive generations of Crabbe men died leaving very young sons and daughters. Joseph lost his father when he was only ten, and he himself died the same year in which his son, Eyre John, was born. The latter, over sixty when his only child, Eyre Macdonell Stewart entered this world, only lived until the boy was seven or eight. In his turn, Eyre Macdonell, after a tough military life, died in 1905 a week before his 53rd birthday and left eight children, Tempest, the youngest being only eight years old at the time.

Eyre John Crabbe, born in 1791, followed his father into the army. After a tough early army life, Eyre John underwent three decades of uneventful peace, as his regiment "policed" British territories overseas. Within the armed forces it was (and still is) quite common for soldiers to experience long stretches of bore-dom with abrupt interludes of fierce fighting. Eyre John was scarcely out of his teens when he sailed with the 74th Regiment of Foot to Portugal and Spain to take part in the Peninsular War. Between 1810 and 1814 he fought in many battles, took part in the siege of Badajoz, and was involved in 'Wellington's masterpiece,' the battle of Salamanca. He was wounded at least once, received an inordinate quantity of clasps (medals) and was promoted to the rank of captain. In March 1814, the 74th was sent to Ireland and never met Napoleon's forces at Waterloo.

Eyre John is a less hazy figure than his father. During the latter period of his army career, while serving in the West Indies and Canada, he wrote letters home to his unmarried sister, Eliza and to Sarah, his widowed mother, who outlived Joseph by sixty years. Between 1840 and 1845, Eyre John scribbled dozens of chatty, inconsequential notes to his family. What emerges from them is his struggle against boredom. In Barbados, he created an ornamental garden on waste-ground outside his barracks.

As a soldier, Eyre John, now colonel of the 74th with 900 men under his command, took physical exercise seriously, both at work and at play. When his regiment moved to Montreal to guard the Colony (as it was termed) against possible American expansionism and threats from the French, based in Quebec, Crabbe tended a garden of exotic blooms and vegetables. Ever a keen traveller he visited Niagara Falls, slept under the stars in a wigwam, and in winter, took up sledging. At Christmas-time in 1840, the sprightly forty-nine year old danced the quadrille at a grand ball "and kept it up until 3 o'clock in the morning and on Wednesday was at another and kept it up again until the same hour."

Like his great-grandson Angus, who longed to return to the UK from Singapore, and never knew where or when he would be posted next, Eyre John in 1842 heard rumours that his regiment might be sent to India or China. But they were false and the 74th headed back to Britain in 1845. Shortly afterwards, Colonel Crabbe retired from the army, after artist David Cunliffe, well-known for his military groups, depicted Crabbe on a bay horse accompanied by his officers. Dressed in red tunics and tartan trews, they stand before a background of supposed Highland scenery. This painting now hangs in Edinburgh Castle Museum. I assumed it was commissioned as a golden handshake to mark Eyre's retirement after he'd honoured the 74th with 38 years' service but its real purpose was to acknowledge the restoration of the regiment to its original status. Although the 74th was founded as a Highland regiment, for over thirty years its officers and men had ceased wearing the kilt, and the unit's association with the Highlands was all but forgotten. Joining up as early as 1807, Eyre John remembered when officers and men wore Highland dress and knew how powerful a connection this Scottish region was with his troops. On his return from Canada, Crabbe asked his Commander-in-Chief (the aged Duke of Wellington) if he could help. The duke lobbied the Crown, who agreed to the restoration of the regiment's original status and allowed the officers and men to wear tartan trews but not the kilt. Many anniversaries hold sway in a nation's mind and it is no coincidence that 1845 marked the centenary of the Jacobite defeat under Bonnie Prince Charlie and the destruction of Highland society. During the aftermath of the rebellion, the wearing of the kilt was forbidden by an Act of Parliament for up to 36 years.

When I investigated Joseph's grandson, Eyre Macdonell Stewart Crabbe (I'll refer to him as EMSC), I also found a wealth of material. Like his grandfather and father, EMSC joined the army but, in his case, it was the fashionable Grenadier Guards. Unlike Eyre John, who began his soldiering in the long, hard Peninsular War and ended it with a period of relative inactivity, EMSC spent his early days in England and Ireland and only later saw active service, first in Egypt where, in 1882 a nationalist revolt prompted Gladstone's government to intervene militarily. Thirty then and married with five young children, EMSC, attached to the Commissariat and transport staff, sailed with the Guards as part of the British army. The Egyptians were soon defeated and my great-grandfather returned with a medal.

EMSC made two more military forays into Africa as the continent became the focus of imperialism from British and other European nations in the late nineteenth century. In 1884 as a captain, my great grandfather volunteered "for the fun of it" to join "the Soudan Expedition," leaving behind his wife, Emily and a brood now of six. Coerced into taking action against the Mahdi in the Sudan (a southern state of Egypt), Gladstone made the decision to send Major-General Charles Gordon to quell this Islamic revolutionary leader. But it was a disaster and, by September 1884, Gordon was besieged 1,600 miles up the Nile at Khartoum. EMSC, serving in the Camel Corps' Guards Camel Regiment as acting quartermaster, set out to rescue the hapless Gordon. On arrival at Port Said, they travelled by train to Cairo, camped near the pyramids, then proceeded upstream in barges to Aswan from which they reached a camp south of Dongola. After a week, the brigade rode 70 miles upstream to Korti, where they prepared to cross a stretch of desert in order to cut off a bend of the Nile. On their way, at Abu Klea, the troops caught sight of the enemy. By daybreak they were attacked. Forming a defensive square the British, including EMSC's section, fought off the far greater number of adversaries. At one point, the defensive square was broken and the battle, though brief, was fierce and bloody. The Guards were lucky in their position, which helped them to avoid many more casualties and deaths than their comrades-in-arms. This battle was immortalized by Sir Henry Newbolt in *Vitai Lampada*, a poem that uses the public school ethos as a metaphor for an idealized form of conduct in war.

> ...The sand of the desert is sodden red,
> Red with the wreck of a square that broke;
> The Gatling's jammed and the colonel dead,
> And the regiment blind with dust and smoke.
> The river of death has brimmed his banks,
> And England's far, and Honour a name,
> But the voice of the schoolboy rallies the ranks,
> "Play up! Play up! And play the game!

When EMSC's contingent reached the Nile and pitched their tents near Metemmeh, they discovered that Khartoum had fallen, so there was nothing for it but to retrace their steps and return to Cairo. Although they failed in their objective, individual Guards officers were amply rewarded: EMSC was promoted to brevet major, mentioned in dispatches, awarded two medals, and was included in a group of officers presented to the Queen at Osborne.

In 1898, EMSC was promoted to the rank of Lieutenant-Colonel in time to lead his battalion into battle in South Africa. Wars have always drawn comment; the Boer War attracted a flurry of famous writers: Kipling was vigorous in his support for the British during the South African campaign, Arthur Conan Doyle wrote about his impressions of the conflict in *Memories and Adventures* and ex-soldier, Winston Churchill turned up as a correspondent. A fair amount of information exists on the part EMSC played in the war: his name appears in general histories, regimental archives, and his own account (posthumously published) of the Grenadier Guards' 3rd battalion. His portrait is reproduced on a Wills' cigarette card as one of a series of well-known figures of the South African war. Perhaps the most valuable material on Crabbe, where the reader may catch a glimpse of the real man, can be found in his correspondence to Daisy, my grandmother. These hastily penned letters, 19 from South Africa, lay unread by Daisy's children and grandchildren (EMSC's Victorian hand-writing was hard to 'decode') until my cousin, Charles Gordon Clark offered to transcribe them. What emerges after Charles' painstaking efforts, is a kaleidoscopic view of Crabbe from the time on board ship, he is the first to accept an innoculation against typhoid, to the occasion when he describes his wounds after the Guards' first battle, as mere 'scratches.' On reading about his looting of enemy ponies, struggle to provide a Christmas feast for his men, and of the day when he was shot at by Boer commandoes I realize how graphic his stories are when compared to his father's accounts of bean-growing in Montreal and of gallivanting in the ballrooms of Upper Canada. At the time each man was writing letters home, both were in their late forties. It says much for EMSC 's fitness and health that in middle age, he was scaling hills, crossing fords, and galloping through the South African veldt as deftly as a man half his age.

This narrative is not a panegyric of the man; he received plenty plaudits, the most distinguished being the Companion of the Most Honourable Order of the Bath, which is conferred to Britons in recognition of conspicuous service to the Crown. It is a given that Crabbe, backed by his mother's fortune, was groomed for a high social position. Professionally, he was tough, even ruthless. In his account of the "Soudan" campaign, a brother officer, Count Albert Gleichen, grandson of Queen Victoria's elder half-sister, wrote that on seeing some Arabs going about their business in a village, Crabbe ordered 20 of his best marksmen to fire at them. During the South African campaign he devised a ruse to trick the Boers into shooting each other. After their first battle, Crabbe sent Daisy a curious memento: a bundle of letters belonging to one of his men and shot through with an enemy bullet. After the battle of Belmont, EMSC relished showing the scene to officers who had not been present. However, the colonel was paternalistic towards his 850 officers and men and referred to them as 'his flock,' 'old boys,' and 'motley crew.' He liked to treat his men at Christmas with a slap-up meal of roast beef, plum pudding and beer. Like most late Victorian imperialists, whose country had seen no major conflict since the war against Russia in the Crimea, he relished action. "The situation in South Africa," he wrote in his history of the battalion, "caused deep excitement to all corps who had any chance of seeing active service." His views were clear: they had to go to war against the Boer, so that Britain could remain a first class power.

For us in post-colonial Britain, Crabbe's unflinching certainty is hard to understand. Even more bemusing is Arthur Conan Doyle's thumb-nail sketch of the commander:

"Here is another man worth noting," writes the creator of Sherlock Holmes. "You could not help noting him if you tried. A burly, broad-shouldered man with full, square, black beard over his chest, his arm in a sling, his bearing a medieval knight-errant. It is Crabbe, of the Grenadier Guards. He reins his horse for an instant while his Guardsmen stream past him. 'I've had my share – four bullets already. Hope I won't get another today,' he says.

'You should be in hospital.'

'Ah, there I venture to disagree with you.'

He rides on with his men."

Some days before his meeting with the Victorian author, Crabbe had gone foraging with a commanding officer of the Cold-stream Guards. Accompanying them were his adjutant, another officer (Captain Trotter) and a soldier. When the party caught sight of four mounted Boers on a hill, EMSC suggested they 'round them up,' unaware that these men were members of the Johannesburg mounted police and 'some of the best shots in the Boer army.' Feigning a retreat, the Boers hid behind a rock and opened fire on Crabbe and his companions. EMSC's horse was killed instantly, its rider wounded in the arm and thigh. A bullet lodged itself in the thigh of the Coldstream's commanding officer, Captain Trotter was wounded badly in the arm, and Crabbe's adjutant was shot through the heart. After the incident, as EMSC was recovering in hospital, Captain Trotter, who described the event in a letter home, saw his superior "weep like a child over his dead adjutant."

In his role as father, EMSC reveals much in his letters. He managed to correspond, not only with Daisy but with Violet, Gladys, and his wife, Emily. He wrote from Gibralter where the battalion berthed for over a month, on board ship, at Modder River, Magersfontein, and Klip Drift. He kept writing until the evening before he was wounded by the Johannesburg mounted police. Crabbe's range of subjects is diverse: he describes the taking of prisoners, the officers' Mess hut, hurriedly built by members of the battalion and the acquisition of coconut matting, so his men could play football; he sends his daughters pressed wild flowers and bird skins and reports the sighting of a secretary bird and springbok deer. My great-grandfather was a man of gargantuan ego with a physique to match. The wearing of a beard denotes achievement (mid-Victorians, like the ageing Charles Darwin, Karl Marx, Brahms, Friedrich Engels, and Johann Strauss championed them); Crabbe was no slouch in that department. During the Sudan Campaign of 1885 and in South Africa he's photographed with generous facial hair. At that time, a beard was associated with the heroic, with men who were independent and resourceful. Beards went with the image of manliness, a cult which some claim grew to such fever pitch that it precipitated Europe into the bloodbath of the 1914-1918 war.

In addition to his ventures to the Dark Continent, Crabbe lost no time in expending both his bullets and seed. His wife, Emily Jameson, was from an Anglo-Irish whiskey distilling family. They were married in Ireland on 25th May 1876; she was eighteen and EMSC six years her senior. Their first child, Colville, was born two years later in 1878. Twin daughters, Daisy and Violet, followed in 1879. Gladys was born a year later. Lewis arrived in 1882, then Ivan in 1884. There was a three year break when Crabbe went off to the Sudan; in 1887 Iris appeared while Emily was still in her twenties. Their last was Tempest, an afterthought who appeared ten years later when his mother was 39.

EMSC's letters to Daisy show strong feelings for those he left behind. Writing after he was wounded in the thigh and wrist at the battle of Belmont after the battalion's arrival in South Africa, Crabbe admits "it is weary work for you all at home." For his wife "it is as bad as 1885" but for Daisy and her siblings "it is a first experience and I well know how hard you find it but you must try and cheer up and remember that everything is for the best and we can only play our part to the best of our ability and trust." While Crabbe senses their anguish (presumably they received a telegram after he was wounded), he makes little of what his wife and three eldest daughters, had to undergo. But at that period martial masculinity, and the practice of extolling qualities associated with the masculine, were predominant. Attributes of courage, stoicism and self-sacrifice were applauded. Women's voices were silenced and their deepest feelings and opinions, of their menfolk going to war, were ignored. The silence, or at best the voicing of a stereotype, hindered the development of a more thoughtful response to women's needs in relation to armed conflict. I doubt if Crabbe ever considered how hard it was for his wife and daughters to maintain their vigil while he was away.

Although she was successful in suppressing her emotions,

Daisy's body was unable to lie. Plagued by eczema, unsightly eruptions on her face, hands, and chest, it is unlikely that she saw her skin disease as a manifestation of the weeping soul, like some people did. Crabbe asks several times during the campaign about his daughter's ailment, the first time when he stopped at Gibralter. He compares her battle with eczema to his struggle against the Boer. At Modder River he wishes upon her its disappearance "not as the Boers do now to the next kopje but thoroughly routed as we hope they will be in the near future." In sum, this uber-masculine figure is ham-fisted and ineffectual in his distant affection. In some letters he encourages Daisy not "to fuss or worry" but to take life easily and be "absolutely idle and become no more Martha but Venus instead." In others, he bullies her into responsibility for her younger siblings. "Mind you try and keep Xmas going allright for the children," he chides. Daisy's duties were to help Iris with her reading, teach local boys their three r's, and organize village amateur dramatics or "tableaux," as EMSC calls them.

Crabbe was anxious that his letters for the twins' twenty-first birthday (15th February, 1900) arrive on time. Writing on 25th January, he expressed a fear also that the celebration will "lack a little in joy and excitement with which we all like to surround it at home." His birthday letter is tender and warm but he complains that his daughter underrates herself; she should be more self-reliant and develop a "contented mind in a sound body." He adds poignantly that he hopes to spend many more birthdays with her (in effect he only celebrated three more before his death in March, 1905). He concludes with "ever my darling Daisy" and hopes her self-denial will be rewarded. This wish suggests that his daughter is expected to give generously to the family and deny her own needs. Perhaps, after giving birth to so many children in quick succession, Emily was unwell and relied on her older daughters to care for the younger children.

I'm fortunate also to have access to images of both Eyre John and his son, Eyre Macdonell. The only picture of the former is the 1845 regimental portrait of the colonel mounted on his bay horse. To paint a man on a horse is to create an impression of authority, even invincibility. If a man wished gravitas, he only needed a mount. As Alexander the Great averred, a horse gives a man wings. For centuries, the horse was seen as an emblem of power. George III had 'Adonis'; the Duke of Wellington fought at Waterloo on 'Copenhagen,' his mount; Napoleon rode to Marengo, Austerlitz, Jena, Russia, and Waterloo on his white stallion, 'Marengo.' In the famous equestrian portrait of Napoleon by Jacques-Louis David, the horse with rolling eyes and flared nostrils, is conveying the Frenchman across the Alps. Although Cunliffe paints Eyre John's unnamed steed with its head held high, he has applied an Anglo-Saxon sobriety to the composition, with none of the drama of David's portrait.

A painted portrait is different to a photograph. While a painting performs a synthesis of a person's attributes, a photograph captures an aspect of an individual or a specific moment of the person's existence. Represented in photographic form, EMSC is first seen as a captain in a line-up of Guards officers in the 1885 Sudan campaign some days either before or after the battle of Abu Klea. In South Africa he is seated by a table in the officers' mess hut. The other two pictures are studio portraits where, in dress uniform, including sword, cocked hat and a row of medals on his front, he is bald and has lost his beard although he displays an extravagant rams-horn moustache. On retirement EMSC's rank was higher than that of his father, but he failed to have a portrait painted of him on a horse (although his favourite charger followed behind his coffin at his funeral in 1905). Britain in late Victorian times, had become a more humdrum, industrialized society than the early days of the monarch's reign, when John Eyre's portrait was commissioned.

It is unknown whether Angus knew much about the careers of his military forebears. Perhaps Daisy supplied her middle son with stories of Joseph, her great-grandfather who, as an East India Company army officer, impressed his superiors in India. In Eyre John, Daisy's grandfather, Angus could dream of the young officer proving his mettle in Wellington's arduous Peninsular

131

campaign. When it came to his maternal grandfather, EMSC, Angus was not only able to listen to Daisy's tales of her father, he could also read about him in history books or even amass a collection of Wills' cigarette cards with his grandfather's picture on one. Here was a Boy's Own alpha male onto whose memory Angus could graft his aspirations. Did Daisy relate her father's adventures in South Africa when the colonel hunted down Boer guerrillas with their crack marksmen? For two long years, the "sturdy" Crabbe, as Arthur Conan Doyle refers to him, "who was wounded four times," flushed out these expert fighters from the mountains of the Cape Colony. On several occasions Crabbe almost met with disaster, when he and his party were besieged by the enemy; only by much skill and subterfuge did they make their escape.

Soldiering, indeed, was in Angus's blood, and in his Crabbe antecedents he had much to live up to. Yet, Angus, given his ancestors, should have known what to expect of warfare and its effect on enemies and allies alike, under dire circumstances.

EMS Crabbe & Officers in South Africa. (EMSC seated extreme right.)

ON 1ST SEPTEMBER 1934, as 2nd lieutenant, Angus joined the 1st battalion of the Argyll & Sutherland Highlanders. It was a regiment and not the British army Angus wished to be part of. His grandfather's Corps, the Grenadier Guards, was of no interest however smart or fashionable. On his application form he wrote, in order of choice, three regiments that he wished to join. The first on the list was the Argyll & Sutherland Highlanders.

Although he was schooled south of the Border, my uncle wished to assert his Scottish identity. As back-up, he wrote down the Black Watch and the Cameron Highlanders. The Argylls were an obvious choice. Before being invalided out, his father had entered its 3rd battalion of Volunteers. Many Argyllshire men from the landed and farming families had served in the Argylls. Together with the Lindsay-MacDougalls of Lunga and Stewarts of Appin, Angus found himself with men whose families knew the Largie Macdonalds and one, Ian Stewart of Achnacone, was to leave a lasting impression on him. Officers were also recruited from south of the Highland line and even from England but the regiment still attracted sons from famous Argyll families. As for the soldiers themselves, they hailed from Scotland's central belt and northeast England. Many sought a route out of poverty by joining up, but in earlier times, men were recruited from Argyll's outlying regions including the islands and, because they understood little English, commands were given in Gaelic.

The Argyll & Sutherland Highlanders' history stems from the final years of the eighteenth century. In 1793 George III asked the 5th Duke of Argyll to raise a kilted regiment of 1,100 men, and in due course the 98th Argyllshire Highlanders (later the 91st) were formed. Less than a year later the new regiment, with men whose grandfathers had fought against Government troops at Culloden, embarked for South Africa to capture the Cape of Good Hope from the Dutch. The 91st returned in 1803 to guard against invasion by Napoleon, English southern shores. In 1808 the regiment moved to Portugal to rout the French. In 1871 Queen Victoria's daughter, HRH Princess Louise, married the Marquess of Lorne (later the 9th Duke of Argyll). The following year, when the princess was appointed the regiment's Colonel-in-Chief, the Argylls became known as Princess Louise's Argyllshire Highlanders.

To mark their allegiance they adopted her coronet and cipher, while adding to their insignia the Argyll boar's head and motto 'Ne Obliviscaris' (Do Not Forget). In 1881 under Cardwell's reforms to the British army, the 91st amalgamated with the 93rd (the Sutherland Highlanders which, after their stand in the Crimea at Balaklava, earned the sobriquet of The Thin Red Line) and became Princess Louise's Argyll & Sutherland Highlanders. She designed the regiment's new emblem which combines the Argylls boar's head with the Sutherland wild cat. In military terms the emblem encapsulates a concept; the American essayist, Ralph Waldo Emerson, claimed that it answers the need for a belief in transcendence and in a higher aim, "an old rag of bunting blowing in the wind, on a fort, at the ends of the earth, shall make the blood tingle under the rudest, or the most conventional exterior." Each former regiment retained its motto, the 91st's 'Ne Obliviscaris' (Do not forget) and the 93rd's 'Sans Peur' (without fear), which signified the regiment's pledge. The Argylls' 'Ne obliviscaris' has a particular resonance when thinking of Angus.

The newly-amalgamated regiment's uniform was still the kilt but in the Sutherland tartan, which was similar to the Argyllshire regiment's dark green Campbell design with its distinctive black line. Officers and non-commissioned officers (NCOs) wore a badger-head sporran, and glengarries were the favoured headgear. Added to their kilt, sporran, bonnet, pipes, drums, emblems and motto, the Argylls possessed a mascot: Cruachan, a dark, brown Shetland pony (originally called Tom Thumb) presented by HRH Princess Louise in 1928.

The Argyll & Sutherland Highlanders served in the Boer War (1899-1902) and Great War (1914-18). The 2nd battalion, to which Angus would be assigned, remained at home until 1927, whereupon they voyaged to Jamaica for two years, followed by a four year period in Hong Kong and China. They moved to India in 1933 where they remained, until just before the outbreak of War when they sailed for Malaya.

For Angus, becoming an army officer in the Argylls was a natural progression from his attendance at Winchester College and Magdalen. A regiment fosters a team spirit and imposes a strict system of hierarchy: officers were set apart from the men, much in the same way as a Highland laird lived close to, but apart from, his tenants and employees.

Regimental protocol was similar to public school ritual which often bewildered newcomers and served the purpose of putting them in their place. However, as they familiarised themselves with the arcane practices, the new officers were able to feel part of the team.

There were no clear-cut rules as such, just rituals that had evolved over the years and the practice of these encouraged feelings of fellowship. Different regiments had different rituals and a Highland regiment's traditions often fostered in its men a strong sense of Scottishness. Within the impersonal institution of the army, the regiment gave a man a home.

Nevertheless, officers were obliged to 'share similar interests,' to enjoy similar sports and pastimes, and even hold similar attitudes to life. In other words, each man had to fit in.

Officers and other ranks occupied separate messes, but they came together as one and shared a common history. Central to the British army is the concept of a family, engendered by the regiment. Although they had to accept a strict discipline, which amounted to silly practises for private soldiers like polishing and ironing bootlaces, they looked after each other. Officers led by example, and they all fought for each other, and not for the army or the nation. Officers grew so close that when they talked of a regimental colleague they referred to him, not as a friend, mate or pal but a 'brother.'

The 93rd, as they were referred to, was a regiment of the foot or an infantry unit, with foot-slogging and little glamour. Importantly, it depended upon a strong link to a geographical locality and history. Angus's choice of regiment reflected his connection with the county of Argyll but also the regiment was more relaxed than the Black Watch (his second choice). "The latter was stiff and formal," explained David Gibbon, son of Aubrey who served with Angus in India. "If someone got divorced (early in the 20th century) they had to leave the regiment." When all was said and done, the Black Watch was snobbish; it was considered beyond the pale for officers to speak with a Scottish accent, especially if it was Glaswegian. On the other hand, Argylls officers had no objection to their colleagues speaking in a dialect. It was common for brothers in military families to enter different regiments. This practice created a leavening effect on the posh Black Watch so that in time it became less stuffy.

Unlike many of my uncle's contemporaries, his family had little continuous tradition with the regiment as his father never saw active service. David Wilson, who joined the 1st battalion from Sandhurst, was a third generation Argyll, his father, Lt-Col A.R.G. Wilson being the 1st battalion's commanding officer and his grandfather, Major-General Sir Alexander Wilson, the Colonel of the regiment. Others, like Jim Cunningham, Jack Hyslop, Kenny Muir, John and Giles Tweedie, and John Lindsay-MacDougall came from families in which successive generations had served in the regiment. Doubtless, a lack of family tradition within the regiment caused Angus to feel somewhat unsupported and an outsider.

Angus received no warning against joining up, unlike Archibald Wavell, another Wykehamist, whose schoolmasters thought he was too bright to be a soldier. My uncle was no dunce and had an intellectual bent, but above all he sought action and adventure. When he joined the Argylls, the British Army was in a parlous state. At the end of the Great War, the number of officers and other ranks dropped dramatically. From 3.5 million in 1918 to 370,000 in 1920. Expenditure also fell. In peacetime, Britain (with its vast Empire) maintained its army as a means of keeping order. "Great Britain has never had a large army in time of peace. She has a small professional force which is little more than an imperial police reserve," wrote Winston Churchill in January 1938. Nevertheless, he warned that the military should be kept at full strength and be equipped with the latest "appliances and fullest supplies."

By the early Thirties, threats from Germany and Japan were real but re-armament only began in 1935. It wasn't until 1938 with a loan of £36 million (supplementing a budget of £87 million) that the army was ready for war. The British Army reached the nadir of its fortunes during the inter-war years. The least glamorous of the armed forces, it lacked the tradition of the Royal Navy and the fresh appeal of the Royal Air Force. After the armistice when the full horror of trench warfare was made known, the British public preferred to forget about the professional soldier and, as Kipling regretted, made "mock o' uniforms that guard you while you sleep." However, the army was necessary as, under the Treaty of Versailles, the empire gained added responsibilities with territories mandated in the Middle East (the former Ottoman empire) and the Rhineland. India was its largest commitment, with 70,000 British troops required. Europe was little threat, until Hitler rose to power, but during the late 1920s and 1930s there was a risk that the Soviets might invade India via Afghanistan. After the First World War, a ten year rule restricted defence spending. All three services planned their expenditure assuming that no war would break out for at least that time (the measure was maintained until 1932). As a result the army was accused of being static and ultra-conservative. To be a soldier was dull and frustrating, and promotion was slow.

Nevertheless the army benefited from the new-found peace. Without worrying about an enemy, reforms and innovations could be made. Mechanisation, including pioneering experiments with the tank, began in the early 1930s. Demonstrations on Salisbury Plain had 180 tanks moved by radio control in dense fog. As the horse was abandoned in field, furrow, and street, it disappeared also from the army; in its place arrived the armoured car and light tank although at first, little attempt was made to develop them, but, as motor transport increased, marching infantry became a feature of the past.

Armoured formations? Platoons? NCOs and other incomprehensible military acronyms? What was it that repelled me about the army? Was it the implicit violence, the uniforms or its uniformity that put me off? My generation had extolled individualism while my mother's contemporaries conformed and were part of mass movements; they were people on the move, especially the march. I belonged to a generation brought up on protest songs like *Blowing in the Wind* sung by Bob Dylan and Joan Baez. Some American contemporaries, although I was never well acquainted with any, were draft-dodgers, runaways from serving in the armed forces in Vietnam. At home, most men a decade older than me were conscripted for National Service before the British Government began to phase it out in 1957. Most found the experience, at best a bore and at worst, unpleasant.

An abiding memory of my youthful attitude towards the military was from visiting Simon, who, on inheriting the Lockhart of Lee property in Lanarkshire, permitted the Territorial Army to practice their manoeuvres in his fields. As I watched men in camouflage crawling in the heather, I sniggered. "These men are defending your country!" my uncle was indignant. But I didn't see it like that. I made a distinction between Angus and his Crabbe ancestors, regarding them as little more than mercenaries, servants of imperial Britain versus men of principle like the medieval crusader, Sir Symon Loccard, my Jacobite Macdonald ancestors, and more recently Nelson Mandela, Che Guevara, and the Irish Republican Army. I may not have agreed with the brutal practices of the latter but they were rebels with a cause nonetheless, not servants of their country policing its interests. When in 1968 Russia invaded Czechoslovakia, I saw the tank as a symbol of oppression, but as the years rolled by I realised that for Paris or inmates of a concentration camp like Auschwitz, the sight of an American, British or Russian tank signified liberation. Soldiers could rape, pillage and kill but, depending upon the situation, they could also save, aid and impose order upon chaos.

But the experiences and attitudes of military personnel were an unknown, at least to me.

When war was declared in 1939 my father joined the RAF. After it was over he and his contemporaries, especially my mother's surviving brothers, wanted to forget it all, and I inferred from their silence that they were antipathetic towards the armed forces. When, in the 1970s a well-publicised campaign was waged to save the Argylls from disbanding, my family made little attempt to support it. To cap it all, no nephew or niece and great-nephew or great-niece of Angus has chosen the armed forces as a career, and it seems that after many centuries of fighting for their country, our family had had enough.

To discover more about Angus, I needed to talk to officers and soldiers. It didn't matter whom, so long as they were military. After several unhelpful telephone conversations with a retired brigadier and a major-general, I came across ex-soldier Henry Hopkinson. A slim man, with a hint of self-mockery, welcomed me at the front door of his bungalow in the southern outskirts of Edinburgh. As I entered I noticed hanging on the wall a picture of Shiva, the multi-armed Indian goddess, but not until we were drinking our third mug of tea did I dare ask Henry if Indian goddesses and warfare combined.

"Is soldiering compatible with spirituality?" I ventured. "I thought they were hostile."

"Read the Bhagavad Gita," he said. "It's all about warfare!"

Thinking it over, I saw that monotheistic religions also embraced armed combat. The Old Testament is full of stories about the Israelites' battles, while up and down the country, church congregations still sing hymns about Christian soldiers fighting the good fight. "But I'm a child of the Sixties!"

Peace and love were the goals of my generation.

"So am I!" he chuckled. "It didn't stop me from joining the army, as a private, mind. My father had me down for Sandhurst as soon as I could talk, but when I was expelled from school, they wouldn't accept me," he grinned. "All that flower power was huge attitude, you know. So, you're a pacifist, Mary?" he said raising an eyebrow. "If someone was about to rape your daughter and you had a gun or a knife, wouldn't you use it?" This question is always posed as the acid test of whether someone is or is not a pacifist. "Yes, I would!" I sighed. "No, I'm not a pacifist." I'd written to Henry to ask him what he learned on joining up and to explain the kind of equipment Angus would have used. "He would've had a rifle." This mild-mannered man was an expert in weaponry. "I can strip one down, clean all the parts and assemble them to order, no bother!" he explained. "Then, he would have had a few hand grenades. They're called pineapples; they're in 16 sections and shaped like the fruit."

I then asked Henry what it was really like to be in the army. As a young soldier in 1966 he helped at Aberfan, a mining village in South Wales, where the contents of a slag heap had engulfed a primary school full of children. He had also seen action in one of Britain's former Colonies. "In battle, rank is forgotten," he explained, "officers and men address one and another by their first names." This closeness nurtured also in pub, club, locker, and boardroom has no female equivalent. But it could turn like a worm and a steely ruthlessness take its place. In a novel by Eric Linklater a sergeant shoots a junior officer when the latter loses his head in the face of the enemy. That's what made me uneasy. What did I want from my deceased uncle? Was he hero or anti-hero, courageous or a coward? When all's said and done, what gave me the right to rake over the embers of his short life? I feared I was no better than a nosy parker inspecting a pile of dirty linen.

After meeting Henry I visited Stirling Castle, headquarters until 1964 of the Argyll & Sutherland Highlanders. Crouching on top of a hill rising steeply from the city centre, the castle was once the home of Stewart kings; Mary Queen of Scots was crowned here in 1543. After its decline as a royal residence, the castle became a military centre (the Young Pretender, Prince Charles Edward Stewart, tried to capture it in 1746, two months before his defeat at Culloden) and in 1881 the regiment's head-quarters. I drove past the church of the Holy Rude, where James VI was crowned and parked my car on the esplanade. Whereas, in the 1930s, the space was used as a parade-ground, today it serves as an open-air concert arena. In spite of the cold wind, I paused to absorb the panoramic view: to the west was Ben Lomond, and on the opposite side stood the Wallace Monument, swirled in mist. I approached a large defence wall and moat, entered through the main gate and crossed a cobbled courtyard. After climbing a slope that led to the palace and great hall, I found a courtyard and on its west side the King's Old Building built for James IV in 1496. Once an infirmary and officers' sleeping quarters, it became in 1988 the Argyll & Sutherland Highlanders museum.

I had come not to gape at medals, photos or kilted uniforms but to see if the museum held any records on Angus. Rod Mackenzie, the museum's deputy curator, ushered me into a room where officers toast their Queen and country. Dominating the space was a mahogany table and on its surface a silver bowl surrounded by silver goblets, plates, quaichs, and cutlery, each object's sheen reminding me of the army's obsession with order and ceremony. As I sat, Rod presented me with the 1st Battalion's diary. "Let's hope you can find something in that!"

I learned, that as a new recruit, Second-Lieutenant Macdonald was not entirely green. The OUOTC had taught him how to clean a rifle, shoot straight, drill with precision, polish a bayonet blade, and fumble through a manual of military law. From the time he became a scout at West Downs until mid-way through his second year at Oxford, when he entered the Territorial Army, Angus had prepared for his career as an army officer. After joining, he'd come to the Argylls' depot at Stirling Castle and took part in ceremonials and drills on the esplanade.

More significant was his introduction to the then commanding officer, Ian Stewart of Achnacone, who belonged to a branch of the Appin Stewarts. They were woven firmly into Argyllshire's social fabric and the Appin laird's wife, a staunch Episcopalian who played the church organ, was a friend of my grandmother. This social ease and recognition helped oil the wheels for the young 2nd lieutenant. Stewart introduced several comforts for his men: a hot water system and a cup of tea after meals. It was here, in late 1934, at the start of Angus's army career that Colonel Stewart noted the qualities of this tall, reserved young officer. For the most part, Angus was based at Redford Barracks on the southern outskirts of Edinburgh. Since the construction of Fort George in the Highlands, Redford had become the largest military installation in Scotland.

I now possessed his dates: vital milestones in his short life. During Angus's first months in the Argylls, the battalion resembled a theatrical troupe more than a fighting force. Pageantry and ceremonials have always preoccupied soldiers. In October, 1934 the regimental pipe band took part in a contest in Italy's Turin (Angus was absent from the competition as he was no piper but his brother Jock was a gifted player). The Italian newspaper, *La Stampa* was extravagant in its praise: "…these flaming reds, those feather bonnets, those cloaks draped from the shoulder and falling in harmonious pleats down the back — what did the public know of all that dazzling ensemble, rendered still more vivid by the inimitable way the men held themselves, and by their marching in that capricious yet most orderly step? These wonderfully fine fellows with beautiful uniforms and bearing. They reaped applause to the full and were both yesterday and the day before the darlings of the public."

Back in Edinburgh, other 'darlings' (six officers and 150 other ranks in conjunction with the Royal Scots Greys) took part in the filming of 'The Iron Duke' and enacted the charge of the Gordon Highlanders and Royal Scots Greys at the battle of Waterloo. To fulfil the complement, the battalion provided a guard of honour for the admiral of the General Fleet when the "Deutschland," a German battleship berthed in the Firth of Forth.

The diary was punctilious in listing each officer, his rank and role. Angus's name occurs when the battalion shifted south to Tidworth, a village near Salisbury Plain, the traditional training ground of the British Army. The Argylls left Edinburgh on 10th January, 1935, and their send-off was tumultuous, as they had been popular during their four year stint in the capital. Ironically, Angus's army career in Scotland amounted to just over three months before he returned to his old stamping-ground (Tidworth was twenty miles from Winchester College).

The garrison was a bustling community, constructed in the early 1900s during the heyday of the British army. By the beginning of the Great War, it was self-sufficient with a railway connection, church, hospital, theatre, recreation rooms, power station and cinema, while Tedworth House was an officers' mess. The Argylls were billeted at Lucknow Barracks. From the outside its main structure (built in 1905) resembled an English country mansion and was a pleasant change from the grim, prison-like building at Redford.

Apart from the appearance of his name in regimental records the only other reference to my uncle at Tidworth is the Winchester College obituary stating that "he looked every inch a soldier when we visited him at Tidworth." I wondered who the obituarist referred to when he wrote 'we'? Was it his housemaster, college prefects, or members of the Officers' Training Corps? In addition to parades and manoeuvres, Angus sweated it out in a series of long-distance marches. In the autumn of 1935, the battalion performed a large exercise over a wide area. While completing the task they made a discovery; if after dumping supplies, administrative vehicles doubled as troop transport, the unit could occupy important ground and gain an advantage. Although this new scheme of 'misappropriating' supply vehicles caused plenty controversy, it set a precedent and the practice was adopted widely between 1939-1945.

Angus's service records reveal that during his first summer in the south, he received tuition in mortar warfare and signed on for a further course the following year. He also learned about air photography at Netheravon Airfield nearby. Some skills were put to the test in his final year in Wiltshire. In June 1937, to mark the new King's birthday, 1st Battalion, as part of 3 Division, paraded on Salisbury Plain. Its open ground was ideal for carrying out experiments in mechanizing the infantry. The event, reviewed by General Sir John T. Burnett-Stuart, Colonel-in-Chief, was the division's first large parade with mechanised transport and many feared it would be a disaster; some vehicles had just been issued and were temperamental, while others were ready for the scrapheap. But the parade went off without a hitch and the Colonel sang the troops' praises: "The fact there were no breakdowns, either during rehearsal or on parade, speaks for itself," he applauded. Burnett-Stuart was one of the few pre-war generals to favour mechanised tactics.

There were less strenuous duties, at times convivial, although the 23 year old lieutenant had to be on his best behaviour when he was invited by the Colonel of the regiment, Major-General Sir Alexander Wilson to attend the Argylls' annual dinner in July, 1936 at London's Naval and Military Club. The pukka establishment still exists but has moved to St. James's Square. Founded in the 1860s for officers of the army and navy, the Naval and Military Club or "The In & Out" is, as its website photograph indicates, hoary and conservative. One public room shows a mortar on a desk, a ship's canon by the fireside, and a portrait hanging on the wall of a bereted general. As a home-from-home for worthies from the shires, it has a strict dress code and expects its members 'to dress in a manner consistent with the character, dignity and standing of the club.'

There was no danger of anyone at the major-general's table slipping up in his attire. Each officer, high-ranking or low, wore dress uniform (kilts and white tie). If Angus was unacquainted with his dining companions, he would soon know them. Ian Stewart, his boss at the Stirling depot, was present, so was Hector Greenfield, who would be his commanding officer in India and John W. Tweedie (adjutant of the 2nd battalion from December, 1936). What the officers ate, drank, and discussed is unknown. Much easier to guess was what was on the mind of the ageing Major-General Wilson. The 88 year old Princess Louise, their Colonel-in-Chief, had just written him a friendly letter congratulating her regiment on being selected for conversion into a machine-gun unit. At that time, neither the Princess, Wilson, nor the officers and men, were aware that this arrangement would cause them many headaches in the future.

On 12th May, 1937, three Argylls officers and 50 other ranks travelled to London to perform ceremonial duties at George VI's coronation. I doubt if Angus pushed hard to attend although if anyone was entitled, it was he, as Archbishop Lang, who had baptised my uncle as a baby, was officiating. The coronation earned a mention in the regimental magazine when the editor warned that 'the handsomest men in the battalion have already been chosen — there are no vacancies left.' Joking apart, smartness and good looks mattered. A soldier's turn-out was commented upon by writers and journalists, as in La Stampa after the Argylls' pipe band visited Italy. A young soldier was expected to be proud of his appearance. As with the plumage of a robin, cock pheasant, or drake, colour plays an important role in an army regiment, particularly a Highland one. Setting aside combat khaki, it's a soldier's dress uniform that wins hearts and sends shivers down the spine, and it should create as much of an impression as the feathered display of any farmyard rooster.

The culmination in military pride and peacock display was the Tidworth tattoo. Battalions took the event seriously, and from July to September training was interrupted so that officers and men could attend rehearsals. Although Angus's stay at the garrison co-incided with three consecutive tattoos it is unlikely he performed in any. In 1935 the Argylls performed a drill display; the following year, two officers and 100 other ranks represented the battle of Falkirk of 1298. The Argylls were accompanied by two bands: the Pipes and Drums of 1st Battalion and the regimental band which, in common with regimental bands throughout Britain, consisted mainly of wind instruments. Established in 1920, the annual Tidworth Tattoo was performed in early August on the polo ground in front of Tedworth House. It drew a mass of spec-tators, who travelled from as far afield as London, Birmingham and Wales. The grandstand had a seating capacity of 30,000. Local firms constructed the scenery, and the garrison theatre became a fitting room for 2,000 performers. Theatrical costumiers supplied the costumes and a Wiltshire laundry was put on standby each evening if it rained. Local boys flogged chocolate sent from the manufacturers by special delivery; NAAFI canteens sold tea, cake and sandwiches. Troops performed to military music before an elaborate backdrop. One year the capture of Quebec was enacted. Other acts involved a motorbike dispatch rider leaping over a gap in a broken 'war-time' bridge (at that time both Norton and Triumph vied with each other to produce a wheel that avoided collapse when the bike landed).

The Tattoo may well have attracted Angus's mother and siblings. A graduate in Forestry from Oxford University, Jock was working for the Forestry Commission which, in the 1930s, was acquiring land to plant trees, so that the country's timber reserve could be replenished after its depletion during World War One. Older sister, Douna and her husband, Henry Rogers, with their infant daughter Shian, were about to leave their parish in London's East End, where Henry had been a clergyman, and move to Gordonstoun. The new school, established by Kurt Hahn, an early refugee from Nazi Germany, was looking for schoolmasters and Henry was a successful applicant. Angus's younger brother, Simon had followed him to Magdalen College, Oxford, and sixteen year old Esther Mary was a pupil at Downe House.

A more likely occasion for a family reunion was Christmas, 1936 (Angus's last in the UK) when he gave my mother a book, Rudyard Kipling's 'The Maltese Cat'. For Angus, it was an obvious choice as it was about polo-playing. Fresh from the press, publisher Macmillan, had hired Lionel Edwards, a painter of horses, to illustrate the narrative. Since Esther Mary was a horse lover, the book was a suitable gift. Or was it? *The Maltese Cat*, subtitled *a polo game of the Nineties*, describes the slick conformity of careless, young army officers at play at the turn of the century. While Kipling coveted acceptance by such circles, he was unable to ignore those who existed alongside this coterie. In *The Maltese Cat* he brings humour and charm to the polo ponies, allowing the story to unfold from their viewpoint, just as he did with Baloo, Shere Khan, and other beasts in *The Jungle Book*. What better gift (for the giver) than a tale about polo playing in India, since the donor might soon find himself in that country indulging in such an activity?

Although we know that Christmas, 1936 was Angus's last in Britain, we are ignorant as to whether he was aware he'd be going overseas. Friends, Angus Rose and David Wilson, were already preparing for their transference to 2nd Battalion; they left in March, 1937. The other unknown is whether my mother's brother presented his gift in person or if he sent it by post? He may have remained at Tidworth, sharing the view of a contributor to the regimental magazine, who claimed that when stationed in England, you profited from two end-of-the-year celebrations: Christmas and Hogmanay (in Scotland the battalion only celebrated the latter).

I like to believe that Angus returned to Largie for his last Christmas with the family and, amongst other gifts, presented Esther with hers.

ANGUS SUSPECTED he would be posted overseas; in the early part of 1937, some close friends transferred to 2nd Battalion garrisoned at Secunderabad in south India. First was David Wilson who sailed on His Majesty's Troopship (HMT) Dorsetshire accompanied by two other officers from the battalion, Ian Stonor and Gordon Campbell Colquhoun. Angus Rose followed in the spring. Voyaging on HMT Neuralia, he arrived at Bombay in early April. Rose, one of four siblings all commissioned into the army, was to become if he wasn't already, a firm friend.

My uncle may well have wondered when his turn would come. He did not have long to wait as on 29 June, the *London Gazette* announced that he and two other officers were to be posted to 2nd Battalion during the first half of the 1937/38 trooping season for India which began in September and finished in March, the reason being that servicemen took the three week sea voyage at the beginning of the cool season, so they had time to acclimatise before the Indian plains became a furnace the following April. Today, when a soldier's home may be reached from any point of the globe in a matter of hours, it's hard to imagine how young men felt then as they prepared for service overseas. During the 1930s, it was usual for troops to spend at least five or six years abroad without any prospect of returning to the United Kingdom.

That September, a host of troopships departed Southampton for the east, the most celebrated being the recently built 1,000 ton HMT Dunera, which on 9 September, began her maiden voyage to China. To see her off, War Minister Mr Hore-Belisha paid the honours. HMT Somersetshire followed on 11 September with a draft heading for Egypt. Three days later, the 9,543-ton HMT Lancashire left Southampton 'with military drafts for India.' This was Angus's ship. Somewhat apt for the modest young man, the Lancashire was serviceable, unspectacular, and no government minister waved her off.

I imagine that some of the family came to Southampton quay

for Angus. Daisy saw to it that her children's rites of passage were observed. They watched Jock row for Oxford, were present at Douna's wedding at Largie, and attended the marriage of Jock to Anne Stirling Maxwell, when Angus was best man and Esther a bridesmaid. Daisy made the long journey from Argyll. Whether Douna was able to travel from Gordonstoun in Morayshire is unknown. Both Simon, still at Magdalen College, and Esther, at Downe House in Berkshire, were not so far away. One or two friends, people connected with Daisy's youth, may have swelled the family ranks, or possibly an aunt. Violet, Daisy's twin sister, lived in the south.

The voyage to India was Angus's first big adventure, possibly his first trip abroad. While he was growing up, the family could not afford to take holidays overseas. It was certainly the young man's first journey away from Europe and, as the band played *Auld Lang Syne* and a posse of photographers lined up their subjects, he must have felt a mixture of emotions. There was the thrill of the new, the foreign, and the East. Fed on Rudyard Kipling, Angus was curious to head to India into the sunset of the British Raj, with its civil unrest and disaffection. He was optimistic. However, if he was happy, was everyone else pleased? He had a terrier (this is how the family story went) that refused to eat, and after he departed it pined and died. Added to this tale, apocryphal though it might be, sister Douna allegedly reported years later that Angus knew he would never return.

From the time when he was nine years of age, when he set off for his first term at West Downs, Angus associated the month of September with departure. However, the young army officer had to go back four generations to Joseph Crabb, his great, great grandfather, before he could find a forebear who had served in the east.

The ship departed at 3 p.m., after the final inspection which ascertained passengers' berths and the stowing of baggage. With the strains of the National Anthem ringing in their ears, passengers watched from the deck as relatives and friends on the quay receded into the distance. As an officer Angus had a roomy cabin, shared with three others. They slept on bunks, had a basin, cupboard space and each a chest-of-drawers. They needed plenty storage space, as they wore uniform and mess kit for dinner. Each cabin had a steward. The other ranks received no such comforts: warrant officers, sergeants, and married people occupied a third of the ship, while the troops were squashed together like sardines sleeping in cargo space on hammocks.

The ship slid past Netley Hospital and its abbey before navigating west through the Solent, separating the wooded Hampshire mainland from the northern shores of the Isle of Wight. Their final view of England was Alum Bay's red cliffs and the white rocks of the Needles, before the ship entered the Channel. Angus's companions were Captain Jack Hyslop and Lieutenant John Lindsay-MacDougall. Hyslop came from an Argylls family, his grandfather having served with the 93rd in the Crimea and during the Indian Mutiny, while his father fought in the Boer War and in France. Hyslop was tall, good looking, well-mannered and, while serving in Cairo in the 1920s, gained a reputation for ballroom dancing, but it was short-lived. Not long afterwards, a main tendon in one of his legs was severed in a shooting accident. John Lindsay-MacDougall of Lunga on the Ardfern peninsula was an Argyllshire laird. The MacDougalls had known the Macdonalds for generations; members of the two families had dined, partied, played sport, and even fought alongside each other. They had breathed the same sea air, tramped similar stretches of heather, and dated each other's sisters. In a photograph of the officers at Trimulgherry, taken in January 1939, the three men, Hyslop, Angus, and Lindsay MacDougall, stand side by side in the centre of the middle row. No doubt their three-week sea voyage helped the trio forge a singular bond.

Passengers were not allowed to remain idle. Before breakfast, officers and men sweated on deck with a physical fitness regime. Officers performed a course of duties taking it in turns to oversee the stowing and drawing of hammocks on the troop deck, attend each mealtime and inspect the mess deck three times a day. The latter, known as 'vomit and sweat,' required a strong stomach, particularly when the going got rough: the pong of unwashed bodies and stench of vomit could be overpowering. David Wilson writes that during their three-week voyage, there were courses in a host of subjects from Urdu, taught by senior Indian Army officers, lectures on India and the Indian Army to small arms training when they fired at a target in the sea towed from the ship's stern. These activities took place as the ship plied the waters from Cape Ushant to the Bay of Biscay; celebrated for its storms and rough waters, the latter can often be as calm as a mill pond. HMT Lancashire reached the coast of Portugal and sailed south; although Lisbon, situated nine miles inland, was not visible from the sea, the Cintra hills and the ancient regal palace were. When they rounded the promontory of Cape St Vincent and Cape Sagres, they changed course and headed south-south-east towards Gibraltar. Lying like a recumbent lion guarding the entrance to the Mediterranean, the island or 'The Rock' encapsulated the might of the British Empire. The historic fortress towering against a cloudless sky was an impressive sight.

After Gibraltar, they hugged the southern coast of Spain; with a pair of binoculars Angus could see the Graeco-Roman towers of Malaga's cathedral and, in the distance, the Sierra Nevada. The young man peered through his glasses at the Andalusian coastline to see a country in the throes of civil war. To starboard was Africa but at Tunisia's Cape Bon, the coastline turned sharply south. From this point until the Nile delta one thousand miles east, land views were obscured. As they sailed towards Egypt, the days became shorter and the sea calmer; fewer passengers suffered from seasickness. With the warmth, soldiers slept on deck while others settled down to guard duty, played tombola, or attended to their mess orderly duties. After reaching Malta on its seventh day at sea, the Lancashire continued until it sighted land. Moving from the familiar blue of the Mediterranean, the ship fetched up in shallow water beneath which were the sands of the Nile. From the deck, the troops saw trees, small houses and minarets. This was Port Said, the bustling gateway to the East.

When the ship docked the troops disembarked and, after performing a route march and taking a bath, they were free to explore. Travelling on the Dorsetshire, David Wilson stopped here for ten days in the sweltering sun. For most young men, Port Said was their first experience of coping with hawkers and vendors who preyed on the passengers and crew of troopships and ocean-going liners. Henry C. Day, a chaplain on a troopship at this period, wrote of Port Said that 'architecturally, socially and morally it leaves much to be desired'. I'm sure Angus was irritated by the molesting guides, amused by the undesirable postcards on display and intrigued by extraordinary scenes in which the 'gully gully men' (local magicians) plied their acts. The canny young officer grabbed the chance to buy duty free goods as there were bargains to be had. What Angus desired was a good camera (in one letter he mentions how he intended to take colour photographs), and it may have been at Port Said that he bought one. The obvious place to go was Simon Arzt's department store on the waterfront. Served by assistants dressed in white with red tarbooshes, Angus bought a 'Bombay bowler,' a khaki solar pith helmet with a flattened crown and a thick brim. As he placed it on his head and glanced at his reflection in the store's mirror, he saw a new Angus, young but with a purpose. He was going places and would succeed. Family tradition expected no less. Unlike the other ranks, officers had to buy their own gear, so Angus stocked up with tropical clothing, bought pills to ward off a queasy stomach, and treated himself to a haircut but drew the line at visiting the photographic studio. That could wait.

The next stage (and the most memorable) was their 86½ mile passage down the Suez Canal. With a speed limit of 6 to 7 knots, the ship's crossing took 15-20 twenty hours to complete, but their transit was delayed by a mass of other craft on the waterway. She had hazards to contend with, such as freakish sandstorms and thick fog. Vessels were forbidden to overtake except when they reached Timsah and the Great Bitter Lakes. Situated at 10 km intervals were stations with high masts giving instructions to passing ships. Mail ships gained preference over oil tankers and freighters carrying dangerous cargo, which sailed only by day. At night the Lancashire was guided by a searchlight fixed to her prow. The diffused light made the water beneath her appear pitch black, while the banks on either side of the liner shone a ghostly white.

At the Suez entrance, the waterway cuts a straight line south for twenty-five miles. On the east bank is the Arabian Desert, and on the west, the vast Lake Menzaleh, where fishing boats bobbed on the water among sandy islands. For centuries, El Kantara (now El Qantara), at the junction of the Palestine and Egyptian state railways, has been a crossing place for travellers between Egypt and Syria. Loaded with biblical memories, it saw Abraham, his sons, and even the holy family pass through on their way to Egypt. This is where the Israelites settled in the days of Jacob, whose son Joseph became ruler of the land.

Halfway down the canal and east of Ismaila is Lake Timsah where crocodiles once teemed. Farther south, and extending for 12 miles, lies the vast Great Bitter Lake which resembles an inland sea. Beyond this gigantic stretch of water, and almost as an afterthought, is the Little Bitter Lake. The final station is Port Tewfik on the Gulf of Suez. Released from the canal, passengers and crew found the Red Sea hot and the atmosphere on board as airless as an oven. The eastern smells were becoming tiresome and tawdry and orderly officer duties irksome, if not downright unpleasant. Even the lectures, physical fitness programme and ship's food began to pall. From dawn to dusk, a bugle announced the daily duties, from sweeper and swabber tasks to the stowing and drawing of hammocks; there was even a sharp blast indicating when troops were permitted to smoke.

The best part of the Red Sea (or Arabian Gulf) passage was a short break at Port Sudan situated midway down the gulf on the African coast. Here, they found a hotel with an open-air swimming pool. Those wishing to sample the local life visited the market-place to watch Arab, African, and Berber traders, and the nomadic Hadendoa tribesmen with their distinctive hair styles, whom the white colonialists described as 'fuzzy-wuzzies,' a term no longer acceptable today as it reflects the casual racism of the time. Angus may well have taken a trip to explore the coral reefs nearby; as it was the habitat of 1,000 different invertebrate species and 200 soft and hard corals, it was an obvious attraction; a glass-bottomed boat conveyed visitors to see strands of coral that grew in the form of bushes, mini ferns and gauze-like sheets, with myriads of fish 'mingling in the living garden of the sea,' as the Reverend Day described this remarkable feat of nature and the world's most northerly tropical reef.

The ship's final stop in the Arabian Gulf was Aden, which occupied a strategic position en route to India. Separating Aden from Bombay was 1,645 miles of water: the Indian Ocean took 4 to 5 days to cross. After the Lancashire weighed anchor at Aden, passengers quickly lost sight of the mainland, their chief interest being other ships, an occasional aircraft overhead, and sea life: flying fish, dolphins, porpoises, sharks, and whales.

On the morning of day five, Bombay hove into sight, with its splendid harbour, immense white buildings, church spires, the university dome, Gothic towers, factories with tall chimneys, parks, hospitals, hotels, and public buildings. The voyage from harbour to harbour had taken three weeks, thanks to the Suez Canal that forged a passage from the Mediterranean to the Red Sea. In the days before the canal, the journey by steamship from London around the Horn of Africa to Bombay took at least thirty days. Angus's destination was Bombay, but his friend, David Wilson, who travelled earlier in the year for Waziristan in the north-west, sailed 400 miles north to Karachi.

For their first night, officers and men remained on board but in the evening some took a stroll around the harbour. They had heard about the night life, its smart clubs like the Bombay Gymkhana, Byculla, the Royal Yacht Club, and the Willingdon. They ambled along the tree-lined promenade, enjoying the cool ocean breeze, and watched a ceremony where, to invoke prosperity, an effigy of Ganesh, the elephant god, was cast into the sea. Fishermen were landing their catch; monkeys lurked on hot tin roofs. Angus had mugged up on Bombay. One day he would explore the city and visit the caves nearby. However, the noise and smells were off-putting, but happily he'd arrived at the end of the monsoons in time for the cool season, which was still very hot and humid; he wondered how he'd manage when it was really hot. They had received plenty of lectures about the hazards of drinking bad water and eating raw fruit. So it was important to pay attention to personal hygiene and drink only water that had been boiled. As for malaria, there was still no satisfactory preventive measure against it and the young man had no wish to come down with a frighteningly high temperature, hallucinate, and even see vibrant colours as he suffered from the tropical fever. For several centuries, the only effective agent was quinine although a new, highly efficient anti-malarial drug called mepacrine had just been invented.

Angus was overcome by the sheer weight of humanity in Bombay and the cheapness of life as stick-like figures begged in the streets. He wanted to escape. Even in his home country he felt uneasy tramping the streets of Glasgow, Edinburgh, or London, so one more night on board the Lancashire came as a relief. The next day he departed from the Victoria Terminus with its extravagant Gujurati-Gothic architecture on a troop train bound for Hyderabad, the capital of the Deccan province. To accommodate the jocks, as the Scottish rank and file were called, the train had special carriages, which consisted of bunks with lavatories at either end of their section and no corridors. Officers travelled first class. Angus's compartment, with lights and fans, had two bunks up and two below as well as two cane chairs, a lavatory and a shower. The occupants also had a bearer to lay out their bedding on the bunks. To prevent dust from entering the space, the window was covered by gauze over slats and glass. A typical dinner in the restaurant car was curry, lentil soup, dhal, chicken or omelette, followed by bread and butter pudding. The next morning, as the sun rose in a cloudless sky, the bearer served Angus and his companions chota hazri or little breakfast, and brought hot water for them to wash in and shave. The train maintained a steady 60 mph instead of the usual 35 mph of the standard Indian engine. Drivers and firemen of the Great Indian Peninsular Railway took a pride in their appearance and worked all day dressed in suits and sola topis. They saw to it that their locomotive was kept spick and span with well-polished brass and steel. As the passengers gazed from their window, they saw that the countryside was flat and dusty. For mile upon mile, they chugged along the even plains, passing oases of trees, houses and fields, and when they stopped at a station, monkeys gathered on the platform in the hope that passengers would throw them food.

There was little for Angus to do inside the stuffy compartment but lie on his bunk, put up with the din of the whirring fans and sip soda water. Before they reached their destination, each officer brought out his best uniform and put on his kilt, red and white diced hose and spats in readiness for arrival. For headgear Angus may have chosen a sola pith helmet. On the other hand he might have erred on the side of tradition and settled for the Wolsey; wound round its crown, with exactly seven folds, was a khaki cloth called a pagri and on the left side a tartan flash with the letters 'A & SH' in yellow capitals, with a white hackle stuck in it.

Now Angus was ready for his new life, one in which a good heart and proper training are not a guarantee against malevolent forces beyond the horizon.

Angus and Peter Farquhar at Secunderabad

HYDERABAD TERMINUS WAS CROWDED. But Angus was now no stranger to the crush of humanity, the lack of personal space, the noise and smells that assaulted travellers in the east. A delegation led by adjutant, John Tweedie, came to meet them.

Outside the station stood a row of horses with their driver, each beast harnessed to a tonga (a two-wheeled carriage). Angus, accompanied by another officer, took one and set off at a brisk pace through Hyderabad, the principal city of the Deccan. Of all the 550 princely states of India, this ancient Islamic province roughly the area of France was the largest. Hyderabad was also very beautiful, its founder having attempted to create in its minarets, palaces and gardens 'a replica of heaven.' They drove 5 ½ miles north to Secunderabad, past a man-made lake, the Hussain Sagar, which separates the two cities. Today the two settlements are one metropolis but previously Secunderabad was a separate town comprising the largest British garrison in India after Poona. From a tiny tented encampment on the outskirts of the old city, Secunderabad, founded in 1806 and named after Sikander Ja, the third Nizam of the Asaf Jahi dynasty, grew into the home of the British army in southern India. Tucked away from the hustle and bustle of Hyderabad, the garrison became self-sufficient with bungalows, open spaces, churches, race and golf courses, and the famous Secunderabad Club founded in 1878. Angus's destination was Meadows Barracks at Trimulgherry Fort. In the nineteenth century, as a response to the Sepoy Mutiny in 1857 when the Hyderabad Residency was attacked, the army built this stout fortress, otherwise called 'the entrenchment,' with a moat.

Accommodation was in blocks but officers and married personnel lived half a mile outside the fort. As the party trotted towards their billet, they saw strange-looking trees like the pomegranate and banana, and native animals, and birds, that Angus had already met in children's picture books or the *Encyclopedia Britannica*.

Entering a new world, he still felt at home in this English military cantonment. Angus was on safe ground here. He and his peers understood each other, spoke the same language, and held similar beliefs.

Not a fresh-faced newcomer like some second lieutenants straight from Sandhurst, my uncle had already made a good impression in the 1st Battalion. His arrival at Trimulgherry coincided with the 2nd Battalion returning from Waziristan where, towards the end of 1936, the Fakir of Ipi, ruler of the province in the North-West Frontier, had provoked a guerrilla war against the British. In April 1937, the 93rd was sent to the region to sort out the Fakir's band of armed tribesmen, but the real danger was in falling seriously ill, not death in battle; during the hottest part of the season, a sergeant had died of heat stroke and disease had killed several men.

On 18 October, the battalion had departed Rawalpindi for its six-day train journey back to Meadows Barracks. Angus had served with some of these men but, as newcomers and old-stagers congregated in the comfortable two storey officers' mess, with its garden and tennis courts, they were aware of a difference: those who had fought in Waziristan and officers like Angus who, to put it bluntly, had not yet been 'blooded.'

Among Angus's first responsibilities was as guard of honour for the Viceroy's visit at Falaknuma Palace to the south of Hyderabad. Built in 1884 in a fantasy European style, the residence was home to the 7th Nizam of Hyderabad, Mir Osman Ali Khan, Asaf Jah. His Exalted Highness, ruler of the province since 1911, the richest man in the world with a fortune of $2 billion. He owned hundreds of racehorses and dozens of Rolls Royces. The prince had his own infantry regiment, currency, and postal service too. The Nizam's private treasury held £100 million in gold and silver bullion and £400 million in jewels, including enough pearls to pave Picadilly. This wealth came from owning the world's largest diamond mine, the source of the Koh-i-Noor, Great Mogul diamond, and the rare £60 million Jacob gemstone, which the prince used as a paperweight.

Decked in full dress uniform, the Argylls provided an inner cordon of 17 sentries and a guard of honour of 230 men with pipes, drums and a military band for Lord Linlithgow, the Viceroy. The British had a special relationship with the Nizam; not only was he the highest ranking Indian prince and therefore entitled to a 21 gun salute, but following his financial contribution to the British war effort in the 1914–18 war, he was seen as the 'faithful ally of the British Crown.' The Argylls' gave the royal salute for the Viceroy, and the band played soft music for the Mizaj-Pursi, a formal Islamic ceremony that welcomed the visitor and bade him good health, after which the soldiers returned to their tented accommodation on the terrace. The ritual was repeated for the Nizam's arrival, only he received a general salute.

The Viceroy's visit lasted several days during which time His Excellency inspected hospitals, schools, and civic schemes in Hyderabad and Secunderabad. After their five day tour, when Lord and Lady Linlithgow departed for Delhi by train, the Argylls, before striking camp, made a tour of the palace. Designed in the shape of a scorpion, with the two stings splayed like wings, the Nizam's enormous residence of 220 lavishly furnished rooms and 22 spacious halls had taken nine years to complete. Faluknama left most European palaces in the shade: the library, a replica of the one at Windsor Castle, had a mahogany and ebony ceiling inlaid with dozens of panels, each in a different kind of wood. This room alone housed 5,900 books, including an illuminated copy of the Holy Quran. While a two-ton hand-operated organ (the only one of its kind in the world) graced the palace ballroom, the Nizam's dining room accommodated a dining table large enough to seat 100 guests, who feasted off gold plates.

As a soldier, Angus was largely insulated from the social life of Hyderabad but judging from photos of dinner parties in the Faluknama dining room, there was much social interaction between Indians and the British. Being a princely Indian state, the Deccan province was separate from British India. The Indians, of whom some were extremely anglicised, and the British met on equal terms: if the British dined in Indian homes, Indians joined

British clubs and both races played golf and cricket together. Hector Greenfield, soon to be appointed commanding officer of 2nd Argylls, wrote to Brigadier Edward Spears that 'The local Indians in Hyderabad are very pleasant and the upper classes, who run the state, are mostly educated in England.' Iris Portal, sister of British politician Rab Butler, lived in Hyderabad in the late 1930s and claimed that most high-ranking Indians from the Deccan province were either anglophiles or francophiles; they rented or bought apartments and villas in London, Paris or Cannes. Portal was not fooled by the Deccan sybaritic ways: 'It was like living in France on the eve of the Revolution,' she remarked; she was aware that life in the villages away from the Nizam's court had not progressed much since the Middle Ages

The Indian elite in Hyderabad were not altogether happy about the gaining power of Congress, the democratic party that wanted home rule. But change was coming, as Mahatma Gandhi's influence in India grew. When he became Viceroy in 1936, Lord Linlithgow, under the Government of India Act 1935, implemented plans for local self-government, which resulted in Congress party governing five out of eleven provinces. The new arrangement was unpopular with many princes, and they responded by affiliating more closely with the British. 'They are enthusiastically pro-British as they are bitterly opposed to Congress whose socialistic ideas alarm them very much,' wrote Colonel Greenfield.

Apart from a wariness of socialism, upper class Indians had often rubbed along well with the British, whose monotheistic religion resonated more comfortably with their Muslim faith than that of the Hindu. Traditionally, the two races preferred to segregate the sexes: in muslim households women occupied purdah quarters while British men herded in all-male clubs. Both cultures had strong military traditions and enjoyed sport, in particular the hunting or shooting of animals and birds.

The special friendship between Linlithgow and the seventh Nizam of Hyderabad may well have been forged on the Deccan plateau where teal, mallard, shoveller, and spotbill settled in their thousands. It is significant that the Viceroy's visit was in January as it was at this time of the year that these birds migrated south, pausing to feed in the surrounding countryside. Linlithgow was a keen shot. When he was not governing India, he visited different parts of India to shoot. Later that year he stayed in a district of Rajasthan (now the Bharatpur National Park), and in one expedition alone, his party shot 4,273 birds. This carnage was common and in grand social circles it was the norm. In his autobiography, *The House of Elrig*, Gavin Maxwell notes that his late father Aymer, uncle of Jock's wife, Anne, née Stirling Maxwell, had taken part during 1907 in shooting parties resulting in the cumulative slaughter of 23,000 birds and small mammals. Maxwell attributes his father's dedication to the sport as a need to belong to a select group that stipulated that its members be an outstandingly good shot. These upper class men demanded no less stringent entry requirements than those posed by a gang of urban youths on their incomers. But the practice of shooting signified more than a fundamental need to be one of the boys. If this was the case, the more peaceful sports like cricket, tennis and golf would suffice. Undoubtedly, the killing of game served to prepare young men for the adult world. The connection between the sporting life and war has little distinction in the minds of some. While he was with the British Expeditionary Force in the 8th Battalion of the Argylls in France, close to the Maginot Line at the beginning of World War II, Jock spent hours watching Germans through his binoculars and 'found them far more interesting to stalk than deer.' Angus Rose would make commando-style raids on the west coast of Malaya and compare his guerrilla tactics against the Japanese to the thrill of wild-fowling on the Solway.

An official shoot was arranged for the fourth day of Linlithgow's visit. David Wilson writes in his memoir of the anxiety it caused him and his friends. The Viceroy's shooting party headed 60 miles north-west of Hyderabad to Nizamsagar. In 1923, as part of the seventh Nizam's modernisation programme, he ordered the inhabitants of 40 villages to be evacuated so that a vast dam could be built. This part of the province was Angus and his cronies' favourite sporting ground, a pleasant place at which to camp and shoot. However, before the Viceroy's visit, the young Argyll officers found that around their chosen jheels (large, shallow lakes), notices had been erected to indicate that these places were reserved for the Nizam. Needless to say, Angus and his party ignored the signs. When the day arrived for the shoot, the villagers who gathered to retrieve the game and some of the officers in the party who had ignored the notices, colluded in not telling. Fortunately, Linlithgow was satisfied. The plateau teemed with duck and teal and by 2 p.m. His party had managed to bag 60 birds.

The usual procedure for their shooting expedition was to set off at 3 a.m. by car in groups of 4 to 6 with servants, bedding rolls, and shot guns, so they could take up their positions by the jheels. There they edged their cars towards the water's edge and waded into the shallow water at the perimeter and waited until dawn. As light appeared, the wildfowlers saw the birds silhouetted and heard their murmuring. The leading gun let off the first shot, whereupon a rush of duck and teal flew into the sky. As the sun rose, the birds disappeared, signifying the point at which the shooters counted their spoils and had breakfast. The best shooting was at dusk, and to take full advantage of it, the officers waited in concealed niches until the moment when the birds returned, and each man was rewarded for his patience and skill. The officers returned to their cars, ate supper served by a camp fire, after which they slept under the stars in their bed-rolls. It was cold at night but the low temperatures warded off pests and mosquitoes. A typical quota during such a sporting spree was 250 birds, which were brought back to Trimulgherry and kept in cold storage.

From photographs, it's clear that Angus's early months in India were happy. Gone are any traces of the overgrown schoolboy or the self-conscious Oxford undergraduate. India held an atmosphere of mystery and excitement, but was unable to offer him his usual sporting opportunities; instead, he went shooting. For an officer of slender means, as a young lieutenant's salary was very small, this sport not only offered Angus the thrill of the outdoors but helped prevent him from over-spending in the officers' mess. Although he played polo (his 1939 Easter Day letter to Esther reveals he owned a pony for this purpose), the cost was minimal. Sport was part of the Argylls' fitness routine, and their team played hockey against the 5/2 Punjabs and the West Yorkshires. The Argylls' excellent football team won the 1938 tournament. Boxing was a favourite for many but not with Angus, as he was to profess to his mother in a letter from Singapore. To a point, he enjoyed team games but my uncle preferred solitary pursuits like sailing, shooting and flying. While his friend, Angus Rose, was captain, Angus was track judge rather than a competitor in the Trimulgherry athletics tournament that summer when they staged contests in running, the long and high jump, pole vaulting, throwing the hammer, javelin, and tug-of-war.

Besides sport, Angus helped edit *The Thin Red Line*. The editorial team rotated every three months to bring out the periodical four times a year, at an annual reader cost of 7/- or 5 rupees. With Angus Rose and Lance Sergeant Andrews, Angus edited the February 1938 magazine. Browsing through back numbers, I'm impressed by the quality of the diary of events, notes on the sergeants' mess, the pipes, drums and military band, not forgetting the 'What the Parrot is Saying!' column. In summer 1939, the parrot asks the identity of 'the sergeant that won the beauty competition and is he really a good looker?' With few bylines, it is impossible to distinguish who wrote what. I suspect that one entry styled in a jocular vein comes from the pen of Angus Rose (in many respects the two Angus's are flip sides of the same coin, one light-hearted and extrovert, the other careful and guarded) who describes an occasion when Professor Gupta, an 'eminent' entertainer, displayed his conjuring feats and snake-swallowing. 'Bigger and better snakes were swallowed this time, even than the time before but the editor's stomach was not strong enough to watch.' When Rose's cousin arrived from the UK at Trimulgherry, he received a welcome with a potted biography. While Jack Hyslop earned a mention, as did E. N. Campbell Baldwin, Peter Farquhar and Bobby Rumsey, Angus had none. Perhaps his arrival was too late to be announced in the November issue, and by the time the following number was published, Angus needed no introduction.

A more plausible reason was Lieutenant Macdonald's modesty: as co-editor, he was reluctant to indulge in self-publicity.

My uncle missed his home and family, but he had friends, both old and new; of the latter, Peter Farquhar, five years his junior, is photographed with Angus standing beside an army lorry at Meadows Barracks. In the background, framed in an archway, are two Indian women in long tunics and trousers while the soldiers, holding batons, are clothed in shorts, shirts, Sam Browne belt, and topi. The men are a world apart from the two young, brown-skinned women. Each pair is hermetically sealed within its socio-racial group, one policing the homeland of the other. When the photograph was developed, did he notice the two young Indian women in the background? Did he wonder at the unfairness? Perhaps he saw it like his friend, David Wilson who, years later, explained that he was young and just got on with the job and in doing so enjoyed himself, made many friends, and saw places that today's tourist is forbidden to visit.

At Hogmanay they celebrated. The officers brought out their silver and in a large punch bowl, prepared a potent concoction of Atholl Brose for the sergeants. Shortly before midnight, the NCOs were piped into the officers' mess where the acting commanding officer, Jim Cunningham, rose to propose their health. Together they toasted, sang, and danced into the small hours. If they had been stationed in Scotland, all would have been well, and they would have been permitted to sleep until well past noon. But this was India. At 6 a.m., Angus rose and dressed in his finery for his first Proclamation Parade at the Maidan, an open exercise area used for polo-playing and ceremonies. Established during Queen Victoria's reign, the Parade held on 1 January demonstrated the armed forces' loyalty to the reigning British monarch, the King Emperor. All notables turned up: the Nizam and the British Resident, who kept tabs on the Nizam and his government.

The three mile march in the fresh air from Trimulgherry to the parade ground helped many sober up. By the time the 93rd found their positions, they were in the company of '5 cavalry regiments': the Royal Horse Artillery, a British Indian cavalry regiment, an

Indian cavalry regiment and two regiments of the Nizam's state cavalry. Spectators thrilled to the gleam of the horses' flanks, the jingle of the bits, the smell of the turf and the colours of the soldiers' ceremonial uniform. Behind the mounted units came the West Yorkshires, 4/19 Hyderabads, a mule transport company and the Nizam's infantry. The National Anthem followed the swearing of allegiance. The Union Jack was lowered, the Royal Standard raised, a royal salute given, and a feu de joie was sounded: soldiers fired blank cartridges into the air. Before offering three cheers to the King Emperor, the troops removed their head-dresses. The 93rd received the command, 'doff your bonnets.' Finally, the formation marched past, 'with eyes right for the flag,' back to the barracks. 'The march past was very good,' was an editor's verdict, 'and steady' which surprised him after the hammering most officers and men had given themselves the previous night.

In 1896, thirty years before Angus attended a Proclamation Parade, Winston Churchill, as a young army officer, noted that a procession of elephants also gave their salute. 'At the end came a score of elephants drawing tandem-fashion gigantic cannon. It was then the custom for the elephants to salute as they marched past by raising their trunk and this they all did with exemplary precision,' wrote the new officer of the 4th Hussars in *My Early Life*. Explaining why the custom was abolished, Churchill attributes it to 'vulgar people tittering' so that 'the dignity of the elephants or their mahouts was wounded.' Soon afterwards, the elephants themselves were discontinued and 'clattering tractors' were brought in 'drawing far larger and more destructive guns.' Needless to say, Churchill mourned the discontinuation of 'the elephants and their salutations.'

Good performances were not always the norm. Conformity is a byword for the military, but the British Army thrived on traditional individualism, which grew through the independence of its regiments; each accrued a unique character of its own. However, this could cause trouble at a ceremonial. On one occasion during the march past, the Argylls led the West Yorkshires whose pace was slower than their highland brethren. Unfortunately, the officer leading the Argylls failed to appreciate the discrepancy and the result was chaos.

Accommodating changing personnel was a prerequisite in the army. In early 1938 the turnover at Trimulgherry was rapid. In February a draft arrived from Stirling Castle depot with Company Sergeant Major (CSM)Munnoch, who would serve closely with Angus. A further draft of one hundred officers and men from 1st Battalion followed. With it came the new commanding officer, Lieutenant-Colonel Hector Greenfield. His wife, Ivy (née Dering), was Angus's second cousin. The couple were married on Armistice Day, 1918. Greenfield had not escaped the Great War unharmed receiving a severe wound to his left leg while serving in Salonika in 1916. Despite fears that the limb might have to be amputated, it was saved, although in photographs of the period, he carries a walking stick and limped slightly for the rest of his life. In spite of this, he managed to pass all medical examinations and retired from the army in his early fifties in 1946. After they married, the Greenfields moved to Paris, living initially at the Ritz for a controlled price, where Hector became assistant to the Military Attache at the British Embassy. Little is known of Hector and Angus's friendship but as his son James Greenfield suggests, they 'were obviously good friends, which is a common occurrence between a commanding officer and his adjutant, despite the age difference.' (Hector was twenty years older than Angus.) Hector spoke often of his regimental colleagues and stressed that Angus was 'one of his best, if not the best, of his younger officers,' claims James. Unfortunately, the two men enjoyed few occasions when they could meet socially while serving in India and later in Singapore, because their routines and dates of leave failed to coincide. In spite of these drawbacks, Angus became Hector's adjutant, which helped cement their friendship.

They also had a family connection going back to the days when Angus was a boy. The Greenfield Visitors' Book reveals that during the 1920s, Daisy often stayed with the couple when they lived in the south not far from Winchester College. Presumably my grandmother used her cousin's as a base to visit her children at school. In February, 1936 when the Greenfields were living in Wilton near Salisbury, Daisy stayed with them again, bringing with her Angus, who gave his address as Tidsworth. The rapport between the families is also confirmed by the existence of several photographs in the Greenfield album of John Ronald Moreton Macdonald, his children, and even Daisy's nephews, Andrew and Martin Willan.

With arrivals came departures: Jim Cunningham headed home via North America. After several years service overseas, officers were entitled to an extensive period of leave. Many returned home via China, America or Canada. Some used the period as an opportunity for an extended visit to Australia or South Africa. The more recent arrivals were permitted two months local leave, which allowed them time to visit the Central Provinces, Kashmir, Ceylon or the Dutch East Indies. On 29 March, Kenny Muir, Angus's wildfowling accomplice, took a nine-month privilege leave before returning home to join 1st Battalion. His departure marked a complete change-over of officers since the time when the unit arrived in India in 1934. 'There is now nobody with us in the battalion who came from Shanghai,' wrote the editor of *The Thin Red Line*.

Coinciding with Muir's farewell was the arrival of the hot season. 'The weather began to tell on our tempers.' That year it was unusually hot as temperatures soared above 100 degrees Fahrenheit. Fans or punkahs whirred in each public room of the barracks 'at considerable danger to human life,' *The Thin Red Line* reported. With the heat came a change in routine: dinner-time was no longer at mid-day but at 6:30 p.m.; all ranks adopted short-sleeved shirts with pockets, collar and shorts; officers put away their kilts. In the mess, they wore a white jacket, a shirt with collar, trousers and a tartan silk cummerbund. Another colonial totem, the Wolseley, chose this moment to bite the dust. Its resemblance to an English bobby's helmet suggests that the army of the British

Empire was one of policing rather than warfare. The army insisted on clinging to outmoded traditions, but one was the need to avoid sunstroke, so from dawn until 6 p.m. it was mandatory to wear a helmet. After 6 p.m., forage caps or glengarries were allowed. While all ranks were permitted to walk out of barracks in white trousers and shirt, the kilt was worn on parade duty, but with a short-sleeved shirt instead of a kilt dress jacket.

The extreme heat, however, was not the only discomfort that officers and men had to bear. When Angus arrived, the attitude of his colleagues was somewhat relaxed, if not complacent. Under the temporary command of the amiable Scottish Borders-born Major Jim Cunningham, the battalion was proud of its achievements on the north-west frontier and in athletics. But as the heat intensified, so did life in the 93rd when the new second-in-command, Major Ian Stewart, appeared. An indication of Stewart's modesty is the failure of the regimental magazine to mention his arrival at Secunderabad. Reluctant in drawing attention to himself, he preferred to promote the battalion instead. Undoubtedly, the entrance of the formidable warrior had a profound effect on all ranks. 'It was as if,' explains David Wilson in his memoir, 'an atomic explosion had hit us,' as the Second-in-Command put into motion his radical ideas on soldiering, that became the heart of what they did for the next four years. The family of Ian Stewart, the 13th laird of Achnacone, were hill farmers and soldiers. Two ancestors were killed at Culloden, another in the Peninsular War, not to mention a naval antecedent, who was Nelson's flag officer at Copenhagen. As an 18 year old platoon commander of 2nd Battalion, Stewart was reputedly the first British officer to land on French soil in 1914. After Stewart led a charge and fell, claymore in hand like his Jacobite ancestors, the sergeant leant over him, saying 'poor kid,' only to receive the caustic retort that he had tripped over his sword. After winning the Military Cross in 1915, a Bar two years later, and being mentioned in dispatches twice, Stewart was wounded but served later in the tank corps and fought at the battle of Cambrai. Writing in *The Thin Red Line* after Stewart's death aged 91 on 14 March 1987, Wilson admits that at first he was none too keen on his programme. 'We certainly looked with disfavour at the increasing tempo of training that was going to upset the somewhat slow and dignified practices that had been the custom of the army in India.'

According to Stewart, the battalion may have looked smart and been good at sport, but the command structure was lacking. In a word, it was unfit for modern war. His credo was to concentrate on leadership, not only for officers but right down to the rank of lance corporal. He believed that training was paramount and upheld the adage of Kutosov, the great Russian general from the Napoleonic period: 'train hard, fight easy.' During the late 1930s, higher command realised how unprepared the British Army was for war. Writing to Hector Greenfield in December 1939, Major General Edward Spears, liaison officer between British and French forces in both world wars, claimed that Britain had not been 'very thorough in its preparation [for war] particularly as far as the army is concerned.' The consequences of such neglect were felt keenly at grass roots level. To create new army divisions, many battalions were 'robbed' of their NCOs, the backbone of their units, who were sent back to the UK to train new recruits. The 93rd suffered in this way.

One of Stewart's innovations was to take groups of NCOs and private soldiers out of their companies for 4 to 6 weeks for specialised instruction on leadership. In India, with fewer officers in a battalion than the equivalent unit in the UK, NCOs often assumed command when the latter were on leave or attending courses. Notwithstanding the losses when his best men were sent home, Stewart's strategy created a core of men who became the powerhouse of the 93rd in Malaya. But he was a hard taskmaster and swept aside the customary 'hot weather routine' in which the battalion, during the hot season, enjoyed a prolonged siesta indoors from 10 a.m. to 4 p.m. His reason was that in war, nobody stopped fighting because of the heat, cold, or wet. As it happened, it wasn't the sun that interrupted the training programme that year but the rain. At Trimulgherry in May, everyone was pleased when the rains came. People sighed with relief as they saw the grass grow, the cattle fatten, and lemonade sales sink by 50%. Stewart was far from happy; his companies had been training 7 miles from the barracks at Kompalli, and the ground there was awash. Furthermore, his programme suffered from troops afflicted with dysentery and malaria relapses, a legacy from the Waziristan campaign. Apart from the monsoon rains and sickness, the battalion continued training until just before Christmas 1938 when the companies took a break to rehearse for the Proclamation Parade.

Stewart was known for his eagle eye. Nothing escaped the legendary Argyll commander's attention and he expected the same from his officers. A platoon commander should know everything about his men down to the condition of their health or footwear. This senior officer was strict with himself too: he was a teetotaller and exceptionally fit. Although well over six feet tall he weighed only nine stone, and because of his extreme thinness, the jocks called him, with irony, Busty. From the start, Angus hit it off with Stewart, otherwise my uncle would not have risen to responsibility with such speed in the battalion. If Angus was none too keen on what some staff and medical officers considered a fanatical approach to soldiering, he complied and thrived in this regime. He may have had reservations about Stewart's disregard for taking a midday rest, refusal to indulge in a 6 o'clock chota peg (cocktail), and gimlet gaze for military detail, but he kept them to himself.

One of my regrets is that when I rented a cottage in early 1975 in Appin at Portnacroish, whose graveyard now holds Stewart's grave, I rubbed shoulders with the Brigadier in the Duror Inn but had no idea of his significance in my uncle's life. Being a teetotaller, he was a rare visitor to the hotel's lounge bar but I remember the hush that descended when this figure of authority entered the room.

Curiously, little mention is made in the regimental magazine of Stewart's seismic change in routine apart from the May 1938 number, in which it reports that instructors from the Somerset Light Infantry, North Staffordshire Regiment and the Royal Tank Corps were staging courses for the benefit of officers and NCOs of the 93rd.

Possibly Angus participated in Stewart's excursions up-country in areas where few British soldiers had been seen since the Mutiny. Although the companies took tents and dry rations, they were expected to shoot game and live off the country. For hot food they used a petrol stove and a nest of black dixies (oval cooking pots) so soldiers could cook for themselves. These expeditions were a combination of public relations stunt, Boy Scout self-sufficiency and a late 1930s equivalent of a Bear Grylls endurance test. Local police acted as guides and interpreters and, in return, the jocks repaired tracks, wells, houses, and the much-needed tanks that held the local water supply. Commanded by captains or subalterns, these parties were an excellent way of getting to know Indian village life and a far cry from the Trimulgherry routine. Away from parades and military duties, the jocks learned how to live from the country, the officers and NCOs discovered how to take responsibility, and respect grew between soldiers and villagers, so that when officers visited later in the year to shoot, they were welcomed as old friends. In the evenings, the jocks and villagers joined together with bagpipe and sithar for an impromptu concert and drank a potent toddy made from the coconut palm.

Stewart's idea of a concert was different and dry, of course. With the aid of bandmaster and pipe major, NCOs entertained the battalion with Highland songs sung in English and Gaelic, which boosted morale and, cemented camaraderie. Coming from a family that owned land since the battle of Flodden in 1513, Ian Stewart had a keen sense of tradition which was demonstrated during the Malayan Campaign when he commanded tunes from his bugler and piper that resonated with each of his officers' and men's hearts.

Early in 1938, each young officer began to specialise in some field, and for Angus it was in signals. 'We are in the throes of specialist training', came a report in the magazine.

'Signallers are learning the mysteries of dots and dashes with the lamp, flag and helio, not forgetting the super-charged buzzer.' On 11 April 1938 he entered a three-month signals officer's course in Poona. In pre-war days, the city was the spiritual home of the British Army in India conjuring up diehard army colonels sitting on verandas drinking pink gins. Angus travelled on a train, known as the 'heatstroke express' and found the landscape dry, brown, and dusty. Now that he was in British India, he noticed that not only was everyone connected in some way to the army but society was more class-ridden than in Hyderabad.

Three weeks after he qualified as regimental signals officer, Angus travelled farther north to Staff College, Quetta in British Baluchistan. Intended for senior command at which Wavell, Montgomery, Auchinleck, and Slim had at one time attended, Staff College was a prerequisite for all ambitious army officers. After the stifling temperatures of Poona, the mountainous region was a relief. But all too soon, he returned to the furnace of the Deccan plains.

Back at Trimulgherry, the 1938 September Munich crisis gave the battalion a chance to test its mettle under Stewart's training programme. At short notice they performed their 'war duties.' Within 4 ½ hours of receiving the warning order and led by John Lindsay MacDougall, B Company took up guard at the Hyderabad Residency 11 miles from the barracks, in a tribute to Stewart's work on transforming the battalion. The men congratulated themselves.

THE BIGGEST SHIFT in my uncle's life came when he was appointed adjutant on 1 April 1939. If nothing else, Angus now knew that he'd be staying with the 2nd Battalion. It was a considerable promotion. Angus had been a likely candidate although some officers, senior in rank, were passed over in favour of him. He had a sharp intellect and being a good all-rounder and mixer he allowed his individuality to be subsumed by duty to the battalion; he was a wise choice, replacing John Tweedie when he and his wife returned to the UK in May. The former adjutant, 'a man of striking good looks and explosive temper,' had taken up the role in December 1936.

Angus was now tucked away from his colleagues in an administrative post, not in the field or on operations, but behind a desk. The adjutant (adjuvare in Latin means 'to help') assists his commanding officer, in Angus's case, Hector Greenfield. The role generally went to a captain who, in many cases, on taking up the position was regarded senior to other captains and ranked just behind a major. Yet, Angus was still a lieutenant and would not be appointed captain until 3 September 1939. His new position put him in charge of personnel and in maintaining discipline among the subalterns, making sure they turned out smartly on parade. He also saw to the administration of the battalion, that orders from the commanding officer were sent to the company commanders and distributed down the line to all ranks, including lance corporals. Until the 1970s, the adjutant also took charge of operational staff work, which meant he planned and carried out operations so that, while he controlled a battle, the commanding officer commanded it.

Indicative of his good manners and wish not to boast, Angus in one of his infrequent communications with Esther, only mentions his promotion ('I am now adjutant of this battalion') in the penultimate paragraph of his 1939 Easter Day letter. He apologises for being a dilatory correspondent: it is 'simply ages since I last wrote to you'. But it's significant that after admitting he had 'at least 2 letters of yours here in front of me, which I know are unanswered,' he grabs the opportunity to make contact only a week after his promotion. Evidently, he wanted to spread the news, not only to his younger sister but, by asking Esther to remember him to their mother and Aunts Violet and Gladys (otherwise called Gim), he meant that they should all know. He's at pains to explain what his new post requires. 'I have a pretty full day's work generally starting at about 7 a.m. and very often not finishing till about 5 p.m. A great deal of this time is spent in my office, I regret to say. If I can get out for an hour each morning, I am lucky.'

For a man who loved the outdoors, being stuck inside was a disadvantage, especially with such a long working day. Still, he was proud and felt that he could now square up to Jock, his older brother, the Oxford rowing blue and Largie laird. A small bonus was that for regimental line-ups he could be photographed, not in a kilt, which he disliked wearing, but in a pair of tartan trews.

Angus was due two months' leave. Generally, families (military wives and children) headed for a hill station: the Murree hills in the north in an area now part of Pakistan or south to Ootacamund, often referred to as Ooty, situated in the Nilgiri hills in the province of Madras. They set off by train at the end of March and stayed until mid June, the favoured destination being Wellington, on the outskirts of Ootacamund. The latter was to South India what Simla had been to the north. At 7,500 feet above sea level, a pleasant temperature change to the plains, it was a home-from-home, reminiscent of the English South Downs with houses or suburban villas surrounded by neat hedges and rustic nameplates on the gate.

For their leave, some officers were drawn to the bright lights of Bombay, but spending hard-earned money in the fleshpots of the metropolis was termed 'poodlefaking' and frowned upon. This expression applied to anything resembling the seeking of women's company like dancing, horse-riding, playing tennis, picnicking, and taking part in theatricals. One author suggests, army officers should pursue animals, not women. If there was to be any passion, it should be for the regiment and not a girl. The tradition was that subalterns may not marry, captains may, majors should and colonels must. However, few junior officers could afford to have a wife as the army paid no marriage allowance until an officer reached thirty.

Nevertheless, some did marry like Angus Rose, whose wife, Alison lived with him at Trimulgherry. So did John Lindsay Mac-Dougall, married to Sheila Sprot. They lived in a bungalow at the garrison which they shared with other officers. Ian Stewart married late. Many were surprised he had a wife at all as he was clearly wedded to the regiment.

As a twenty-six year old bachelor, Angus planned to spend his two-month leave in Kashmir on shikar. The shooting of big game there was popular among army officers. It not only symbolised British imperial manliness but was in direct contrast to the emasculated pastimes of fox-hunting and pheasant-shooting where birds were bred for the sport. For virile young men seeking adventure, shikar in India was the counterpart of wildfowling in Britain, where salt marsh estuaries were swopped for the solitary mountains of Kashmir. For some time, the army in India had used this form of sport as a cover for gaining intelligence, particularly in the north-west of the sub-continent where, in the latter part of the nineteenth century, the British and Russian empires vied for supremacy in Central Asia. There is no reason to believe that Angus went on shikar for any other purpose than recreation, as did David Wilson in 1938.

Shooting was a favoured subject for the pages of *The Thin Red Line* and many articles claimed that Srinagar, Kashmir's capital, was full of agencies for sportsmen. One voluble writer explains the vagaries of shooting a bear. Although amusing, the subject-matter was distressing for me to read. However, David Wilson and Angus were thrilled at the prospect of shooting one. Evidently Kipling's *The Jungle Book* had had little effect on them and they had no hesitation in knocking off a Baloo or two. 'The village', writes the author, 'will be delighted.' Bears did much damage as they lived on grass, apricots, berries, Indian corn, and chutra gald (golden syrup). The feature apprises the reader of the correct footwear for bear-stalking: felt shoes covered with grass rope and the big toe separated from its neighbours by rope inserted between it and the other toes. These ingenious coverings, the writer informs, are ideal shoes 'for the police, cat burglars, soldiers breaking out of barracks and nurses'.

Angus's Easter letter expresses a hope that he would shoot a red bear, as had David Wilson, who killed two. Whether my uncle succeeded is unknown as the regimental game book in which officers recorded their spoils, was 'lost in the ashes of Singapore.' However, I remember that a russet-coloured animal skin used to hang over the banisters on the landing at Ballure. Remaining in this position until 1966 when my grandmother died, this pelt may well have belonged to a red bear or, more prosaically, to a highland cow. It's likely this object was a trophy from Angus's Kashmiri trip. When travelling to and from the UK, officers and their wives often carried parcels for and from the families of others. Perhaps when leaving Singapore in February 1940 to return to the UK, Ivy Greenfield took the bearskin with her as a present from Angus to his mother.

My uncle wrote in detail about his plans. He was to leave by train on 9 May and travel from Secunderabad to Lahore via Delhi. 'This takes me through the hottest parts of the plains of India at the hottest time of the year and Indian trains can be perfectly beastly when it is really hot.' Angus wasn't exaggerating. Trains in his day had no air conditioning but within a few years, some contained in each compartment blocks of ice placed in tin containers to help lower the temperature. As he travelled north by rail he suffered intense heat, was plagued by dust, and at night, had no sheets on his bed. The journey began on a Saturday evening, when he boarded the Grand Trunk Express to Delhi, which he reached on Monday. Perhaps he contacted his old chum, Bobbie Rumsey, and lunched with him in the light tank company's mess at the Red Fort. From Delhi he boarded the Frontier Mail for Lahore and reached the city on Tuesday morning. For the final two hundred miles, he boarded a bus for Srinagar and reached his destination on Wednesday at noon. At best, the journey was fearfully uncomfortable and at worst, hair-raising. In his letter, Angus bemoans the fact that he had the choice of a 'native bus...in acute discomfort' at a cost of 10 rupees or of hiring a car for 80 rupees; 'a question of two evils,' he surmised.

Travelling on Indian buses needed a strong stomach. With their American chassis, these vehicles possessed a wooden body fashioned by a local carpenter and painted in garish colours with pictures of fierce Indian gods, temples, tigers, or cows. Beside the driver was one first class seat, and behind it was a row of second class seats which consisted of a padded bench with a wooden back rest and 5 inches of knee room. Behind this row were 2 to 3 more wooden benches with 3 inches of knee room and no backrest. Storage for wood, rice and kerosene was at the back where the driver's assistant crouched. The Sikh driver arrived to start the journey 30 minutes after the advertised time for departure and the journey was interminable; passengers were forever boarding and alighting. The bus stopped more than once for fuel and had to halt for inspection at octroi posts, points on the road where heavy vehicles paid a toll.

Hopefully Angus found a front seat, as a perch with 3 or 5 inches of leg room would have been very uncomfortable. Whatever niche he was allotted, he may well have seen the funny side of the experience as he watched the driver negotiate the precipitous bends on the road with one hand on the rubber bulb of his horn and with the other changed gear, steered the bus and operated the brake. Accompanying these feats, the driver also freewheeled downhill and replenished the radiator, which had boiled dry, with water. Possibly Angus treated himself to a night or two at Nedou's hotel in the centre of Srinagar, then a favourite place for officers on shikar. Architect Adam Nedou from Dubrovnik arrived in India during the last quarter of the nineteenth century to construct a palace for the Maharajah of Gujarat. In 1880 he opened his first of a chain of hotels in Lahore. Eight years later he established one at Gulmarg in Kashmir and another in Srinagar. Forty years after Angus made his trip to Kashmir, a guide book stated that the hotel was 'a little decrepit-looking,' The hotel exists today but after the ravages of civil war in Kashmir, it suffers from neglect, much like other heritage buildings from the heyday of the British Raj. Most probably, the young adjutant stayed in a private house, as the only photo I found of his shooting expedition shows him in tweed jacket and plus fours. My uncle stands by a large deciduous tree and an exotic shrub with cascading blooms in the garden of a diplomat and his wife, Sir Peter and Lady Clutterbuck, who welcomed travellers to the Himalayas and young men on shikar. In 1937 Clutterbuck and his wife 'kindly and generously entertained' a party of explorers before they set off on expedition to the Shaksgam Valley.

In like manner, Angus prepared for his four week expedition to the beautiful Sind Valley north of Srinagar. Acting as agent, a Srinagar merchant arranged everything for him: a shikari (a local big game hunter who served as a guide) and coolies from a nearby Kashmiri village. The agent also obtained a licence so that his client could shoot in a valley between Kashmir and Ladakh, and supplied camping equipment and ponies for the first stage of the trek. These merchants owned large shops in the centre of the city where they sold rugs, pashmina shawls, and carved wooden boxes. Daisy had a box measuring thirty square inches and thirty inches high. It came from the East, its surfaces were intricately carved, and it had a pungent smell of patchouli. The box, now in my younger sister Elisabeth's possession, was discovered after my grandmother's death at the back of a cupboard under the stairs at Ballure. Its top opened to reveal a row of small compartments, each with its own lid and a circular ivory handle. Was this Angus's souvenir from a shop flanking Srinagar's Jhelum river and brought back to the UK by an obliging officer or his wife?

Kashmir rose in Angus's imagination as a far-off magical dream, especially when he was sweating in Secunderabad. Like the Deccan, the country was an independent Muslim principality, and its different customs and traditions must have appealed to Angus after travelling through British India which was official and dull with snobbish colonials throwing their weight around. In topography, this province was as different to Hyderabad, as the Argyll-shire countryside is to the fields of the English Home Counties. Angus was aware of Kashmir's beauty. The young adjutant had seen pictures, even railway posters, of the famous houseboats on the Dal Lake in Srinagar and of the wonderful Mughal gardens. This hidden valley, 10,000 feet up in the Himalayas, had a transcendent, watery beauty. That was why Srinagar, with a river flowing through its ancient streets and the lake on its north side, was called the Venice of the East.

There was also something instinctive about choosing this region. Like a migratory bird, Angus was accustomed to making journeys from north to south and south to north. Since he was a boy he'd travelled from Kintyre to the south of England for study or work but had always returned home to the north for rest and freedom. Likewise, India's north meant empty spaces, solitude, and quiet.

The two month Kashmir holiday was a high point in Angus's short life. In his two page letter to my Mum, written in a small, neat hand indistinguishable from the script of his commanding officer, Hector Greenfield, he describes his prospective leave. 'The wild flowers are marvellous in May and June, I believe; iris and all sorts of lovely flowers and apricot trees in full blossom. I imagine it will be rather like Switzerland in summer.'

After departing from Srinagar, Angus set off with only his retinue for company. Officers were unable to go on holiday together. Because of their limited number in India, they had to stagger their leaves. Angus's caravan consisted of ten ponies, which carried the tents and stores, two shikaris, a cook and his helper, called the 'tiffin coolie.' Although they took food, Angus shot for the pot and let his shikari attend to other matters like selecting where they camped each night. In the late 1930s the un-metalled road up the Sind Valley was beautiful. Today it's a motorised highway supplying the needs of the Indian Army. Angus's plan was to walk 80 miles north until he reached Dras. They arrived first at rice and maize fields as they tramped past the villages of Ganderbal, Kangan, and Gund. After three days, in which they trekked 60 miles, they reached Sonamarg, which means Meadow of Gold, given the hosts of flowers that grow there in spring. The name could have a metaphorical meaning also, as the town held a strategic position in the days when it was on a major trading route into Central Asia.

Undeniably, Angus was as impressed as Wilson, who commented that the 'loveliest wild alpine flowers I have ever seen' grew there. My uncle fully anticipated carpets of gentians, saxifrage, alpine aster, rock jasmine, and mountain orchid, warning Esther in his letter that 'I am going to try and take some coloured photographs.' He may well have achieved his aim and even sent them to his mother but, like the carved box, they were pushed out of sight because their existence only reminded her of her lost son. When my uncle reached the foot of 'an 11,000 foot pass,' the Zoji-La, marking the entrance into Ladakh, he found the lush, green Kashmiri countryside gave way to a barren, lonely scenery. Even in late May the Zoji-La is still covered in snow, and a track passes through the region where the Dras River has its source. The Zoji-La climb was steep but for a fit young man it presented little difficulty. Four hours from the summit they reached the rest house at Matayan but their destination was Dras, famed for its freezing temperatures and heavy winter snow. Here, Angus took up his nullah or beat. 'I hope to be able to wander about for about 10 days and shoot,' he wrote. Wilson dismissed his retinue and got down to 'some serious stalking.' Compared to the stalking of red deer at the father of his sister-in-law's efficiently-kept deer forest at Corrour in Inverness-shire, Angus's Kashmiri experience was less productive. But the thrill of shikar was not so much in the kill but in being alone in the fresh air on the mountainside. And all at a price he could afford. Angus was unaware that he was one of the last of his kind to enjoy such a privilege, and that he was witnessing a world that would soon disappear. In 1947 India gained independence and these northern regions came under hot dispute. Both India and Pakistan claimed Kashmir. When China invaded Tibet in 1959, tension in the region increased, resulting in a heavy military presence.

This fact was not lost on me when, on a visit to Kashmir in

1983, I saw convoys of army vehicles choking the roads. At that time, 18 years before I discovered Angus's letters in my mother's desk, I was unaware that I was following in my uncle's footsteps. Like him but 44 years later, I wished to escape from India's hot plains and explore the mountains and valleys of Kashmir and Ladakh. I followed a similar route but travelled in the opposite direction to Angus. From Simla in north India I headed north to Manali, a town in the foothills of the Western Himalayas, and joined a trek into the Zanskar valley east of Kashmir. I walked west over the Phirtse La Pass as far as Padam. From this town, I jumped into the back of a truck which conveyed me, other trekkers, and local road-workers to Kargil, a village on the road from Leh to Srinagar. The roadmen were carrying home the corpse of their colleague. When these sombre men reached their village and alighted, 'we all fell silent as the body took its leave. The men carried it shoulder-high up the hill in the moon-light. Nobody wanted to occupy the space where the corpse lay, except for a pushy Swiss guy!' I wrote in my diary. I found Kargil 'a dump and much like a wild-west frontier town. Dirty gutters and expensive!' The next day I sought a bus and after depositing my rucksack on the roof of the bus, I entered and was horrified by the lack of leg room by my seat.

'It's impossible for someone as tall as I to sit comfortably! When we get moving, it's hellish. None of the windows stays open. My knees rub against the back of the seat in front. The countryside is like Zanskar with steep mountains, fast rivers and few trees. Soon we move into alpine-type scenery with wild flowers and fir trees. It is early morning, and people in the fields are harvesting some form of grain. The roads are very rough. At one stage the bus follows a hair-raising descent, and I hope the brakes won't fail and we all go careering over a steep precipice. We stop at Dras, which is not much of a place, and at Sonamarg where I wait in a café to be served an omelette. When we approach Srinagar it becomes more wooded with old, wooden houses; then we reach the city's outskirts with the Dal Lake, covered in green slime, and see the houseboats.'

I stayed in Srinagar for at least five days and enjoyed the comforts of a decent hotel overlooking the lake. Noisy, with car and scooter-taxi horns blaring, it was hard for a woman in a Muslim country. 'Srinagar is where you are harassed sexually, commercially and by beggars. These people can be really cheeky. One had extraordinarily twisted limbs so that he stood on all fours.' If I had known that Angus had preceded me, I would have realised that he too would have had to handle the Kashniri hard sell: in a government-owned shop on the Jhelum river I inspected carved wooden objects, basket-work, needle-work, woven rugs, and clothes in wool and silk. In his time, there was no tourist centre. Today, the state-controlled organisation fixes the price of anything from houseboat rates to sport. Shikar is strictly regulated, and endangered species like the snow leopard and tiger are protected.

I'm sure that when I viewed the Dal Lake in the early 1980s, I saw a similar scene to the one that Angus came across in 1939. At that time, many houseboats were moored in the water. From the beginning of the century, the British hired them when they visited, as they were denied ownership or rental of houses on dry land. Many of these fine vessels, fashioned in cedar with walnut facings, still bobbed on the water in the reeds by the bank and had names like Omar Khayam (de luxe), Miss England, Sun Flower, and Rosemary. The lake was always busy: a shikara laden with vegetables floated past, one man at the bow and another on the raised stern. Another, more ornate, was fitted with a brightly-painted hood and had silk streamers. Looking up to the top of the hill was a fort and an expanse of trees, which lent greenness to the scenic view. I went for a walk past a garden in which grew a pomegranate tree. Goats grazed on the grass verge; sheep and cows blocked the road. Groups of women, dressed in black, their heads and faces covered, passed as I tramped towards old Srinagar with its narrow streets. Here, there were houses with carved verandas, balconies, and mughal-shaped windows. Hens and ducks scavenged in streams choked with litter.

I could not visit Srinagar without seeing the mughal gardens. The first was 'disappointing as the grass is scorched,' I wrote.

Because of its superb position between the mountains and the lake, the Nishat Bagh with its ponds and waterfalls, was the best. However, the garden's lay-out resembled a municipal park with rows of chrysanthemums, dahlias, phlox, and marigold. The gardens were perfect for family outings when fathers took photos of their children and bought from vendors soft drinks, masala dosa, samosas, Indian sweets (all tasting similar), tea, and knick-knacks. When we finished with the gardens, we drove round the lake through a number of villages. The tall houses, with intricately carved wood-work, had brick, thatched, or corrugated roofs. But the drains were open, and livestock roamed wherever it wished. I saw men beating metal and embroidering cloth. In a beautiful setting on the north-west shores of the lake, I stopped to admire a white marble mosque. 'What with the women covered up and the mosques,' I scribbled, 'Srinagar feels like a real Muslim, non-Indian city.'

Angus returned to Srinagar, not by bus but by foot, and headed for Gulmarg at 8,000 feet above sea level to play golf. 'It is the place where anyone in Srinagar goes when it begins to get a little hot,' he explained. Meaning a meadow of flowers, Gulmarg boasts one of the world's highest altitude golf courses and has plenty of scenic walks but it was unlikely that Angus had time to indulge in many. His last activity was a week's fishing but he does not say where. 'Then, I have taken a rod on a trout stream. As you know I am told that even the most ignorant novice can't help catching fish in Kashmir.' Kashmir, the Happy Valley, yielded willingly its bounty and from its teeming rivers, reminiscent of the Highlands, came an abundance of trout. With its snow-capped mountains, fast-flowing rivers and steep slopes covered with pines and other evergreens, the country captivated Angus and reminded him of home; perhaps not Kintyre but the central Highlands, and part of Inverness-shire where Sir John Stirling Maxwell's deer forest lay. With its carefully planted pine forest, river, hills, and loch, Corrour, at the head of Loch Ossian, had much resemblance to Kashmir.

Unlike David Wilson, Angus had no father to boost his bank

balance after his two-month holiday. 'The snag of this trip is that it will be expensive and uncomfortable travelling there,' he wrote. To defray the cost he sold his polo pony, 'as I don't want to have to feed it while I am away in Kashmir. Also I shall need a good deal of ready cash for this trip. So for this reason I have also sold my car.' After his fishing interlude, he had 'to scuttle back' to Trimulgherry. By this time the hot weather had abated and 'the gardens looked green again,' claimed the editorial in the last edition of *The Thin Red Line* before its publication ceased for the duration of the war.

On return, Angus took over as adjutant again, replacing Captain Morgan who had stood in for him. Within weeks the battalion was put on short notice to move but they did not know where. As part of the 12th Indian Infantry Brigade (of the 4th Indian Division), it was debated whether they would be sent to the Middle East with the rest of the division but they soon learned that they were to go to Singapore.

At the beginning of August they received orders to move to Madras and embark on the SS Egra. Early on the 2nd, the battalion assembled with weapons, kilt and full pack and said goodbye to their Indian servants and staff and marched to Secunderabad railway station, past the 2nd West Yorkshires, who came out in their pyjamas and lined the road to cheer them past. It took a day to reach Madras and a four-day voyage on the SS Egra, before they reached their destination.

ANGUS ARRIVED at Singapore's Keppel Harbour on 8 August 1939. Looking down from the deck he saw, bobbing on the water, wooden sampans, navigated by Chinese men in faded blue, wearing peaked straw hats. Dominating the island's approach was a mass of concrete: pillboxes, searchlight emplacements and coastal gun batteries on Blakang Mati, where sometimes new arrivals spent a few days in quarantine. Today, this islet, now called Sentosa, is a pleasure island with golf course, malls, beaches, and a museum showing Singapore's past and the 1942 British surrender to the Japanese.

Similar in shape and size to the Isle of Wight, Singapore lies off the southern tip of the Malayan peninsula. The Malacca Strait separates the island's southern shores from the east coast of Sumatra. Here the Indian Ocean meets the South China Sea. On 29 January 1819, an East India Company servant, Sir Stamford Raffles, set foot on the island and saw immediately its potential as a trading post. In realising his ambition, the enterprising Raffles enabled the British in South East Asia to compete with the Dutch. However, trade only boomed in the following century. To supply the most important ingredient for the manufacture of car tyres, planters in Malaya began to cultivate rubber sending the raw material to Singapore for storage before being exported.

As the twentieth century progressed, Japan became a serious threat to British interests and sought to advance its influence in Asia. The rising far-eastern power coveted Malaya's rich reserves of rubber and tin. These assets then had to be protected. Britain decided to build a naval base in the region but was uncertain where to put it. Hong Kong was too close to Japan while Sydney in Australia was too far. Eventually they chose Singapore. In 1926 Britain agreed to spend £60 million to build a naval base on the north-east coast of Singapore Island. Costing £60 million, it was opened the year before Angus and the 2nd Argylls arrived. With its floating dock towed from Britain, barracks, enclosed town, and depots, the structure answered to the propaganda of being the 'Gibraltar of the Far East.' Singaporeans believed they were safe from invasion as few suspected an army could reach the island by land. Not all were fooled. The guns protecting the southern approaches and the naval base on the north-east were only outward signs of defence. The front door may have been locked but not the back. In reality, the Malayan mainland was far from impassable and the jungle, as found later, was penetrable.

At the time of the Munich crisis in summer 1938, the Argylls were poised for embarkation to Singapore, but at the last moment they were reprieved. This time, however, most Argyll officers realised the situation was worsening in the region. Sent to Singapore 'in a hurry,' as Ian Stewart expressed the situation, the 2nd Argylls were part of the 12th Indian Infantry Brigade (formerly the Secunderabad Light Infantry Brigade) alongside two Indian battalions, the 4/19 Hyderabads and 5/2 Punjabs. After their tour of duty in India, the 12th Brigade was chosen to reinforce Malaya, where they expected to stay for three years. Other British battalions at the Singapore garrison of Malaya Command were 2nd Gordon Highlanders, 2nd Loyal North Lancashires, and 1st Manchesters.

After the Argylls disembarked, they marched down Pasir Panjang Road, a long avenue running parallel to the harbour on the outskirts of the city, to Gillman Barracks. These were modern, well-designed, three-storey blocks with huge windows that looked out on to the sea. Shared with the Loyal North Lancashire Regiment, the battalion found these premises a distinct improvement on their accommodation in India. Officers and sergeants used the same mess, had hot and cold running water, flushing lavatories (a 'thunderbox' became a feature of the past), excellent playing fields, and all Singapore's attractions within a twenty minute bus ride.

Singapore was a huge change for the troops. This flat, tropical island, situated 85 miles north of the equator, was unbearably hot and humid, with no escape. The enervating heat overwhelmed my daughter, Julia, and me when visiting Singapore in July 2010.

'Wear natural fibres and carry UV umbrellas!' we were advised. 'Take it easy for the first few days and use taxis; the fares are regulated.' 'It will be very different to how it was in 1942,' warned Professor Brian Farrell of the National University of Singapore. Nevertheless, some aspects never change: the hours of sunset and sunrise (dawn and dusk are non-existent in the tropics), the sea, the vegetation, and wild life. Some Singaporean landmarks still stood: St Andrew's Cathedral, Singapore Botanical Gardens and Raffles Hotel. Farrell was correct; much of the traditional architecture had disappeared and we needed not only maps to discover Angus's haunts but a guide, as we failed to register that the Presidential Palace off Orchard Road was the old Government House.

Our arrival on the island was different to that of Angus. As we circled in the aeroplane above the city waiting to land at Changi airport, we gazed upon islands scattered like jigsaw pieces in the sea. Here was this South-East Asian metropolis with oceans of skyscrapers, their smoked glass windows winking in the fierce heat. I had read about Singapore's modernity and cuisine, even its recent claims that each grand hotel employed a pastry chef to create sumptuous afternoon teas. Our first encounter with Singaporean futurism was the airport loos, so sensitive that they flushed at the approach of a finger. On a more sinister note, notices at immigration control said 'Death to Drug Traffickers.' As we stepped out of the air-conditioned airport building, we felt we were entering a sauna. Finding the climate hard to cope with, we began to sympathise with Angus having to work in such heat. He found the island's humidity challenging. My uncle was not the only one to complain; when writing home, Hector Greenfield called the island 'very steamy,' Although he found Singapore much more efficient than India, he soon began to hate the place.

In common with Greenfield, Angus disliked Singapore and in a letter to Daisy in January 1940, wrote that he hoped not to stay there long. He missed India's open plains which offered space and solitude; he could no longer escape to the Western Himalayas.

At that time this Asian city was not as clean as it is today. Anyone straying from the colonial centre was assailed by a cocktail of unpleasant smells like stale urine, rotting cabbage and garlic. By the late 1930s, although the island's shores were still wild with mangrove swamps, impassable rivers and jungle, the city was crowded and suburban. 'It resembles Wimbledon,' wrote Greenfield, 'all tarmac roads and houses.' Elsewhere, the jungle was tamed into parks, golf courses, and playing fields to serve the population of one of the British Empire's richest cities. At its nucleus were the Singapore Cricket Club, St Andrew's Cathedral, the municipal building and the Supreme Court. Across the river were Raffles Hotel, the bund, modern office blocks and department stores. Singapore was the first twentieth-century global city, inhabited by myriads of different ethnic groups: Chinese, Indians, Arabs, Armenians, Jews, White Russians and, significantly, a population of 3,000 Japanese. This plurality would pose challenges in the not too distant future. In 1939, as it is today, Singapore's inhabitants were obsessed by technology, consumption and ultramodernity, including the latest gadgets: telephones, refrigerators and air conditioning. Asia's first skyscraper was opened two months after Angus's arrival. The Cathay building, 83.5 metres high, was the first premises in Singapore to be air-conditioned, and it sported a 1,300 seat cinema in which the audience, unusually for that time, sat in armchairs to view a film.

Singapore has at least one hotel that provides the ultimate in tropical chic. Since 1899 when it was founded by the Armenian Sarkies brothers, Raffles has been a magnet for the rich and also for writers. Joseph Conrad was an early patron as was Kipling, who advised visitors to 'feed at Raffles.' Between 1910 and 1915 in the Long Bar, Chinese bartender Ngiam Tong Boon invented the Singapore Sling; although the hoteliers profited from selling their Asian employee's popular cocktail, they would not permit Boon's compatriots to patronise their establishment until the 1930s. By the time Angus stepped past the palms and rickshaws lining Raffles' luxurious entrance, the hotel was recovering from a period of decline that began during the Great Depression.

Angus explored not only the colonial centre and residential

areas, but also the narrow streets of Chinatown. However, the battalion had to prepare for war which, for Europe, was only weeks away. Ian Stewart took command while Hector Greenfield was on leave and wasted no time in galvanising his officers and men. He had a good idea what to expect from the enemy as in 1932, when serving with the Argylls, he had guarded the International Settlement in Shanghai. Stewart stood in as commanding officer until Greenfield's return.

As for Angus, his adjutant, Kenneth McLeod remembers in 2010 that the Colonel must have been quite satisfied with him. This elderly gentleman had been one of four officers who, in August 1940, sailed from the Stirling depot to Singapore. 'Stewart was very selective in building up his team and when officers arrived in Singapore, he would interview them to see if they were suitable and those he didn't fancy just disappeared into other jobs.' Angus fitted the bill; at twenty-six he was mature, with five years' experience as a commissioned officer in the regiment, and he was unmarried.

The first task was to adopt the Bren gun, their old Vickers Berthier light machine guns having been decommissioned and abandoned in India. Introduced in the 1930s, the Bren soon became the workhorse of the British infantry. Firing up to 500 rounds of .303 ammunition a minute, the weapon was designed by Czechs in Brno and manufactured in Enfield, hence its name. Unfortunately, not many personnel knew how to operate one and their problems were compounded by a shortage of officers and an absence of Bren carriers. Happily, ten carrier vehicles did arrive in Singapore but were difficult to steer.

Within days, the Argylls earned a reputation for toughness and came to be known as 'the jungle beasts.' Unlike the commanders of 2nd Gordon Highlanders and 1st Manchesters, Stewart stuck to his strict programme. Some senior staff objected; younger officers resented it. As adjutant, Angus could not complain and on 3 September, the day war was declared in Europe, he was rewarded for his loyalty by being promoted to the rank of captain. Soon afterwards, Peter Farquhar and Angus drove the length of the Malayan peninsula making notes on existing and prospective defences.

By the end of the month, 12th Indian Infantry Brigade became a command reserve responsible for the defence of Johore, the south-eastern Malayan state, which was ruled by its sultan. A causeway, two thirds of a mile in length, crosses the narrow stretch of water that separates the state's southern coast from Singapore Island. With the two other brigade battalions, the Argylls were to guard the mainland at Endau and Mersing and prevent the enemy from attacking its south-east coast, and making headway into Johore. The battalions trained in the pleasant countryside around Mersing; when off duty, they bathed and went fishing. Usually one company stayed there for a month at a time but sometimes they remained there for two.

Angus had to learn Malaya's topographical features, acquire a feel for the new country, and familiarise himself with jungle conditions. On the way up the coast were rubber plantations with trees planted three to four feet apart, a similar distance to the positioning of apple trees in an English orchard. Sections of jungle with thick vegetation edged right up to the road. To the uninitiated this terrain appeared impenetrable. When a belt of jungle was cleared, the new vegetation grew much thicker than the original. Once a person had passed through this dense screen, he reached primary jungle which had no need to be cut and visibility was possible up to thirty to forty yards. The problem was that the British had little knowledge of jungle warfare. Up until that period troops stationed in Singapore were static and employed beach defences. The Argylls had already proved their prowess in mountain warfare against the tribesmen of Waziristan but Malaya was different. What they learned in north-west India would not stand them in much stead here. Wearing plimsolls, they learned to advance through the terrain in single file, the lead man cutting a way forward, the second widening the path and the third checking the route with a liquid compass, although Kenneth McLeod claimed that these instruments were useless in the jungle because the high tin content in the ground affected their accuracy. 'We had to discover how to find our way by taking our bearings from the sun, stars or just get lost!' They also used landmarks like rivers, roads and other natural features to find their way.

In July 2010, when my daughter and I motored down the old trunk road from Kuala Lumpur towards Port Dickson on Malaya's south-west coast, we stopped to inspect the trees with wide-spread canopies and the vegetation: ferns, palms, bamboos and creepers, some that hugged their host so tight that they killed them. On the ground were fretworks of shallow roots. The jungle was far from quiet: water tumbled over root and stone while an unidentified bird called from the branch of a tall tree. The area reminded me of the grounds at Largie as Angus would have known them, with their sculpted shrubs, banks of bamboo, and large ferns. The jungle's most striking feature was its earthy smell, not unlike the steamy atmosphere of a heated greenhouse. The ground was passable but uneven and I could see how easy it would be to get lost. We did not venture far, as the prospect of hosting a leech or some other jungle parasite was uninviting. Angus and his companions had no choice. The army failed to appreciate that wearing shorts up-country was unpractical. The remedy, then, was to take a lighted cigarette and burn off unwelcome guests that had fastened on to the skin.

At first, jungle navigation was difficult because of inadequate maps (one inch to the mile), unworkable compasses, and no wireless. At that time, if someone was injured there was no available casualty evacuation or air supply. Other hazards were predators: 'We never saw tigers,' writes Kenneth McLeod, 'they were there in the jungle but if you were in a party they would take no notice and skedaddle. It was the older fellows that became man-eaters as they couldn't run fast enough to catch their prey.' Vipers and pythons also lived in the jungle, and monkeys were ubiquitous and tribal with a male leader. By taking a note of what they ate, the jocks could discover which plants were safe to consume.

Jungle training was one thing but adapting fighting skills to a rubber plantation was another. The uniformity of these areas was dispiriting when the troops confronted row upon row of tall trees whose leaves cast looming shadows. If soldiers trained for too long under these conditions, they became depressed and suffered from 'rubberitis.'

No matter what kind of ground the Argylls trained on, it was exhausting, particularly in the Malayan climate. But Stewart was inspiring and managed to get his men to advance 1,000 yards an hour in the jungle. If nothing else, they became fighting fit and the regimental spirit always remained strong. Stewart never failed to provide essential rations such as hot, sweet tea five times a day to prevent dehydration.

After training the Argylls marched back to Singapore from Mersing, taking eight days to complete the 116-mile journey. Officers accompanied the men, and the ultra-fit Stewart, twice the age of his men and officers, maintained his position at the head of the column. On these marches, the commanding officer wore a Glengarry. The march not only toughened the men, but proved that Singapore was vulnerable to a rapid infantry advance from the north, as there was no jungle barrier protecting the northern coast of the island from the mainland.

In December 1939 the jocks handed in their kilts but officers still wore them for special occasions. Many peacetime parades were abandoned.

That same month the Argylls moved camp to Tyersall Park close to the Botanical Gardens. On my map I managed to find the old entrance; the rusting gate into the precinct, once owned by the Sultan of Johore, is close to the National Orchid Garden off Tyersall Avenue, not far from St. George's Church, where Anglican congregations worship. Now weed-ridden, Tyersall's entry was uninviting and too risky to negotiate, as it was late afternoon when the mosquitoes are active. 'Unlike the Gordon Highlanders who had stone-built barracks, we lived in bamboo huts three feet off the ground. This was to repel snakes and other wild life,' wrote Kenneth McLeod. The roofs were made of palm leaves stitched together to resemble tiles laid on bamboo struts. Tyersall was make-shift and hurriedly built in order to accommodate two battalions (the other was 4/19 Hyderabads). These barracks also held the brigade headquarters and the Indian military hospital. The huts were 40 feet long with a veranda running along the outside wall. There were thirty beds in each and junior officers lived in similar accommodation but in cubicles with a cold water section for their ablutions. These had overhead water buckets that served as showers.

While the jocks had to keep their sleeping quarters spick and span – blankets just so and clothes on a peg – officers were let off lightly. A Chinese 'boy' looked after them. In the morning he brought tea and a snack, sometimes a bunch of delicious bananas. Angus Rose writes about his and Angus's Chinese 'boy,' Ah Ling, who spoke little English. On his first day, Angus asked Ah Ling to lay out their mess dress for dinner, but when the two officers returned, they found that the new servant had laid their shot guns on their beds. Angus Macdonald worked out that Ah Ling had mistaken 'mess kit' for 'musket' When Ah Ling made mistakes, the two Angus's fined him. Angus Macdonald kept an account with meticulous calculations based on the Chinese servant's misdemeanours so that, when Ah Ling's first pay day came, he owed his bosses $25. Although Angus, in a letter to Daisy, makes no mention of Tyersall and its primitive facilities, he refers to his quarters as 'a shed' in his correspondence with Esther. Shed or no shed, Tyersall had its amusements. Officers liked to rag in the mess, diving head-first through the flimsy partition erected between their ante-room and dining room. Angus's letter to Daisy, written after his first Christmas in Singapore, never mentions anything to do with training or manoeuvres. Censorship regulations prevented it. They were at war even if at that time it was phoney.

But it was not just back-breaking manoeuvres and long-distance marches. Off duty, my uncle found plenty to entertain him even though it was expensive. 'In Singapore, almost any game was played on first-class grounds.' Now a captain, Angus joined the Royal Singapore Golf Club. Its course at Bukit Timah on the road to the causeway, was beautiful; the tropical trees on the perimeter had all been removed and it reminded one of home. This extirpation of the tropical did not stop at the club's vegetation; it also included humans. The Royal Singapore Golf Club was for Europeans only.

In May 1940 Angus gave up his membership at the golf club. He could have taken up flying but that was costly. Like Captain Michael Blackwood, he joined the Royal Singapore Yacht Club. 'I had neither the money nor the time to belong to both the golf and yacht club,' Angus confessed in his letter to Esther. After his land-locked life in India, buying a yacht was very welcome. It was a pleasure to escape from the stuffy metropolis and feel the fresh sea breezes and swell of the waves. A sail around the tropical islands was a different experience to the dank, cold forays he was accustomed to in Kintyre.

Singapore was expensive. However, the island, as a duty free port, had a favourable currency rate (in Secunderabad a bottle of Scotch cost 8 ¼ rupees but in the Colony it was only 5 rupees). Angus earned more than the other ranks, but his salary was not large. It's intriguing, therefore, that after he arrived in Singapore, he bought a car. 'It's the first new one I have ever had.' Obviously an important purchase, Angus wrote to his mother in detail in his letter of 11 January 1940. 'I decided that taxis were costing so much that it would pay me to get a car, provided it was a small one and I could get some ready cash. So I bought the smallest on the market, a six horse power Fiat, and it is quite tiny.'

As this vehicle would play a crucial part in the defence of Singapore, I was determined to find one and, if possible, drive it. A friend suggested I write to the Craigie column in the *Dundee Courier* to ask if anyone owned a Fiat 500, otherwise known as a 'Topolino,' which means 'little mouse' or Mickey Mouse in Italian. In no time, Craigie informed me that a vintage car enthusiast from a village outside Dundee had a 1937 Fiat 500, which I could inspect. When I arrived, I found, parked in the courtyard, a dark red Topolino. To my eye, accustomed to the Morris mini and other models of today, this Fiat was not the smallest car I had ever seen but compared to most vehicles of Angus's day, the Topolino must have seemed miniscule. With a more curvaceous body than its British counterpart, the Fiat's front headlights, positioned on either side of the engine at the bonnet, did resemble a mouse's ears. I knew exactly why Angus had bought it: the vehicle was cheeky and stylish. From its crest, in elongated Art Deco letters, to the sunshine roof and the word 'olio' on the oil gauge, the two-seater, though tinny, with rexine seats and an open boot for storage, exuded a youthful bravura. This model had languished in a shed belonging to a Dundee policeman and given a complete overhaul by its new owner, who spent £1,700 on renovating the car's engine. As I sat behind the steering wheel, I pictured Angus beetling through the streets of Singapore and cruising along a Malayan jungle road at its top speed of 53 mph. When I scrambled inside I saw how cars of the Thirties permitted limited visibility to the driver; the Fiat's front windscreen was much smaller than its modern equivalent and the same applied to the back window. Poor Angus! How cooped up he must have felt. As I stretched my legs out in the recess, above which lay the petrol tank to the rear of the bonnet, I realised he would have had his work cut out fitting his longer legs into the cramped space.

By all accounts, the Fiat 500 was an important acquisition. To his mother, he was at pains to justify the purchase, reminding her that with petrol costing $1.10 (2s. 7d.), the car was economical to run (it managed 39 miles to the gallon). Anxious to convince Daisy that he had made a wise decision, he stressed that, by buying the car new, it would be more likely to retain its second-hand value. Judging from the lengthy explanation as to how he would meet the cost, Angus must have feared his mother would be concerned. He was buying the Fiat by hire purchase over a twenty-month period, or on what was then euphemistically termed the 'Never-Never System of Easy Payments.' Writing to his sister, he adopted a more frivolous approach, describing how absurd he looked. 'As you may imagine I look a bit of a sight driving about in this tiny little car with my head sticking out several inches through the sunshine roof (I find it very difficult to drive with the roof closed), but I think Singapore is getting used to the sight, as I have been driving about there for over 18 months now.' He was disappointed that he was unable to avoid paying what he owed. 'When Italy came into the war, I thought I would get away

195

without paying any more instalments but unfortunately Fiat owed a lot of money to their American bank here and all their hire purchase rights had been mortgaged to this bank. So I had to go on paying the bank instead of paying Fiat. Most annoying!'

The men and officers from the Argylls saw Angus and his Fiat as inseparable and long after the war he was remembered as 'Angus Macdonald in his wee Fiat.' 'Your uncle did look odd with his head protruding through the sliding roof, especially when he wore his pith helmet and white hackle!' Kenneth McLeod suggested that Angus chose the headgear on purpose when he could have worn something less ostentatious like a Glengarry or Balmoral. That Angus had to use his car for military duties suggests how overstretched and under-resourced the armed forces were in Singapore although he obviously claimed for mileage on the vehicle. For a tall man with an important job to drive such a diminutive car suggests an element of self-parody, as Angus sped along the Singapore roads and cocked a snook at the ultra-materialistic, sophisticated comunity. Other officers like Michael Blackwood bought a Lagonda open tourer, which more than likely turned ladies' heads. Captain Balbir Singh of the 4/19 Hyderabads bought a Morris 8 in which he toured the Malayan peninsula.

Angus still enjoyed himself while off duty in spite of having to watch his pennies. Many officers did. 'Most of us took an active part in the night life of the city,' wrote Angus Rose. Nevertheless, Singapore, although racy and modern with its air-conditioned Cathay building, had an exasperating prissiness which in some ways still exists today, with enclaves of born-again Christians, a strong work ethic, and an obsessive attitude towards cleanliness. In Angus's day, if he and his brother officers wished to live it up, they found that all bars and clubs closed by midnight. This was the wife of the governor, Lady Clementi Thomas's doing. On Saturday nights it was different and Europeans dressed up and caroused until the early hours of the morning. First, they congregated at Raffles for a drink before dinner, after which they proceeded to the exclusive Tanglin Club, situated in Stevens Road not far from Tyersall. Founded in 1865 by 'forty good men,' the Tanglin was one of Singapore's oldest social clubs and boasted the best dance floor in the Colony. Angus and his friends took advantage of the greatly reduced fees for officers. The following morning they played golf or went sailing, then indulged in long drinking sessions followed by a curry tiffin (a light lunch), by which time all but the toughest underwent a period of 'lying-off.'

Although officers were allowed into clubs and invited to play on residents' tennis courts and swim in their pools, these offers did not apply to NCOs or Indian officers. In general, the Singaporeans were not overly friendly. Some officers resented these people's stand-offishness, especially when 'up country' in Malaya the planters were 'incredibly hospitable.'

Away from such sprees with his brother officers, Angus Macdonald attended more formal social engagements. In his 1940 New Year missive he informs his mother that he and Jim Cunningham (shortly to be replaced as A Company commander by a younger officer), were invited to a reception at Government House. Officers regularly received invitations to tea parties and dances there and they usually accepted as this was one way of getting to know 'suitable' young women. This time it was to meet Lord Willingdon on his way to New Zealand, as the country was celebrating its centenary and the retired Viceroy of India was representing Britain in this event.

Angus would have strolled on the Padang, patronised Raffles and worshipped in St Andrew's Cathedral with its array of whirring fans hanging from the neo-Gothic ceiling. However, Europeans were only a part of the Singapore community. Not far from the plush, residential precincts of Orchard and Holland Roads were narrow, crowded streets with impermanent dwellings where transient workers and their families eked a living. Angus Rose visited these parts where Singapore's Entertainment Worlds (New World, Happy World, and Great World) were situated. Angus Macdonald was sure to have accompanied him to places where reputedly 'no white man came.' In this part of the city, Chinese, Muslim, Malay, and Japanese plays were staged. When, in 1936, the French playwright, Jean Cocteau, viewed these different examples of oriental drama, he described them as 'interminable monologues with no sign of a beginning or an end to the performance.' He observed that some plays lasted five hours. At these 'Entertainment Worlds,' men could buy ten dances with a pretty Chinese girl for 50 cents but he was not allowed to touch her. On one occasion, Rose and his friends sampled a Japanese dinner in a Singapore restaurant. In a spotlessly clean room, guests sat, tailor-fashion, around an 18 inch high circular table with a hole in the centre. First they drank rice wine, followed by a dish of bamboo shoots, vegetables, chicken, raw eggs and soya-bean sauce sautéed in butter. After the meal, geisha girls (professional entertainers and not prostitutes) performed. This agreeable ceremony with its display of the gentle arts was Angus's introduction to Japan. If my uncle had cared to learn more about the oriental nation, he would have discovered Japan's other customs: its tea ceremonies, pottery skills, calligraphy, flower arrangements, poetry, courtesy, discipline, truthfulness, and honour. However, Angus, his brother officers and, not least, the jocks themselves, were only to learn about Japan's more brutal att-ributes.

13 horsepower Fiat - the 'Mickey Mouse' model

WITH ALL his responsibilities, it was unsurprising that Angus's letters home were infrequent. However, the odd one or two were important as letter-writing was the only way men serving overseas could keep in touch with their families. When war broke out, it took up to two months for a letter to reach Britain by surface mail from Singapore. A speedier alternative was to use airmail which was prohibitively expensive or, in an emergency, to send a telegram. Angus's method was to encourage all female family members, his mother, sisters, and aunts, to pass his letters around; when he wrote to Daisy, she let Esther read his news. In a similar way, his sister shared Angus's correspondence with her mother and aunts.

When he wrote to Daisy in early January 1940, Angus attributes his busy life not to the rigorous jungle training he and his battalion were undergoing, but to the New Year's festivities. 'New Year,' he wrote, 'was celebrated in the usual fashion. On New Year's Eve, the sergeants came and saw the New Year in with the officers in the officers' mess. On New Year's Day the men ate heavily off turkey, plum pudding and beer. The Fancy Dress ball at the club was a great success.' For Daisy there was a sense of déjà vu as she read what the jocks feasted on; as a twenty-year-old, she had received a Christmas letter from her father, then Colonel Crabbe, when he was serving with the Grenadier Guards at Modder River in South Africa. Like his grandson 40 years later, Crabbe had told Daisy what his men ate on Christmas Day also.

Angus communicates well on paper and although we do not have her letters to him, we receive an impression that Daisy is an interested correspondent as her son offers snippets of gossip and discloses what is happening to his friends. Giles Tweedie, newly arrived from Glasgow and brother of John, Angus's predecessor, was in hospital for an undisclosed injury or ailment. Angus explains that he paid a visit to Tweedie, 'Someone goes down to see him every evening now for half an hour.' Tweedie was sent back to

Britain the following month. Hector Greenfield's son, James disclosed that Giles had suffered a mental breakdown. It's a tribute to Angus, as adjutant and the other officers of the battalion, that they treated this young officer with sympathy and respect.

Angus Rose left again on 2 January to Staff College, Quetta to attend a six-month course. 'I shall miss him as he is always cheerful company,' writes Angus. On 20 February, Greenfield returned to the UK on promotion to Colonel to take up a staff post, although at the time Angus wrote that nobody, including Greenfield himself, knew his destination or the exact nature of his posting. With his departure, Colonel Stewart took command of the Argylls. The continual comings and goings of officers and men had to be accepted. Angus said goodbye to a number of friends when the battalion left Secunderabad. John Lindsay MacDougall was due to sail with 2nd Argylls to Singapore but at the last minute was sent to Britain to train 8th Battalion destined for North Africa. His trunk was left on the ship and put in storage in Singapore until the end of the war, when it made its way back to Lindsay MacDougall's home at Lunga in Argyll. Aubrey Gibbon, who was to marry Lindsay MacDougall's widow, went to 1st Battalion and to the Western Desert.

Surprisingly, these moves did not badly affect the battalion's esprit de corps. But the Argylls had built up a proud image. 'I cannot believe I shall ever enjoy anything so much again,' wrote Hector Greenfield to the then Brigadier Edward L. Spears early in February, eleven days before he departed Singapore and the battalion. 'One of the attractions is the feeling that you are your own master, within reason, and another the charm of being among your oldest friends. I have been lucky to have it [command of the 2nd Argylls] for as long as two years in these days of rapid change.'

Plenty of changes came during this period of relative calm: the phoney war lasted from September 1939 until May 1940. Unlike Europe and the UK, life in Singapore continued as usual with no blackouts or rationing. The government and the press tried to lull the population into a sense of security. After all, this was Fortress Singapore, but the army was under no illusion as to the island's safety. Incoming soldiers were regarded with irritation by civilians who felt overwhelmed by servicemen in their streets. Some expatriates felt guilty that Singapore was so unaffected, while others in the army felt especially cut off as home leave was forbidden in wartime. 'We are so far out of the world here,' wrote Hector Greenfield to Spears' wife in November 1939, 'that we have almost ceased to realise we are out of touch.' Angus Rose hoped that when his course at the Staff College, Quetta, ended he would be sent to the Middle East or back to the UK. Greenfield himself was relieved to get 'something more active as this is a complete backwater,' and Angus 'sincerely hoped' he would not be in Singapore very much longer. Nevertheless, Stewart continued to keep his battalion fit for war with route marches and jungle training. Throughout this time, drafts of men and officers sailed from Scotland to arrive many weeks later in Singapore. As adjutant, Angus welcomed Kenneth McLeod to the Tyersall mess. 'We were all very pally,' McLeod recalls, and he found Angus 'a very good chap.'

In May 1940, disaster hit Europe. Hitler invaded the Low Countries and France, routing Allied units including the British Expeditionary Force, before being evacuated from Dunkirk. The fall of France caused consternation among officers in 2nd Argylls whose brothers were caught up in the debacle. Rose's eldest brother, Rhoddy, adjutant of 1st Highland Light Infantry, was fighting in France, while the youngest, Neil in the French Foreign Legion, was missing. Cables tumbled in not only for Rose, whose anxiety was allayed, but also for Angus, as Jock, a captain in the Argylls' 8th Battalion, was also serving in France.

On 16 April Jock's battalion was sent to Metz in north-east France to help the French defend the Maginot Line. By 23 May the situation became critical when the German forces reached the Channel. The Division moved west to support the French on the Somme at St Valery. As soon as Jock's battalion reached its destination close to the River Bresle, which runs parallel and a little south of the Somme, Jock and his men blocked the roads with farm carts and tree trunks and relieved a French armoured car regiment already in contact with the enemy at Sallenelle. Before the regiment left the area, a French officer showed Jock the neighbouring wood which, he warned, was laid with German booby traps, set off by a wire as soon as pressure was put on them.

On 3 June, when a German patrol arrived in the west part of the wood, Jock and his men set off towards the enemy to try to cut off their retreat. As he approached the wood's perimeter where a path ran into a field, he heard a deafening report and looked down. Seeing that his left leg was badly damaged he staggered back to his party of men and lay down. The leg was broken above the ankle and he had a wound close to his knee but it only caused pain when he moved. He lay there for two hours until a stretcher arrived. At a nearby farm they found a truck which drove him to Sallenelle where he was laid on the ground and given a bottle of champagne to drink but, because he was shivering violently, he was unable to. Orderlies in a local school gave him chloroform and dressed his leg, before he was conducted to the advanced dressing station seven miles away. By now it was dark and, without headlights, which were forbidden, the driver was unable to find his way. Jock advised him to stop the vehicle so that he could study the signposts properly by the side of the road. When this measure was unsuccessful, Jock grabbed the man's map and found out, in the nick of time, that they were heading for Abbeville, which by that time was occupied by the Germans. The following day they arrived at the casualty clearing station at Rouen. Jock suffered from a long, uncomfortable journey in an ambulance but was moved to a hospital train where doctors operated on his leg, sending word to the driver not to brake too suddenly. Finally at a hospital in Le Mans, where he was put in a ward with four other officers, and that evening, before he performed the operation, the young surgeon, Jack, warned him that 'he might have to have his leg off.' At this point, he kept it. 'I was relieved to wake up and find I still had two legs,' he wrote. Jock stayed in the hospital for a week then moved to La Baule on the mouth of the Loire. Two days later at St Nazaire, he boarded a hospital ship, the Dorsetshire, which arrived at Southampton on 15 June. His destination was the Royal Victoria Military Hospital at Netley. The vast building, a quarter of a mile long, accommodated 138 wards and 1,000 beds and was constructed at Victoria's behest after the Crimean War. Soon after his arrival, Jock returned to the operating theatre and this time his leg was amputated. For several days afterwards, the doctors were unsure if Jock would survive the operation.

We know that Angus wrote to his brother as soon as he learned of his injury but, like so much connected with him, the letter can not be found. On the other hand, we have access to Jock's reply (dated 10 October) in which he comments on the speed with which Angus's letter arrived, a month from 'pillar box to door.' Jock wrote from Keir, the home of the Stirling family (cousins of his wife Anne), whose large house had become a war-time auxiliary hospital to Gleneagles (in 1940 the luxury hotel stored its finery, filled in the golf course bunkers to evade enemy detection, and adopted its bridal suite as an operating theatre). 'My leg,' Jock writes, 'has now quite healed over but it is a slow process. I have got to wait a bit and then get a wooden one or rather an aluminium replacement. I can go about quite well on crutches all over the house and up and downstairs, but it is too slow for going far out of doors. So, I have got a pony cart which I go about in here which is a great advantage.'

Jock is lengthy and meticulous in recording his experiences in France from the day in early February 1940 when his battalion arrived at Le Havre until the time when he was evacuated to Southampton four-and-a-half months later. He evidently valued his 40 page account written in a small, even hand, and had it typed and copied three times. Apart from being ignorant of Angus' response to Jock's injury, we have no idea if the latter sent this long letter to his younger brother. Perhaps he suspected the disclosed details would not pass the censor, so he kept the letter to show Angus on his return from the war. The contents are an extraordinary source of primary material and read in part like a war diary, which units were expected to maintain. Most of the missive is packed with accounts of his battalion's itineraries, its military exercises, operations and hilarious vignettes such as the occasion when a drunk Argyll cook staggered down a station platform, his behaviour being noted with amusement by officers and men from the Black Watch. Most poignant are his observations of French villagers being evacuated from their homes. 'It was a sad sight to see the old people and children setting off down the road carrying what they could of their belongings…They left all their livestock behind: cows, calves, horses, sheep, rabbits, dogs and hens. A lot of these were left shut up and we sent the men round to let out everything that had been shut in before it starved.'

Jock's account of his time in France with the British Expeditionary Force is at all times understated: this display of insouciance, if not sang froid, was instilled in him from an early age. We gain not only an insight into the organisation of his company but also its social character. The officers and men were of a similar mixture of personalities found in any Argyllshire community and this gives Jock's narrative the impression that they were off on a continental spree:

> We had a very successful concert here in a barn, at which we had two Mod medallists singing in Gaelic – Sgt Lamont of C Coy, a native of Mull, and Lance Corporal McLennan from Islay – and also Pte Kerr, who joined us with a batch of militia, who had a really professional Paul Robeson voice. We also had songs from the Padre, Rev Archie Beaton of Lochgilphead, and the Quartermaster, Hugh Campbell.

By discussing his military exploits, Jock attempts to assert his seniority over Angus when he explains that he has already been in contact with the enemy: 'It is extraordinary how discipline goes when you get into the front-line,' he writes. When Jock describes a gruelling march, it appears a doddle when compared to the extremes of heat and jungle hardship that Angus endured. 'It was the worst thing I did in the war from the point of view of exertion. It was not very far, perhaps twelve miles all told, but we had done twelve miles the night before, and had no sleep for two nights and days and had been shelled in the Hartbuch into the bargain.'

As for the bizarre, nothing beats his story of arriving on France's west coast at Ault, south of the River Somme, and being told by the shopkeeper that the Germans had already stopped there and, when they found no British or French soldiers in the village, they bought cigarettes and beer and went to the beach where they parked their tank and bathed in the sea. But it's when Jock launches into a tale of his visit with his General and a number of other officers to a girls' convent school in Loos that he excels as a storyteller. The pupils greeted them with a rendition of *God Save the King* (all four verses) and the *Marseillaise*. Following these, was a speech by the head girl, after which she curtsied to the General, who had to reply in his bad French. Next was a concert that ended with a solo by the dancing teacher who held a bouquet of flowers in each hand. The officers hoped she would finish her routine by presenting them to the General but this was not in the plan. They were expected to admire the girls' handiwork, at which point Jock and his companions thought that 'a whisky and soda might go down very nicely.' Instead, they were led off to have tea with the Mother Superior and eat indigestible cakes baked by the girls.

It is particularly strange how Jock in his account avoids expressing his feelings after such a calamitous experience. The lack of self-pity and displays of reserve and courage are impressive as he represses his emotions, denies his pain, and demonstrates a remarkable calm at the prospect of a difficult future. Reading between the lines, his volubility suggests he has not yet registered the full implication of his disability. Full of ebullience, generous anecdote and amusingly depicted scenarios, his letter is an attempt to be cheerful before his brother. The observant reader, who can pierce the thicket of cheerful obfuscation, will see that Jock only refers obliquely to his greater loss and dwells more on the minor ones. He wishes he had kept a diary and taken photographs while serving in France but they, amongst everything else, would have been lost to the enemy. Serving as an early step towards healing, the letter as substitute diary recovers some of the loss, just as soldiers in captivity often write in detail of the sequence of events that lost them their campaign.

Jock's injury was, of course, ineffably catastrophic, not only for him but for all his family. It was the first of a chain of family disasters. Here was an active thirty-two year old, easily the most athletic of all the brothers, reduced to an invalid who would never again run, swim, jump, ride a horse, or bicycle, dance, row, play football, rugby, cricket, tennis or golf; neither would he be able to indulge in any field sport like shooting or stalking. The implications of his wounding at the start of World War Two were that it made him not only a casualty but also a problematical focus. People rallied around the wounded warrior, particularly women. Anne bore the brunt and Esther was given compassionate leave from the Auxiliary Territorial Service (ATS).

Although Jock's misfortune led him towards taciturnity and self-absorption, he was not beyond kindness and would invite sons of friends killed in the war; one such visitor was Colin Lindsay MacDougall, whose father, John was killed in 1944 during the Salerno landings in southern Italy. My uncle showed the young boy his new dairy farm and amused him by using his artificial leg to hammer nails into a post. However, Jock's injury dented the family image; its identity was no longer confident or assured as the figurehead was lame. We saw instead a man, the head of our tribe in pain, often silent, distant and preoccupied. Of course, our uncle's predicament was not unusual. Maimed men with severed limbs were the consequence of war. Captain Trotter, a close associate of Colonel Crabbe, Jock's grandfather, lost his arm in South Africa at the turn of the century. These losses were as ancient as the gods themselves: Achilles with his vulnerable heel and Hephaestus, son of Zeus, and Hera, lamed by rejection.

Stationed in Singapore, 7,000 miles from Europe, Angus felt even more cut off than before. 'He kept rather to himself,' writes McLeod, 'but we were in difficult circumstances.' We will never know if Angus's reserve was due to his being naturally self-contained or a response to the bad news from home. The 'difficult circumstances' were, however, plain to see although the governor, Shenton Thomas did his best to conceal them from the civilian population. The far-reaching consequence of France falling to Germany was that it sealed the fate of Malaya and Singapore. Now that French Indochina came under the control of Vichy France, Japan was able to use these territories as a base to invade Malaya. Hitherto, the peninsula was too distant for Japan to launch an attack. By June 1940, with the fall of France and Italy's entry into the war, people became aware of the possibility of invasion. Then the UK itself came under a real threat in the autumn when the blitz began on 7 September. Throughout the rest of 1940 and well into 1941, the Chief of Imperial General Staff, Sir John Dill, was loath to send troops to the Far East, even though he claimed earlier in the year that after the UK, Singapore was the most important strategic post in the British Empire. His idea was to increase the Far East garrison with troops from India and Australia. Early in 1941, military reinforcements were stepped up: the 11th and 9th Indian Divisions, which formed the 3rd Indian Corps, and the 8th Australian Division (later called the Australian Imperial Force) arrived in February of that year. Additionally, two British battalions from Shanghai swelled the numbers. Anti-aircraft defences also were reinforced.

As the Australians arrived, tension in the city increased. There had always been uneasy relations between the different British and Scottish regiments. The Gordon Highlanders found the Argylls testing. The former, from the Aberdeen area, were more rural in outlook, while the Argylls, many of whom hailed from Scotland's central urban belt, were considered to be quite streetwise. The Argyll jocks had a reputation for brawling with English battalions so they were paid on Wednesdays instead of Fridays to avoid confrontations with other soldiers. The arrival of the Australians created more problems. There were famous fights between the Diggers and the jocks. Although the Scots were smaller in stature, they were fitter than many Australians. Discipline was an issue with both the jocks and officers. The latter may not have resorted to fisticuffs after they had had one or two drinks, but they still needed to be kept in order. As adjutant, this was Angus's responsibility but, Kenneth McLeod relates, 'he was never heavy-handed or 'the type to domineer.'

As the situation became more critical, new recruits (either from Sandhurst or the Territorial Army) arrived to replace older men. Stewart needed a complement of fit, young platoon commanders and NCOs. Modern equipment was not so easy to come by. In vain, the General Officer Commanding (GOC) of Malaya, Lieutenant General Sir Lionel Bond, asked for more modern equipment. He received little, and when his replacement, Lieutenant-General Arthur Percival, took over in May 1941, he knew there was no point in asking. Tanks, for example, went to defend Russia and the Middle East. The 4/19 Hyderabads, an Indian battalion in the brigade, were short of rifles. Those that were available were old, a proportion of which had been used in World War One. They also lacked steel helmets and other operational equipment. As for transport, the Argylls had armoured vehicles: five Lanchester armoured cars and three South African Marmon-Herringtons. Additionally, they had fourteen Bren gun carriers and a .45 Thompson machine gun. They also possessed three-ton support vehicles which carried ammunition and rations. Although past its sell-by date and designed for the Middle East, the Lanchester was the best vehicle the Argylls had at their disposal. It may have been cumbersome but it was powerful and well-armoured. These vehicles took two months to arrive in Singapore and when put to the test, they would not start. However, they were suitable for use on the roads and were therefore vital for Stewart's tactics. Fitting the bill as an anti-tank weapon, the Lanchesters, after being fixed, became mobile forts and were named after Scottish castles.

On 29 April 1941, two months before his twenty-eighth birthday, Angus was appointed brigade-major of the 12th Indian Infantry. The brigade-major's role involved similar duties to those of adjutant, but more of them. In World War Two, a battalion's personnel amounted to 845 men and officers. The 12th Indian Infantry consisted of one British battalion (2nd Argylls) and two Indian battalions. The first was the 5/2 Punjabs, a regiment raised in 1798 during the Madras Presidency and a run-of-the-mill

Indian army unit comprised of Punjabi Muslims, Sikhs and Dogras. The second battalion was the 4/19 Hyderabads, instituted in 1788 by Nawab Salabat Khan of Ellichpur to protect the northern borders of the Hyderabad state. As chief of staff to the brigadier, Angus became responsible for several thousand men, a position that only went to the best officers. While the brigadier was away from headquarters, the brigade-major assumed responsibility, which included the supervision of staff work (intelligence, logistics and personnel) at brigade headquarters. Angus must have been very good at his job. It was essential for the commander of a battalion or brigade to have a stalwart right-hand man backing him up in all matters, such as providing direction to operations and sometimes going up to the frontline. Implicit in the position of brigade-major was an attention to detail, the skill to write clearly, and be able not only to command, but also to possess the independence of mind to make important decisions off his own bat.

Archibald Paris was Angus's brigadier. Rose describes him as having a deep knowledge of human nature and as an experienced, fighting soldier keen to discuss morale and training. 'Our Jocks were very fond of Archie Paris.' He could talk to them in a straightforward manner on such widely differing subjects as prostitutes, drink, and administration in the field. His unruffled manner under fire had also won their admiration. Indeed, one jock, Corporal Gibson, wrote of Paris in glowing terms: 'He was a powerfully built, handsome officer, his face deeply tanned through years of service. His iron grey moustache was always neatly clipped and his eyes shrewd and quizzical. Like Colonel Stewart, Paris was athletic, very strong and took pride in his physical fitness. He could outmarch men many years his junior.'

To be brigade-major of the 12th Indian Infantry Brigade was to be responsible for far more Indian soldiers than British. In fact, half of all troops sent to defend Malaya were from India. At the beginning of World War Two, the Indian Army was 200,000 strong but by the end of 1941, it had grown to almost 900,000 officers and men, expanding to well over 1.8 million by the end of 1942.

The Indian Army was organised like the British Army; an infantry battalion had four rifle companies, a headquarters company, and a specialist platoon. Dominating the infantry were Indian recruits who were all volunteers. They came from races noted for their physique and martial prowess, the most renowned being the Gurkhas from Nepal but also the Sikhs, Rajputs and Pathans. The majority of recruits hailed from the Punjab; mostly very young, they came from families with a military tradition. Discipline, training and strong traditional ties generated loyalty and service in the Indian recruit. An Indian infantry battalion was a mixture of races and religions organised into separate companies. The 12 to 16 officers who held a King's Commission were almost all British. After World War One, a few places were made available for Indians at Sandhurst where, on successful completion of the course, they too were awarded a King's Commission. In 1932, an officers' training academy opened at Dehra Dun on the subcontinent, where graduates became Indian commissioned officers. This process was known as 'Indianisation' and the 4/19 Hyderabads was one of the first regiments to be involved in it. By 1939, one in seven officers in the Indian army was Indian and were concentrated in certain units.

As brigade-major, Angus served alongside Indian officers in the 12th Indian Infantry Brigade but he possessed no more than a smattering of Hindi, Urdu or any other Indian tongue as the English-speaking Indian officers he commanded were able to translate his orders for their men. It was rare for an Argyll officer to learn Urdu, the official language of India. Judging from Angus's workload, the courses he attended, his promotion to the position of adjutant, and his off-duty interests, his 'knowledge of the language would have been rudimentary.' Out of all Angus's brother officers at Secunderabad, only Aubrey Gibbon passed a lower standard Urdu exam in 1935.

We know nothing of Angus's relations with the Indian officers of the brigade but it must be understood that he and most other young men of his class and era spent their formative years influenced by formidable figures: doughty, devoted schoolmasters and dons, whose outlook and morals harked back to the Victorian age. These men, in knowing that their charges were born to lead, encouraged them to conduct themselves well and exercise a sense of service and responsibility towards those placed in their care. It was axiomatic, therefore, that my uncle applied a sense of duty towards his responsibilities as an officer.

The Indians who amounted to 36,920, greatly outnumbered the 20,900 personnel of the British Army in Malaya. The other sizeable presence was the 8th Australian Division, numbering 15,160, under Major General Gordon Bennett. Different to the British, the Australian Army was a citizen militia, which received reasonable pay and had no staff-trained officers. Many were volunteers, their units comprising friends, brothers, and workmates. The Australian officer was less formal than his British counterpart and spent more time on field craft, weapon training, and tactics than on drilling and turnout. Undoubtedly Angus had contact with the antipodeans and in a less fiery manner than the jocks who not only clashed with them in clubs and bars but also in Lavender Street, the red light district of Singapore. It was to 'the Aussies,' as they were chummily termed, that Angus made his famed two-mile dash up Bukit Timah Road on the north-west of Singapore city during the last-ditch attempt to save it from invasion by the Japanese.

The task of brigade-major in this polyglot, pluralistic garrison was complex, not least because amongst the Indian troops and officers there was considerable unrest. Some were close to mutiny. The political situation in India was delicate; nationalism was growing, and although the army had always been insulated from politics, these elements of subversion were reflected in the views of many officers who were beginning to 'tire of drinking the King Emperor's health each night.' From 7 to 9 May 1940, almost a year before Angus's appointment, two companies from the 4/19 Hyderabads refused to obey orders and were disarmed; the 2nd Argylls had been placed on alert. The battalion had returned an Indian officer to India because 'he expressed views considered to be highly objectionable in an officer holding a commission in the service.' Lieutenant General Sir Lionel Bond (General Officer Commanding, Malaya) regarded the incident seriously enough to launch an enquiry into the extent of discontent within the Indian Army in Malaya. With the influx of Indian troops into Singapore and Malaya, fears grew that resident nationalist parties were infecting officers and men with a sense of grievance. For some time there had been dissatisfaction in the Indian Army, but the only significant mutiny of Indian soldiers between 1857 and 1941 was in Singapore in 1915 when soldiers from 5th Light Infantry ran amok. To avoid mutiny, a company was made up of soldiers from different religions and races with each community having their own holidays and eating arrangements. One reason for a heightened sense of resentment among Indian officers was the operation of a colour bar in Singapore, forbidding them entry to clubs and other forms of social life in the city. This was a shock as these officers fully expected to be treated like their British counterpart. It says something that Angus was appointed brigade-major at this critical time. His promotion to chief of staff of a brigade with two Indian battalions was because he was valued for his social confidence and level-headedness and was guaranteed to relate well with the Indian officers.

As the year continued, the threat of invasion grew. When Germany invaded the USSR, the situation changed in East Asia. This was the moment that Japan had been waiting for. On 2 July 1941, at an Imperial Conference in Tokyo, Japan decided to expand its troops in South-East Asia and set up bases in south Indo-China, where the French authorities accepted Japanese demands. Three weeks after the conference, the first batch of Japanese forces arrived in southern Indo-China. Japanese warships entered the colony and its air force made a base near Saigon. The eastern imperial power was now within easy reach of Malaya and the sought-after oil-fields of the Dutch East Indies. On 25 July, two days after Japan's action, the US banned the export of oil and other materials that aided Japan's military purposes. When the British and Dutch followed suit, it caused surprise and anger within Japan (80 per cent of its oil was imported from America and 10 per cent from the Dutch East Indies). Japan, however, was undaunted; the country was stockpiling oil and had enough in reserve for eighteen months. Its war-machine was poised for an opportune moment to launch an attack on Imperial Britain and its allies in the region. Nevertheless, few of Japan's potential enemies knew when that moment would be.

An Argylls' route march

Before the Storm

IN AUGUST 1941 Angus took a break from his duties. 'I have not had any leave for exactly a year,' he wrote to Esther on 11 August, 'and I was beginning to feel that I needed one.' There was no question of him returning home. Not only did the war prevent it but even in peacetime, soldiers were seldom granted home leave while serving overseas. Because of Japan's recent aggressive policies in South East Asia, Angus and his brigade were expected to be ready for the enemy to invade at any time. With this in mind, he chose a place within easy range of his Singapore headquarters for a three week respite. 'Things are a bit tense out here as I write, and I am quite expecting to be called from leave any moment.'

As in India, there were bolt-holes in Malaya for army officers wanting to get away from steamy Singapore. The longest established was Penang, an island off Malaya's west coast. As early as 1786, tired Europeans congregated there to enjoy the mild climate of Penang Hill. Over 2,500 feet high, this green oasis stretched as far as the island's western shores. Angus probably knew Penang which, with Malacca and Singapore, was a crown colony of the Straits Settlements. It was to Penang that his friend Angus Rose was posted in December 1940 to take care of the island's defence plans.

Penang or Pulau Pinang was not that far from Singapore: a 12 hour ride on the night train to Kuala Lumpur and then a journey by steamship from Port Swettenham to the island. Angus would have been impressed by the sight of colonial Georgetown, its classical fronted civic buildings, clock tower dedicated to Queen Victoria, and all within spitting range of ships berthed in the harbour. This tropical island was rich, compact and only a few acres smaller than Singapore. It had sumptuous palaces owned by Chinese trading magnates, large colonnaded churches, mosques, Buddhist temples, and shops, whose verandas extended the length of their frontages, so that the public could amble along covered walkways protected from the sun or the monsoon rain. Where the

214

Roses lived is undisclosed. The most fortunate found accommodation on the forested hill in elegant mansions where their comfortable lifestyle was maintained by fleets of servants.

Elegant though it was, Penang was too suburban for Angus. He needed a more open, people-less space in which to relax. There was a chain of hill stations stretching the length of the Malayan central range, each with a golf course cleared from the jungle and other provisions for outdoor recreation. One of these resorts was good for trout fishing, the fish ova having been cradled in ice and trundled uphill to supply the local streams. Angus chose Malaya's Pahang province in the Cameron Highlands to get away. Deriving its name from William Cameron, a British surveyor who came to the region in 1885, the plateau, which nestles close to the peaks of Banjaran Titiwangsa, is between Penang in the north, Kuala Lumpur in the south, and about 400 miles from Singapore. More than 4,700 feet above sea level, it was an ideal 'home-from-home' for Europeans, and by the mid 1920s it attracted a steady flow of visitors who enjoyed the cool breezes and clean air; they came also to admire the waterfalls, tea plantations, and terraces of strawberries.

Although Kenneth McLeod claimed it was 'ideal for those serving in Malaya,' the Cameron Highlands (fondly termed 'a little corner of England in Asia') was a poor second to Largie. In his letter to Mum, Angus comments with envy on her good fortune in being able to take three months' leave there. 'I would give almost anything to get home even for three weeks, let alone months. But I'm afraid there is no chance of that till we have fixed up this wretched fellow, Hitler!'

At the outbreak of war in September 1939, my mother was ready to read English Literature at Somerville College, Oxford where Margaret Roberts, who later married Dennis Thatcher, was an undergraduate. Delaying her entry into academia, Mum joined the Auxiliary Territorial Service (ATS), originally The First Aid Nursing Unit (the FANYs) of the army in World War One. By 1938, the FANYs formed into the Women's Transport Service or ATS; a small section of the Corps contained women who undertook espionage work for the Special Operations Executive.

During her war service my mother drove convoys of lorries, chauffeured senior army staff, and operated anti-aircraft guns (ack-ack). At the beginning of the conflict, she was stationed at Inverness, where as a new recruit she learned to march and drill. The sergeant, appointed to train the women, was so unimpressed by their efforts that he insisted they perform their drills in a concealed area, behind the Nissan huts.

Inverness on the north-east coast of Scotland was near enough for Esther to visit Largie occasionally. But life at her childhood home was very different now. The rationing of food and fuel affected everyone. After a long period of convalescence, Jock returned to the castle but found its steep, winding staircase, from the ground floor to the upper ones, difficult to negotiate. Owners of big houses were required to accept evacuees, children from Glasgow whose homes were threatened by heavy Clyde-side bombing. In addition, friends and relatives from other cities, particularly London, took refuge at Largie. Daisy's nieces, Barbara Gordon Clark and Anne Swann stayed with their young children as did Violet, Daisy's twin sister, whose son Martin was killed at Calais in June 1940. Ever active, Daisy also helped with the war effort by taking part in schemes to support the armed forces and prisoners of war with the Red Cross and the Women's Rural Institute (WRI). Although Esther could enjoy three months' leave at the castle, I'm sure she had little time to sail, go for leisurely walks, or ride a horse. Angus, however, harboured longings for cool, soft rain, delicious, wholesome Highland food like roast grouse and fresh raspberries, the smell of the bracken and heather on the Largie hills and a relaxing evening with his family and friends.

As with most servicemen in Malaya, the fairish-skinned Angus struggled with the heat. In two letters to Esther (the first from Secunderabad and the second from the Cameron Highlands), he devotes space to the subject, an indication that the climate of each country was a problem to him. Of the tropical heat in Asia, he writes 'in the whole of Singapore there is no such thing as a fireplace, and I have not used a blanket for over two years, and very often don't use a sheet or the top half of my pyjamas either!' A three week reprieve in the Cameron Highlands was very welcome. 'It is quite reasonably cool here,' he writes, 'which is a great relief as I have not been cool since June 1939 when I was up in Kashmir.' Casting aside wartime censorship regulations, it is what Angus omits in his brief letter that is revealing. Beyond the cheerfulness and reserve, there are traces of nostalgia and homesickness. The correspondent refers to towns (Inverness), friends (Neil Ramsay, David Dundas Robertson and Ralph, whom Angus had not heard from in a while) and the seasons (a Scottish summer that, after four years absence, had become but a memory), in a manner that strikes the reader as wistful, as if Angus feels shut out of normality, his service life in the Far East a prison sentence to which he has resigned himself. 'It does not look now as though there is much chance of my being posted to a job at home.'

The nostalgia is activated by a frustration, that he is not in charge of his destiny. He is a cog in an institution whose rules are made by faceless men in Whitehall. Even Greenfield's letters indicate that his career is subject to someone else's decisions. For expatriates and members of the armed forces serving in Malaya, homesickness was rife. Little wonder, then, that in the hill stations of India and Malaya the British built mock Tudor cottages. These fake wattle and beam homes helped nostalgic rubber planters and tin miners to feel they were back at home living in an English shire. After all, many civilians were only allowed six months home leave every four years. From the foothills of the Himalayas to Singapore's Orchard Road, these expatriates, adept at carrying their customs, architecture, and culture wherever they went, also constructed for themselves neo-Gothic church buildings and baroque facades for department stores and town halls.

Homesickness was a rather recognisable complaint. As early as 1763, a Dutch professor, Jerome Gauba, wrote: 'Do not even the sturdiest races, exhibit men who are troubled by peculiar ailments when assailed by a yearning to which they do not yield soon enough, to return home after having tarried overlong in foreign parts; ailments that may end fatally when all hope of return is lost?' By 1943 homesickness in troops serving abroad was taken seriously. An important factor in attaining morale among fighting men was the prevention of nostalgia. Believed to be contagious, troublesome epidemics of the problem swept through companies and camps, and whenever a division moved, men and officers were affected. No wonder Angus's letters home are less cheery after his move to Singapore. As circumstances become harder, home-sickness increases, and what was more challenging than Colonel Stewart's training or the threat of a Japanese invasion? Accompanying nostalgia is a tendency to idealise the home environment. 'Distance lends enchantment,' wrote Sigmund Freud, 'so that one forgets the many unpleasantnesses of one's home or usual surroundings and can think only of the more desirable aspects.' As with his grandfather, Lieutenant Colonel Eyre Crabbe, who served in South Africa at the turn of the previous century, Angus was exiled from Europe. While Crabbe was away for over two years, his grandson spent a longer period overseas, from September 1937 until his death on 2 March 1942.

Angus does not say how he travelled to the Cameron Highlands. He may have driven there in his Fiat. The old trunk road, still in existence, was steep and twisting and the motorist felt swathed by clouds as he climbed towards his destination. Mile upon mile of dense forest (strictly speaking, at 4,000 feet it is no longer termed a jungle) surrounded him. This huge carpet of green, largely untouched and very ancient, was inhabited by native people and mammals like the tiger, wild pig, and tapir. As the motorist negotiated the road's corkscrew bends, he saw, growing beyond the verges, tall trees with wide leaves and a mass of vine-like creepers hanging from their branches. Angus's destination was The Smoke House Inn situated high in the hills near the village of Tanah Rata. Opening for Christmas 1937, the hotel was small and exclusive with, initially, only six guest rooms. It was the brainchild of William Warin, 'managing director of the biggest firm of advertising agents in Malaya,' explained Angus in his letter. The Smoke House, constructed in a mock-Tudor style, was one of the first permanent buildings erected in the hill station.

Warin was clever – 'he ran the place more or less as a hobby' – and knew how to make expatriates feel at home. An early advertisement claimed the inn was a place that Europeans in Malaya 'have yearned for ever since they left the homely shores of Britain.' Combining 'architectural beauty, modern fixtures and a crazy-paved garden,' it was 'the first of its kind in the Far East.'

At last Angus could feel cool. 'They have fires in the evening and sometimes in the middle of the day as well and I have two blankets on my bed.' The food was good and, as advertised, there was 'roast beef of Old England as only Old England knows it.' The beds were comfortable and the bath water hot. It was Warin's décor that Angus found overwhelming. Homesick he may have been but he failed to fall for the over-stated decoration. 'The general style of the architecture is "olde worlde" as is also the furniture. You know the sort of thing. Open fireplaces with warming pans hung about the place and a spinning wheel by the side of the fireplace. It is all very well done but myself I think there is a little bit too much of the olde worlde stuff.' The Smoke House was a ragbag of 'let's pretend' and more like a stage set than a hostelry. Its décor owed much to cliché: pictures of the Charge of the Light Brigade, the death scene of Horatio Nelson, scenes of foxhounds in full cry, cricketers on the village green and ladies in crinolines; also chintz-covered armchairs and sofas, a grandfather clock, and horse brasses pinned to the wall.

Angus gave the garden the thumbs up – 'it is exactly like an English garden, say in Surrey, with roses and all the usual sorts of flowers that grow at home, all complete with crazy pavements, sundials and a particularly bogus well, which on close examination proves not to be a well at all!' This bogusness pervaded Angus's experience here, making his last leave not entirely satisfactory. He played golf on the Highlands' nine-hole course close to the hotel but, because he had not played for over fifteen months, his game was 'very painful indeed.' Apart from his rusty playing, his golf balls kept disappearing. 'One expects to lose them when one hits them into the rough, as I frequently do. But on this course you can quite easily lose a ball in the centre of the fairway, as in many places the ground is damp and peaty and the ball not infrequently sinks right in and you never see it again! Rather expensive! Fortunately, there were second-hand balls on offer at ten cents each. 'These are the ones that people like me hit into the rough and which the caddies collect in their spare time and sell to the caddy master.'

Up in the Cameron Highlands, he wished to take exercise and see the countryside. 'When one does so, one is disappointed as there is no view at all on account of the jungle. Even with paths cut through the undergrowth, there is no view worth speaking of, so I could get no photographs except for snaps of the hotel, its garden and dogs.' Nor did Angus have much luck at riding, although there were horses for hire and he'd packed his riding breeches. 'I thought it might be rather fun to have a ride, as I have not ridden at all since I arrived in Malaya. But I find that there is literally nowhere in this place where one can break into a canter, except on the golf course, and that might not be very popular with the golfers.'

Perhaps his complaints of the 'impenetrable jungle' and having to 'cut through the undergrowth' are associated with the tough training he underwent in Johore and on Singapore Island. By this time, he'd had enough experience of the Malayan hinterland to be wary of it with its parasites, poisonous snakes and difficulties in navigation. Had my uncle been a botanist or, like his mother and aunts, interested in gardening and plants, he would have been happier. If he'd climbed a further 2,000 feet he would have found himself in the clouds, close to tall trees that allowed creepers with flame-red blooms or purple convolvulus-like flowers to encircle their trunks. He would have seen wild bananas, the tough wide leaves used for clothing by the native Orang Asli who today sell honey at the roadside. Here he'd have seen virgin forest, trees with huge canopies, palms, ferns, lichens and other genera that produce medicinal plants to combat flatulence, backache, indigestion, menstrual pain, insect stings and bruises, while the bamboos, if cut correctly, provide water for a person's survival.

Seventy years on, The Smoke House still thrives. Indeed the

building has been extended so that it has sixteen rooms or suites, each with a quintessential English name: Squire, Fairhaven, Ambleside, Gwenlaura, Hazelwell, Hermitage, Spencer and Croft. The Smoke House was so renowned that for years it appeared on all Ordnance Survey maps of the region. It is now an attraction for Malaysian families who choose to take tea at the inn while they relax to the gentle strains of canned Mozart, or stay for dinner to feast on large steaks and bombe Alaska. The inn retains its 'olde worlde' atmosphere and some of the original furniture like the grandfather clock in reception. Although, six months after Angus's visit, the Japanese took over the hotel and used it as an officers' mess, the invaders preserved the Warins' effects. 'The Japanese destroyed people, not property,' said William Warin's son, Tony who, on the eve of the invasion, escaped with his mother to Australia to spend the war years there.

When my daughter Julia and I visited the Smoke House in July 2010, we were appointed a room with wood panelling, gate-leg table, candelabra electric lights, crimson furnishings, brass fire implements and a four-poster bed. Our furnishings were reminiscent of a Terence Rattigan stage set. However, all was not what it seemed; the beds were unaired, the food, although promulgated as English fare, was not properly so. Strangely, just as in Angus's time, second-hand golf balls were on sale at reception. Outside, in the flower bed were abundant blooms, as if a collection of garden-centre house plants had been plonked in it: poinsettias, busy lizzies, and other plants that would only thrive in a house or conservatory at home. The bogus well mentioned by Angus had a palm tree growing in it, and the summer-house was crammed with excess furniture. On the roadside next to the hotel was a British telephone kiosk, an attraction for Asian visitors, who like to photograph each other standing next to it.

On his way back to Singapore, Angus stopped at Kuala Lumpur to stay with his cousin Clare Langworthy, married to H. B. Langworthy, the Deputy Commissioner of the Federal Malayan States Police. During the Japanese invasion of Malaya, the Langworthys were evacuated on the SS Duchess of Bedford and arrived safely in the UK on 4 April 1942. Langworthy returned to Malaya in 1945 after the end of the war and became Commissioner of the Malayan Union Police until the formation of the Federation of Malaya on 1 February 1948, whereupon he retired. Clare (born in 1900) was the youngest of three sisters, the eldest being Ivy Greenfield. Myrtle was the middle sibling and their brother, Anthony, the youngest of them all. Since the sisters all lived in Malaya at the time when Angus served in the 2nd battalion, he became acquainted with them. The Langworthys lived in a select area of Kuala Lumpur in a roomy colonial bungalow. Built in a manner that kept its occupants as cool as possible, it possessed an open-air courtyard in the building's centre. There was little need, therefore, for Angus to stay at either the Station or Eastern Hotels, situated on a hillside near the minarets of the railway station designed by A.C. Norman. Today, both hotel structures still stand: the first functions as a hostelry, part of which is recognisable as the old stables; the Eastern is a ruined husk, its exterior walls coated in flaking green paint.

The expatriate community in Malaya worked and played hard, their social life revolving around the club, the Royal Selangor (or 'Spotted Dog') on the Padang. Had Angus stayed in a hotel rather than a private house, he might have been invited into this exclusive precinct by a member, but only because he was a responsible young army officer and came from a pukka social background. Junior officers and other ranks were not permitted. At that time, 18,000 Europeans, many of Scottish descent, lived in Malaya, some from well-established families who had lived there since the nineteenth century; others were rubber planters and tin miners, a number of whom would join the Federal Malay States Volunteer Force to defend the country against the Japanese. Perhaps his hosts arranged for Angus to meet some Scots; there were even a handful who had served in the Argylls before turning to civilian life. Kuala Lumpur was the capital of the Federated Malay States and therefore different from the Straits Settlements. It was a new city but had a strong colonial bureaucracy. Angus noticed the difference between the more relaxed British Malayans and the formal

Singaporeans. The latter were concerned with trade; they held the seats of power of the commercial companies and had a more sophisticated lifestyle than the rural, isolated Europeans on the mainland. The peninsula was ruled by the Malayan Civil Service (some 300 members) and 200 white police officers of whom Langworthy was one.

Kuala Lumpur today is different: the streets are filled with women in the hijab (some are on holiday from the Middle East). Above the sound of traffic you can discern the amplified Muslim call to prayer. Streets have been renamed – the former King's Road, where the town hall is situated, now has a Muslim name. Although the mayor of Kuala Lumpur wishes to rid the city of its architectural past, some buildings still remain like ghosts of the former imperial power. Nowhere is this more obviously demonstrated than at the Coliseum Café, one of the few colonial places not demolished in the past ten years. Dark and dingy, its entrance swing-doors suggest a Wild West saloon bar: the lighting is dim, the white tablecloths and napkins grubby. A diminutive, white-coated waiter, nicknamed Captain Morgan, welcomed us; many of his colleagues, only recently retired, began serving there before the war. The café still produces similar fare to that consumed in Angus's day, although strict Muslim dietary rules are observed and pork is no longer on the menu. A throwback to colonial times, the menu is aimed at homesick soldiers, planters and tin miners: pancakes, ice cream, crème caramel, steak, chips, fish, sliced white bread, HP sauce, Lea & Perrins Worcestershire sauce, and a selection of alcoholic drinks. Adjacent to the café is the grey-walled Coliseum Theatre where, during the 1920s and 1930s, planters watched performances of London hits and, on a balcony outside, actors stood to be viewed and applauded.

Entertainment and applause were soon to become a feature of the past. It was obvious from Angus's last letter that he believed a Japanese attack was imminent. 'By the time you receive this letter we will know whether or not Japan has decided to commit national suicide.' Was Angus so sure of the allied forces' superiority or could it have been his way of concealing his fear? Certainly the remark echoed the attitude of Ian Stewart and other officers in Malaya Command. 'I do hope, Sir, you are not getting too strong in Malaya because if so the Japanese may never attempt a landing,' said Stewart. There was a common, somewhat racist assumption that the Japanese, like the Italians, were inefficient warmongers: small, myopic and technically backward. The problem was that military intelligence was unable to obtain much evidence on the Japanese military machine. Most people believed that this eastern power had little chance of success because of its isolation from Europe, its failure to defeat China, and the fact that its economy was in tatters as a result of America's sanctions. Some sources even suggested that Japan was intending to attack Russia and not Malaya. Lastly, Churchill believed that the US, with its Pacific fleet, would be the ultimate deterrent against a Japanese attack on Malaya.

On his return Angus found life in Singapore very tense; with its troops now in Indo-China, its warships in coastal ports, and its air force near Saigon, Japan was closer than ever to Malaya, the Philippines, and the Dutch East Indies. In London, General Sir John Dill informed Lieutenant General Arthur Per-cival that he was unable to spare more personnel, ammunition or war materials as he needed to build up Britain's defences. He believed that Germany, which had invaded Russia in June 1941, would soon overrun the Soviets. In spite of the latter's success in holding out against its enemy, Dill was unwilling to risk compromising the defence of the UK. As far as military resources were concerned, the War Office decided to prioritise Britain and the Middle East and sent no further troops or equipment to the Far East.

In August 1941, Lieutenant General Percival insisted that he receive at least five divisions and an armoured brigade for Malaya. Three months later, in November, additions arrived but Percival still only had four divisions and they were under strength. However, during late August and in September, the 27th Australian and 28th Indian Brigades arrived in Singapore. From the latter part of August 1941, Churchill urged the Admiralty to send a small force of ships to Singapore. But the Royal Navy was hard pressed to spare more than two capital or leading ships after supplying the needs of the Home Fleet, Gibraltar, and the Mediterranean Fleet. By the end of October 1941, the Prince of Wales, a modern battleship, joined the old battle cruiser, Repulse, and headed towards the Far East.

At the time when Angus was enjoying his leave (August 1941), Churchill and Roosevelt held their Atlantic Conference in which it was agreed that the United States, the UK, and the Dutch would issue a warning to Japan regarding further aggressive actions. On 6 September 1941, the Japanese also held a conference at which they decided to go to war while there was a chance of victory, otherwise they'd be strangled by the U.S. trade embargo. Japan's objective was to seize the raw materials of South East Asia, particularly oil from the Dutch East Indies. However, during the closing months of 1941, Japan tried to reach an agreement with the U.S. to end the trade embargo, but the latter refused to lift it until the eastern power promised to retreat from the Asian mainland. These were harsh terms, and on 14 October 1941 the Japanese Army Minister announced that the withdrawal of troops was unacceptable as their position in Manchuria, Korea, and China would be endangered. The Japanese cabinet resigned, as it was reluctant to embark on another war; three days later, General Tojo was appointed Japan's Prime Minister. His cabinet resolved to pursue negotiations with America until 30 November. This date was strategic as Japan knew that if it were to make a successful attack, it would have to be made at the approach of the winter monsoons. Tojo believed that war was necessary to preserve the Japanese empire although he was aware that an invasion of Malaya and the Dutch East Indies was a gamble.

This bellicose prime minister envisaged Hitler and Mussolini taking care of Britain and the Soviets, while his country might do a deal with the isolated U.S.. However, Admiral Yamamoto, the Commander-in-Chief of Japan's combined fleet, was more ambitious. He saw it as a plus point that the U.S. Pacific fleet's base had recently moved to Hawaii. If Japan could deliver a decisive blow and knock out the American fleet, it would help them to forge a Pacific empire. If successful, the Imperial Japanese Navy's 11 battleships and 10 aircraft carriers would be more than a match for Allied naval forces. Japan's southern army headquarters were already established at Saigon. This army was divided into four smaller armies (a Japanese army was equivalent to a European corps-sized formation). The XXV Army would seize Malaya and the XVI, the Dutch East Indies. Their plan was to carry out an invasion with speed and approach with stealth, surprise, and infiltration. The Japanese soldier, who possessed a spirit of self-sacrifice, displayed huge endurance and with an unbreakable morale, he regarded surrender dishonourable, even treasonous. He also understood that indiscipline would earn him severe punishment. Lieutenant General Tomoyaki Yamashita took over XXV army command on 15 November, but his chief of planning operations, Lieutenant Colonel Masanobu Tsuji had been studying tropical jungle fighting for months: sea landings, transport, equipment supply and training took place on Hainan Island. During 1941 Tsuji sent Japanese officers disguised as commercial travellers to Malaya to gather intelligence. Having established a good espionage network on the peninsula, he also arranged that Jap-anese residents should help with intelligence.

While this was happening, the allied powers were watching. American code breakers intercepted Japanese signals on 24 November. The U.S. Chief of Naval Operations signalled Pearl Harbour that Japanese attack was a possibility. On 29 November the War Office in London passed a message to Air Chief Marshall Robert Brooke-Popham in Singapore that Japanese negotiations had broken down and an offensive was likely. On 1 December volunteer forces mobilised and a sigh of relief was made when, on the following day, the Prince of Wales and Repulse arrived in Singapore. On the third, the Admiralty informed Singapore that the Japanese Embassy in London had destroyed their cipher machine. At dawn on 4 December, the first Japanese transports bound for Thailand and north-east Malaya left Hainan Island. Another transport left the next day, planning to join up with the previous one on the morning of 7 December in the Gulf of Siam.

To prevent detection, they relied on bad weather or the breaking monsoon. Nevertheless, RAF reconnaissance sorties attempted to fly into the South China Sea but bad weather stopped them on 4 December.

On 5 December, the British Chief of Imperial General Staff advised Brooke-Popham he could launch Operation Matador if the Japanese sailed to the Kra Isthmus in Southern Thailand. This operation was a plan to mobilise allied forces across the border into Thailand to intercept the Japanese before they were able to invade Malaya. The next day, No. 1 Squadron Royal Australian Air Force took off from Kota Bahru at midday and sighted three transports and a cruiser approaching the Gulf of Siam about 185 miles from Kota Bahru on the north-east coast of Malaya. Shortly afterwards, they sighted the main Japanese convoy (twenty transports) and signalled back to base. Brooke-Popham hesitated in putting into motion Operation Matador by ordering troops into Thailand. The transports could, after all, be a ploy by the Japanese to induce the allies to attack. Meanwhile, the enemy transports split up, one heading for Kota Bahru and the others for Singora, Patani and farther north in Thailand.

For some time 12th Indian Infantry Brigade was positioned in reserve south of Kuala Lumpur, but during the last week of peace, the Argylls and the 5/2 Punjabs spent an intense period of training on the south-west coast, first at Seremban, then at Port Dickson. The Argylls trained on firing ranges and on Saturday 29 November were put on second degree of readiness. That evening Angus Rose and his wife, Alison, who had returned from Penang in September, held a party in Singapore. After a buffet supper in their house, the party-goers danced at the Tanglin Club. With the elegant female guests and handsome officers, they contrived to create an atmosphere reminiscent of the Duchess of Richmond's ball on the eve of the Battle of Waterloo in 1815, but updated to 1930s tropics dress. 'It was the last evening on which we danced and gallivanted together,' wrote Angus Rose in his memoir.

WHEN THE JAPANESE invaded Malaya on the night of 7 to 8 December, Angus was with his brigade at Port Dickson on the southwest coast of the peninsula. The brigade staff learned of the landing when, shortly after 1:15 a.m. on the 8th, a motor cycle dispatch rider arrived with an order for the battalions to man their positions. The news was far from unexpected: two days earlier the brigade had been put on 'Action Alert' when Japanese ships were seen approaching the Thai coast. There was little surprise that an attack would come from the north-east. As early as 1937, when Lieutenant General Percival was stationed in Singapore as General Staff Officer 1, he predicted the Japanese would land at Patani or Singora in southern Thailand, and Kota Bahru in north-east Malaya. However, it was not until France fell in mid 1940 that Malaya's fate was sealed as Japan could now use nearby French Indo-China as a base for its troops. Even more serious for Britain was the secret pact made between Japan and a hitherto neutral Siam (now Thailand). Prime Minister Pibul Songgram, although appearing pro-British, ignored Churchill's appeal to forbid Japan permission to land its 5th Infantry Division at Patani and Singora.

Percival knew that Japan was planning an assault on Malaya, but had no idea it was so imminent. Invading British, American and Dutch territories simultaneously seemed inconceivable. The assault on Kota Bahru on the night of 7 to 8 December was timed to coincide with the bombing of Pearl Harbour in Hawaii, only it happened an hour earlier. When the news of the attack reached Sir Shenton Thomas, he reputedly said to one of Percival's staff, 'Well, I suppose you'll shove the little men off.' Angus's brigade, 12th Indian Infantry with its three principal battalions, were to shoulder most of the responsibility of shoving the Japanese out of Malaya. As a highly-trained, jungle-savvy mobile reserve, used when extra force was needed, the brigade was tested to its limits during the ensuing 2½ months. Angus served continuously throughout the campaign. For 70 consecutive days he was heavily involved, sometimes in the front line while many colleagues were killed, lost in the jungle, or taken prisoner.

Within hours of landing on the beaches of Kota Bahru, Japanese troops made inroads into northern Malaya, their objective was to seize the main north-south trunk road in the west. From two directions, additional Japanese divisions surged over the Thai border: the first from the west where they engaged with the 11th Indian Division led by Major General David Murray-Lyon at Asun and Jitra. The other, after landing at Patani on the Kra isthmus, a sliver of land that separates Thailand from Malaya, advanced south farther inland, and crossed the border north of Kroh, and began its assault on the narrow, remote road to Grik. There was even a third division which headed south from Bangkok. For the 11th Indian Division, 'shoving off the little men' proved harder than anticipated. They needed backup. 12th Indian Infantry Brigade came to their rescue and blocked the main road on the west coast, that ran from the north to the Straits of Johore, a stone's throw from Singapore.

The grimness of the situation for the British Imperial forces intensified when in the early hours of 10 December, HMS Prince of Wales and the cruiser HMS Repulse were sunk by the Japanese off the east coast of Malaya. 'Blown clean away at one fell swoop was one of the main pillars on which our sense of security rested,' wrote Ian Morrison, a correspondent for *The Times* newspaper. On that day, 12th Indian Infantry Brigade was ordered north. The Argylls travelled by train to Jerantut in the Central Highlands of Pahang where a Japanese landing at Kuantan was expected. 'The Jocks were in very high spirits,' wrote Angus Rose, 'and were spoiling for a fight.' The occasion remained firmly in the memory of the then Lieutenant Gordon Smith when he wrote his memoirs in 1995: 'I vividly remember the train journey and how unreal the situation seemed, and the thoughts that went through my mind as they did, I'm sure, through the minds of all of us...at least we all had confidence in our state of physical fitness and training.'

While some soldiers relate the experience of battle with sport,

I compare it to the discipline of the theatre. Militarists describe armed conflict as 'the theatre of war:' facing an enemy is not unlike the occasion when an actor confronts an audience. Adjutants, ADCs or brigade-majors, assisting commanders, are termed understudies. To realise their objective in battle or on stage, both soldier and player undergo exhaustive drilling or strict training in performance techniques. Each, assisted by weapon or prop, has solely his body and mind as a means of achieving his end, whether in hand-to-hand fighting, driving a tank, operating a machine gun or in moving an audience.

That morning, the 5/2 Punjabs followed from Singapore. 'The men are in very good heart, yelling out their respective religious cries as the train steamed out,' wrote the commanding officer, Colonel Deakin, who had trained recruits before he arrived in Malaya. With the intention that it be used as an instruction manual for young officers, he wrote a diary of the campaign while imprisoned by the Japanese in Kuala Lumpur Central Jail. The Indian battalion's progress was interrupted by trains carrying hordes of European refugees from Penang, which was being bombed by the Japanese. The third battalion of 12th Indian Infantry Brigade, the 4/19 Hyderabads, was posted to Kelantuan State on the east coast of Malaya to block the Japanese advance south from Kota Bahru.

After a meeting on the 12th with commanding officers at Brigade HQ in Singapore, Angus departed for Ipoh, a mining town and army base in Perak State. The Argylls and Punjabs followed the next day, arriving in the large town lying on the banks of the Kinta River 125 miles north of Kuala Lumpur. As staff officer, Angus was not employed in armed combat but his job at Brigade HQ put him in danger. During the ten week Malayan Campaign, when the brigade made lightning withdrawals down the 400-mile length of the peninsula, its headquarters was set up in different places and moved many times, sometimes twice in one day. In one battle, it was camouflaged in a rubber plantation, and in another, a jungle clearing. For effective communication with fighting units it was best positioned near a road. A requisitioned tin miner or planter's bungalow was welcome; invariably the owner, in his hasty evacuation, left well-supplied refrigerators and larders and some houses were replete with magazines and other comforts. But, up country in the north, all they might have for a headquarters was a tent or the back of a lorry. Whatever the location, it was best to be inconspicuous and that, generally speaking, ruled out large, recently vacated luxury homes.

Angus was the brigadier's most senior staff officer. After deciding what to do, the brigadier created the orders and the brigade-major wrote them down and carried them out. With his boss or alone if necessary, Angus would leave the headquarters and confer with commanders of combat units and provide directions. He also controlled the battle, sat on the wireless (during the Malayan campaign this device was very unreliable), receiving information from fighting units, and saw to it that they had reinforcements, ammunition and other supplies. Occasionally, if the brigadier was called away, the brigade-major would take over. However, if it was for a long time or if his commanding officer was killed or wounded, a battalion commander would take command. Angus's role was complex and, during the campaign, exhausting because of the fast pace of each battle. He should have felt proud of himself; after the war Lieutenant General Percival claimed that 12th Indian Infantry Brigade 'having been over two years in Malaya when the campaign began, was probably the best-trained and most experienced brigade in the country.'

How much was Angus aware of the disasters that met the defenders of Malaya? Angus would have learned of the 11th Division's defeat at Asun on the 11th and at Jitra on the 12th, as the reason his brigade was sent north was to aid the beleaguered formation. As for the sinking of the two British battle-ships, HMS Prince of Wales and HMS Repulse, not only was Malaya aware of the debacle, it was also front page news in the UK. It meant the Japanese had gained mastery of the seas. Enemy assault on airfields in the north resulted in allied aircraft being withdrawn from Alor Star and Sungei Patani in the west and Kota Bahru, Machang and Gong Kedah in the east. By 9 December, the British had only ten operative aircraft at Butterworth aerodrome. By contrast, the

Japanese possessed 150 making frequent sorties into Malaya from the Singora-Patani area. Within days of landing on the peninsula, the enemy had gained control of the skies.

It was up to the army alone to repel the enemy. On 14 December, the bulk of the brigade departed Ipoh by train or bus and travelled north into jungle and mountainous terrain to Baling in the northern state of Kedah. Legend has it that the town was founded by a cannibalistic monarch who, after being banished from his kingdom, recanted, tore out his teeth and threw each to the winds. The place where they landed was Baling. There was a danger that the retreating 11th Division might be cut off by the Japanese 42nd Infantry Regiment advancing from Patani across the Thai border. Here, in a remote, mountainous region where tigers roamed, Japanese infantrymen threatened to pour down the narrow road from Kroh to Grik towards the Perak River in Central Malaya. To deny the enemy access to Malaya Krohcol, a British force, was sent across the border to occupy The Ledge, a piece of high ground 35 to 40 miles into Thailand. But the Japanese moved too fast, nabbed The Ledge, pushed back Krohcol and crashed southward towards Grik. It was crucial, therefore, that this road be blocked, so Lieutenant General Sir Lewis Heath, commander of III Indian Corps, sent the Argylls' C Company to deal with it. At this point, Heath, who had distinguished himself earlier in the year and in the previous one when he commanded 5th Indian Division against the Italians in Eritrea, decided to take under his control Paris's 12th Brigade, normally attached to Malaya Command.

Meanwhile, another Japanese formation was expected to advance south along the main road on the west coast. So 12th Indian Brigade (Argylls' A, B and D Companies and the 5/2 Punjabs) was ordered to hold the road at Baling. Effective communication was one of the challenges facing brigade staff. Having attended signalling courses in India, Angus was practised in this field but his skills were sorely tested in Malaya. Communication was by wireless, cable, runners or dispatch riders who travelled by motorbike. Wireless communication in Malaya was unreliable, as transmissions broke up or were limited because of the humid climate, frequent tropical storms and jungle-covered hills. As with ammunition, weapons and vehicles in Malaya, signalling equipment was in short supply also; infantry battalions possessed one signal set only to communicate with Brigade HQ. Forward companies and platoons used cable but this form of communication was vulnerable to shelling, and there was a shortage of telephone cable. Another ploy, while fighting in the north, was to use civilian telephone lines, which were often disrupted by enemy attack; during fierce rear-guard battles, the forces were not given priority over civilian use. Often the only solution was to use dispatch riders (important people like Lieutenant General Percival had a team of liaison officers) on motor bikes but too frequently congested roads impeded progress.

On 16 December the Argylls withdrew to Titi Karangan village on the Karangan River 30 miles east of Penang. Titi Karangan was the brigade's first proper battle or 'blooding.' When at 10 a.m., Japanese troops emerged from the jungle in native clothes, the Argylls hesitated, unsure if they faced the enemy or local rubber tappers. Nevertheless, the Japanese, in trying to outflank the Argylls, turned off the road onto a hill and fell into a trap set by B Company, which caught some 200 of them at close range with machine guns and rapid rifle fire. That morning, the 5/2 Punjabs took up position six miles north of Titi Karangan at Pekaka bridge, which crosses the Muda River. Whereas the Argylls' first contact with the enemy was successful, the Indian battalion's experience was less note-worthy. When the Japanese attacked the bridge in the late afternoon, there was 'far too much excitement and shouting,' wrote Deakin in a disgruntled schoolmasterly fashion. His adjutant showed a lack of calmness, especially on the telephone. One mortar section, on being shelled, withdrew without orders and as a consequence, an NCO was put under arrest. C Company had distinct signs of the 'jitters although at the time enemy fire was not heavy.' One of the reasons for the men's fears was Japanese mortar shells had a high bursting charge and made a tremendous noise. By the end of that first day facing an experienced enemy, the Punjabs were reliably chastened.

The British imperial troops not only had to square up to an implacable enemy but also cope with their surroundings. Major General Barstow, who commanded 9th Indian Division, likened jungle combat to fighting blind or having a hood over the eyes. The enemy could be anywhere: very close, to one side, behind or even up a tree and above you. Jungle sounds were intimidating, especially during the night when men could not tell what was there. A leaf rustle could be an animal or a Japanese soldier. Added to their discomfort was the monsoon rain which fell in torrents. To keep dry, each man wore an anti-gas cape that served as a complete waterproof covering. Like a cycle cape, only longer, it was roomy enough for a soldier to wrap himself in and use as a ground sheet to lie on. Although effective in the monsoon rain, the cape was too hot to wear when dry, so it was rolled up tight and packed away.

Farther south at Titi Karangan, after the successful attack by A and B companies, the Argylls noticed the remaining Japanese soldiers had drawn together swiftly to continue their attack, at which point Colonel Stewart had to think fast and anticipate the enemy's next move. In spite of heavy casualties, the Japanese kept up the pressure with wide, outflanking moves. To avoid encirclement, Stewart knew that his battalion had to make an attack, which meant the Argylls must leave their positions and engage in hand-to-hand fighting, a move that would result in heavy casualties. In a letter dated 14 March 1942, he described his tactics: 'We fought a mobile war for the road (the only tactical feature) from the road.' Stewart knew that defending a fixed 'position' was no use as the enemy could encircle them. They needed to control the road directly as this feature was crucial for supplies and communication. They also had to hold it in depth so they were not outflanked or blocked. So the Colonel in his glengarry (ever reluctant to wear a tin hat) called Pipe Major John McCalman to discuss the tune he should play to accompany the advance. Stewart suggested the Gaelic tune *Gabaidh Sinn a Rathad Mhor*, which translates as 'We'll take and keep the highway.'

Stewart ordered Drummer Hardie, his bugler and batman, to

blow the signal for attack and the young soldier sounded the first part of the call; then, as Hardie wetted his lips to prepare for the second, a dispatch rider hove in sight with a message from Brigade HQ. 'You may withdraw at any time at your discretion,' it said. So Hardie continued to blow his bugle but sounded the 'stand fast' instead. Had the battalion been asked to delay another 15 minutes, their counter-attack would have cost the Argylls' two companies, as encirclement by the enemy would have resulted in defeat. 'Fortunately we had a brigade commander who understood these things,' wrote Stewart. Paris, the longest serving senior commander in Malaya, was a wise one and always reluctant to take risks when it concerned his troops. However, credit went also to his staff who, with split-second timing and efficiency, carried out their commander's orders and saved the two Argyll companies.

The brigade handled itself well in its first contact with the Japanese. For the battle-hardened enemy, the fighting at Titi Karangan was but an interlude in a series of conflicts, as the Japanese soldier had been fighting in China since 1936. Seasoned for years by a real war, these forces, including their weapons and aircraft, had been tried and tested. This was not the case with the soldiers of the British Empire. Except for 12th Indian Infantry Brigade, the young allied armies were no match for the Japanese. The battle of Titi Karangan lasted two hours. Great damage was inflicted on the enemy — an estimated 200 Japanese soldiers were killed. One Argyll officer figured that A Company's Bren guns killed between 200 and 400, while his battalion suffered eleven casualties, two missing and nine wounded.

After their first contact, the battalion was clear on the enemy's tactics. Speed was of the essence. They should fix frontally and encircle to a depth of 1,000 yards while Stewart launched a wide (four mile) encircling attack with a reserve battalion to cut the road in the rear. The Japanese employed similar tactics to the Scots and carried out their plans with considerable swiftness. From the way the enemy fought at Titi Karangan, the Argylls noted that they operated in dispersed, mobile self-contained groups, each with freedom of action within the battalion plan but all understanding and operating the same standard technique. However, the Argyls dealt the first blow to Japanese invincibility. The Japanese soldier stuck rigidly to a plan and, if rattled, became disorientated: fierce, noisy bayonet charges unnerved him. After their first battle, Stewart decided that anyone coming on to the Argyll lines in native dress would be shot. Locals, they assumed, would go away and not come into contact. But this was wishful thinking. The Japanese often co-opted locals at gun or bayonet point into doing things for them.

It's claimed that British Imperial forces, comprising British, Indian and Australian divisions, were of greater number than the Japanese. This may have been the case when allied troops took their last stand against the enemy on Singapore Island but not on the mainland. The Japanese vastly outnumbered the British and Indian troops, and not until the fighting reached the south of Malaya were Australian troops deployed. When 12th Brigade moved north on 14 December, Lieutenant General Heath could spare only one Company to defend the vital area north of Grik. While the bulk of the brigade (the Argylls and Punjabs) positioned themselves at Baling, on the afternoon of the 13th, Captain Bobby Kennard with 62 officers and men from Argylls' C Company, proceeded up the narrow road north, to staunch an avalanche of three battalions from 42nd Japanese Infantry Regiment advancing south. Popular memory is often uncomplimentary about the British Imperial forces' performance during the Malayan campaign, the opinion being that neither the British soldier, nor the Indian nor Australian, was a match for the fierce Japanese fighters. People forget about the David and Goliath-like contest of Bobby Kennard and his Argylls' C Company who, on a 25 mile stretch of single-track, twisting road, delayed a force many times its own number. The road was vital; the Japanese wished to seize it as it led to Perak State's royal capital, Kuala Kangsar. If they succeeded, they'd be able to control the junction of the main north-south trunk road and sever supply lines to the British forces in north-west Malaya. The Upper Perak region, 1,000 feet above sea level, is remote, and the roads, mere jungle tracks, hard to access.

Fortunately for C Company, on account of the heavy rain and poor road surface, the Japanese were forced to abandon their tanks. Kennard's men were unlucky when it came to enemy aircraft which attacked them. Starting their retreat in a truck that ran into a monsoon ditch and got stuck, the men disabled it and made off in an old Chinese lorry. With this vehicle, the Company fought down the Kroh-Grik road, running ambushes on steep hills and narrow bends. Numbering only 35 now, Kennard's company ambushed the enemy by positioning seven men 100 yards apart. Each group went into action for ten minutes, at which point it advanced to its next position. This leapfrogging of seven men here and seven there, went on for a day and a night. C Company suffered 50 per cent casualties and rejoined the battalion 'absolutely exhausted and sleeping on their feet' after the battle of Titi Karangan. It was a sobering lesson to the Argylls on the swiftness of the Japanese advance but it was a great achievement. They had stopped the enemy from advancing west into South Kedah and Province Wellesley, so avoiding the 11th Division being cut off in retreat. 'For four days,' wrote Colonel Stewart in his history of the Argylls, 'this company with gallant assistance of some volunteers, delayed the advance of at least three enemy battalions until the remainder of our regiment was moved to that particular front to back them up. They did their job and did it very well.' In 1943, while Duncan Fergusson from C Company was a prisoner of war, a Japanese officer who had fought with 42nd Infantry Regiment, asked him how many men ambushed their regiment on the Kroh-Grik road. Fergusson scratched in the sand with a stick the number 35. The Japanese officer angrily added two zeroes to the figure but Fergusson erased them.

Following Titi Karangan, the Argylls repeated their success in six major battles at Sumpitan, Lenggong, Kota Tampan, Chemor, Gopeng-Dipang and Telok Anson. In these, the Argylls (some 500 men) and other battalions like the Leicesters took on Japanese regimental groups of close to 6,000 men. Fighting the battle for the road, they bought precious time for the retreating 3rd Indian Corps and inflicted, on a numerically superior enemy, casualties that far exceeded their own. Writing some years after the end of the war, Lieutenant General Percival praised the troops of the Malayan campaign. 'All ranks courageously faced a situation which was prejudiced from the outset through lack of resources to complete the magnitude of the task.' Japanese domination of the air was total, and the brigade under regular attack from enemy aircraft. Not once did the battalion see any allied aircraft. In the latter part of 1941, British commitment elsewhere stopped the government from bolstering the Royal Air Force in Malaya, whose total stock was 141 serviceable aircraft, the best of which were 42 Brewster Buffalo fighters. In comparison to the Navy 'O' fighter, its Japanese counterpart, the Buffalo was slow and flew no higher than 10,000 feet.

On 17 December, Heath ordered 12th Indian Infantry Brigade to Kuala Kangsar to staunch the enemy's farther advance down the Grik Road. In the small hours, behind the rear of the 2nd Argylls, the 5/2 Punjabs withdrew from their Pekaka position; three hours later they reached Merbau Pulas. But the Japanese tried to rush the bridge before the sappers were able to blow it. Deakin complained that his men retired 'without due cause' and had to be forced back. Reports of the battle and the intensity of the enemy's assault suggest that there had indeed been enough cause to retire. 'The enemy were in the swamps, up trees and, on both sides of the road, and there was tommy gun fire coming from the village,' wrote Deakin, who wondered if fifth columnists were responsible for the shooting. In the northern unfederated state of Kedah, there was considerable opposition to British rule and disaffected Malays were hostile towards the British. Fifth columnist stories were rife; a Malay was shot for hanging a red sarong out to dry and it was rumoured that one anti-British faction could be distinguished by its black clothes. So that intelligence officers could inteview suspected fifth columnists, battalions employed interpreters, as few officers or men in the British forces in Malaya spoke Chinese or any local language. On 18 December, the battalions arrived at Kuala Kangsar and enjoyed a much-needed rest. It made 'a marvellous difference,' Deakin scribbled. 'It seemed that I was commanding a completely different battalion. The men had a snap in their walk, were cheery and alert.' (Throughout the campaign, the troops were plagued by exhaustion, which could sometimes be more threatening than the enemy). Lost or broken vehicles and ammunition were replaced and personnel received a change of clothes and boots.

For 3 to 4 days until 11th Division completed its withdrawal, 12th Brigade blocked the Grik road and denied the Japanese entry to Kuala Kangsar. At dawn on the 19th, the Argylls advanced 30 miles up the Grik road past Chenderoh, a 3 mile long, 3 mile wide artificial lake with a hydro-electric power station. After passing through Lenggong village, they stopped 4 miles farther north at Sumpitan. Helped by the newly formed 1st Independent Infantry Company, the Argylls' unblooded D Company smashed into the village and confronted the Japanese who, although superior in number, suffered heavy casualties. Fighting continued until early evening. By the end of the day the Argylls lost 3 men to a count of 100 Japanese casualties. The Japanese responded by sending 3 strong battalions from Sumpitan to Lenggong. Stewart ordered Captain 'Bal' Hendry's A Company (helped by 1st Independent Infantry Company) to ambush the Japanese as they moved south. The following morning (20 December), Hendry's men attacked the enemy, killing 12. However, in the late afternoon reports came from Chinese farmers that the Japanese were heading down the fast, wide, and muddy Perak River towards Kota Tampan on rafts and in boats, which they had carted overland from the east coast. Their intention was to encircle the Argylls and cut them off with a road block. Negotiating the river past Kota Tampan, they intended to bypass Kuala Kangsar, which would deny withdrawal of the Argylls (farther north at Sumpitan) and the retreat of 11th Division. Colonel Stewart sent reinforcements and alerted his battalion's rear.

On 21 December, Heath ordered the brigade west of the Perak River and arranged that 12th Indian Infantry Brigade be put under the command of 11th Division. By now Angus and the staff's heads were spinning, their brigade like a parcel being passed from one commander to another. First, 12th Indian Infantry Brigade was under Percival's Malaya Command, then it became the responsibility of Heath's III Indian Corps. It was now under the control of 11th Division, commanded by Major General Murray Lyon. The latter arrived that day at Brigade HQ to discuss sending his Division behind the Perak because of the Japanese use of the river which threatened the brigade's lines of communication. While the Division could handle the enemy by day, it was difficult to prevent the Japanese from rafting down the river at night and reaching Kuala Kangsar. Fortunately, 4/19 Hyderabads met this threat on the east side of the Perak River.

Argylls' C Company performed well and Japanese casualties were heavy. Some of the enemy fired from trees where they took up sniping positions but they were not particularly 'good shots as their rifles weren't great.' The Argylls responded by spraying the trees with Bren gun fire. The battle was successful; the Argylls had obstructed the Japanese from advancing down the road and their casualties numbered 3 officers and 50 men, mainly wounded. The Japanese figure was 350. At 8 am on 21 December, the Japanese attempted another assault on Kota Tampan, attacking the left flank of the Argylls' A and D Companies. Stewart ordered a withdrawal. The two companies were not keen to give up, but withdrew six miles down the road under cover of darkness. By this time both sides were quite tired. During the preceding days, 12th Indian Infantry Brigade had delivered the Japanese Ando Regiment some nasty blows. Lieutenant General Yamashita removed his forces from North Malaya and replaced them with the Imperial Guards Division, stationed in readiness in Thailand.

The 5/2 Punjabs also did well. D Company repelled a heavy Japanese attack and inflicted numerous casualties on the Japanese, receiving none themselves. Morale was high, the Companies fighting with a purpose. 'It appeared as if the battalion had at last found its fighting legs,' wrote Deakin proudly. Angus was busy with a meeting between the divisional commander and Paris. Murray-Lyon noticed that the Japanese offensive had eased off and suspected the enemy was moving south across the lake and down the Perak River as far as Sungei Siput, north-east of Kuala Kangsar. Murray-Lyon visited Brigade HQ a second time that day to discuss plans for withdrawing the Division behind the river that night. At 6 p.m. on 22 December, David Murray-Lyon issued his orders. 12th Indian Infantry Brigade was to head for Salak North in the Sungei Siput region. The Argylls and Punjabs departed that evening in very good heart and arrived at their destination at 2 a.m. the next morning.

The moment of elation was not to last; the following day was difficult. Salak consisted of one short street with small Chinese and Malayan houses or shops. The troops billeted in these dwellings. The armed forces in sparsely populated Malaya faced a scarcity for billets of large houses or farm buildings. There was little time during the Malayan campaign for the army or Public Works Department to construct hutted camps. Instead, civilian houses and schools (generally Chinese) were commandeered. Nevertheless, fighting the length of the country, many men and young officers never once found a bed to sleep in and had to curl up on the ground or find a space in a building and lie on the floor. The Salak billets were unpleasant and also a death trap from the air. Both battalion commanders, Deakin and Stewart, decided to quit at dawn the next day. This manoeuvre would not be easy as enemy recce planes were flying overhead and would spot any large troop movement. Hitherto, the brigade had been untroubled by enemy aircraft, as in thick jungle country 'it was impossible to make even the remotest guess as to the location of our own or the British lines,' wrote the Japanese Colonel Masanobu Tsuji.

The Malayan countryside was variable: apart from jungle-covered hills, there were acres of rubber trees. There were paddy fields where villagers from nearby kampongs grew and harvested rice; the flat, open country of central Malaya had tin mines where the ground resembled a lunar landscape blistered by mounds of tin tailings, the name given to the industry's waste. When the soil was removed, the rain eroded the rocks beneath. Red and ochre in colour, they rose like cliffs on whose surfaces grew bracken, Straits rhododendron, elephant grass, and ground orchids. When the dive-bombers flew over, the battalions took cover in a rubber plantation and dispersed. For seven hours, these planes attacked from high altitudes and machine-gunned the Argylls and Punjabs. 'They flew in at 300 feet and you could see the pilots,' explained Deakin. 'It was a ghastly experience.' For the first time, the Indian soldiers asked their commander why no British aircraft was available to protect them. Writing in his diary, Deakin admitted the question 'was difficult to answer.' On that day alone, the bombing raid cost the brigade 60 casualties. At Brigade HQ, where personnel also ran the gauntlet of dive-bombers, the 5/2 Punjabs' commander found a dissatisfied staff grumbling about Divisional HQ's lack of policy and orders. A possible reason was that Murray-Lyon was about to be fired. The following day (Christmas Eve), he was relieved of his duties. After three days, brigade staff experienced another change of senior command with Paris taking over 11th Division and Angus's old boss, Stewart, commanding 12th Indian Infantry Brigade. Major Gairdner became temporary commander of the Argylls. Most of the jocks regretted Stewart's promotion as 'he couldnae be with his ain boys.'

On the 23rd the two battalions moved to Chemor, a tin-mining and rubber-growing area 14 miles south of Kuala Kangsar and seven miles north of Ipoh. Deakin disliked the idea of another night move. 'This was the third time the battalion was made to position itself in the dark,' he complained. Later, the 5/2 Punjab patrols reported that they had encountered enemy soldiers on bicycles. Many Japanese infantrymen travelled in this way, often acquiring a bike and spare parts en route. If a soldier's bicycle tyre suffered a puncture and he had no time to repair it, he carried on cycling nonetheless. When the tyre disintegrated, he pedalled on the metal wheels which made a terrible din on the asphalt road. Cycling in parties of 40 to 50, riding three abreast, they chatted and laughed as if they were heading for a football match. Travelling as lightly as they could they wore green, grey, khaki, or white, some in baggy trousers while others favoured shorts. Their head coverings were felt hats, caps, eye shades, or even a piece of cloth tied round the head.

Christmas Eve marked the British Imperial forces' struggle to hang on to central Malaya. It was essential to retain the states of Perak, Selangor, Negri Sembilan, and Pahang, as they provided security for Singapore. However, this region was harder than the north to defend because much of the ground was open. Nevertheless, central Malaya had obstacles for the invader like wide rivers such as the Perak, Bernan and Selangor. While Japan's aim was to press farther south and take Singapore, the British employed delaying tactics in an attempt to stall the enemy until reinforcements arrived. Knowing how tired the British troops were from having to fight for more than two weeks without rest or adequate equipment, General Yamashita strengthened his forces by adding an extra Division and engaging two more in the west. He also arranged for air raids to increase.

Positioned at Chemor, 12th Indian Infantry Brigade aimed to hold the Japanese on the Perak River's west bank by guarding the main road and railway. On Christmas Eve, the troops rested and celebrated with delicacies from Ipoh. While they celebrated, the enemy pasted posters claiming Japan wanted to free Asians from British rule and distributed pamphlets in Chinese, Malay and English with scurrilous accusations against the white race. On Boxing Day, the brigade faced the inexperienced, but numerically superior, Japanese Imperial Guards Division. In spite of their weariness, the Argylls and two Indian battalions fought well. However, nobody, least of all Arthur Percival, was under any illusion as to the reality of the brigade's situation. Percival wrote: 'The 12th Indian Infantry Brigade on the main road front, however, had now been in action continuously for twelve days. The men had fought well and knew it, and their morale was unbroken, but their condition was like that of troops who have had twelve strenuous days of manoeuvres under foul conditions. Tired troops against fresh troops, inspired by success and capable of exploiting to the full the mobility conferred on them by their ability to live on the country, to eat its rice, and to move on its cycles; fighting blind against an enemy in possession of detailed information of our strengths, movements and dispositions and enjoying also the advantages of freedom of the seas and supremacy of the air. That was the picture.'

To see the Japanese soldier is to realise that much of his equipment was second-rate, often commandeered as he progressed down the country. He either drove a car or truck with a local number plate or rode a bicycle, and when it rained he produced an efficient mackintosh cape with a hood. This was his only standard uniform. As for his cooking, he used light gear and lived off the country, collecting rice, fowl and vegetables from villages. Each man possessed a cigarette tin with a loop of wire attached. After cutting a stick, he hung the tin from the wire and boiled his rice over a communal fire and added a small can of fish or concentrated food to his meal. Others consumed rice alone but, whatever they ate, it only took half an hour to produce and eat.

The brigade now fought in the Kinta Valley in open terrain suitable for artillery; it was their good fortune the Japanese were not so good at this form of weaponry. When the enemy attacked the brigade's right flank on 27 December the Punjabs' A, B and C Companies engaged in hand-to-hand fighting. Although the Japanese also suffered heavy casualties caused by British artillery, brigade staff were troubled at the prospect of having to leave behind the dead and wounded. Battalion commanders were well aware of the troops' fatigue. The men had had little rest since the night of the 19 to 20 December at Kuala Kangsar. Since that date they had been in constant touch with the enemy, fighting every day but one. Brigadier Paris, as temporary Divisional Commander, was also concerned. An eye witness wrote: 'The troops were very tired. Constant enemy air attacks prevented them from obtaining any sleep by day. By night they either had to move, obtaining such sleep as was possible in crowded lorries, or were compelled to prepare yet another defensive position. The resultant physical strain of day and night fighting, of nightly moves or work, and the consequent lack of sleep was cumulative and finally reached the limit of endurance. Officers and men moved like automata and often could not grasp the simplest order.'

The young Argylls' officer, Gordon Smith, longed for a proper night's sleep and 'to stop the killing, go home and be normal.' If front-line troops were engaged at night fighting or preparing a defensive position, the brigade staff were also extremely busy. Whereas a jock might be able to snatch 40 winks, commanders found it much more difficult, and progressively so, the higher the rank the officer held.

To stem the enemy's advance south, Paris ordered the brigade to guard the northern approach to Kampar situated some miles farther south; the newly-formed British battalion (the Leicesters and East Surreys), the Gurkhas and companies from the Federated Malay States Volunteer Force, prepared a defence of Kampar. Brigadier Paris hoped that, with the move from Chemor to Gopeng and Dipang situated south of Ipoh, 12th Indian Infantry Brigade would have three days respite. But it was not to be. The Japanese followed up rapidly and on the afternoon of the 28th, disaster struck. By 3 p.m., the 5/2 Punjabs withdrew, 30 men to a lorry, and fell in behind the Argylls and Hyderabads so they could rest. The men were exhausted but unable to nod off; continuous attacks from the air rattled the Indian troops especially when enemy planes descended to the level of the tree-tops and took aim. The Indian soldiers realised the RAF would never appear and stopped asking. Before noon on the same day, Japanese mortars pounded the Hyderabads and two hours later enemy patrols managed to reached their forward Companies. The idea was to withdraw from Gopeng, allow the Japanese to occupy the town that night and shoot them with artillery early the next morning but the enemy pipped them to the post. Battle commenced and raged on until mid-afternoon when the Japanese, supported by eight tanks, launched an attack against the tired Argylls, who were unprepared and without anti-tank backup. Although the tanks failed to break through the brigade's defence, the Argylls were forced back on to the 5/2 Punjabs.

Morale in12th Indian Infantry Brigade fell to an all-time low; the troops had contended with increased enemy artillery, greater air activity and Japanese tank assaults. Although the brigade held the enemy at bay for 48 hours they'd no alternative but to withdraw to Bidor. The retreat began before noon on 29 December, but ended at 6:15 p.m. 'in the midst of terrible confusion.' Major Gairdner and the rest of his battalion 'were coming back in confusion and some panic amongst the troops was discernible,' wrote Deakin. In their disorderly retreat, the Argylls had brought with them two of the Punjabs' forward Companies. Panic was spreading and Deakin, his second-in-command and Captain Luck, an officer in the 5/2 Punjabs, had to stop any further withdrawal of the men at the point of their revolvers. 'It was heart-breaking after the battalion had found its battle legs for it to break at Dipang. The only excuse is the weariness of the men and the bad example set by the other two battalions, including a British one [he meant the Argylls]. It was panic that caused them to break and not the number of casualties, which were relatively few.'

That afternoon, as it passed through Dipang, the leading Japanese tank fired shots at Stewart's Brigade HQ, which stood 1,000 yards south of the hamlet. The brigade intelligence officer, Lieutenant Gordon Shiach, driving towards the invading tank, was shot in the groin: he died a month later in Singapore's Alexandria Hospital. Now the brigade, 'which had so doggedly borne the brunt of the attacks by the greater part of the Japanese 5th Division, withdrew to Bidor,' explained Woodburn Kirby in his official history of the campaign. The 5/2 Punjabs were delighted now to receive anti-aircraft Bofors, the first time anything had been done to counteract the enemy in the air.

Ian Morrison of the press visited Stewart's HQ. From the time the Argylls began their training in Singapore and South Malaya, Stewart made use of press publicity. He liked his lads to be photographed in the jungle, on parade and on route marches through the local kampongs. The meeting between Ian Morrison and Angus might have looked like an old boy's reunion: both were old Wykehamists, the same age, and keen athletes who had competed against each other in house rowing contests. Morrison appeared at a critical time for 12th Indian Infantry Brigade, now famous for its staying power and its ferocious attempts at delaying the superior Japanese forces. He saw himself how overworked the staff were at Brigade HQ, providing instructions for dispatch riders, communicating with staff at divisional HQ and disseminating orders to brigade battalions and companies, sitting in on conferences between the commanders, not to mention providing instruction to teams of men responsible for transport, equipment, ammunition and rations from one place to another and over a huge area. Perhaps Morrison was thinking of Angus when he wrote the following. 'Tired and worn after several days of pretty continuous action, but still amazingly cheerful, they were drawn from the oldest families in Scotland...When I hear people inveighing against the degeneracy of my contemporaries, especially those contemporaries who come from the old families of England and have been to the old schools, I like to think of those young officers of the Argylls.'

Many Argylls' officers came from old Scottish families: my uncle, the Colonel, David Boyle of D Company, Angus Rose, and his cousin Michael Bardwell of B Company. Morrison wanted to talk to the men, so he could counter false rumours and write encouraging words about the campaign. Captain 'Bal' Hendry was top of his list and Sergeant-Major Bing, who had taken on a number of Japanese soldiers at a railway station. After a hand-to-hand fight, when not only fists but also teeth were used, Hendry finished off a couple by beating them senseless with his army hat while Bing grabbed the barrel of his tommy gun and used its handle to club a few more.

In the evening on 30 December, Deakin asked Brigade HQ about the summaries of evidence on men charged with cowardice but the staff told him they had no time to deal with them. As brigade-major, Angus was responsible for disciplinary issues such as these. The brigade bussed 25 miles south to Bidor for three days' rest which turned out to be only two. To get from A to B, the troops either marched or rode in a lorry driven by the Royal Australian Service Corps whose drivers were older men (often Great War veterans) who were fearless, dedicated and cheerful. In March 1942 Ian Stewart, in a broadcast from Bombay after he escaped to India, stressed that motorised transport did not mean that the troops had an easy time. 'It usually meant six hours in the dark to do 20 miles, for the traffic congestion on the roads at night was simply dreadful.'

At Hogmanay, the Argylls celebrated with a slap-up dinner when officers and men drank whisky, quaffed champagne, and ate tinned ham and chocolate. They even improvised a concert in a Chinese school. On the last day of the year, the battalions received a special mail delivery when letters and news bulletins, dated 15 December, arrived from Port Dickson. Missives from friends and loved ones had been sorely missed and the absence of communication from the outside world had been bad for troop morale. Not one soldier had seen or read a newspaper since operations began in the second week of December.

Before the New Year, Percival and Heath decided 'to hold the Kampar position' for as long as possible so their forces would not fall back behind the Kuala Kubu road junction before 14 January. It was essential to delay the enemy as far as possible from Singapore before the reinforcements arrived. The market town of Kampar was where they would do it. Their position lay on either side of a steep, wooded hill called Bujang Melaka, covering an area of nine miles by six and stretching south from Dipang between the main road and another thoroughfare. To the north was an open tin mining area and on the south-west lay a rubber plantation. The vulnerability of the position was that from Telok Anson in the west, enemy forces could make a sea landing and bring their small boats up the Perak River which flowed into the Indian Ocean. Paris put the brigade in reserve with orders to prepare positions at Bidor for the troops defending Kampar to retreat through. The brigade had to keep an eye out also for attacks from the coast particularly in the Telok Anson area, fifteen miles west of the Argylls' position up the Perak River. Early on 2 January, the Japanese infiltrated the countryside around Telok Anson. 1st Independent Infantry Company and two Argyll armoured cars forced them to withdraw. 'Bal' Hendry and the Argylls' A Company positioned themselves south-east of Telok Anson but by 8:15 a.m. they were in danger of being outflanked by the enemy so they withdrew. That afternoon, yet again the Japanese attacked the brigade with fighter planes and bombers. Enemy fire did not discriminate. A number of senior officers had already been killed or wounded in battle so that when Paris became Divisional Commander, he had to replace several brigadiers as the original ones were either dead or in hospital. There was a sigh of relief when the day was over. The men could eat at last, since food was only brought to them in darkness, and although there was a full moon that night, aircraft were absent as the Japanese were not night-flyers. The next morning the bombing began again with a vengeance. It was the worst the soldiers had ever experienced. 'This ceaseless air activity and heavy casualties were visibly affecting morale and consequently lowering the battalion's resistance to enemy ground attack, which was bound to come by the evening.'

At 8 p.m. the attack began. Deakin was amazed that some Japanese had not only managed to cross the river but had also negotiated the neighbouring swamps. 'It seems that no natural obstacle will ever stop a Japanese soldier. A number of them had climbed the trees that bordered the road and made things very unpleasant for the troops.' On 3 January, the Argylls, under heavy bombing, successfully leap-frogged their Companies back before the advancing Japanese. Finally, on that night 11th Indian Division withdrew from Kampar. As a reserve, the brigade, including the Argylls, covered the defenders' retreat until 11 p.m. In darkness, the exhausted Argylls, Punjabs, and Hyderabads, headed 20 miles south for Slim River, where they stopped at the village of Trolak. It had been an exhausting 25 days. Angus was on the move from 10 December until 3 January as his brigade withdrew 176 miles from northern Malaya to the central region. With no air support, the brigade had been subject to intermittent air attacks. With the Prince of Wales and the Repulse destroyed, the Japanese now controlled the sea around Malaya and were free to infiltrate the country via its estuaries and rivers. Because of swift enemy action, Brigade HQ had to be set up and struck frequently. Angus may not have earned a high profile during this part of the campaign unlike Captain Bobby Kennard of C Company, who ambushed the enemy on the remote road north of Grik, or the intrepid

'Bal' Hendry and Sergeant Bing, or even David Boyle with his un-blooded D Company, who caused considerable damage to the Japanese at Sumpitan on the Grik road. But Angus's role as brigade-major was vital, requiring a particular flair that embodied courage, versatility, and sangfroid, as well as meticulous consistency.

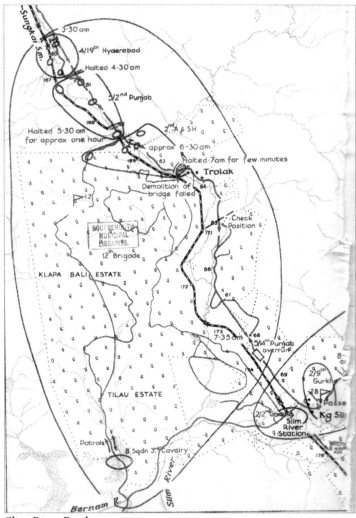

Slim River Battle

BLUE HILLS on the horizon and in the foreground, a wide river, its banks crowded by palm and jungle creeper; on the left, a narrow track encroached on either side by thick, lush vegetation: this is Slim River, an hour's drive north of Kuala Lumpur and a stone's throw from Malaysia's north-south highway. The small town situated in Perak, Malaysia's central state, owes its name to an eighteenth-century Englishman who mistook the local river for the Perak and got hopelessly lost while trying to navigate it. Surrounded today by palm and rubber estates, the locality attracts visitors to its waterfalls, theme park, and hot springs. With a temperature of 104°C, they are reputedly the fifth hottest springs in the world.

On New Year's Day 1942, before they departed from Kampar, the personnel of 12th Indian Infantry Brigade felt the heat when Stewart called a conference for staff and commanding officers to discuss whether Trolak, a few miles north of Slim River, was a strong defensive position. While the brigadier and brigade-major thought it was, the battalion commanding officers were unhappy and not keen on the positions allocated their troops. Slim River was crucial for the British. When Percival and Heath visited the brigade on 31 December, they informed Stewart and his staff that British troops must hold on to ground north of Kuala Lumpur and protect the airstrips of Malaya's capital and at Port Swettenham until 16 January when ground (the British 18th Division) and air reinforcements were expected to arrive. Although Slim River had natural strengths as a defensive position, the problem for 11th Division was that the Japanese, now arriving in numbers on Malaya's west coast, might make a landing between Kuala Selangor and Port Swettenham. From here, they could advance towards Kuala Lumpur, south of Slim River, and block the British line of retreat.

As 12th and 28th Indian Infantry Brigades took up their positions in the Slim River area in the early hours of 4 January, 12th

Indian Infantry Brigade appointed 3rd, 6th, and 15th Brigades to cover them, after which these troops advanced to the mouth of the Selangor River. Meanwhile, Heath sent Indian and volunteer groups to guard the coast at Kuala Selangor, a move which helped scotch a Japanese landing on 2 January. Most senior officers believed the Slim River area was an excellent position. Thick jungle and high mountains covered the east side while on the west was more jungle, behind which lay a dangerous swamp that extended as far as the coast. The ground was an excellent anti-tank obstacle as a narrow corridor 20 to 30 miles long, ran from Sungkei to Rawang. Stewart claimed this natural feature 'was designed to force the enemy into defiles on the road and railway, thus allowing economy of troops on our part, and a concentration of targets for our powerful artillery; in the case of the rear battalion, it was to take advantage of the good lateral communication to meet any wide encircling move through the jungle, as soon as it should emerge.'

Nevertheless the area needed two separate forces to defend it: the first, at Trolak in the north, where the road and railway ran parallel and close to each other, and the second at Slim River as the road looped east for about five miles and did not rejoin the railway until it reached Tanjong Malim ten miles south. If there was any hope of the enemy desisting from its air strikes, it was soon dashed. The Japanese Zero and Oscar fighters ruled the skies, 'bombing and machine-gunning the Indian troops all the time.' The day the brigade arrived at Trolak, the Japanese bombed and machine-gunned Tanjong Malim, where Paris set up his Divisional HQ, and destroyed several vehicles on convoy duty. The following day at Trolak, enemy aircraft bombed and machine-gunned the jungle bordering the road and railway even when there were no visible targets. There were few casualties, but the attacks had a demoralising effect on the soldiers, as Deakin confirms: 'I found a most lethargic lot of men who seemed to want to do nothing but sit in slit trenches. They said they could not sleep because of the continued enemy air attacks. In fact, they were thoroughly depressed. There was no movement on the road, and the deadly ground silence emphasised by the blanketing effect of the jungle was getting on the men's nerves. The airmen could not see the troops but knew they were there and continually attacked the road and railway areas in which the defences were sited.'

On 5 January the troops prepared their defences but, to avoid attack from the air, they worked at night. 'However,' wrote Deakin, 'the battalion was dead tired, most of all the commanders whose responsibilities prevented them from snatching even a fitful sleep. They had withdrawn 176 miles in three weeks and had had only three days' rest. The battalion had suffered 250 casualties of which a high proportion had been killed. The spirit of the men was low, and the battalion had lost fifty per cent of its fighting efficiency.' That afternoon, a large group of Japanese advanced down the railway line towards the Hyderabad's Ahir Company, which held its fire and then inflicted 150 casualties on the enemy. Here, for the first time during the campaign, Angus is mentioned in Major General S. Woodburn Kirby's *The War Against Japan, Volume 1*, not by name but by rank. The Hyderabads' left forward company grew nervous, which prompted their commander to request permission to withdraw. As Stewart was absent from Brigade HQ, Angus, as chief-of-staff, granted the company their request. However, when Stewart returned he reversed Angus's decision.

By the morning of the 6th, the brigade had made ready their defences including the erection of wire and tank obstacles. Later that day, some Tamils on their way south reported that they had seen at Sungkei, eight miles north, a column of 'iron land-ships.' The ever-optimistic Stewart believed they were lorries. The 11th Division's two northernmost brigades took up delaying positions; Stewart's 12th at Trolak to the north, and Selby's 28th in the south at Kampong Slim and along the river as far as Slim River Bridge. Stewart positioned his three battalions in the following order along the seven-and-a-half mile sector: 4/19 Hyderabads, the lead battalion, at milestone 60; 5/2 Punjabs behind them at milestones 61 and 62; and the Argylls to the rear in a rubber plantation along an estate road at right angles to the trunk road, less than a mile north of Trolak bridge. The Hyderabads' sector was 3½ miles long. A Company went astride the railway, C Company astride the road and B Company to the rear on a track between the railway and the road. The Hyderabads were weak. The young, undertrained troops were unsettled by their long retreat. Their commanding officer, Lieutenant Colonel Wilson-Haffenden, had been wounded in an air attack on the 3rd, and their rifle companies now numbered only three. On the plus side, they had anti-tank guns, concrete blocks, barbed wire and had dug slit trenches. Stewart ordered the road in the 5/2 Punjabs' sector (positioned to the rear of the Hyderabads) to remain undamaged so that carriers and armoured cars might access the Hyderabads farther forward. 24 anti-tank mines went to the 5/2 Punjabs and, for additional support, they received a single troop of anti-tank guns and a battery from the 137th Field Regiment. The remainder of this battalion was positioned in the Cluny rubber estate between Slim River Station and Slim River Bridge. Brigade HQ was west of the railway and road in the Klapa Bali estate nearly two miles west of Trolak village, as was the Argylls' battalion HQ, on a plantation track off the road. After the battle, Brigade HQ's position was criticised. To avoid attack from the air, Stewart had chosen a secluded location but it prevented the commander and his staff from seeing properly what was happening.

Angus's decision to withdraw the Hyderabad Company on 5 January was wise as Major Brown, acting commander of 4/19 Hyderabads, rang Brigade HQ to say that A Company had noticed that the Japanese were attempting to outflank the battalion on the east side of the road and railway. A havildar (a non-commissioned officer in the Indian Army equivalent to a sergeant) from Deakin's battalion had also seen the enemy close by, so the commander advised Stewart that they should withdraw. Because Brigadier Paris, positioned at Divisional HQ, suspected the enemy were trying to work their way around 12th Indian Infantry Brigade at Trolak, he planned to withdraw the 12th behind 28th Indian Infantry Brigade on the night of 6 to 7 January, and leave the 28th for another night's rest, before they took up positions north of

Slim River at noon on the 7th.

As a result of the Japanese 42nd Infantry Regiment's failure to rout 12th Indian Infantry Brigade down the railway on 5 January, their colonel prepared a deliberate assault. He told his battalion commanders that on 7 January, a section of his troops would advance through the jungle around the enemy's right flank towards Trolak. The rest of the regiment would attack down the road with tanks. Their commander, Major Shimada, persuaded Colonel Ando to launch the attack that night. As 12th Indian Infantry Brigade settled in for the night of 6 January, the Argylls' B Company, billeted in huts once belonging to Tamil estate workers, tried to rest. They washed their clothes, swam in the river and ate stew and drank hot, sweet tea but were harassed by enemy planes. The Argylls had suffered 25% casualties – 250 men including 13 officers – and had received no replacements, unlike the Japanese who brought up fresh troops every 36 hours. Although Stewart under-estimated the report that Japanese tanks were approaching, he decided to play it safe and have his two forward battalions (4/19 Hyderabads and 5/2 Punjabs) complete their withdrawal by first light the next morning. For added security, he also ordered his reserve battalion, the 5/14 Punjabs, to position themselves south of Trolak village at the same hour.

Within hours of the battle's commencement, reinforcements arrived: seasoned Argylls and 30 to 40 new men, whose short training in Singapore was to serve as a bulwark against the rigours that were to follow. Amongst the veterans were Captain David Drummond Hay, a convivial, affable fellow, tough Platoon Sergeant Major Jimmy Love, who fought tigerishly in C Company up the lonely Kroh-Grik road, and Lieutenant Kenneth McLeod: some recently recovered from wounds received earlier in the campaign; others were 'milked,' taken from the battalion for non-combat duties in Singapore.

At midnight on 6 January, the 4/19 Hyderabads began their withdrawal and shortly afterwards, their forward companies came into contact with soldiers from the Japanese 42nd Infantry Regiment on the road. British artillery and mortars met the enemy attack. By 3 am., and in brilliant moonlight, a column of 30 Japanese tanks, followed by infantry in lorries, attacked straight down the trunk road. Nobody in their wildest dreams had conceived of a tank attack at night (not even in Russia or the North African desert was this form of assault considered) but during the early hours of 7th January, Japanese tanks performed this feat at Trolak. The procession was too fast to enable an observation officer of each forward company to alert in time other units. The tanks made mincemeat of the obstacles before them and within 20 minutes had crashed through barbed wire barriers, removed concrete cylinders serving as roadblocks ,and put out of action the battalion's anti-tank guns. Still in the dark, the tanks blazed away unimpeded, with enemy infantry following them. While the quartermaster and some drivers from the beleaguered Indian battalion threw grenades at the column, most of the men from the remaining Companies were cut off in the jungle on either side of the road and were never seen again. Rab Kerr, an Argyll writing after the end of the war, claimed that as the Hyderabads withdrew in trucks and tracked vehicles, they noticed to their horror that their last vehicles, were not Bren carriers but enemy tanks. Stewart's plan was to have a row of half-sawn trees dropped across the road immediately after the last tracked vehicle had passed through and, while clearing the obstacles, the enemy would come under heavy fire. However, in the pitch dark the Japanese tanks drove through before the roadblock of fallen trees could be implemented. After the battle, Stewart admitted that he was culpable for failing to employ anti-tank measures like road-cratering and the laying of mines. The acting brigade commander's response was that his forward Indian battalion had sufficient tank obstacles in front.

The leading 20-ton medium tanks advanced at 10 to 20 yard intervals and had .303 machine guns and a light mortar, which fired indiscriminately to one side. Behind these came light tanks, each armed with one .303 machine gun. The vehicles' speed was between 3 and 6 miles per hour although they could reach 28 mph. Their machine gun and cannon fire were intense but ineffective except against targets actually on the road. Major Shimada may well have suspected that 12th Indian Infantry Brigade's forward battalion was a cinch, but he was under no illusion that the other two would fall away so easily. At 4:30 a.m., just over an hour after the tanks made their first contact, the column halted. Stewart had seen to it that the Punjab's foremost defended locality (D Company north of milestone 61) was mined. Fierce fighting followed when the Japanese leapt out of trucks and fought Deakin's Indian soldiers, who destroyed three tanks but no anti-tank artillery was available to exploit the situation. When the Japanese came under attack and felt threatened, they began to shout and yell, employing a fearsome noise to intimidate the enemy. One moment the night was still but the next, all hell broke loose. Men yelled, automatics fired, engines roared, tins clattered. It was nerve-shattering. Deakin writes: 'The din which followed belies description. The tanks were head-to-tail, engines roaring, crews screaming, machine guns spitting tracer, and mortars and cannon firing all out. The platoon astride the cutting threw grenades, and one tank had its track smashed by an anti-tank rifle. The two anti-tank guns fired two rounds, one of which scored a bull, and then retired to the Argylls' area. One more tank wrecked itself on the mines.'

Today, local inhabitants claim the area is haunted and individuals report that they have heard wailing and yelling, particularly at night. The Punjabs stalled the enemy until he discovered several loop roads which, before the Public Works Department straightened the thoroughfare, had been part of the main road. Using these loops, now obscured by jungle and tall grass, the Japanese outflanked the defenders. It is unclear how the invaders knew about these detours. Some claim they were included on Japanese maps but not on the British, which suggests that enemy agents were active in gathering information for some time before the invasion.

Although the Punjabs' reserve company held back the enemy for an hour, it was encircled at 6:30 a.m., when the Japanese discovered the second disused road loop. In sum, this brave Indian battalion managed to delay their adversary for two hours not only through the support of a couple of minefields, an anti-tank battery and a few anti-tank rifles, but through their determination to fight on until the end of their moral and material resources.

The third battalion to stand in the enemy's way (the Argylls) was unable to take advantage of the delay. Communications broke down shortly after dawn, so there was nobody to say what was going on. This meant that the gunners could not shore up the trapped tanks in the Punjabs' sector. Dispatch riders and field telephones failed to operate for several hours and wireless links rarely existed below brigade level. Deakin rang Brigade HQ to report that the Japanese had penetrated the Hyderabads and pushed back his leading company. But by 5 a.m., when the railway bridge was blown, the telephone wires were cut in the forward area. Back at Brigade HQ, Stewart knew only that the 5/2 Punjabs' most forward company had halted the enemy. News of the battle had not reached units further south, including the Argylls. Stewart ordered Deakin to 'hang on at all costs,' the Argylls to erect road blocks at Trolak and the 5/14 Punjabs to move forward to milestone 65. As the Argylls were about to eat their breakfast, they saw the Indian troops streaming towards them. It was 6:30 a.m., before contact was made with Paris at Divisional HQ on 12th Indian Infantry Brigade's unreliable wireless, by which time the two forward battalions were overrun. The acting divisional commander sent his principal staff officer, Lieutenant Colonel Arthur Harrison, to find out what he could. Travelling up to Slim River in his brand new Ford V8 he collided with a tank at Cluny estate. Fortunately, before Harrison set out, he had sent a message to Brigadier Selby of 28th Indian Infantry Brigade to deploy his troops immediately. The latter also received a visit from an officer from 12th Indian Infantry Brigade (since Angus was Harrison's counterpart at Brigade HQ, it could have been him) informing him of the bad news.

Although Angus was not fighting, he worked in a dangerous place at Brigade HQ situated 1¾ miles west of Trolak village. At 9:30 a.m., the enemy attacked on the west flank close to Brigade

HQ. For either side, bagging a brigadier and his staff was a feat worth considering; in his undercover activities behind enemy lines on the west coast, Angus Rose ambushed a Japanese brigadier in his car. Staff officers, especially when contacting in person forward companies or carrying orders, were especially vulnerable as was the case with intelligence officer Gordon Shiach, machine-gunned by a tank at Gopeng-Dipang. Angus was having a very difficult time trying to contact combat troops and Divisional HQ. Much equipment from 11th Division signals was already lost during the retreat. The only means of communication between Divisional and Brigade HQs was the telegraph line along the railway but this was cut when the railway bridge was blown up over Slim River and it remained out of action during the battle. The alternative was to use dispatch riders on motor bikes but they were often too slow within the swiftness of the battle situation.

By now it was daylight. At 6:30 a.m. four medium tanks reached the first road block and swept it aside. 'Our chaps could do nothing. They just looked helplessly at the passing tanks which were firing hard; a few threw grenades,' reported an officer. The column proceeded straight down the road and at 7 a.m., it reached the second road block at Trolak, where armoured cars and anti-tank rifles checked it, but not before it knocked out two cars and smashed the roadblock. There were further problems for the Argylls. The sappers failed to reach the Trolak bridge in time to demolish it. A number of Argylls gathered at the bridge, where more enemy tanks and infantry arrived at 9 a.m., and destroyed the remaining armoured cars and carriers. For two long hours, the Scots fought bravely for the bridge. Finally, as the demolition charges failed and they found no sappers to blow it up, the jocks blockaded the bridge with an armoured car, but the bridge fell intact to the enemy.

In spite of all the tumult, the ever-optimistic Stewart informed Selby, whose HQ farther south was on a gentle slope and promised better wireless reception, that the situation was serious but not critical, and that he would withdraw his brigade at noon. As for Paris ten miles south of the river, he only learned at 8:30 a.m.

that tanks had broken through the Trolak sector but by that time they had almost reached Slim Road bridge. By 8:30 am., the Argylls B and C companies and HQ reassembled near Trolak but within half an hour, more Japanese tanks and infantry arrived, so the Highland regiment established a perimeter 200 yards south of Trolak. By this time, Stewart was in touch only with the Argylls D Company positioned on the estate road. After ordering them to delay the Japanese advance, the enemy surrounded D Company and most officers and men were killed or captured. Later in the morning, Lieutenant Colonel Robertson, now commanding officer of the Argylls, ordered his men to push through the jungle towards Slim River. Few men from B and C Companies ever rejoined their battalion. Dozens lost their way, died of disease, were captured after being betrayed by Tamils or killed. Robertson was eventually ambushed and killed. The surviving Argylls and men from the other battalions retreated towards Kampong Slim, while the tank column and Japanese infantry bludgeoned their way towards Slim River Station, then followed the road that looped eastward towards Slim River Bridge. As the Argylls fought on, Brigadier Selby made his way to 12th Indian Infantry Brigade's HQ, its isolated position hard to reach. Trolak would have been better but this was where Paris had established his HQ before moving to Tanjong Malim, and Stewart was reluctant to make another move as his staff were tired. The tanks moved steadily forward at walking pace, mowing down the unprepared 5/14 Punjabs then the 2/1 Gurkhas, until the 155th Field Regiment halted them at 9:30 a.m., two miles south of Slim River Bridge.

While the tanks rampaged slowly south, Stewart re-established his HQ close to Selby's on a hill near Kampong Slim but at midday tanks shot at them. Sometime after noon, 25 bedraggled Argylls, separated from their battalion, scrambled through the jungle and reached Brigade HQ where they found Stewart, Angus, and Lieutenant Ian Gordon (an Argyll on the brigade staff). Later, Donald Napier arrived with a dozen men. The Japanese were still very active close by, but with his customary sangfroid, Stewart told the men 'to pay no attention to these people. They are firing any old where.' Together, Stewart, Selby and Lieutenant Colonel Harrison decided that the remnants of the two brigades should hold out until nightfall by which time they could withdraw across Slim River and retreat down the railway line to Tanjong Malim. Before they made their retreat, the two brigadiers held a perimeter around their HQs and collected stragglers. All transport north of the river was destroyed. In the evening, swathes of tired and hungry troops crossed the Slim River, trudged down the railway line and arrived at Tanjong Malim at midnight where transport was waiting to drive them south. Others staggered in to Tanjong Malim during the early hours of the next morning.

The Argylls' survivors of Slim River numbered fewer than 100 (4 officers and 90 other ranks) from the original 576. They were mainly from Donald Napier's A Company and the transport section. It had taken the Japanese 6 hours with a Company of 30 tanks, an infantry battalion, motor transport and engineers (with the rest of the tank battalion and remaining 2 infantry battalions in reserve) to cover 9 miles and wreak mayhem amongst 11th Division's 2 northernmost brigades. With the withdrawal of the remaining troops from these brigades came the loss of the Division's transport, guns and the equipment of 2 field batteries and 2 troops of anti-tank guns. The Japanese also captured a month's supplies for 2 brigades, 50 light armoured cars including Bren gun carriers, many vehicles of great value to the transport-starved Japanese, sixteen 25-pounders and 7 anti-tank guns. Additionally, valuable sappers, gunners and medical personnel were captured.

Slim River was a major disaster. 12th Indian Infantry Brigade was annihilated – on 8 January, the Hyderabads could only account for 3 officers and 110 men; with Deakin, their commanding officer, captured, the 5/2 Punjabs were left with 1 officer and 60 men. Two-thirds of 28th Indian Infantry Brigade was destroyed, their 2/1 Gurkhas decimated. Of 12th Indian Infantry Brigade's personnel who were lost in the jungle, 14 officers and 409 men escaped the Japanese and returned to British lines: 800 were killed, 1,200 captured and 2,000 went missing, many of whom were captured. Of the 576 Argylls, 40 died in the jungle, 75 were killed, 30 reached Sumatra, 300 were captured and 94 returned to British lines weeks later. The number of Japanese casualties was a fraction of the losses suffered by the British and Indians. The battle of Slim River lost central Malaya to the Japanese and threatened the British chances of holding northern Johore long enough for reinforcements to arrive.

Above all, 11th Division ceased to be effective.

There were many reasons for the disaster. It is obvious that Japanese tanks caused much of the problem. Neither Paris nor Stewart were present at the battles of Asun or Jitra farther north where tanks were used by the enemy. These officers underrated them and their potential in thickly wooded terrain. Tanks were not involved along the rugged Grik road where 12th Indian Infantry Brigade earned its reputation. After the end of the war, Stewart wrote that he had never taken part in an exercise of co-ordinated anti-tank defence. The use of tanks on a road at night was a surprise but it was not the first time that the Japanese had employed this measure.

Other factors contributed to the defeat. Communications broke down so that the rear brigade defending the Slim River area was unaware that the Japanese had engaged with the forward battalion of 12th Indian Infantry Brigade. Brigade HQ was positioned well off the main road, so they lost touch with the situation. There was also a failure to make full use of anti-tank weapons. 11th Division possessed an anti-tank regiment and 1,400 anti-tank mines, yet 12th Indian Infantry Brigade only possessed one troop of anti-tank guns, 24 anti-tank mines and a few concrete obstacles. The brigade had a field regiment and, although it could not be used to support the forward infantry Companies because of the wooded country, there was no attempt to use it in an anti-tank role. Added to all of this, the brigade relied too much on demolitions as a delaying factor, yet in some cases bridges were not successfully blown up. Above all, some proportion of the blame should go to Percival, who paid a heavy price for not swopping an exhausted Division with fresh troops, namely his 9th Division positioned at Singapore and in Johore. Afraid of exposing these areas to attack if the forces were moved, Percival kept them in reserve. But 12th Indian Infantry Brigade was exhausted and at the limit of its endurance. It had little time to adjust its defences to the demands of the different terrain at Slim River, and the hasty manning of Slim River failed to protect them against armoured attack. While the British and Indian troops stuck to the tracks, estates, and trunk road south, the Japanese exploited this area by bombing them, firing into jungles and plantations on both sides of the roads, and by occupying the crossroads and road junctions.

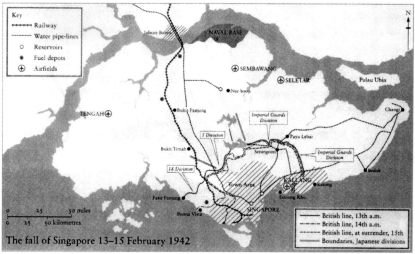

Singapore before Surrender

ON THE MORNING of 13 January, the brigade departed by train for Singapore where, after a month of frantic fighting, they settled back in Tyersall Park. A poignant moment for the survivors came on their first Sunday when 100 officers and men, mainly Argylls, assembled in the gym with the families of those who failed to return. In amongst the ropes and fitness tackle they held a simple service when Colonel Stewart read from the New Testament and Lieutenant Donald Napier accompanied the sombre group on the piano as they sang the *Old Hundredth* and fortieth psalms.

If Angus expected a slackening of pace in his duties, he was mistaken. On his first day back, he discovered that his old boss, lost to 11th Division for the past three weeks, was returning. Once again, Percival had re-shuffled his pack of senior command, replacing Paris with Major General Key. At this stage Heath advised Percival, who stressed the move was not due to a lack of confidence in Paris, but that an Indian Army officer was needed to re-establish confidence in what remained of the 11th Indian Division. Ian Stewart thus relinquished his post as brigade Commander and returned to command the Argylls while the brigade left 11th Division and reverted to its original reserve role. For Angus, the change of bosses presented a similar challenge to that which a civil servant meets after a general election when Ministers from an out-going government are replaced by the incoming one. We'll never know if Angus chafed at his desk job like his close friend Rose, who found his staff appointment at Singapore Fortress not at all to his liking. At this time, Rose became second in command of the battalion while my uncle remained the brigade's chief-of-staff. There was some snobbery about staff appointments. In general, the British Army preferred officers to have experience of both staff and command but unlike the U.S. military, they regarded staff jobs as subordinate to those of command.

A huge amount of reorganisation needed to be done. The battalion wanted back Argyll officers and men employed outside the regiment, for administration and staff appointments, but many were unable to be spared. Yet, they amassed 200 officers and men, swelling the ranks with officers from the Straits Settlement police, the Malayan Civil Services, and some wounded and released from hospital. They salvaged ammunition and pirated vehicles. By the time the Japanese invaded Singapore, the Argylls had 250 men, two 3-inch mortars with 700 rounds, 4 Bren carriers, 6 armoured cars, including a pirated Lanchester (Stirling Castle), machine and tommy guns (the latter good for fighting at close range in jungle and rubber plantations).

From 15 January, they trained hard; efforts to keep the men occupied and entertained, by watching films, participating in sport, and taking limited leave in town, were difficult, with so many lost officers and NCOs. But fun was to be had, and word got around that Singapore fell on pink gins and parties. The allegation was unfair, as higher command and staff officers were abstemious, quiet and conventional. Contrary to popular rumour, the predominant atmosphere in officers' messes and clubs was one of gloom and despondency, which some Argylls did try to expunge in any way possible.

While this was happening, the Japanese constantly strafed and bombed the island. During the second week of January the enemy intensified their daylight raids with the purpose of destroying allied air defences. The loss of the Royal Observer Corps post on the mainland and inadequate radar cover meant the period of warning of an air strike was woefully insufficient. At least 30 minutes were needed to allow the fighter Buffaloes to reach 24,000 feet, the height at which the enemy aircraft flew. During the latter half of January, air attacks increased so much, that by the end of the month the whole allied bomber force had to withdraw to Sumatra.

As many as 27 enemy bombers, escorted by fighters, conducted raids on Singapore at least three times a day. The leader plane would give a signal whereupon each aircraft dropped its bombs simultaneously, which meant that one small area was hit by 200 bombs. These were termed 'diarrhoea' attacks and the blast and splinter were deafening. One officer took the attacks in his stride. Angus Rose, a keen cricketer in his leisure hours, regarded the conflict between the British Imperial Forces and the Japanese as a game. 'He gave the impression that he almost enjoyed it!' wrote Wilson, who recounted Angus's remark after a bomb dropped near them, while they occupied a slit trench, 'Well, that just missed the off stump!'

The purpose of the air raids was to destroy buildings, ground aircraft, and the naval base. To counteract this, newly-arrived Hurricane fighters engaged the Japanese Zeroes. The greatest strain was between 21 and 30 January when convoys bringing reinforcements gained priority; six Buffaloes, supported by bombers and torpedo-bombers, performed the task.

There's no mention of Angus taking part in the withdrawal across the causeway that connects Singapore Island to Johore. Whether or not he lay in a slit trench, trying to avoid bombs raining down on him, we'll never know, nor if he took his place next to Stewart in the Argylls' rearguard, as their commander made the historic retreat across the water to the doomed island. Because the withdrawal was such a significant event, my daughter and I wanted to cross the causeway when we visited Singapore. We boarded an express train. Situated off the expressway east of Keppel harbour, the station building is a monument to early 1930s engineering with each concrete pillar at the entrance dedicated to commerce, industry, and agriculture, aspects of what once made Malaya the industrial diamond of the Empire.

The railway travels north-west until it meets and runs alongside the Upper Bukit Timah Road that merges into Woodlands Road. Farther along the line at Woodlands Point, the train halts at a check point before it traverses the causeway spanning the Johore Straits that separate mainland from island. From the train window, I saw a stream of cars and men on motorbikes flying past and imagined the night in January 1942 when Angus, the Argylls and 30,000 British, Australian, and Indian troops withdrew over this causeway from the mainland.

At a conference on 28 January, Percival put Ian Stewart in

charge of the withdrawal. Much later, Stewart wrote to David Wilson: 'What ought to have been done was to have Archie Paris and 12th Brigade in the job of commanding the whole rearguard, i.e. someone with a proper staff.' All Stewart had were a few trusty Argylls and marines like Lieutenant Jock Hayes, who were ordered to find a flotilla of boats and small craft for a quick getaway if the enemy scotched their plan. From his HQ in a bungalow on a hill overlooking the Straits east of Johore town, Stewart, with Rose and David Wilson as adjutant, arranged an outer perimeter of 4 miles held by the Australian 22nd Brigade and the Gordon Highlanders, while his 250 Argylls managed an inner perimeter, less than a mile in depth. This was risky. Intending to thwart III Corps' retreat, the enemy's aim was to advance inland from the west and, if their plan succeeded, Singapore, with its small garrison, would have to surrender and a costly assault for Japan across the strait could be avoided. But by the end of January, III Corps, albeit minus several units including the entire 22nd Indian Brigade lost in remote jungle on the east coast, reached the northern side of the causeway in south Johore. Writing decades after the event, Wilson remembers his feelings of anticipation as he and his companions prepared their positions two days before the withdrawal. 'We knew we had been given a vital job and for the first time if things went badly wrong we would be Horatius holding the bridge at all costs.'

Built in the early 1920s, the causeway was a gargantuan stone structure with broad foundations that descended many feet below the water's surface. 1,100 yards long and 23 yards wide, it accommodated a road and railway line. For the British and Indian sapper it'd be a nightmare to demolish, although they had gained plenty of experience. These men made elaborate preparations to blow a sizeable hole, sixty yards wide, into the causeway. In the end, the demolition was only partly successful, resulting in a fordable gap of 4 feet at low tide. As it was the largest, most important demolition job of the campaign, personnel from the Royal Navy laid depth charges to destroy the steel road, railway bridge, and pipeline that supplied Singapore's reservoirs.

The weather preceding the withdrawal was beautiful, with brilliant, cloudless days and a waxing moon at night. As the troops assembled on the north side of the causeway, Japanese aircraft rained down British bombs acquired from captured airfields. 'It was a long night for us all,' remarked Lieutenant Hayes, 'We could not believe the Japanese did not understand exactly what we were doing...why didn't they knock hell out of us?' David Wilson compared the cleverly-orchestrated withdrawal to the last act of the Aldershot Tattoo. As darkness fell, trucks, ambulances (Percival, Heath and Bennett rode across in one to observe the event from the Singapore shore), carriers and motorbikes began the exodus. These vehicles passed over with no headlights, as it was a full moon. Next came row upon row of infantry, with the persistent thump of their boots on the asphalt road. The Australians followed and then the Gordon Highlanders. As the sun rose, an Argyll piper stepped up, set his drones astir, and began to play *Blue Bonnets over the Border*. The skirl rose high in the early morning air, as the remarkable strains caught not merely the imaginations of the marching Gordons but their Digger companions also, not to mention the ears of the Japanese. Half an hour after the Australians and Gordons crossed over, the Argylls began their withdrawal to the piping of Charles 'Boy' Stuart and Piper McLean, who played *A Hundred Pipers* and the Argyll quick march, *Hielan' Laddie*. 'They came swinging past behind the bagpipes, mostly small men, I noticed. Hard, dour and as tough as leather, they marched with a long supple stride, and there was an arrogant confidence about them,' wrote Geoffrey Brooke, RM. The Battalion HQ, and Signals followed with Wilson and two platoons of their rearguard, leaving Stewart, Hayes, Tam Slessor, Drummer Hardie and Company Sergeant Major Bing as the final group to withdraw, covered by Harry Nuttall in Stirling Castle with Michael Blackwood. When they were all safely over, Stewart, who made sure he was the last man across, gave the signal for the Indian sappers to blow the causeway and at 8:15 a.m., a colossal explosion was heard all over the island.

They had miraculously succeeded in transferring over all 30,000 men with their vehicles from the mainland. 'Lars Porsena missed his cue and Horatius had to take his bow alone!' wrote Stewart. When Major John Wyett, an Australian officer, asked Stewart why his soldiers marched over to the sound of the pipes, the phenomenal warrior replied, 'When the story of the Argylls is written you will find they go down in history as the last unit to cross the causeway and were piped across by their pipers.' Stewart's aide from the Royal Marines, Jock Hayes, unstinting in his admiration for the Argylls, said. 'If there were to be sticky moments, then there were none with whom I would more gladly have shared them than with those tough, courageous, and business-like officers and men of the Argyll and Sutherland Highlanders. The country does well to honour them.'

From 23 January, a week before the withdrawal, Angus took part in another arrangement: Percival instructed Singapore Fortress commander Keith Simmons, assisted by staff under Paris, liaison officers from III Corps, and 8th Australian Division to make plans for the island's defence. The island, shaped like an overblown rose or an elephant's head, was divided into three parts, south, west, and north: the Australians in the west, the British 18th Division in the north, and the Indians in Command Reserve. At the end of January, 210 Royal Marines, survivors from the Prince of Wales and the Repulse, joined with the 250 remaining Agylls and became one unit, the Plymouth Argylls. The successful union was the inspiration of Lieutenant Colonel Alan Warren RM, who introduced the tommy gun to Malaya for jungle fighting and organised Special Operations Executive (SOE) stay-behind parties on the mainland after the surrender. Having arranged the evacuation of Penang, he now devised a strategy for a major exodus of personnel from Singapore. Warren may have seen a role for the Argylls and Marines in this exercise. With their knowledge of boats and sea craft, the marines would've been useful. During their first week as a combined unit, the Argylls, already acquainted with Singapore Island, showed their new colleagues the areas where they'd most likely be fighting.

Higher Command agonised where and how the enemy would attack. Percival was under no illusion that the Japanese might delay, as speed was their hallmark. In any case they needed to free troops and aircraft for operations elsewhere and open sea routes to the Indian Ocean. Malaya Command was certain that the main offensive would come from the mainland but had little idea as to which side, east or west. The Japanese might even launch an airborne or sea attack; in respect of defence, no part of the island could be neglected. The consensus was that the attack would come from the west as the main communications were on that side. During the first week of February, Australian patrols reported Japanese activity on the mainland's west bank opposite Singapore Island. If the Japanese did invade from the west, they could combine their assault with a seaborne attack via the straits of Malacca. However, they might approach from Mersing down Johore River and attack the Changi area on the north-east side of the island. Percival believed the enemy would come from this side; so did Stewart as there were feints on Pulau Ubin Island. But Paris thought the enemy would come from the north-west.

Singapore Island's coastline measures 72 miles and, at the beginning of February, the island's garrison numbered 85,000 men though not all were fighting personnel. More accurately, the armed and equipped fighting force reached 70,000, an equivalent of 4 weak Divisions, not a great number for the defence of such a coastline. Percival organised his defence into 5 commands: northern, southern, western, anti-aircraft defence and command reserve, the last being Paris's weak 12th Indian Infantry Brigade. As the sole reserve of Malaya Command, it consisted of the 5/2 Punjabs, strengthened with raw recruits from India, and the 4/19 Hyderabads, which were no luckier. With neither of these battalions in a fit condition to fight, it was up to the Argylls to bear most of the brunt of the assault. However, Percival planned to strengthen his reserves. 'It was my intention as soon as the direction of the attack was known and this reserve was committed, to create a new reserve by withdrawing troops from parts of the front which were not threatened.' The General Officer Commanding had his eye on using battalions of the newly-arrived 18th British Division once they were acclimatised. Percival knew that if the enemy succeeded in landing on the island, they must be stopped on or near the beaches. On 3 February he instructed commanders: 'All ranks must be imbued with the spirit of the attack. It is no good waiting for the Japanese to attack first. The endeavour of every soldier must be to locate the enemy and, having located him, to close with him.'

The first week of February was very tense. Because beach defences had not been erected, hard-pressed army and Singapore Public Works Department personnel had to put them in place mainly at night. At 6 p.m. on 5 February, enemy artillery attacked with a heavy barrage. 'The bombardment...is said to have been the heaviest concentration of fire ever put down by the Japanese army. The guns used were of all calibres, but the main punch came from modern 240-mm howitzers, specially built for this very purpose' Two days later, Australian patrols saw a large number of enemy soldiers in a rubber plantation on the mainland opposite the island's western shores. That night, the Japanese staged a diversionary attack on Pulau Lubin, a small island to the northeast of Singapore Island. Confused as to whether or not this move was a feint, Malaya Command responded by bombarding it. While the defenders' attention was distracted, the real Japanese assault was launched in the north-west section held by the Second Australian Imperial Force's 22nd Brigade.

The Argylls knew the terrain well. It had been their training ground before the invasion, where Stewart, Angus and Sandy Munnoch were famously photographed as they trudged through the swamps. Much of this country west of Bukit Timah Road was completely undeveloped. As 12th Indian Infantry Brigade was put on a state of readiness to counter-attack a possible landing in the western sector, Rose and Stewart argued over which shore the enemy would arrive at. Rose wrote that at that time Stewart looked grave: 'our beach defences were poor in the west, troops were too thin on the ground and they had inadequate reserves.'

They guessed the enemy would attack on the night of 8 to 9 February as conditions of the moon and tides (a waning moon which did not rise until 2 a.m. and a flow tide at the same time) were similar to those under which the Japanese amphibious operations at Kota Bahru and in China had taken place. They surmised that the first arrivals would beach under cover of darkness and allow the moon to help them encroach inshore.

As it happened, Rose and Stewart's guess was correct. The enemy arrived late that night, Sunday, 8 February: 'The Australian battalions had by this time become alert and were convinced that the enemy had attacked the land on their front, and consequently they too started firing upon the crossing-points, raising pillars of water from the straits, sinking Japanese boats and killing many men. Then the battle began on the island itself. The Japanese soldiers with white bands around their heads and the ashes of their comrade-in-arms in bags hanging around their necks, rushed the Australians, in spite of concentrated fire of machine-guns and mortars, and started a hand-to-hand fight under the moonlit sky.

By 12:05 a.m. on the 9th, the Japanese had pushed back the Australians in the north-west sector of the island and were floating their tanks on ingenious pontoons over the Malacca strait. During the small hours of that morning, 12th and 15th Indian Infantry Brigades were called in and placed under Major General Gordon Bennett's command. 12th Indian Infantry Brigade was ready by 6 a.m., but nobody at the brigade knew where they were to go. Communications failed because the bombardment cut the wires. Rose indicates the difficulties that faced my uncle and his staff at Brigade HQ. They had to deal with orders from Major General Bennett at North-Western HQ and disseminate them coherently to the battalions. While Bennett was an unknown quantity to the staff, officers in the Argylls were trusted friends.

The trouble was that Percival at Sime Road (where he ate, worked, and slept) was unsure if the early morning attack was the genuine thing or not, so he was unwilling to commit his reserve brigade until he was certain. Percival's aim was to cover the approaches with defended localities and hold the mobile reserves ready for a counter-attack. While Rose, Wilson, and others waited for orders, they heard on the wireless a news bulletin saying the Japanese had landed in strength on the north-west sector of the island and the British imperial forces were dealing with the situation. Then the phone rang and the unruffled voice of the Argylls' brigade-major announced that the troops should be on parade (prepared for action) immediately.

12th Indian Infantry Brigade was to move to Choa Chu Kang Road near Tengah airfield and take up position at the Neck, a spot of ground to the right of the Kranji-Jurong line that runs north/south-west, between the sources of the rivers Kranji and Jurong. The brigade, consisting of 440 Argylls of which 150 were marines, was accompanied by 440 officers and men (many were reinforcements) from the 4/19 Hyderabads. The third battalion was absent; the battle of Slim River had wreaked such havoc on the 5/2 Punjabs that they ceased to function as a fighting force. The job of 12th Brigade was to prevent the enemy surging from the island's western shores towards Bukit Timah and deny them entry to Singapore city. With its two large petrol depots and supplies of food, weapons and vehicles, Bukit Timah was tactically important. Situated in the centre of the island, if captured, it would give the enemy command of the hilly northern sector but also Pasir Panjang on the south coast as well. As the two battalions took to the road, moving at 20 mph and 15 vehicles to the mile, the Japanese dive-bombed them. Drivers from other battalions panicked, which caused fear in the Argylls and Hyderabads. The brigade was there to strengthen the 22nd Australian, being driven back by the Japanese 18th Division. There was every chance it would advance as far as the main road leading from the north of the island to Singapore city itself. Bennett ordered the brigade to hold positions astride the road but, disappointingly, not to counter-attack. Both the Argylls and Hyderabads knew this country well but their Australian commander had other plans. Brigade HQ was in the PWD buildings at the entrance to a quarry off Bukit Timah Road. Angus and staff had difficulties in making contact with the two battalions. Communications were not helped by each battalion being given only one telephone, as wires could be cut by the Japanese army 'Gwens,' their medium Mitsubishi Ki-21 Type 97 bombers, equivalent to a German Stuka. However, Hurricanes seeing off enemy aircraft heartened the troops.

The situation was worrisome with the brigade ordered to hold night, defensive positions until 9 a.m. the next morning. The western area's crucial Kranji-Jurong line was now manned by a weak 12th Indian Infantry Brigade on the right, the special reserve battalion in the centre, and the 44th Brigade on the left, reinforced by 22nd Australian Brigade with 15th Indian Infantry Brigade in reserve. The Japanese, firmly established on the island now, began to bring over their reserves, transport and tanks. The night of 9 to 10 February was exceptionally dark and wet. As the rain fell, it was black from the oil that blazed from the Kranji oil tanks. These had been demolished earlier in the day. The men's trenches filled with water; they sheltered under trees, huddling in their roomy, waterproof capes. Their provisions (enough for 3 full days) cheered them but they were dispirited by passing groups of Australian stragglers and the incessant croaking of bullfrogs in the neighbouring swamps.

Realising how serious the situation had become, Percival issued a plan at 12:50 a.m. on the 10th for an inner defensive ring around Singapore city to include Kallang aerodrome, the MacRitchie and Peirce reservoirs and Bukit Timah village. The next morning, Rose shaved in ditch water, unaware that, at first light, the Japanese had attacked the 4/19 Hyderabads which resulted in a withdrawal down the road to a position north-west of Bukit Panjang Road junction. Disturbingly, the staff at Western Area HQ were also unaware until 5 a.m. that the enemy, having repaired the partially-demolished causeway, had landed at Kranji and were advancing towards Mandai village only two miles farther north. Since 27th Brigade had made an unexpected retreat from the area west of the causeway, Key (commander of 11th Division) sent his reserve 8th Indian Infantry Brigade to recapture the high ground that the Australians had deserted. At 8 a.m., 12th Indian Infantry Brigade, on Choa Chu Kang Road east of Bulim, successfully checked the enemy, who mortared and machine-gunned the Argylls before moving round their right flank. Stewart asked Paris if he could withdraw his battalion to high ground behind Peng Siang River. By 9:30 a.m., the Argylls were astride the road behind 2/29 Australian Battalion.

Meanwhile, Paris, concerned about the missing 27th Brigade, sent patrols to make contact with the Australian force but did not find it. Equally ominous was a report that the trunk road as far as Kranji Road junction (now held by the Japanese) was unprotected. Realising that the enemy was free to move unobstructed down the main road to Bukit Timah, Paris withdrew his brigade and 2/29 Battalion to defend Bukit Panjang Road junction with the 4/19 Hyderbads remaining astride the road and west of the village. Paris had no authority to withdraw from the Kranji-Jurong line, but his flank had been endangered by 27th Brigade's unauthorised retreat the previous night. The lack of strong leadership demonstrated by Percival and Bennett made brigade and battalion commanders decidedly nervous.

By early afternoon, 12th Indian Infantry Brigade had abandoned the Kranji-Jurong line, leaving the special reserve battalion and 44th Brigade farther south uncovered. The Argylls took up position halfway between Bukit Panjang village and Bukit Timah. On that day (10 February) Percival, accompanied by General Wavell, recently appointed in overall command of American, British, Dutch, Australian (ABDA) Command, visited Bennett's headquarters. When the Generals learned they had lost the Kranji-Jurong line, Wavell ordered a counter-attack to recapture it. The latter had flown to Singapore from Java after receiving a forceful cable from Winston Churchill who urged the defenders of the garrison 'that the honour of the British Empire and of the British Army was at stake,' if they failed to repulse the Japanese invaders. Later that afternoon, Bennett ordered 12th, 15th and 22nd Indian Infantry Brigades (numbering 4,000 infantry) to re-take the all-important line, to safeguard the Bukit Timah area. The counter-attack was to be conducted in three stages, starting at 6 p.m. on the 10th. It was to continue at dawn the next morning with an attack by 12th Indian Infantry Brigade and would finish at 9 a.m. with the re-occupation of the Kranji-Jurong line.

But the Japanese forestalled it, as Yamashita had other ideas. With the bulk of his infantry safely across the Strait, the Japanese general planned to seize Bukit Timah by dawn on 11 February, as the day was special, known as Kigensetsu, the anniversary of Emperor Timmu's coronation and the founding of the Japanese empire. If Yamashita's forces could take Bukit Timah, it would not only be a gift to his ruler but the defenders would have to abandon Singapore's reservoir area and the garrison's fuel, food, and munitions. The Japanese XXV Army's night attack with bayonets was planned to be two-pronged: their 5th Division advancing east along the Choa Chu Kang Road and the 18th down the Jurong Road. Meanwhile, 12th Indian Infantry Brigade settled in and prepared for its intended counter-attack at dawn the following day. During the late afternoon, Stewart and Rose went for a walk in the fields on the government Dairy Farm east of the Argyll position on Bukit Timah Road. Stewart suspected the Japanese would break through that night and, if they succeeded, the battalion should rally at this spot where there were good fields of fire. His orders were to remain in position facing outward, desist from firing and use the password of 'Argyll.'

Shortly after dusk the Japanese infantry did attack and dispersed 12th Indian Infantry Brigade's 4/19 Hyderabads on Choa Chu Kang Road. The Australians staunched the Japanese advance just before a column of between 50 and 75 medium tanks drove down the road. They destroyed three but the remainder broke through the Australians' defences, turned right at the end of the road, and headed towards Bukit Timah. Standing alone between the Japanese and Bukit Timah depots, the Argylls, using all their vehicles and anti-tank mines at hand, improvised roadblocks. Sometime later, when Paris and Angus were sitting down to eat at Brigade HQ, a Japanese tank appeared out of the darkness and fired at them. The brigadier responded by shooting back with his revolver. As the tank turned round and withdrew, Paris exclaimed,

'I expect he'll be back soon with a few pals.' Indeed, the Japanese tanks advanced determinedly down Bukit Timah Road. When the leading vehicle reached the first of the Argylls' hastily erected roadblocks at 10:30 p.m., it was knocked out but the 50-strong column, supported by infantry, broke through the obstacle, forcing the Scots and 12th Indian Infantry Brigade HQ to withdraw to the east of the road and to the Dairy Farm.

Before the tanks broke through, Paris sent Angus to warn other defending companies of the attack. 'You go off to Bukit Timah,' he said. 'Tell the Aussies what's happened and get a proper obstacle covered by anti-tank guns fixed up. We'll hold 'em here as long as we can.' With his customary insouciance, echoed no doubt by the other officers, including his brigade major, Paris added 'and after you've done that put some soda on the ice.'

Angus gained his 15 minutes of fame when, late at night on Tuesday, 10 February 1942, he made a historic 2½ mile dash in his tiny Fiat. Pursued by 50 enemy tanks with the leading vehicle firing at him, he rammed his foot down on the accelerator, shot under the railway bridge, past the Ford factory and fire station until he came to a halt 300 yards south of the Bukit Timah Road junction. Here, he alerted the Australians, whose liaison officer organised a third road block covered by anti-tank guns. Under the fire of the leading Japanese tank, Angus contributed the last vehicle, his baby Fiat, to the roadblock. At around midnight, and in true David and Goliath fashion, his car, as part of the obstacle, knocked out the tank. This roadblock, supported by two anti-tank guns, held and prevented the Japanese tanks from ploughing into Singapore City. Angus's drive along Bukit Timah Road was an apt swansong. Not only did he and the Australians save the city from invasion that night but they also denied Yamashita the satisfaction of capturing Bukit Timah for the anniversary of the Japanese empire.

Before dawn on Wednesday, 11 February, the brigade withdrew to the Dairy Farm rendezvous. The Argylls' Battalion HQ departed first, then Paris moved off in the early morning with B and

C companies, edging their way down the pipeline that ran from the causeway to the centre of the city. Stewart stayed at the farm edge, waiting for his missing Companies. When they arrived at their meeting place by Sime Road golf course, they found transport to return them to Tyersall Park.

In July 2010, my daughter and I boarded a bus along that 2 ½ mile stretch beginning now at Bukit Panjang plaza and ending at a gigantic shopping centre in Bukit Timah. It's easy to miss the railway bridge, as it can be confused with overhead passes festooned by cascades of tropical purple-flowering plants. In amongst the ugly modern high rises and public buildings are palms, coconut trees, and bushes with a riot of pink blooms. Providing a vital lung for the populated island on the east side of the road is Bukit Timah nature reserve.

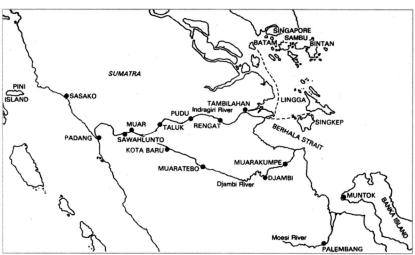

Escape Route (map by Mike Wainwright)

THURSDAY, 12 FEBRUARY 1942. A young child lay dead on a pile of rubble while two women crouched by the body weeping: in the background was a bombed rickshaw, its hood akimbo with broken shafts and buckled wheels. This still is the face of Singapore days before the surrender. Japanese bombers dropped their deadly cargo while men, women and children dived for cover in the monsoon drains as there were insufficient air raid shelters. As soon as a bomb exploded, each victim found himself covered with dust and choked by cordite fumes. It was only when the din stopped and their ears ceased ringing, that they noticed the dead child, sobbing mother, and wailing grandmother by the rickshaw. Some troops straggled, others deserted; still others went on a rampage of looting and raping. Dozens got tight on gin and whisky. Chinese families, Malays also, trundled their remaining possessions through the streets away from the approaching front line. At street corners, firemen wrestled with hoses. Down by the river, the rubber stores were alight. The flames, fanned by the breeze, threatened to leap the river and set fire to the houses on the other side. As the government closed down its departments and burned official documents, extravagant rumours abounded. The broadcasting station and local newspaper were no longer of any help with firm news, as their producers and editors had fled. Even the government broadsheet ceased publication. So, people fooled themselves: an armada would rescue them at the 11th hour. Was this not Singapore? How could the 'Gibraltar of the East' fall?

By mid afternoon at Tyersall Barracks, exhausted survivors from the Argylls' A and D companies, who had been fighting in the racecourse area, confronted another disaster. The Indian military hospital, a part of which was situated within the Argylls' barracks area, suffered a direct hit from the Japanese bombers. Many patients and staff were unable to escape from the wooden huts with thatched roofs. Others, too injured to move, needed to be rescued. The fire burned furiously and although fire services were summoned, the message failed to arrive as the telephone lines were down. Army personnel transferred vehicles and armoured cars and removed ammunition from the guard room, by which time the fire had progressed to the officers' quarters and mess. By the end of the afternoon, the whole of the camp was a 'smouldering ruin' and everything was destroyed except weapons, ammunition, and equipment. Pipes, drums, band instruments, and kit had gone up in smoke. All that remained was 'the spirit of the regiment,' wrote one officer, and a certain nonchalance displayed by officers like Angus who, on viewing the extent of the damage at Tyersall, announced that he was delighted to see the 'ruddy officers' latrine had burned down' and, what was more, 'in fine style.'

With this spirit, some 50 Argylls and 4 officers (all that remained at Tyersall of the original battalion of 860 men) re-formed into sections to hear what their Colonel expected of them. He asked (not ordered) them to re-join the battle raging in Reformatory Road in the south-west region of the city. Abandoning the charred remains of Tyersall, they marched through Argyll Gate but when they were a mile down Holland Road, Angus drew up in a staff car and stuck his head out of the window. 'Haven't you heard?' he bantered. 'It's all been changed!' Angus alluded to Malaya Command's most quoted cliché. He had been sent by Singapore Fortress's commander, Major General Frank Keith-Simmons, to tell the Argylls to halt and await further orders. Archie Paris had argued strongly against his 50 men going back into battle. These troops returned to Tyersall and took up residence in huts unscathed by the fire. While the officers sipped a whisky and soda and waited for their dinner of cottage pie a signaller entered the room and handed Colonel Stewart a message from General Wavell. The commanding officer was to evacuate Singapore with two of his most experienced officers and NCOs. The Colonel chose Angus Rose and David Wilson. Sergeant-majors Colvin and Bing were his choice of NCOs.

Stewart, Rose, and Wilson bade goodbye, Angus wished them well. 'I give you a couple of weeks longer than us,' he said, when he heard that they were making their escape by ship to Java, 'before finishing up in the cooler.' 'Old Angus,' wrote Rose in his personal account of the campaign, 'might have been seeing us off after a dinner party with the same humorous chuckle, the same quick wit and generosity.' The summons for these officers to leave Singapore at the 11th hour was a result of Wavell's plans to let a number of army, navy and air force personnel (including civilians) escape. 'Just before the cessation of fighting,' he advised, 'opportunity should be given to any determined bodies of men or individuals to try and affect escape by any means possible. They should be armed.' Men were selected from the Argylls, Sherwood Foresters and other regiments, to offer their fighting expertise to combat the Japanese outside Malaya. Many personnel grabbed a craft and headed for the mouth of a river on the Sumatran east coast. From there, they proceeded overland towards Java or travelled upriver, then across land by lorry or car, finally boarding a train for the last lap of their journey over the Sumatran mountains, until they reached Padang on the west coast, where they boarded a ship for Ceylon or Australia. The next morning, Friday, 13 February, the day Ian Stewart's group slipped out of Keppel harbour, a total of 1,800 army officers and men of merit were evacuated from Singapore. It was done with secrecy so that the bulk of servicemen would not attempt a last-minute dash for freedom and seize the remaining available vessels. It was also important to keep these plans from the enemy. The summons to escape was often unexpected: some men were still in the front line of battle, while medical staff might be in theatre performing an operation, when an order arrived for them to report immediately to the docks.

On Saturday, 14 February, Brigadier Paris was ordered to escape. To accompany him, he chose Angus and Captain Michael Blackwood, also Stewart's batman, Drummer Hardie. The group reported to the operations room at Singapore Fortress headquarters, a bomb-proof bunker 9 metres underground at Fort Canning, located in a park overlooking Orchard Road in the heart of Singapore. Battlebox, the name given to this underground warren, was General Percival's lair to which he and his staff moved on 11 February when the Combined Operations headquarters at Sime Road, close to the golf course, was in danger of capture by the enemy. This unique site from war-time Singapore, with 22 rooms filled 3 foot deep with water and an old motor-bike rusting in the corridor, was sealed off from the public gaze until it was rediscovered in 1988. With help from veterans and staff from London's Imperial War Museum, Battlebox was restored. On arrival at Fort Canning, my daughter and I bought our tickets, designed to resemble war-time security passes, and were led towards a heavy iron door in the side of the hill. Recorded sounds of air raid sirens and bomb blasts met us as we descended a flight of concrete steps into a maze of underground rooms. It was cool but our guide assured us that when it was in operation and filled with army personnel, it would have smelled like a midden in spite of its recycled air supply.

Battlebox is more than a World War Two site; with life-size wax models of important figures in Britain's Malaya Command, it offers the spectator a chance to re-live that fateful morning of Sunday, 15 February 1942 when Lieutenant General Percival and his staff surrendered to the Japanese. Using animatronics, these 24 life-sized wax figures move (albeit jerkily), talk, and some even appear to breathe. However, the overall effect borders on the absurd, as a serious historical event is brought to the level of a second-rate puppet show. The first room has a telephonist at the switchboard (the telephone was more reliable than the wireless and, to safeguard codes, Malaya Command changed them every 48 hours). We followed the arrows until we arrived at the Surrender Conference room where, seated around a large table, were wax models of Lieutenant General Percival and senior staff: Lieutenant Generals Heath and Bennett, Brigadiers Torrance and Newbigging. In the neighbouring room, under the glare of a bare light, we saw hieroglyphics scrawled on the wall by the Japanese Kempeitai (the military police), who chose this place as their headquarters after the surrender. 'But they soon changed their mind and moved to the YMCA building on Stamford Road,' said our guide. It was hardly surprising, we thought, as we peered around a corner and found a row of urinals. Beyond these was the air filtration unit that could, if necessary, handle a poison gas attack.

Each evacuee had permission to carry a small suitcase containing their belongings but, after the fire at Tyersall, most men possessed few personal effects. Angus's golf clubs, cricket bat, fishing rod, shot gun, not to mention his letters, photographs, camera and clothes, disappeared in the conflagration. Stewart lost his family documents and David Wilson, a regimental sword passed down to him from his father and grandfather. With his brigadier, Angus and others approached the camouflaged entrance to Fort Canning's Battlebox. As they descended the flight of cement steps and entered the operations room, they felt they were being sucked into the jaws of hell. It was hot, and the cramped rooms smelled of sweat. At the top of each door a section of iron had been sawn off to allow a greater flow of air to pass into the room from the corridor. The machinery vibrated, and it was noisy with male voices at the switchboard, stenographers at their typewriters, and constant requests from senior officers asking to speak to commanding officers. The man at the switchboard kept calm, army discipline having been so firmly instilled in recruits that it helped keep a semblance of order at this terrible time. Major General Keith Simmons entered the room and handed each man a signed chit giving them permission to leave Singapore.

Unlike the Colonel and his staff who escaped a day earlier, Paris's band was unable to embark for their getaway on any cruiser or known ship. All they could find was a small craft such as a sampan, tonkan, junk or launch. Some days previously, Angus, Michael Blackwood, David Wilson and Angus Rose agreed that when Singapore fell they would collect a sampan and row it in the dark to the Singapore Yacht Club, where Angus and Michael's yachts were moored and stocked with food and water. In one or other of these vessels, they would make their getaway. Oddly, if a serviceman attempted an escape one minute before the official surrender (8:30 p.m. on Sunday, 15 February), he was deemed a deserter and liable to be shot. If, on the other hand, he made a bid for freedom two minutes later he was seen as a hero and congratulated for his pains.

As it happened, all four officers received orders to evacuate the island but their yachts had already been snitched. A few days before their departure, as the enemy advanced from the island's northwest towards the yacht club in the south, where many private boats were moored, the authorities realised these could be used for escape. On the eve of Tuesday 10 February, a call went out for airmen with basic seamanship skills to use them as their aircraft had been sent for safe-keeping to Sumatra. So Angus and Michael's yachts had gone and were likely to have already been sunk by Japanese bombers. The rush, then, was on for anything that sailed or floated.

Up until the 11th hour, the authorities had insisted there was little to fear. Singapore was a great naval base with guns on the island of Pulau Blakang Mati guarding the south-west, while those on the north-east repelled assault from the east. Sir Shenton Thomas was determined that panic be averted. For this reason, newspapers and broadcasting stations were censored so that Japan's rapid advance down Malaya's east coast was kept a closely-guarded secret. This move was so successful that even by the beginning of the second week of February, civilians in Singapore could not believe that the enemy had not only landed on the island but had reached the outskirts of the city.

As evening fell, Angus's party made a dash for the docks. On the waterfront there was a smell of tar and burning wood as dozens of godowns (storage sheds) burned down. Flames from burning oil tanks on the nearby island of Pulao Samboe made the sea look crimson. Keppel harbour was cluttered with abandoned cars. Surrounding them was the flash of shells, an occasional flare-up marking a demolition and, in the background, coastal batteries firing northwards at the enemy. 27 men who had sheltered from the bombing at the YMCA joined them. Like Paris and his staff, these servicemen came from a variety of units to form a new army in India later. Each man waited in an air of unreality for a berth in a vessel. This was their last chance to escape, as official evacuation was to be suspended that night. Heading out into a mine-laden sea aiming for the Sumatran coast was a risky business. If caught, the Japanese would show little mercy. Tokyo Radio warned the British that they would not be permitted another Dunkirk and Japanese planes (now based at Tengah on the island) switched their attacks to the docks and allied shipping.

In the end, Angus and his brigadier found the Celia, a small well-made harbour launch with a twin diesel engine. She was 50 foot long, 10 foot in her beam, and had a seating capacity of 30. As darkness fell they departed Singapore with 67 persons on board. The passengers included Brigadier Paris, the Commander of the Royal Engineers, another Colonel, Angus Macdonald, Michael Blackwood, the Commanding Officer of the Indian Army Medical Corps, 40 British other ranks (sappers, signallers, gunners, including Sergeant Macdonald of the Argylls, and a sergeant major of the Gordons) and Captain N. W. Frisby, adjutant of the Federated Malay States Volunteer Force. Because they had no naval personnel on board, Angus and Michael Blackwood took charge of the navigation. But they were ill-equipped for a sea voyage; all they carried was a map (80 miles to the inch) and a military pocket compass but they had no torch, chart, or plan of the area's minefields. Apart from Michael Blackwood's knowledge of the inner field, they trusted to luck and their small draft of 3 foot to carry them out of danger. They knew that Japanese fighter, bomber and reconnaissance sea planes were hovering in the sky above them. In their favour, however, these planes did not often attack small vessels but the escapees took the precaution of following the example of larger ships, which laid up in day-time on the banks of an island, and camouflaged the Celia by covering her with branches.

Seen from the sea, their last view of Singapore was horrific as the whole city appeared to be enveloped in fire. The night of the 14th was moonless and the pall of smoke coming from Singapore made it feel even darker. Sumatra's east coast had three river mouths, up which evacuees could travel: the Kampar, 80 miles south of Singapore, was the closest followed by the Indragiri and the Djambi, opposite the Banka Straits. The Celia headed for the first. They were given a bearing of 210 degrees to take them to the Kampar's mouth but it was not until they detected an error of 50 degrees that the deviation was noticeable. Being overloaded (the Celia was carrying double her recommended quota of passengers), the launch was hard to steer and she swung off course. While negotiating the minefield and within sight of Singapore, the boat's engines failed. As they floated close to a blazing ship, beached on a small island, they feared they would be caught the next day in this exposed condition. But after an hour, an engineer managed to re-start one engine, and they carried on using that. However, steering the Celia became even more difficult. Looking to their rear they saw, silhouetted against the flames of another burning ship, a rocky island they had just missed blundering into. Other hazards included coral reefs, mines, storms, and even sharks, although these creatures hid because of the explosions. The men's worst fear was detection by a Japanese fighter plane or bomber. Evidently, the party was unaware of the food dump at Moro Island in the Durian Straits, where they could have collected provisions stashed in 4-gallon petrol cans (each containing enough food and water for 6 men for 2 days). Also available were vital navigational instructions to Priggi Raja at the mouth of the Indragiri river.

An hour before daylight on the 15th, the fugitives sensed they were near land as the water appeared shallow. Rolling in an uncomfortably heavy swell, they anchored, waited until dawn and found themselves in a bay with no outlet and realised they had strayed northwards from their course; to right themselves, they had to turn south-eastward, skirting round an island until they could reach the proper channel. Later that morning, two single Japanese reconnaissance planes hovered over them, followed shortly afterwards by seven Japanese bombers flying south at 2,000 feet. The helmsman took evading tactics but the Celia was doubtless too tiny to interest the enemy. By this time, they were about 50 to 60 miles from Singapore, they could still see clouds of smoke in that direction.

Because they had no charts, they failed to find the mouth of the Kampar river and sailed eastwards off course. In the distance they saw a ship which they hoped was a Dutch patrol boat that might help them. But when they reached it they discovered it was a wreck. However, close by lay an island that looked as if it was inhabited. Several passengers swam ashore and made contact with the Malayan lighthouse keepers on the summit. These men gave them charts and fresh water telling them they were on South Brothers Island and they should make for the Kateman estuary, the nearest part of the Sumatran mainland. From there, they could find their way by land to Rengat, a town on the Indragiri river. Taking the lighthouse keepers' advice, they headed for the estuary where they found a launch, the Mutiara, had run aground. It had on board a number of employees from the Singapore Asiatic Petroleum Company, who were unable to restart their launch's engines, as it required the expertise of a marine engineer. They warned the Celia passengers that as Kateman was a small fishing village, it would be of little help and suggested they continue farther south towards the mouth of the Djambi where the town of the same name had an Asiatic Petroleum Company Depot from which help could be sent to the stranded Mutiara.

Having dissuaded the Celia from heading up the Kateman river, it appeared that the Mutiara crew were asking a lot from the party to proceed far farther south than they needed. After Kateman, the best route was up the Indragiri with provision at varying stages of the journey for transport, fuel, food, and accommodation. On the other hand, the Djambi estuary was 40 miles south of the Indragiri and offered no direct route to Padang. The Celia agreed to contact the depot at Djambi, taking on board Mr Faber who, being Dutch, could act as an interpreter, a Mr de Souza, a 65 gallon drum of diesel fuel and a chart for Djambi to ensure they reached their destination. They followed the coast closely as far as Tanjong Datok on the equator, and from there across the open sea (60-70 miles) until they reached the estuary. All they possessed to keep them on course was the pocket compass, and for this task, navigators Angus and Michael Blackwood applied intense concentration. At 3 a.m. on 16 February, they approached land and anchored. When dawn came, they were delighted to find themselves only ¼ mile from a buoy marking the entrance to the Djambi river, which was a triumph, for Angus's and Michael's navigation skills!

Two small coastal trading vessels hove in sight, heading for Djambi; the Celia followed them upriver. Passing through a small town with a custom house and a water boat anchored mid-stream, they meandered up the broad river through mangrove swamps, keeping a watch out for water snakes. Each passenger was exhausted, having spent over 48 hours crammed in the launch. Many were suffering from insect bites and all were thirsty. However, they soon found fresh water and drank it with relish as it had been strictly rationed during the voyage. At dusk the Celia tried to moor mid-stream but her anchor failed to hold against the strong current, so they tied up alongside a larger ship and made more room for themselves by transferring half their men onto it.

The next morning, 17 February, the Celia pressed on to Djambi, which they reached in 3 or 4 hours. The sight that met them — burnt-out launches and smoking oil tanks — was far from cheering. The cause was not enemy bombing but allied demolition as they feared the worst. Sure enough, they learned that Singapore had fallen and the Japanese had taken Palembang, the next big Sumatran town to the south. The men had no other choice but to head north-west to Padang, the chief port on the west coast of Sumatra. Cars, vans, and lorries were unavailable as they had been evacuated and all petrol stocks were destroyed. But the District Officer suggested they steer the Celia upriver as far as Moearatebok to a military camp there, a journey of at least two or three days. He gave them plenty of tinned food and biscuits and even allocated them a paddle steamer. These were particularly welcome as a number of Australians had swollen their number to 81.

Approximately 50 boarded the paddle steamer while the 23 volunteers with Paris's group remained on the Celia. Anxious to waste no time and use the remaining hours of daylight, they navigated upstream, mooring by the river bank for the night. The next morning, 18 February, at daybreak, they departed and spent the entire day following the innumerable bends in the river until they reached Moeara Tembesi at 5 pm. On that day, they made better progress than they expected because the water was high, which helped them to keep to the inside of the bends where the current was less strong. Realising they were in imminent danger of being captured or having their route blocked, they pressed on anxiously. But it began to rain and the night was dark and moonless. A barrage of logs, branches, and other debris brought down by the floods presented more risk in the dark. The men were glad to find a deserted rest house to shelter in until the next morning.

They rose early the following day and found navigation easy; the current was weak but as the day advanced, it became stronger and they made little headway. The fugitives found the upper reaches of the Djambi fascinating. 'There was a feeling,' wrote Geoffrey Brooke, a young naval officer and evacuee who took a similar route across Sumatra, 'of unreality engendered by this unholy alliance of danger and beauty that was so often with us.' Sumatra's interior was wild. On their approach pigs retreated into the jungle. Large birds (possibly a species of crane) flew overhead. In the water close to their bow swam fish with fins the shape of rabbits' ears, and by the riverbank lurking in the slime were crocodiles. Well after dark, at 9:30 p.m., they saw the first sign of human life. A light flickered ahead but it was extinguished as soon as the Celia's 'searchlight,' an old car lamp, bought at Moeara Tembesi and rigged in the bow so they could dodge the logs and debris floating downriver, was seen. 'Who are you?' a voice called from the darkness. This was Moearatebok with its small garrison of Sumatran troops and a half dozen Dutch NCOs, who made the fugitives welcome. That night, before Paris's group went to sleep on board, the Sumatran soldiers cooked them a meal of vegetables and rice.

The following morning, 20 February, Paris, who had gone ashore immediately on arrival to find transport for the journey's final stage, told the evacuees of the Celia that he and his staff were taking the last available car for Padang and that on arrival he would send transport for them. Not long after Paris's party left Moearatebok, Lieutenant Ian Forbes, RM, one of the survivors of the Prince of Wales sunk by the Japanese in early December 1941, bumped into them. They were drawing away in their large car from an inn after having had lunch and were heading for the coast. Paris's breeziness irritated Forbes so the latter decided that he and his group would overtake them. He was so determined to keep up that he managed to pass Paris's car parked outside a rest house.

Paris and his staff drove north to Rengat on the Indragiri river. Here, Major Jock Campbell had made his headquarters and with help from the local Dutch Controlleour (district commissioner), he provided food, accommodation and transport for servicemen passing through. Campbell was part of a team set up by Colonel Alan Warren, the aforementioned royal marine, who was attached to the Far East Special Operations Executive. They assisted escape groups to reach Sumatra and cross the mountains to Padang by organising aid en route. The team provided rest places and food along the 250-mile route and appointed doctors and nurses to tend the wounded. Warren's headquarters, on the west coast of Sumatra, was where he organised escape attempts, made financial handouts for local fishing boats, set up routes by foot and, when it was too late to obtain help from the Royal Navy, commandeered other ships to convey the escapees to safety.

When Paris's party reached Rengat, they bumped into a handful of Argylls, who had made their way to Sumatra after being cut off from the battalion in Malaya. They were Sergeant Willie Macdonald, badly wounded at Dipang, Lance Corporal Jock Gray, and Corporal Walter Gibson. At this time, overcrowded Rengat was being substituted as a meeting point for Ayer Mollek, farther west. Here, a Dutch rubber plantation was requisitioned as temporary accommodation. It was a welcome change for the evacuees, to be free from mosquitos, and they took baths in the latex tanks and slept between latex sheets. That night it rained heavily and the river flooded, which made it impossible to navigate the following morning. Colonel Dillon, the man in charge at Ayer Mollek, had food for one more week and little transport as the Dutch were using it in their withdrawal 200 miles north-west to Fort de Kock. A few fugitives became belligerent; exhausted, hungry and afraid they demanded supplies at gun point.

Paris and his staff were disadvantaged by their inability to speak either Dutch or the local language. However, at Ayer Mollek they met Lieutenant van de Gaast from the Malay Regiment, who volunteered to be their interpreter until they reached Padang. As a junior officer, Van de Gaast found it hard to communicate instructions from senior Dutch officers that Paris's authority was now limited to the control of his own troops and not to any others. Many feared that they were now trapped as news came that the Japanese were trying to cut off the mountain roads. Transport, mainly lorries, came trickling in but in the end, half the camp travelled upriver in an old steamboat and two barges, while the remainder went by bus to Taloek. Abandoning their car, Paris and his Argylls moved off in two lorries provided by the Dutch. On leaving Taloek they climbed 4,000 feet into the Sumatran mountains, a range extending from north to south of the country's western region. Arriving on the banks of a bridgeless river, they crossed it on a raft attached to a wire operated by a hand wheel. It was beautiful countryside with miles of thick jungle beneath a jagged mountain chain, streaks of silvery lakes, and flat cultivated land.

They finally arrived at the coal mining town of Sawahloento where the Dutch community had organised blankets, food and even converted a shed into a shower room. As officers, Angus, Blackwood, and Paris booked into one of the town's two, small, overcrowded hotels. Here, at the end of the 19th century, the Dutch had constructed a railway line that extended all the way to Padang. Usually the cargo was coal but at this critical period it was people. At the station, when the ancient-looking train drew into the platform, the passengers climbed up several steps to enter the carriages. After a puff and a jerk the train began its four hour journey to Padang over mountains, past deep lakes, and terraces of paddy fields, where workers wearing straw hats, laboured. The train took its time, halting at innumerable stations where passengers bought duck eggs and fried bananas from platform vendors. They followed the east bank of Lake Sinkarak and began the steep climb up to Padang-Panjang, at which point the train descended to the plains lying between the mountains and the sea.

When my daughter and I visited Sumatra in 2010, we flew from Malaysia to Medan on the country's east coast instead of catching a ferry from Singapore. Flying over one of the world's largest islands, a land mass the size of California, we looked down on mountainous, forested country and a patchwork of cultivated land. But our stay was scarcely ten months after a major earthquake had hit Padang in September 2009. As we rode in a taxi from the airport into the city we saw large, modern buildings with shattered walls and collapsed roofs. Most probably, Padang looked more like a war zone than it did in early 1942 when Angus arrived. However, there were plenty of undamaged structures that boasted the local two-pronged Minangkabau roofs resembling buffalo horns; the buildings' curved base resembled a ship's hull. This strange but graceful architectural style is not restricted to domestic houses and is used for school buildings, hotels, and even police stations.

"Nothing but broken houses!' said our driver who could not understand why we were visiting his city. The language barrier prevented us from giving him our reason. But it did not stop him from halting his taxi, shaking our hands and introducing himself. 'You go to Mentawi' he advised. 'Very beauty!' Lying like a sparkling necklace off the coast, these islands attract surfers from all over the world. We drove past a church, its west side looking as if it had been hit by several canonballs. But down in the old town, untouched by the previous year's earth tremors, were several old Dutch colonial houses, their teak verandas uncared for but still intact. Gazing down on to the river bank, we saw, among the brightly painted fishing boats, a team of six men paddling a canoe that sliced swiftly upstream.

Paris's party arrived in Padang on 21 February, a week after they left Singapore and a few hours before Lieutenant Forbes who, although he lost the race, managed to joke about it with his opponents. Angus and his brother officers either booked in at the Orangji Hotel near the seafront or at the Enderaach Club, which the Dutch had turned into quarters for British officers. Two local schools accommodated the other ranks. Flanked on its western side by the Indian Ocean, Padang was the biggest community the evacuees had encountered on their escape through Sumatra. It was a well laid out town with huge, yellow camphor trees lining the main streets. There were Dutch colonial bungalows with wide verandas, well-kept lawns and tidy gardens where families sat and dined in the evening. The local people lived in the old town with its narrow streets and back-to-back houses close to a river that ran down to the sea front. Here, long sandy beaches backed by coconut palms met huge rollers that arrived unimpeded from the Antarctic.

The influx of servicemen and civilians had interrupted the usual calm of this attractive town of 60,000 inhabitants. Each street seethed with refugees, as the Dutch termed the escapees, waiting for a berth on a ship bound for India or Australia. Their condition was desperate. Many arrived with nothing and some, who were in rags, had lost their shoes. They needed food, clothes, footwear, a roof over their head and, in some cases, medical attention and a barber. All lacked cash so each serviceman received money, eight guilders for an officer and five for the other ranks. However, many of the troops were in an ugly mood and the Dutch were worried to learn that some servicemen had sold their weapons on the way over. Relations between the colonials and the local population had been far from cordial ever since the latter had tried to overthrow their European rulers in the late 1920s. To avoid trouble, the Dutch disarmed refugee troops when they arrived and, in spite of some soldiers' bad behaviour, were helpful and generous.

It was not only the other ranks whose attitude and actions left a lot to be desired. The highest-ranking officer of the Australian Imperial Forces, General Gordon Bennett, had decided just before the surrender to leave Singapore without consulting his peers, particularly Lieutenant General Percival. Bennett's actions angered many, in particular Brigadier Paris. On his arrival in Padang, the Brigadier took over as senior officer. When Bennett's British aide-de-camp approached him for funds for his Australian superior, Paris let rip, 'Let Bennett collect the bloody money himself!'

I've wondered how Angus occupied himself during those five tense days before his departure for Ceylon. The British officers listened to the calamitous news on the wireless; each officer and man knew how desperate their situation had become. Padang was sealed off both from the air (Japanese reconnaissance planes appeared daily), and at sea by surface ships and submarines, while the enemy was only 60 miles away by road. They were virtually trapped. On 24 February, Colonel Warren returned to Padang. The following day, Paris relinquished his post as the region's senior British officer when he learned that he was to sail with his Argylls on a Dutch ship called the Rooseboom. It arrived that morning from Batavia in Java en route for Ceylon's capital, Colombo.

In our taxi one late afternoon, we followed scores of people as they left Padang's centre. Seated on scooters, women road pillion behind men, some carrying huge parcels, others babies or large bags of shopping. Small boys or girls, clasped by the driver, propped their chins on the vehicle's handlebars. Most were unhelmeted. All streamed southward out of the city in the direction of Teluk Bayur harbour. Before we hailed our taxi, I asked the travel agent in our hotel if Teluk Bayur was the old Emmahaven, the port Angus sailed from on the Rooseboom. A woman at the counter laughed when I asked if anyone there could remember as far back as 1942. 'I could have asked my grandmother,' she said, 'but she died last year.' I consulted my Lonely Planet guide that indicated Padang had three harbours: one on the mouth of the river that handled boats to and from the Mentawai islands, another 45 minutes from the centre at Teluk Kabung, and the third was Teluk Bayur, the commercial freight port two kilometres south of the city. This had to be the old Emmahaven.

Since I spoke no Indonesian and our driver no English, communication was made through an intermediary, the taxi man's colleague on his mobile phone. Agreeing to take us to the harbour and back for 30,000 rupiah (about £6), he followed the river; at its mouth we discovered a beautiful, natural harbour somewhat marred by a large coal depot, storage sheds and a lot of waste.

There were shacks and other dilapidated habitations and, by the road, barrow vendors selling soft drinks and snacks. We drew up at the harbour entrance and saw through the locked gate several docked ships. Then our driver conveyed us round the left side of the horseshoe-shaped bay where on one side was a forested precipice and on the other, a mountain range. This was Emmahaven. I had read accounts written by fugitives who claimed their journey from town to harbour was made by train; and there before us was the railway line, now disused, hugging the road.

Flanked by sandy, palm-fringed beaches, Emmahaven in Angus's time was an important port, as it held warehouses stocked with tobacco, rice, and tin. At this unhappy period, the harbour was a mess, and, although the city had only been bombed once, the buildings at the docks were destroyed and stained black by the fires. Few vessels in the bay were intact and a flurry of masts from sunken ships stuck out of the water at different angles. Arriving in the early afternoon of the 26th were lorries with escapees — nurses, wives, children, soldiers and businessmen. As they alighted, they clustered in small groups waiting for the time when they could climb the ship's gangway. At 3:00 p.m. Paris entered the docks with his Argylls who wasted no time in setting up on deck Bren guns and rifles, which they were to man in case of an enemy air attack. At 5:00 p.m., as evening and, most importantly, darkness approached, the Rooseboom weighed anchor and sailed out of the harbour. As one of the Argylls, Corporal Walter Gibson states in his ghost-written memoir composed at least eight years after the event: 'We could see the half-submerged ships, victims of the Jap raid, which dotted the entrance to the harbour. But even so I found myself caught up in the spell of the sunset's beauty — for the dying rays fell on a lush growth of tropical vegetation on the dozens of islands round about us, and there are few more beautiful approaches in the world than Padang's Bremmerhaven.' Gibson was referring to Emmahaven.

DURING THE EARLY months of the war my grandmother Daisy, now 60 years of age, felt her sons were reasonably safe: Jock was a captain in the 8th Argylls, Simon an officer in the Lovat Scouts, and Angus served overseas in Singapore. Back at home friends like Edna Greenfield, mother of Angus's former commanding officer admired Daisy who was president of the local branch of the Scottish Women's Rural Institute (SWRI) and during the war served as President and Secretary of the Argyll Federation, which supported the war effort. It was a period of unusual calm and as autumn turned into winter, my grandmother could be forgiven for wondering what all the fuss was about. Then it changed. On 3 June 1940, while in France with the British Expeditionary Force, Jock was severely wounded. Following her eldest son's injury and hospitalisation, the only one of Daisy's five offspring free to help was Esther, my mum, so she was granted compassionate leave from the ATS. Subsequently, each summer she returned to Largie for three months to work on the farm, tend the garden, and manage the castle filled with evacuees.

Secreted away from any city, you might think the war hardly impinged on the community. This was far from the case. On 16th September, 1940 German aircraft spotted, close to Rathlin Island off the northeast coast of Northern Ireland, SS Aska, a British steamship sailing towards Liverpool from West Africa, with French and British troops and 600 tons of cocoa on board. The enemy bombed the converted liner three times after which the beleaguered ship drifted eastward towards the Kintyre coast until it ran aground on the north shore of Cara. Some weeks afterwards, Daisy's nieces, Barbara Gordon Clark and Anne Swann with their young children took a day trip to the island. Four year old Charles Gordon Clark was thrilled to play on the beach's fine, white sand, see the wild goats and sit on the Broonie's chair. Looming before them in the water was the wreck of the Aska, its cargo strewn along the shoreline and floating in the sea. Most tantalising was the sight of dozens of oranges bobbing on the water's surface but these were uneatable, contaminated by salt water.

I can't help wondering if the spoiled fruit wasn't a joke played on the children by the Broonie. After all, Cara was his island and the Highland fairy could be possessive, moody or just plain obstreperous. Were Daisy's nieces disrespectful towards him? Perhaps they patronised or laughed at the idea of the Broonie, in which case he wouldn't have hesitated in retaliating. It was mean to tease hungry girls and boys by placing dozens of inedible oranges within their reach. Barbara's children could scarcely remember the last time they had seen, still less tasted an orange or for that matter, a banana, peach or grape. Recently, all they could lay their hands on was an apple, pear, or plum, and a variety of berries: strawberries and raspberries mainly. Sweets and chocolate, of course, were strictly rationed. Conversely, the Highland fairy was quite capable of indulging people, especially lovers. In Spring 1947 my recently engaged parents visited Cara. During their excursion my father dropped his wallet and only discovered it was missing after his return to the castle. Two days later he received it in the post. A retired doctor found Dad's wallet on the island and posted it back to him. Mum was convinced the Broonie had helped them find it.

Closer to Largie and more intrusive was the wartime range at Rhunahaorine Point where RAF training squadrons fired at and bombed land and sea targets. So that they could view the firing range, Jock's young sons, John and Donald climbed to the top of the castle's tower where they peered out over the fields towards the Point. Nobody avoided wartime rationing and coupons for clothes, fuel, and food. Sugar, tea, and coffee, were limited, and imported foods were banned. Diets became simple and restricted but at Largie, there were treats: honey from Daisy's beehive, raspberries from the kitchen garden, trout caught in the loch, a rabbit stew or jugged hare.

Just as life at Largie became more manageable with Esther's prolonged summer leaves, Jock's slow recuperation from his injury, and the occasional war-time entertainment when neighbour,

Naomi Mitchison, arrived with her theatrical troupe of local fishermen and farmers, news came that Japan had invaded Malaya. Daisy waited anxiously for word of Angus. Astonished by the lightning speed with which the eastern power's forces advanced down the length of Malaya, she was appalled to hear that the defending army had retreated to Singapore Island. As for the surrender, it wasn't much of a birthday present. On Sunday, 15 February, Daisy was 63 years old and that evening, shortly after Lieutenant General Percival signed the surrender papers in the Ford Factory on the outskirts of Singapore city, the prime minister of Great Britain, Mr Churchill, announced in his BBC broadcast from London that Singapore had fallen. The following day, Daisy discovered more when she read the newspapers. 'Singapore Forced to Capitulate,' declared *The Times*. News from the Far East took precedence over columns on Rommel's desert advance, the RAF's Rhineland targets, and Germany's invasion of Russia. Singapore had surrendered unconditionally. The pill could not be sweetened even if *The Times*' headlines stressed the courage of the British Imperial Forces. 'Gallant Resistance Ends' and 'Stubborn Fighting to the End' introduced accounts of British, Australian, Indian, and Malayan troops trying to check the Japanese advance.

The fall of Singapore was an unmitigated defeat, the likes of which the nation had never seen since the American Revolutionary War (1775–83), and Angus was caught up in it. Growing up in a military family, Daisy was used to the business of war; her father was injured in South Africa when he fought the Boers, her grandfather also suffered an injury in the Peninsular war against Napoleon; as for her great-grandfather who made his mark as a young soldier in India in the late 18th century, he did not escape unharmed either. Finally, in the 20th century, her youngest brother, Tempest was blown to pieces in 1915 in the 'war to end all wars.'

Worst of all was the waiting. Daisy wrestled in her mind what had happened to her son. Angus might be dead, worse still, badly injured. Even worse, he might be lost and starving in the jungle.

If he was still alive, where was he? Now that Britain had surrendered, he might have joined the ranks of the 100,000 servicemen taken into captivity. Considering the news of atrocities committed by the Japanese in Hong Kong and China, this didn't augur well. On a more hopeful vein, the authorities may have ordered Angus out of Singapore and at that moment he was making his way to safety. Daisy could only guess; all she knew was her son was in Malaya. That in itself was an advantage over others who had no idea where their loved ones had been posted. So she waited. The month of March arrived and still no news. The lack of information was far from positive; if Angus had been successful in his escape, he would have got in touch.

On 26 March, a War Office telegram arrived at Tayinloan post office and general store, situated close to the smithy and mill. Those buff telegrams were no respecters of class and were equally likely to arrive at the front door of a castle or cottage. Ronald Reid, the Largie gamekeeper, was to receive his telegram when his son James, of 7th Argyll and Sutherland Highlanders, was killed on 21 July 1943. 'They drew lots at the post office,' my mother told me, 'as to who would deliver the telegram.' The postmaster and mistress were Dougie and Jeannie McFater, a couple who, at Christmas two years previously, had sent Angus a tin of shortbread. Perhaps, because of the gravity of the situation, they sent Dougie because a man's shoulder, they say, is broader. Or did Jeannie insist on going? By all accounts she was kind and had taken care to wrap Angus's present carefully, swaddling the tin well with layers of paper lest the contents break. Yet, Mrs Macdonald would prefer the feminine touch, and, if the shock proved too much, it was better that Jeannie break the news.

All was not lost. Hope was still there. The telegram stated Angus was missing, not dead. Two months earlier, another family member had received a war office telegram. On 6 January 1942, Douna, who was farming at Ellary and raising her three children alone, learned that her husband Henry, a military chaplain, was missing in action. The young mother awaited further news and six days later she received a second telegram indicating that her husband was alive but a prisoner. (On 27 March 1940, Henry had joined the Royal Army Chaplains Department and been appointed to 2nd battalion, Royal Tank Regiment, 1st Armoured Division, based at Ringwood in southern England. Six months later on 25 September 1940, he was sent with his battalion to the Western Desert in North Africa where he served in 13th Corps, 7th Armoured Division, Desert Force; a few months later he joined 30th Corps. On 8 July 1941 he was mentioned in dispatches and promoted on 10 November that year).

As soon as Esther, who qualified as a motor mechanic the day Singapore fell, learned about Angus's loss, she returned to Largie. In his letter dated 11th August, 1941 Angus had congratulated his younger sister on her knowledge of motor vehicles. "You must know an awful lot about cars now. After the war you will be relied upon to put our cars right when they go wrong, that is, if any of us can afford to have cars when this war is finished. I am afraid I never even lift the bonnet of mine if I can help it." It was up to the 21 year old to support Daisy, as Douna was tied up with her family, Simon had married Caitriona Gordon on 28 February, and Jock was learning to live a new life as an amputee.

Scarcely a week later (3 April), a letter arrived. 'Madam,' was the abrupt salutation. 'In confirmation of War Office telegram of the 26th March, 1942, I am directed to inform you, with regret, that a notification dated 23rd March, 1942, has been received that your son, Major C.A. Macdonald, The Argyll and Sutherland Highlanders, has been reported missing at sea in the Far East as the result of the loss, through enemy action, of the ship in which he was travelling. All possible enquiries are being made with a view to obtaining further information concerning your son, and any information obtained will at once be sent to you.' The letter's euphemistic language — 'as the result of the loss through enemy action' — was familiar to her but the gut-wrenching feelings were not. This stark written communication contrasts sharply with the one Douna received some months earlier on 16 January from C.D. Symons, the Chaplain General, who warmly, if not guardedly, congratulated her on the news that Henry's name had been removed from the list of 'missing.' 'My Dear Mrs. Rogers,' he began, 'I am sure it has been a great relief to you to hear that it has been officially established that your husband is a prisoner of war. I am so glad to hear that he is safe. The official reports concerning prisoners of war come through very slowly, but should I receive any further news of particular interest it will be passed on to you immediately. I pray that God may give him strength and guidance in this very difficult sphere, and that He will abundantly bless his work among those with whom he is sharing imprisonment.'

In comparison with Douna's letter from the Chaplain General, Daisy's missive from the War Office offered few words of consolation. She read the words over again, trying to find something hopeful in them and a host of questions arose in her mind. Where had Angus set off from? When did it happen? Was it a submarine that blew up the ship or a plane? Most of all, she wanted to know what had happened. Was he alive or dead? Did he manage to climb into a lifeboat or on to a raft? Had he reached dry land and if so, was he free or had he been captured?

Like many Britons, Daisy was familiar with seafaring tales. For centuries, ships were the principle means of travel and faraway lands were known as countries 'overseas,' not one sea but several. In many stories hope featured and even scenes of redemption when the storm, once abated, deposited its human flotsam on terra firma — foreign, admittedly, but largely hospitable — with water to quench thirst and food in the form of fruit growing on trees. In Shakespeare's *The Tempest* the castaways find respite. Daniel Defoe's *Robinson Crusoe*, based on a Scottish castaway called Alexander Selkirk, lived for four years on an island in the Pacific. However, these stories are vastly outnumbered by tales of those who perish. Testifying to the cruelty of the sea on the west coast of Scotland are many graveyards containing the final resting places of unidentified seamen.

Within a fortnight of receiving the War Office letter, Daisy placed a notice in *The Times*. In the West Highlands, living far from her siblings and friends in the south, she used the newspaper as a notice-board, its personal columns announcing family births, marriages and deaths. This time, on 20 April, it was to announce the loss of Angus alongside the 'Deaths' and 'In Memoriam' columns, in a new category starkly named 'Missing.'

'Officially reported missing at sea,' the notice states, 'after the Fall of Singapore, Major Charles Angus Macdonald of the Argyll & Sutherland Highlanders. Information gratefully received by Mrs. Moreton Macdonald, Largie, Tayinloan, Argyll.' My grandmother was not alone; nine other entries accompanied hers, all from relatives, some parents, others brothers or sisters, seeking the whereabouts of loved ones who had served in Malaya. Most were young officers in the Royal Artillery or Indian regiments. One was from a female subaltern in the ATS asking for information on Brigadier Ivan Simson, General Percival's chief engineer. Byron's death (19 April 1824) is commemorated with a verse (very apt when considering Angus's fate) from his poem, *The Bride of Abydos*.

> The winds are high on Helles wave
> As on that night of stormy water
> When love, who sent, forgot to save
> The young, the beautiful, the brave

The notice elicited response. Although little of Daisy's wartime documents and correspondence still exist, John Maxwell Macdonald, Jock's eldest son, possesses the Largie Visitors' book. Her address book of that period demonstrates who was important to her. In amongst utilitarian entries of plumbers, beehive makers, osteopaths and stockists of jam jar covers, my grandmother allocated a page to Angus with the addresses of the Argylls' HQ and the Far East Prisoners of War (FEPOW) Association. Another was inserted soon after Angus was reported missing. Joanne Hawtrey Woore's husband, David, an air force friend of Angus, was also lost after the Fall of Singapore. I like to think that Mrs Hawtrey Woore saw Daisy's notice in *The Times* and got in touch. For a while, the two women maintained their vigil. Then the other lady heard that her husband was alive but in captivity. Daisy duly updated her entry for Angus's air force friend by substituting the words 'husband missing in Java' for POW. The name

Hawtrey Woore is unusual, which was an advantage when I tried to find the couple's descendants. I wrote to Georgina Hawtrey Woore whose name was on a list of editors from a London publishing firm, but it wasn't until I found her brother, Simon on Facebook that I was able to make contact. He replied that David and Joanne were his grandparents but he knew little about that period. David had set off from Singapore (possibly in a yacht belonging to somebody like Angus) and was captured in Java. Nobody talked about it in his family. Daisy included other names and addresses on her 'Angus' page, possibly people who responded to her notice in *The Times* like Brigadier Paris's widow, who lived in Sussex, and his cousin from Northumberland. I searched for more clues: names and addresses of Angus's regimental friends and found a New Delhi address for Angus Rose and an Edinburgh one for Alison, his wife. This couple occupied a space, not in the 'Angus' column but on a page of similar importance to Daisy's friends and family.

Although the burden of Angus's disappearance weighed heaviest on his mother, sisters and brothers, others were anxious to discover what had happened to him. Two days after Daisy placed her notice in *The Times*, Hector Greenfield, now commanding a brigade in the Middle East, enquired again from his mother in Argyll (the first time was on 2nd January 1942 when he asked 'has anyone heard news of Angus Macdonald & Co?'), 'If you have any regimental news, particularly of the 2nd battalion, please let me have it, as I know nothing beyond Ian Stewart's *BBC* broadcast from Bombay at the end of March and I wonder what happened to Angus Macdonald and all of them.' It is hard for our generation accustomed to instantaneous global communications to grasp that during the war news travelled slowly. Hector, serving in the Middle East, was poorly informed about what was going on in other parts of the world. There is a poignancy here in Hector's plea; it resembles strongly another relationship between two army officers, that of Angus's grandfather and his adjutant, Lieutenant Lygon, who was killed in South Africa. After Colonel Stewart's broadcast, the Macdonalds could be under no illusion as to what had gone on in Malaya with the Argylls. But where was Angus? The Colonel was in little doubt as to what had happened to The Rooseboom, but Daisy was yet to hear officially of its fate.

Colonel Stewart, Angus Rose, and David Wilson reached Colombo in Ceylon on 2nd March, 1942, the day the Rooseboom was expected. After three days' rest at the Galle Face Hotel, the officers caught a train to Delhi where they formed a 'jungle training team.' During his voyage and after reaching dry land, Stewart prepared a talk on the Argylls and the Malayan Campaign, broadcast and read by a senior army officer in Bombay on 10th March. Stewart's party departed Singapore on the morning of 12th February on The Durban, a Royal Navy cruiser and arrived the following evening in Batavia, Java. From there, they boarded The Pankor, a small, bomb-damaged Malayan steamer and sailed up the west coast of Sumatra and, after dodging enemy aircraft and submarines, they reached Colombo 10 days later.

Returning to the War Office letter, perhaps the disinterested correspondent had some prescience when he or she advised Daisy to notify the department of her new address if she moved house. Maybe grieving widows and mothers tend to up sticks and move. For this is what Daisy did. Early that summer she 'flitted,' but not far, just a couple of miles up the road to Ballure. At that time Cosmo Lang was the tenant, so Daisy asked if she could have the house back. They came to an agreement that, provided Daisy let Lang stay there each summer for as long as he liked, she could live at Ballure. Daisy moved with the bow tie-wearing Robert in a horse-drawn cart piled with her furniture. The move was easy; she had made many when she let Largie for the shooting.

Still, my grandmother clung to her hope that Angus was alive. The worst of it was not knowing. At least Violet was certain of Martin's fate. Because his death was unequivocal she could grieve properly and even visit her son's grave. Her twin sister had no such 'luxury.' It was as if the ancients returned to haunt her but in their case, as in Homer's telling of the story of Troy, the family was fortunate to possess the body of their loved one. When Achilles killed Hector, he humiliated his victim's family by refusing him a proper burial and dragging his body through the streets. In all cultures, grieving families wish to retrieve the remains of their fallen servicemen so they can bury them with honour. In Angus's case, because his body was never found, there was no certainty and Daisy was left in limbo poised between hope and despair. As she received no official recognition or death certificate, she could hold no funeral ceremony, burial, entombment, or scattering of ashes for Angus. So the grief cycle of shock, numbness and disbelief was suspended. There was a stop-go effect on the family's consciousness and they were unable to break ties with the deceased, which is necessary for mourning. They were also unable to reintegrate the loved one's memory into themselves and thereby find closure. The confusion as to what had happened to Angus froze the grieving, and Daisy was unable to move forward. What was she to think? Was her loss final or temporary? Were there not tales of men, long after they were reported missing, emerging alive from the jungle or found on desert islands?

There was, however, plenty to divert the lady's attention. She redesigned a border on the house's west-facing wall and planted tulips and lilies and read books in the summer house that looked out on to the islands. By mid June, Ballure's tenant returned. Lang hadn't visited since before the outbreak of war. Driven in his old Morris by Mr Wells, his chauffeur, he arrived wearing a plain collar and tie. He stayed for 2½ months, drew strength from his visits to the Cell, the small room he used as a personal chapel, and excursions to Rhunahaorine Point, but was peeved to find his favourite walk spoiled by the Admiralty's firing range. The prelate's visits helped Daisy by providing her with spiritual stability and a means of strengthening her faith. He was a trusted friend who, in spite of his high ecclesiastical position, was also a good companion. Their High Anglican orthodoxy was a given, yet they resorted to a monastic simplicity when celebrating the liturgy in the Cell. Anglo-Catholicism was a comfort to Daisy; it protected her from more extreme religious practices such as spiritualism. A friend suggested she consult a medium, to see if she was able to find out anything about Angus but she refused. My grandmother had a horror of 'contacting the dead' even though her generation, who lost so many young men during The Great War, were keen on occultism. While her father campaigned in South Africa, Daisy's older brother, Colville experimented with 'table-turning.' This alarmed the Crabbes, especially when 'messages from the other side' proved wildly doom-laden and inaccurate.

On 8 May 1945, the war in Europe ended but the Prime Minister, Mr Churchill's address to the nation that day was cautionary. The conflict in the Far East was far from over. Only after America dropped an atom bomb on Hiroshima and another on Nagasaki did Japan surrender. Indeed, on 2 September, on board the US Missouri, she signed an unconditional surrender. Closer to home, Daisy's son-in-law Henry Rogers was repatriated on 23 April from a German prisoner of war camp. But there was still no news of Angus. In late October, ships full of Far East prisoners of war and internees arrived at Liverpool's docks. The Japanese had held them in captivity in countries as far flung as Hong Kong, Sumatra, Thailand, Malaya, Singapore, and Japan. Before these men and women, weak from starvation, disease and other forms of physical abuse, shuffled to freedom down their ship's gangway, they agreed to swear an oath of secrecy about the treatment they had received. They were the lucky ones; thousands had died building railways, working down mines, and constructing roads, buildings, and bridges. When peace came, some were so weak that they died on the voyage home while survivors suffered for years afterwards: malaria, hepatitis, an enlarged heart, and ulcerated intestines were some of their medical conditions. The worst legacy was the psychological damage. The horrors of that period never left the former POWs. When Daisy learned about the torture and starvation these servicemen suffered, she was relieved that her son had not worked on the infamous 'death railway' or laboured down a Japanese mine. She was convinced that Angus would have died in captivity. 'He was too tall,' she said. 'It was the short, wiry type who coped best.'

On 5 March 1943 Captain Frisby, who had served in Malaya with the Federated Malay States Volunteer Force (FMSVF), wrote to the War Office from Sydney, Australia. Having escaped from Singapore on the Celia, he was only able to offer a comprehensive list of his own battalion, the Volunteers, but not Paris's staff. 'I'm afraid I can't help much,' he wrote. 'I made a note of them at the time, but somehow or other, this note has disappeared.' He added that as Paris's brigade major, Angus was put in charge of the British other ranks on board the motor launch until he deputed Frisby to take over. Frisby and most of his colleagues in the FMSVF boarded ships bound for Australia via Java.

The problem was that much of the official documentation and papers were destroyed or lost. A nominal roll of all who had embarked on the Rooseboom was handed to the British troops' headquarters at Padang, but within a couple of weeks (18 March), Padang fell to the Japanese and only a list from memory could be submitted to Ceylon Command, the Rooseboom's intended destination. Angus's name appears on this list with Brigadier Paris and a number of other senior officers from a variety of regiments. The problem of identification and knowledge of who had boarded which vessel was heightened by the fact that so many Allied ships were sunk by the enemy. Those who survived were invariably captured so they were, in the main, unable to offer information on what had happened until after the war.

Towards the end of hostilities, when the tide of the war was turning against them, Japan allowed internees and POWs to make humanity broadcasts. Much of their content was information on the fate of civilians and service personnel in the Far East. One such broadcast was made by the sole British survivor of the Rooseboom, Corporal Walter Gibson. On 15 June 1944, he divulged on Tokyo Radio the names of a number of British personnel who had perished after the ship went down. These were Brigadier Paris, Angus, Captain Blackwood of 12th Indian Infantry Brigade and several other soldiers from the 2nd Argylls. The broadcast, transmitted between 0400 and 0430 hours GMT, was picked up by a monitoring station in Western Canada, Vancouver's Point Grey area. Stations such as this intercepted enemy wireless traffic and by 1943, Vancouver's Point Grey had started to crack Japan's

KANA code. Undoubtedly, the station passed Corporal Gibson's message to an interested British War Office department. Was Daisy aware of the broadcast and if she was, did she believe it was authentic? After all, it could have been a hoax. Information about the war in the Far East was scant, unreliable, and confused. Added to all the uncertainty was the poor, physical and mental state of the returning POWs. It would have been grossly insensitive to grill them for news of missing servicemen the moment they reached British soil. So Daisy, along with many other anxious mothers, wives, and children, waited for concrete information.

On 5th December 1945 a service of thanksgiving was held in St. Paul's Cathedral, London to commemorate the end of the war in the Far East and the homecoming of prisoners and civilian internees. On that same day the Macdonalds' long-standing friend, Archbishop Lang died and his funeral took place five days later in Westminster Abbey. Lang was always a trusted friend of Daisy and had officiated at her marriage in April 1906 to John Moreton Macdonald. He had been a comfort to her when, 15 years later, her husband died after a short illness (Lang conducted the burial service). He baptised several Macdonald children including Angus in the summer of 1913, and in the castle chapel married Douna to Henry Rogers in 1932. Most of all, Lang was a support to Daisy during the last three years of the war, when she had needed it most. I like to think that the reason for his visits to Ballure in the summers of 1942, 1943, and 1944 was that he wanted to give Daisy, younger than him by 15 years, his support. His duties as archbishop had ceased on his retirement.

Finally, on 3 January 1946 an Argyll soldier offered information on Angus to staff at the War and Colonial Office in London. This was the aforementioned Walter Gibson. After his humanity call in June 1944, the War Office had suspected that there was at least one British survivor from the ship. The difficulty was in ascertaining who had boarded it when the only record they possessed was a list made from memory.

Almost two months after Walter Gibson gave his testimony, a gentleman named Mr Stuart, an employee of the Hong Kong

Shanghai Bank, confirmed that Angus had embarked on the SS Rooseboom at Padang and therefore must have drowned. Now that these fragments of evidence were known, Daisy could no longer hold out much hope for Angus's return, and on 13 April 1946 she inserted an announcement in *The Times* in the 'On Active Service' column. 'Missing after the fall of Singapore and now officially presumed killed in action at sea, in the sinking of SS Rooseboom...' Still the words suggest equivocacy. Angus was 'presumed' killed but not known to have been. Daisy was now able to state that officialdom had deemed her son was dead.

They say that the population increases after a war. Certainly, the Macdonald family helped swell what we now term the 'baby boom' generation. The first Macdonald baby born in peacetime was to Caitriona and Daisy's youngest son, Simon, on 17 August 1946. Like many other grieving families such as Mrs Wainwright, sister of Captain Michael Blackwood, the couple named their son after his lost uncle. In Simon and Caitriona's case, it was a gesture, not only of fond remembrance, but recognition that one day, this boy would inherit the property that Angus would have possessed. This was the Lockhart land of Lee and Carnwath in Lanarkshire. After two world wars, it was quite common for property designated for older sons killed in war to be passed to their younger brother. Henry Rogers' inheritance would have gone to one of his two half-brothers had both not been killed in the Great War. In a similar manner, when Angus was lost, it was expected that Simon would become the owner of the Lockhart estate. Significantly, the baby's parents chose affection over dynastic affiliation when they named their first son Angus. Uncle Angus's first name was Charles, chosen in respect of his paternal grandfather and because he stood in line to inherit a property, headed by Charles Lockhart who married Elizabeth of Largie. However, Angus, and not Charles, was the name Simon and Caitriona preferred for their first son. In choosing it, they selected the name our uncle most closely identified with, the one he wished his friends, family and, above all, his army colleagues to use.

Unlike the regal-sounding Charles, and its Jacobite roots, the name Angus strikes a demotic, very Scottish note. Steeped in mythology, Angus as a name straddles the old world and the new. No more so is this demonstrated than in the original words of the beautiful traditional lullaby *Dream Angus* which continues to enthral (in modern arrangements by singers like Donovan and Annie Lennox).

Can ye no hush your weepin'
All the lambs are sleepin'
Birdies and beasties are nestled together
Dream Angus is hurtlin' o'er the heather

Dreams to sell, fine dreams to sell.
Angus is here wi' dreams to sell.
Hush my sweet bairn and sleep without fear,
Dream Angus has brought you a dream my dear.

List' to the curlew cryin'
Faintly the echoes dying,
Even the birdies and the beasties are sleepin'
But my bonny bairn is weepin' weepin'

Dreams to sell, fine dreams to sell.
Hush my sweet bairn and sleep without fear
Dream Angus has brought you a dream my dear.

Associated with the god of dreams, Angus is a timeless figure in folklore. The mythical Angus offers forgiveness and reconciliation through his gift of love and dreams. As I conducted this search for Angus, I discovered that I too was finding a way of reconciliation. In digging up and turning over so much of the past I realised that our family story, its bones and flesh, was lost when my uncle drowned. In discovering who Angus was and what he had experienced and suffered, I was able to understand why my elders had behaved in the way they had done.

Just as Simon and Caitriona's son would one day take on the mantle of his dead uncle and inherit his land, another boy born two years later on 18 March 1948 became a symbol of hope. He was the fourth and last child of the Rogers and they too named him after Douna's missing brother. What was more, the boy bore an uncanny resemblance to his dead uncle. He grew up tall, dark haired, with large, handsome brown eyes. Daisy wasted no time in showering him with love and admiration. Little Angus became her favourite grandchild, much to the incomprehension of the others and particularly me. I was born three months after Angus Rogers. I have photographs of us as toddlers playing and squabbling over a honeypot standing on a table placed on the gravel outside Ballure's front door. In each snapshot, Daisy holds Angus on her lap or has her arm around him. In another she helps him complete a jigsaw. She is all eyes for Angus but not for me. At the time, I resented it even though my mother tried to compensate for Daisy's neglect. It wasn't until I returned recently to those photos that I saw things differently. As I pieced together the events leading up to my birth, I realised why Daisy had a particular fondness for my cousin. By favouring him above me and possibly her other grandchildren, she relived the childhood of Angus, her son. When at breakfast she ordered from Robert McKinven a soft-boiled egg for Angus and not for me or my sisters, Daisy was merely apportioning love and attention to the boy who represented her lost son. I can now see how this fondness she felt for my cousin, was nothing to do with him per se or me, but a need for this old lady (now in her late 70s) to feel close to her own son.

If eggs for breakfast were a treat, so were other foodstuffs, particularly imported goods. All around were signs of austerity as the war against Hitler and the axis powers had to be paid for. Not only did Daisy try to move on, but the rest of the world was also doing its best to put the past behind it. At this time, Lieutenant General Percival at his home in Hertfordshire received a letter from an old friend in Malaya. 'The Japanese,' he wrote, 'are not hated here, as I expected they would be. Today, the first consignment of Japanese toys arrived and were being sold to Malays and Tamils by the Chinese shopkeeper, clearly labelled MADE IN JAPAN. I speak of Mersing where thousands of Chinese were slaughtered by the Japanese less than three years ago.'

This was 1948 when Daisy stayed with my parents in their Berkshire home after my birth on 15th June. 1948 saw the founding of the welfare state by Atlee's Labour government, while overseas the birth of Israel occurred. There was a mood of optimism in spite of continued food rationing and a scarcity of resources. The past, at last, was being wrapped up and laid to rest. However, in the Macdonald family this was far from the case. Just as Angus Rogers and I were beginning to talk and try our first baby steps, something happened in Edinburgh to shatter my family's equilibrium.

The lid of Pandora's box suddenly flew open.

The Rooseboom

WHO WAS WALTER GIBSON?

WALTER GIBSON LIVED up to his alias, which was 'Hoot' Gibson, after a Hollywood silent movie star of the 1920s and 1930s. The original Hoot Gibson rode bareback in rodeos and, as a side-line, was an actor and stunt-man performing dramatic, dare-devil acts. Renowned for his he-man, cowboy image, the Hollywood star made a lot of money and spent it in self-publicity, shouting about himself and his daring. He painted his name on the fuselage of his private aeroplanes, which he raced regularly and dangerously.

In sum, the original Gibson was neither silent nor passive but an exhibitionist.

So, Walter Gibson earned himself an apt nickname, as he too was well-known for his braggadocio and self-aggrandisement, and little else, at first. Perhaps he was trying to compensate for his size; he was small in stature and weighed only 7 stone (98 lbs).

Born in Glasgow in 1914 Gibson was reputed to have been 'a Mossbank boy,' which meant he went to Borstal or a reformed school for young offenders. His peers in the Battalion would tease him by asking "what were you put in for, Hoot?," which angered the young recruit. In 1929 Gibson joined the Argyll & Sutherland Highlanders as a piper boy and at the end of that year sailed to China to join the Argylls' 2nd Battalion. Four years later he accompanied the Battalion to Secunderabad in south India and served in the Waziristan campaign in north-west India. From 1937 when Angus joined the 2nd Argylls in India, the two soldiers' paths crossed but they came from different social backgrounds, one from an old Argyllshire family and the other a poor, if not deprived, environment. In physique they were poles apart. Angus measured 6 feet 3 or 4 inches, Gibson was a foot shorter.

In 1997 during a conversation with Audrey Holmes McCormick, author of *Moon over Malaya*, which covers the 2nd Argylls' Malayan Campaign, Major Eric T Moss (regimental sergeant-major in India) said, Walter Gibson, whom he knew well, was very intelligent. For this reason he was employed in the Battalion and

Brigade's intelligence sections, and Angus, as adjutant and later Chief-of-Staff of the Brigade, worked closely with Gibson.

Gibson served with the Battalion in Malaya. When the Japanese invaded on 14 December 1941 he was with his unit, as it fought the length of the peninsula in an attempt to prevent the invaders from capturing the country, especially Singapore island. From the start of hostilities, the Argylls were in continuous action but it wasn't until the battle of Slim River on 7th January, that they reached breaking-point. Gibson was among 300 officers and men who were separated from their Battalion and lost in the jungle. For six weeks they stumbled through the inhospitable countryside in an attempt to re-join their colleagues. Finally, after dividing into small parties, three soldiers only reached the coast arriving at Port Dickson in the south-west, the town from which the Argylls had set off barely two months earlier at the start of the campaign.

In the interim the fugitives suffered from all manner of privation: many died of malarial attacks, dysentery, 'jungle sores,' exposure, starvation, and exhaustion. Some, already wounded, gave up and invariably died. Others were taken prisoner by the Japanese. Their diet was unrefined tapioca which, when boiled, tasted like potatoes, unripe bananas, and 'jungle stew' consisting of bamboo shoots with slugs. They made progress by night, sometimes achieving as many as 10 miles but usually only two or three. By slashing their way through the undergrowth under cover of darkness, they gained protection from the Japanese patrols. However, the Malays and Tamils were unreliable and would sooner betray them than help. The Chinese though were invariably kind to them. Sometimes these troops found refuge in secret huts in the jungle, where the local population brought them food and from which they bartered their few possessions for road maps and rations. Maps and compasses, of course, were invaluable to them.

The other soldiers who reached Port Dickson with Gibson were a fluent speaker of Malay and Chinese, Captain Douglas Broadhurst from the Straits Settlement Police and attached to the Argylls, and Lance Corporal Jock Gray. On February 13th two days before the British surrender in Singapore and the day before Angus departed the island, Gibson and his companions emerged from the jungle six miles north of Port Dickson. Thanks to Broadhurst's language skills, they acquired a Chinese sampan and sailed it to Sumatra where at Rengat they met Brigadier Paris's party. By this time, Sergeant Willie or 'Toorie' MacDonald, one of the Battalion's best NCOs and badly wounded at the battle of Dipang, joined them. They reached Padang on 21st February.

After Angus, his brigadier, and 500 passengers and crew, five days later, boarded the Rooseboom, we have only Gibson's account of what happened. In 1949 with the help of a Scottish journalist, Gibson wrote an article infused with heroism, murder, pathos and self-sacrifice about the 26 days he spent on a lifeboat adrift in the Indian Ocean. Shortly afterwards, his dramatic story appeared in *The Reader's Digest* and in 1952 on the 10th anniversary of the night when he was cast into the sea, Gibson published a book *The Boat*, translated into many languages, about his trials after the Rooseboom sank.

As a 1,000 ton KPM steamer with a crew of Dutch officers and Javanese seamen, the Rooseboom plied coastal runs between Sumatra and Java. During the final week of February 1942, the ship, en route from Batavia to Ceylon, received orders to pick up passengers at Padang. Soldiers of all ranks, officials, policemen, traders, miners, planters, also women and children crammed on to The Rooseboom, which lay perilously low in the water. Departing at dusk the Dutch vessel headed west towards the open sea, looking out for enemy aircraft. After two nights, the Dutch captain told the evacuees that the ship was now out of bombing range and they were relatively safe. All on board heaved a sigh of relief. In his book, Gibson introduces some of the passengers, such as Brigadier Paris, Captain Mike Blackwood and Angus. Florid in his praise of the first, he also admires the second whose yacht, he claimed inaccurately, was used by Paris's party to escape Singapore. Angus, he narrated, was 'a member of a famous Argyllshire family, heir to a £200,000 estate.'

The author also states that these officers 'were involved in hand-to-hand fighting on Singapore island.'

On their 3rd evening at sea, Paris invited the officers to toast their safe arrival in Ceylon expected to be 48 hours later. Within five hours of their celebration at 23 hours 50 the torpedo struck. Gibson was sleeping on deck next to Sergeant Willie Macdonald who was killed instantly. Chaos was immediate, the din deafening: screams, the hiss of escaping steam, the gush of water rushing into the craft and the frantic bellowing of a bullock in the hold. Gibson's collar-bone was broken and a piece of metal lodged itself in his shin. Within minutes the ship sank, but before it went down the corporal managed to throw himself into the sea and find a chunk of debris to cling onto. Then he saw the lifeboat, the only one out of four on board that the crew managed to launch. It was 28 feet long and 8 feet at its widest part but its bow had a gaping hole which the captain and officers repaired. After letting three women (no children managed to escape the ship) and five wounded on board, 80 survivors including Gibson clambered into the boat, built to hold a maximum of 28. Each person stood shoulder to shoulder with no room to change position or sit down. In the water, their heads bobbing, were more survivors. Most gravitated to the life boat so that it eventually supported 135 persons, many of whom remained in the water clinging to the outside of the vessel.

The next morning senior officers took a tally of their food and water; much had floated away as the boat was launched. They had a case of bully beef (48 12 oz tins), two 7 lb tins of fried rice, 48 tins of condensed milk and 6 Bols gin bottles filled with fresh water. Each person received one tablespoonful of water at sun up and a spoonful of milk and water at night. A tin of bully beef was to be shared between 12 people daily. The wife of a Dutch officer produced a tablespoon as a measure and shared out her thirst-quenching tablets.

Paris stood in the boat's stern and told the evacuees that the captain was in command while he was responsible for discipline. He tried to reassure them that since the Rooseboom was expected to arrive at Colombo the following day, a search party would soon be sent to find them. He expected they'd be rescued within four days. Paris then ordered each uninjured man to spend four hours a day clinging to a lifeline in the water. On the first day sharks approached but the survivors scared them off by yelling at them. A fish stung a soldier in the water and he died in agony an hour later.

The three women on board were Mrs Nunn, wife of Group Captain R. L. Nunn, director of Public Works in Singapore who, after pushing his wife through the port-hole of his cabin, went down with the ship, the wife of a Dutch officer and Doris Lim, a young Chinese woman who had worked for British Intelligence in North China and escaped from Tientsin before the Japanese occupation. They sat close together surrounded by sweating, groaning Jocks, Cockneys, and Javanese. Half the occupants were 19 to 20 year old conscripts of the 18th Division, sent just before the Japanese invasion to bolster Malaya's defences.

Towards dusk, Lieutenant Colonel Douglas of the Indian Army Ordnance Corps swam from a raft floating one hundred yards from the boat. He was at breaking point. With him on the raft was a white woman whose leg had been blown off, lance-corporal Jock Gray, and Angus. My uncle had carried from the ship a flask of what he thought was water but instead was brandy. He had spent the day on the raft drinking from it.

"Angus Macdonald is raving mad," jabbered Lieutenant-Colonel Douglas "I had to leave him. He was trying to push me off the raft." Douglas's voice rose excitedly, and as darkness fell he shouted one sentence in English, the next in Urdu, in a crazy, high-pitched babble. He struck out wildly. "Put him over before he tips the boat up!" screamed a number of voices. Colonel Douglas struggled as they ejected him. He gripped tightly the gunwale, but they fended him off with an oar. In the blackness, he slipped away, shouting a stream of Urdu oaths.

From the second day, hunger, thirst and the cramped conditions began to tell on the survivors. Their skin blistered, especially that of the far-haired Dutch. Many tore off their clothes, dipped them in the sea and put them over their heads to keep cool. All on board were subject to hallucinations. They imagined they saw ships on the horizon. Some had vivid dreams of food, drink, and friendly gatherings. Many of the young drank sea water and those who swallowed a lot fell into a coma and never emerged from it. Gibson gargled with salt water and each morning he cleaned his teeth with it and by the end of the first week he started to drink it in very small quantities. On the third day, some drank their own urine, but it tasted acidic and failed to quench their thirst. Suspicions arose as people disappeared after dark. The following night, they heard screams and shouts, and in the morning 20 people were missing. Then they realised a murder gang was on board. At this time, their rations were cut. A tin of bully beef was shared between 20 and the water ration decreased to one spoonful a day.

At the end of their first week, Brigadier Paris collapsed into a coma and died. Throughout those terrible days, Mike Blackwood had shared his water ration with his superior. Now he tried to hold a simple funeral service for him. The following day Blackwood collapsed and drowned in the bilge water lying at the bottom of the boat. Before his death, Blackwood told Gibson that the brigadier wanted to recommend him for a Distinguished Conduct Medal, an award presented to other ranks in the British army for gallantry in the field. At this time one of the engineers stabbed to death the Dutch captain and a number of suicides occurred. Invariably before the individual threw himself into the sea, he tried to grab the rations and fling them overboard as well.

Gibson now took charge of the water bottles, but by this time there were only two left. When all the Dutch officers were gone (either drowned or had committed suicide), the Javanese crew began quietly to take over the boat. At this time all the senior army officers had expired, and Gibson saw discipline was maintained on board. On the 7th evening they ran out of water. Just as critical was the fact the murder gang in the bows had become more powerful. The rest of the boat realised they had to kill them, so Gibson led an onslaught on the group and rushed them overboard but not before they killed Drummer Hardie, Colonel Stewart's batman. Hardie's courage was legendary. At no time was he ever known to run, not even under threat from the Japanese.

Along with Colonel Stewart, Hardie was the last soldier to cross the Johore Causeway before the sappers demolished it.

One of the high points on the lifeboat was a cloud-burst which lasted for three or four minutes. As the rain fell into the boat the survivors knelt down and lapped it up, filling their bottles with water. On another day when a dozen gulls landed on their bows the people pounced and caught seven after which they tore them to pieces and devoured the raw flesh. But the most horrendous occurrence happened on their penultimate day at sea when the four crew members (all Javanese) with a rowlock struck repeatedly the head of a gunner, weakened with thirst and starvation. Using a tin as a blade they slashed his body, dug their hands into the wound, and extracted chunks of his flesh, which they devoured.

The following morning the survivors saw land. It was Sipora, part of the Mentawis, a chain of islands running north to south 60 miles off the west coast of Sumatra. The living numbered five: Gibson, Doris Lim and three members of the crew although one drowned in the surf trying to reach the shore. As soon as they were on dry land, the non-Europeans quickly disappeared. In 26 days they had drifted 1,000 miles across the Indian ocean and fetched up 100 miles from the port at Padang. After receiving food and water from the islanders and resting for six weeks, Gibson and Doris Lim were handed over to the Japanese who sent them to a prisoner-of-war camp at Padang. They arrived on May 18th, 79 days after they had set off on board the Rooseboom.

This is Gibson's story, as we have it. In his book he explains why he was the only white man to survive. Having been a regular soldier in foreign service for 13 years, he was thoroughly acclimatised to the east, having served in hot places like India and Malaya. When the torpedo struck and Gibson suffered from a broken collarbone, he realised it was a blessing in disguise, because senior officers ordered him not to go into the water but remain in the boat. He adopted a mood of passivity, which helped him save valuable energy and he had a dogged determination to survive. Also, he insisted, his daily ritual of gargling and cleaning his teeth with seawater helped raise his morale.

TUCKED BEHIND St. Giles' Cathedral off the Royal Mile in the old part of Edinburgh is the Court of Session which deals with civil matters. The building is often referred to as Parliament House because, before the Act of Union (1707), it was the seat of the Scottish Parliament. It was to this address that Simon on 11th June 1949 presented a petition to determine the death of his older brother. Although he was certain that Angus had lost his life after the Rooseboom sank, he had to wait until 1949 before he could obtain legal confirmation of that fact. Under an Act of Parliament, a person may be presumed dead if he or she has not been heard of for seven years and since Angus disappeared in 1942, this was the opportune moment for Simon to present his petition. In order to inherit the Lockhart property of Lee and Carnwath, left in trust to Angus by Sir Simon Lockhart in 1919, Simon was obliged to go through this legal process. Sir Simon's widow, Hilda Maud (née Moreton) was a first cousin of John, my grandfather and for 25 years after her husband's death she received a life rent from the Lockhart estate. In 1919 John became a trustee but after his death two years later, nobody else was found to represent the interests of Angus, the Macdonald heir, and the estate fell into disrepair. When Hilda Moreton died on 25th April 1944, the trust lapsed and because of Angus's disappearance, Jock stood in as   factor for the estate.

On that morning the court procedure promised to be simple. After a war it was not unusual for relatives of a serviceman killed in action to bring a petition such as this to the courts. But Simon's plea involved an old Scottish family with a large fortune. Angus's inheritance was £200,000 which in today's currency amounts to several million pounds (when in late 2015 Angus Macdonald Lockhart, Simon's eldest son who inherited the Lockhart estate, died, he left £18,000,000 in his will). The public benches in the court were filled with journalists, notably a reporter from *The Scotsman* and Macdonald Daly, a popular Scottish writer and radio (later television) broadcaster. He was also editor of *The Scottish*

Sunday Express. Undeniably, the family fortune drew the hacks who, that day, must have believed that all their Christmases had come together, especially when they suspected a harrowing, but colourful story would be told.

Crucial to the hearing was a 35 year old Argyll & Sutherland Highlanders corporal from Paisley: Walter Gardiner Gibson. Ever since January 1946 when the War Office in London sent his statement to the Casualties Department of the Colonial Office, Gibson was known to be the Rooseboom's sole European survivor. Before the judge, Lord Sorn, Gibson stated that he had served with Angus for a number of years in the east. He explained that on 26th February 1942 Angus embarked at Padang, Sumatra on the SS Rooseboom with British officers, other ranks and some civilians, all of whom were being evacuated to Colombo in Ceylon. On 1st March, a Japanese submarine torpedoed the ship and almost two thirds of the crew and passengers went down with her. In spite of receiving a wound in the head and shoulder Gibson managed to escape from the ship. Only one lifeboat was successfully launched but at least 135 passengers and crew attempted to cram themselves into it. One of these individuals was Walter Gibson himself. Those who failed crowded around it clinging in the water to its sides. At about midday on 2nd March 1942 a raft with four people on board drifted close to the lifeboat. Lieutenant-Colonel Douglas from the Indian Army Ordnance Corps swam from it to the boat and climbed on board. He stated that the other occupants of the raft were Major Angus Macdonald, another British officer, and a woman. He told them that Angus, "as a result of the heat, thirst and exposure was not in his proper senses". Lieutenant Colonel Douglas died about 24 hours later and on the morning of the 3rd, the lifeboat occupants saw that the raft, which had remained close to them, was now empty. They assumed that Angus and his companions had died during the night. Gibson stated that, at the end of his 26 days adrift, only three people and himself had survived the ordeal. Thanking the corporal for his evidence, the judge said, 'You had a remarkable escape.' He summed up the hearing by telling the court that he had arrived at the conclusion that Angus had died on the night of 2nd/3rd March 1942.

I would like to know what was in the mind of 53 year old Gordon MacIntyre (Lord Sorn) when he told Walter Gibson that he had had a remarkable escape. Three generations of MacIntyres, incidentally have entered my life since that date. In the 1970s I knew Bobby, Sorn's son and in 2013 Gavin, Bobbie's son, as a student of a course I taught at Edinburgh University. I make this observation because it illustrates how Scotland was, and in many respects still is, a small, largely rooted, cohesive society. Wasn't there a hint of irony or even of suspicion in Lord Sorn's comment to Gibson? Perhaps. I'm sure the judge would have at least got wind of the confusion surrounding Gibson's rank. Writing in January 1946 in response to Gibson's statement on what happened after the Rooseboom sank, the War Office advised the Enquiries and Casualties Department of the Colonial Office that 'it is unlikely Gibson will be confirmed in his commission so if you have occasion to write to him he had better be referred to as Corporal!' The Court petition, however, referred to the Argyll soldier as a sergeant and *The Scotsman* report on the court proceedings on 13th June 1949 claimed he was a lieutenant.

With the help of Macdonald Daly, Gibson wrote an article about his experience on the lifeboat. Its serialisation in late 1949 in *The Scottish Sunday Express* provoked anger within the Regiment, which prompted General McMillan, Colonel of the Regiment to write on 15th November of that year to Daly stressing that Walter Gibson, a corporal in the Argyll & Sutherland Highlanders had never been granted a commission either by Lieutenant-Colonel Robertson (one-time commanding officer of The Argylls) or Brigadier Paris. It's significant that Gibson named these two senior officers and not Colonel Stewart as they were killed in action and were unable to refute the claim. As for the moment, when shortly before his death on the lifeboat, Captain Mike Blackwood allegedly confided to Gibson that Paris was going to recommend him for a Distinguished Conduct Medal, this also could never be verified as both officers died on the boat. In his letter to the newspaper editor General McMillan emphasized that Gibson was discharged from the army as a corporal and that in a War Office missive dated 25th January 1946, AG (Adjutant General) officers categorically refuted his statement that he ever held a commission.

Gibson's colleagues in the 2nd battalion regarded him more with amusement than with indignation or anger. Major Eric Moss remembered him strolling around the barracks modelling himself on his superior, Lieutenant-Colonel L B Robertson. At the end of the war, Moss was released from captivity. When he reached Rangoon he found Major Gairdner, the Argylls 2nd in command, in hospital. From his bed Gairdner advised Moss that if he saw Corporal Bloody 'Hoot' Gibson, wearing two pips on his shoulder, he should get them off him. But Moss never caught up with the Corporal, who was 'swanning around' as a 2nd lieutenant. When, after their long voyage home, the released Argyll captives arrived at Southampton and gathered in the transit camp, Moss leafed through a visitors' book and saw the name, Captain W. G. G. G. Gibson. 'Every time he promoted himself he added another 'G' to his name!' said Moss. He next heard that someone had seen Gibson in a railway carriage in Glasgow with the MC (Military Cross) ribbon and three pips on his shoulder.

A month after the Japanese interrogated Gibson and Doris Lim in Padang, the former made a journey of 900 miles lasting five days by lorry with 1,600 British, Dutch and Eurasian captives to Medan on the north coast of Sumatra, where they were imprisoned for two years. With Gibson was planter John Hedley, a Johore Volunteer Officer commissioned as a lieutenant in HM Forces General Service stationed with 1st Mysore Infantry in Singapore. Hedley confirmed that on arriving in the prisoner of war camp in Padang, Gibson claimed he was an officer, which aroused the anger of a number of Australian prisoners who gave him 'a sound drubbing,' and not the light-hearted play he referred to in his books.

Doubtless the reason for the corporal masquerading as a commissioned officer stemmed from his desire for self-promotion and aggrandisement. Notwithstanding the disrepute officers and men of the battalion held him in, Gibson in the account of his lifeboat experiences, strikes a note of megalomania or, as Eric Moss suggested, psychopathology. While testifying in court, however, under oath and chastened by the solemnity of his surroundings, his responses to questions posed by Counsel and Judge were cryptic and restrained.

Nevertheless, in not needing to expatiate on the occurrences in the boat, the witness gives an incomplete picture of what actually happened. Gibson refers to Lance Corporal Jock Gray as a British officer, which is untrue. Gibson claims that Lieutenant-Colonel Douglas died 24 hours after he clambered on board the boat but, after being pushed off it, he died soon afterwards.

It is understandable that Gibson failed to divulge Angus's drunkenness or the volley of oaths Douglas uttered as he fell into the water. Opposite page 16 of the British edition of 'The Boat,' is a sketch of the author wearing a Glengarry with its double dice pattern around the rim and a large Argyll badge pinned on its side. Gibson holds a pipe to his mouth above which grows a resplendent handlebar moustache. The American edition has a photograph of the soldier in an identical pose. In each, he appears strong, manly, managing and accomplished. But something isn't right. From the way he holds his pipe to the jaunty manner in which he wears his Glengarry, Gibson appears thoroughly theatrical and phoney, in his attempt to impersonate an army officer.

Without question, Gibson promotes himself as leader of the pack and the boat's boss. In *The Boat*, the author explains how, after Slim River when he accompanied Captain Lapsley in the jungle, the officer appointed him as his right hand man because he read maps so well. On the boat, Colonel Acworth put Gibson in charge of ensuring survivors received the correct measure of rations. Gibson also claimed that Captain Mike Blackwood asked him to help look after the brigadier. At all times, Gibson gives the impression that he is in the centre of things and in charge. He writes that it was he who took over discipline on the boat after the officers died. In his War Office statement, he explained how they collected the rain water on the boat and, as the sole surviving officer, he rationed it out.

Many asked how the corporal survived while all, except three others, did not. His wounds, he admitted. helped prevent him from having to spend time in the water clinging to the side of the boat. In court, he explained that when the torpedo struck he received an injury to his head and shoulder but omitted to mention his other wounds such as his shin damaged by a piece of metal that had lodged in it. This begs the question, that if he had admitted to any more injuries in court, the judge might have asked how he could have survived at all. It's possible that from the very beginning, Gibson feigned his injuries so that he could receive better treatment on the boat.

When reading Gibson's account, we learn that the detail in *The Scottish Sunday Express* and *Reader's Digest* articles is fuller than what was revealed in court but the book published in 1952 has much more information in it than the articles.. This points to the fact that the author embroidered and embellished his story step-by-step from the court testimony to the articles and finally the narrative of *The Boat*. But memory in general, is usually fuller at the outset of recall. One must take into consideration that Gibson was writing at least seven years after the event took place and after he had experienced unimaginable trauma: a brutal trek through the Malayan jungle, 26 days on the boat, and four days' interrogation by the Japanese after his capture on Sipora island. His captors flung him in an empty cell without food for three days, punched, pummelled, and forced him to kneel for hours on a block of wood three feet long, four feet wide, and two feet thick. Shortly before the end of the war when Gibson was a passenger on a cargo steamer, the Americans torpedoed his vessel conveying him and other prisoners of war from Sumatra to Thailand.

The Times reviewer wrote that *The Boat* was 'sensational on the face of it' and certainly it played to the lowest possible denominator. Gibson refers to the Japanese as pederasts although admittedly during the late 40s and early 50s attitudes towards homosexuality were very different to what they are today. In his attitude towards the young Chinese woman, Doris Lim, he is unabashed. He admits to being attracted to her, "I was seized with a male urge towards the girl as she lay in my arms. I began to fondle her." "Please let me die in peace," was her telling rebuff. The reader might well wonder if his approach was as decorous as he described. Apart from bashing a number of occupants over the head and pushing them overboard, he may well have felt entitled to force sex on the young woman. Gibson explains that he and others on the boat were forced to rush 'the murder gang' off the boat but who is to know which group or person did the killing? And if he was in charge of the rations, who could stop him from grabbing them for himself? It's my guess that if he established himself as alpha male, the woman had no other option but to submit. In such circumstances, it is not the virtuous who survive but the most ruthless. Gibson gives his reasons why he remained alive but we only have his word on that issue. When members of the Javanese crew on the boat, slashed a dying soldier and plunged their hands into the wound and drew out some flesh, which they ate, who is to know if Gibson also joined in? If the Javanese were the wolves, Gibson may well have been the hyena. Even his peers in the Battalion suggest he was capable of such an act. "Do you know," suggested Eric Moss, "what most of us think happened to that wee Chinese girl who was in the boat with Gibson. We think he ate her! " As the saying goes, many a true word is said in jest.

NEEDLESS TO SAY, Daisy and her four surviving children were deeply affected by the publication of Gibson's story in which he describes the final moments of Angus's life. It had been a long wait to know the truth, from the time when my grandmother received the War Office telegram in March 1942, announcing her son was missing, until the moment in June 1949 when Gibson gave his court testimony. During those intervening years, the family had tried to come to terms with their predicament. First, they entertained hope, which soon gave way to despair and finally acceptance that Angus was dead.

While they struggled with the uncertainty, his siblings got on with their lives in a manner similar to Vera Brittain who, after the end of the Great War during which her fiancé and brother were killed, wrote in *Testament of Youth*, that "if the living are to be of any use in this world, they must always break faith with the dead." In September 1947 Mum married a man, the same height and age as her lost brother, who had attended the same preparatory school and, as an undergraduate, learned to fly not at Oxford but Cambridge. There the similarity ended; after leaving university, my father continued to fly, by serving during the war in Bomber Command as a squadron leader. My parents' wedding photograph reveals a delighted groom and a reserved but beautiful bride with 'sad eyes,' observed sister Lis when, many years later, she studied the image. Post-war austerity allowed Mum no bouquet of flowers; she carried instead a small prayer book, its end covers lined in ivory, and the impersonal Edinburgh church where they tied the knot was a far cry from the intimate Largie chapel where the wedding ceremony of Esther's older sister had taken place between the wars. In June 1948, Esther gave birth to me and adjustment to motherhood was hard especially as her father-in-law, Hugh Gladstone died in spring 1949 and his wife, Cecil three months later.

My father was thus unable to offer Esther substantive support with the devastating outcome of Simon's court petition in June of that year. Hugh's will deemed Dad would inherit little from his sizeable estate, the lion's share going to John, his older brother.

I have a framed photograph of me taking my first baby steps in a hayfield on Dad's farm in Berkshire. I had always regarded the occasion as idyllic with an attentive mum, slim and elegant in her Macdonald tartan skirt, and in the background the benign presence of an old cart-horse called Captain, but this domestic scene belies the tales of mayhem and horror spewed up by Gibson at that time in Edinburgh's Court of Session.

After Gibson's disclosures Angus, it seemed, suffered not one death, but two; his actual demise when he died of exposure, thirst and exhaustion, before falling off a raft at night into the Indian Ocean and a more insidious death: the killing of his reputation. It goes without saying that Angus had no resting-place, headstone, or funeral. His death also robbed him of the inheritance, held in trust for him since he was six years old. On leaving the army, therefore, he could have looked forward to owning an ancient title, the laird of Lee and Carnwath, a magnificent castle surrounded by farms of fertile fields, hills, lochs, moorland, and woods. Most importantly, Angus as inheritor of the Lee and Carnwath estate, was to unite the Lockharts and Macdonalds. After Charles Lockhart and Elizabeth Macdonald married in the eighteenth century, the two families fell out. Angus would unite them again just as he, the Macdonalds' third child, acted as a bridge between his older siblings (Jock and Douna) and the younger (Simon and Esther). In fact, his role of connecting and liaison was what he excelled at. As an army officer and chief of staff of his brigade, his job was to provide a link between higher command and the fighting companies in the field.

For Angus's 'other' death, his descent into obscurity and embarrassed silence, I accuse Walter Gibson. It i my belief that commanding officers or colleagues of fallen servicemen 'sugar the pill' when communicating the death to close relatives. They stress the dead soldier's courage, valour and self-sacrifice and try to comfort the bereaved, omitting mention of blood, gore, severed limbs, broken jaws, battered skulls, and the man's possible expressions of fear, lapses of courage and failings in battle. They couch their loved ones' ends as decorously as they can. The shock of death is bad enough so why cause more anguish? To break that code, one of honour and common decency, is heinous and flies in the face of all respect. But Walter Gibson did it, aided and abetted by the opportunism of various newspaper journalists, when he wrote about the events following the sinking of the Rooseboom.

Gibson received assistance from the tabloid press, a branch of the newspaper industry that has always preyed on the famous like Diana, Princess of Wales. The less famous are also fair game and because of their connection with some tragedy or other, they are catapulted into the glare of publicity. In late 1949 Daisy, my Mum, her sister, and brothers found themselves in a similar position, their late brother the subject of ghoulish curiosity and entertainment. Back in 2010, while considering writing a book about Angus, I wandered into an Edinburgh charity bookshop where I discovered a pile of books on World War Two, including a volume of portraits by war artist, Eric Kennington of British fighter and bomber pilots, stories of Rommel in the desert, daring escapes from Colditz and Walter Gibson's *The Boat*. On the cover Gibson was described as 'the man who survived' and author of 'one of the most dramatic sea stories ever told.' I was furious. Here was a man backed by a team of disinterested hacks and editors, creating entertainment out of my family's misery (and many others besides). The book's back cover advertised other 'adventure' stories: 'North for Danger' about gold smuggling, espionage and murder, 'Gentlemen Spies' on the Soviet spy system, 'an authentic document that has all the excitement and drama of fiction' and 'Inside Broadmoor,' a first person narrative of imprisonment in Britain's greatest criminal asylum. The owner of the book collection had been, I imagined, a respectable lawyer or financier, born in the late twenties or early thirties, too late to see active service in the war. His books were a means for him to achieve a vicarious thrill and the story of the Rooseboom was one that he could revel in, wonder at, and congratulate himself that he had not been on that.

Whether it was Gibson, Macdonald Daly, the ghost-writer of the book, the translators of the story, or the readers themselves who were most blameworthy, the effect of these publications was enormously damaging. With this rupture of their code of honour, my family clammed up. The regiment refuted Gibson's claims and in 1954, after the publication of a sequel to 'The Boat,' Walter Gibson emigrated to Ontario in Canada and lost touch with the Argylls.

Our family was not the only one affected by Gibson's story. While conducting my research, I contacted Margaret Gibb, niece of Drummer Hardie, bludgeoned to death on the lifeboat. I wanted to ask Mrs Gibb what she knew about her uncle who served with Angus in the battalion. She had grown up in ignorance of what had happened on the boat and had been unaware of Gibson's account. Brave Drummer Hardie, Colonel Stewart's batman, was her Mum's brother. While Margaret was a child her mother gave little away about him, but she had been very close to her brother. Like me, it was only as a mature woman that Mrs Gibb had tried to find out about her uncle by visiting in 2002 the Argylls' museum in Stirling. In a similar way to my Mum, it caused Margaret's mother too much distress to discuss with her daughter her brother's death.

I hold Walter Gibson and the editors of his articles and book responsible for the silence that lasted for six decades. Written for fame and financial gain, the corporal's account of what happened on the lifeboat, contaminated the grieving families' memories of their lost men with hideous images and details of their deaths. Gibson wrested from Margaret Gibb, myself and many others, our true heritage and birthright, leaving a besmirched wasteland of pain. He prevented us from possessing a sense of pride and knowledge of these officers and men, and in his lurid narrative he associated the names of Angus and Drummer Hardie with, as *The Times* reviewer had observed, "human nature at its vilest." Hardie's exceptional courage and faithful soldiering and Angus's labour in a distinguished military position, especially during the Malayan Campaign, when he toiled for ten weeks in brutally difficult conditions, were kicked aside by Gibson for a sensational scene where Hardie was bludgeoned to death and Angus got blind drunk on brandy. Yet up until the very end, these two men had acted with decency and honour. Can we say the same for Gibson?

When in 2009 I visited Winnie Byrd, daughter of Ronald Reid, once the Largie game-keeper, she showed me a photograph of her brother in full dress uniform: Lance Corporal James Reid of 7th Battalion, Argyll & Sutherland Highlanders, killed in action on 21st July 1943. It's significant that his sister kept his photograph in her living room in a special place. By contrast, Granny placed a photograph of Angus in her bedroom and we never saw it till well after her death. Mum also kept her memory of Angus in a private place. Both of these images displayed Angus in civilian clothes and at no time could a photograph of our lost uncle be seen in a public room. I blame Walter Gibson for Angus's concealment and for the way Daisy and Esther folded their memory of him into their wounded psyches. I also hold him culpable for the evasive way my 103 year old Aunt Anne, in 2009 when I visited her, responded to my enquiry about Angus. "It was so sad," she said, then swiftly turned the conversation to another subject. The cryptic reply implied that his name was still associated with Gibson's calumny.

No wonder my mother was rendered speechless, unable to express or talk coherently about Angus. Her only recourse was to carry on, gain a life, rear her children and try to lead a 'normal' life. In many ways she succeeded. Silence was her way, so much so that Angus and his death eventually became side-lined, sanitised and 'normalised,' so that in 1977, when I watched a BBC television programme on Isaiah Berlin, a British philosopher of Russian/Jewish descent who believed he was exceptionally lucky to have survived two world wars when so many had not, I failed to recognise that my family, although not Jewish or from another group or race persecuted by Hitler, had been tragically affected.

We know that Daisy's three sons failed to escape the war

unharmed. Even Simon, her youngest, was injured. On 24th November 1944 while serving in Italy west of Rimini, an exploding mine wounded him in the shoulder. Each of my grandmother's three sisters lost their second son: Violet's Martin at Calais in 1940, Iris's Roger who, as an escaped prisoner of war, was shot in Italy by Italian Fascists, and Gladys's Hew, who was killed in Normandy after the allied landings in June, 1944. On my father's side of the family, Cousin Dossie, (Dorothy Parrish, nee Drew) reputedly the Victorian prime minister William Ewart Gladstone's favourite granddaughter, lost two sons during the war. Sir William Gladstone of Hawarden informed me of this fact as late as 2015 and although I knew Dossie when I was a child, nobody had mentioned it. They all wanted to forget.

In their attempt to put the war behind them, my parents buried so much that we, the following generation, should have learned about. My family wasn't unusual in this respect. Throughout the country there was a reluctance to remember these men and women. Of the institutions that memorialised them, schools were the first. In 1948, Winchester College added the names of the fallen to War Cloister. In Singapore, disagreement as to the 'rightness' of the British Imperial forces' cause, slowed down the procedure; even in Kintyre it wasn't until 1954, twelve years after Angus was lost at sea, that his name and those of seven others were inscribed on the existing monument that stood opposite Cara. No doubt the Broonie saw it, took note, and even sighed with relief that only eight names were added to the monument. When John, my grandfather, arranged the construction of the memorial after the Great War, the list of dead men was very long. The new one revealed that these young men were brought up near Largie. One was the ploughman's son from the Ferry farm, another was brought up at the forge, his father the local blacksmith. Magdalen, at Oxford University failed to remember its World War Two fallen until 2001. For this college, the Great War hogged the lime-light as far as memorialisation went. It was postulated that nobody could come to terms with the reality of having to go through it all again after the 1914/18 conflict, the war to end all wars.

When my generation came of age at the end of the sixties, it re-acted strongly against militarism. At that time, I had little interest in Angus, why he joined the army and how he died. I was too much caught up with my own life, loves and, aims. But, like Margaret Gibb with her uncle, there came a time when I wanted to find out about my lost relative. I no longer dismissed out of hand his apparently conventional attitudes nor his conformism to army discipline. From having debunked for so long my family's conservatism, approach towards religion and its adherence to traditional values, I realised that these objections failed to detract entirely from my uncle's talent, dedication and strength. In 2010 a Scottish journalist wrote an appreciation of an elderly lady who had lived for many years without disclosing that she worked for the Special Operations Executive and had parachuted into occupied France during the war. In praising the lady's modesty, her reluctance to publicise her achievements, and self-sacrifice, the journalist made a plea for forgotten values, attitudes of my parents' generation that were now regarded by many as old-fashioned and redundant. I saw how my parents and their contemporaries had forfeited their youth to fight for freedom from tyranny and had been willing to give their lives for a just cause. Perhaps the triptych of Eleanor Fortescue Brickdale, presented to Winchester College the year Angus entered the school, had influenced him, in spite of its patrician, elitest message. These ideals of gallantry and dedication to serve others were enacted by men and women, their accomplishments becoming engraved in the minds of many. Captain Oates was one who, during Captain Robert Scott's doomed 1912 Antarctic expedition to reach the South Pole, walked willingly from his tent into a blizzard in order to help his comrades survive. His famous words, 'I am just going outside and I may be some time,' belie his less than gallant behaviour towards young women, especially those from the 'lower orders.' In 2002, Michael Smith published a biography of the captain claiming that, before he set off on his polar escapade, Oates fathered a daughter with a 12 year old girl. Notwithstanding the officer's act, which today would be termed rape, honour of a sort was an accepted aspiration for most young men of the empire and Rudyard Kipling's legendary poem, *If*, embodies these impossibly altruistic ideals. Significantly, he ends with the requirement that men demonstrate empire's primary demand: manliness, nobility, self-sacrifice and endurance without complaint. This was Angus's code. In addition, under dire conditions, he displayed humour, a sardonic wit, understatement, dignity, and sang-froid. Jock dealt with life's blows in a similar fashion: with an extraordinary insouciance towards the amputation of his leg by using his artificial limb to hammer nails into a gate-post. His courage, absence of self-pity, repression of emotion, and disregard of pain should be remembered too.

Those who dishonoured this code, men who dressed as women to gain a place in a lifeboat as some did before the Titanic sank, and air crews who, during a tour of operations, avoided the target, dropping their bombs in a safe place instead, weren't 'playing up and playing the game.' These were the men and women who profiteered from others' privations. I remember a tale told by Mum that illustrated her feelings towards such an individual. During the war, at Oban livestock market in Argyll, a farmer sold his cattle for a phenomenal price. On receiving his cheque the farmer was so delighted that he shouted at the top of his voice, 'Long Live the War!' His jubilation was short-lived; the auctioneer, whose son had been recently killed in action, sent him from the ring and banned him from ever coming back. The code of honour upheld by my family, the regiment and much of society, required always that each man and woman 'play up and play the game.' Some may allege this was the modus operandi of a select few, who could afford to be altruistic, and given his privileged upbringing, this form of conduct was expected of Angus. The memory, however, of him and my entitlement to appreciate his courage and self-sacrifice, in what was an arduous campaign, were obliterated. For six decades I was denied knowledge of his accomplishments.

If Walter Gibson destroyed Angus's reputation he helped to stunt my mother's development. She was nineteen when Jock lost his leg and 21 when Angus was reported missing. Within months of casting off her school uniform she adopted another one in khaki. After her efforts during the war to console Daisy, Gibson's articles and book had the effect of corralling Mum into timidity and fear. She could have achieved much and her failure to realize her potential amounted to another death, a death of the spirit. At the outbreak of war, Mum was about to enter Somerville College, Oxford to read English literature but she postponed entry. Although she could have studied there after hostilities ceased, she was unwilling to grab the opportunity. Mum had seen and suffered too much for her to become an undergraduate at the age of 25. War had made her take cover and flee from education and progress. So, she married and gave birth to four children in a space of six years. But Mum kept her entrance exam papers for Somerville, a letter from the principal congratulating and offering her a place at the college, references from her army days, and her books: leather-bound volumes with gold hand-tooled lettering on the covers and marbled inside end pages of Shelley, Keats, Swinburne, Wordsworth, and Coleridge. From one decade to another, they remained on a shelf unread. After the loss of her brother Mum abandoned her dreams, and I hold the war and Gibson as culpable. Considering the importance of the mother/daughter relationship, we three sisters learned from her example; we hesitated to go out into the world and make something of our lives.

When we as children fought and complained that we had been treated unfairly, begging Mum to intervene, she would say "life isn't fair!" Only now, after finishing my research on Angus do I appreciate what she was thinking when she pronounced those words. Only now do I understand how hard it was for her when in the early sixties we stayed with Dad's sister, Jean and her husband Roddy, then between British ambassadorial postings. I loved to leaf through Aunt Jean's photograph album in which beside family snapshots she had illustrated in pen and ink scenes from her family life. At the beginning of the war, Roddy, as a diplomat in the Foreign Office, was posted to Washington in the USA. To cross the Atlantic he, Jean and their three infant daughters boarded a liner that sailed unaccompanied and not as part of a convoy. In mid-ocean, a German U-boat surfaced but fired no torpedoes at their ship. After the war, Jean illustrated this frightening event in the war-time section of her album. Life isn't fair, is it?

Like the timbre of his voice, the cut of his jacket or his food preferences, I can only guess what Angus thought of his future.

When he wrote months before the Japanese invasion of Malaya, 'after we've dealt with this wretched fellow Hitler,' did he conceive that the end of Empire was so imminent? Before he drowned, my uncle was aware that along with gaining an ancient Scottish name, property and castle, much had to be dismantled so that the past could be distilled into something more essential and relevant. Neither the severely wounded Jock nor Angus could assume properly the role of laird or maintain their castles. Jock pulled his down and Simon, who became owner of the Lockhart inheritance, sold his. Like crusader, Sir Symon Loccard, who held the key to the casket that contained Bruce's heart, Angus failed. Waging battle 700 years after his ancestor, he also fought on foreign soil, confronting an enemy, not from north Africa but from Japan. These two warriors may have lost, but Loccard recovered from the battle-field Bruce's heart and returned with it to Scotland, while Angus's intended inheritance remained intact, going to Simon, who took over the Lockhart name, line and property. This legality, rooted in feudalism, enabled a chain of hereditary incumbents to hold on to a property, as the survival of a name and family took precedence over the interests of any individual. As a result of Angus's death Simon, his sons and daughter maintained the Lockhart line in major part.

It may be senseless to write about a lost man but I was struck by the fact that Angus was Mum's favourite brother. Jock was much older and remote from her, while Simon, four years her senior, bullied her. Angus, seven years older, would intervene on her behalf. By all accounts he was kind, if not a bit dilatory in his correspondence while serving overseas. He took the trouble to write to Mum when she gained entry into Somerville College, Oxford and in his letter from Malaya two years later he is impressed that she is learning how to be a car mechanic.

With his medieval knightly ancestry was Angus an anachronism? His education, with its arcane language and practices, was hardly relevant to a man sent to an overcrowded island in southeast Asia to become chief-of-staff to some 3,000 men. Whatever else, his manner of speaking, choice of words, and conduct were synonymous with loyalty to King and country. Both brothers took part in campaigns that lost spectacularly, Jock at the Fall of France and Angus in the Fall of Singapore. Both found themselves in the wrong place at the wrong time.

One lost his leg, the other his life and each lost his castle. This kind of destruction was not exclusive to my mother's family. Up and down the country, old landed families were falling apart. Although the Largie Macdonalds and Lockharts forfeited their castles, they themselves failed to disintegrate or fade away. Dented though they were by the war they survived.

Unlike Jock with his casual brilliance, Angus was a good foot soldier for the Establishment. My regret is that I have found so little about him. No juicy letters, confessional diaries or searching memoirs. Just a few letters. We will never know what he thought of his regiment and the part Britain played in the war. Because Angus took his secrets to a watery grave, we can only surmise. Did he have a girl? Was he a virgin when he died? How did he feel about his future after the war? Did he look forward to owning his castle?

The displays of courage by Angus and his 'brother' officers in battle and their nonchalance towards danger, are to be applauded. No other fighting unit in the Malayan campaign earned greater respect than the Argylls, but their bravery and disregard for personal safety had, in the end, its limits. Psychiatrists affirm that men and women, when put under duress, invariably break. It's just a matter of time. It's not my place here to name the officers and men who cracked up, often many years after the end of the war. But there were many. Some suffered from years of depression. One or two even committed suicide. Often the bravest most afflected. Those who fought in the Malayan Campaign were indelibly damaged particularly as so many were imprisoned by the

Japanese, forced to build the Thai-Burma railway. Kenneth McLeod survived but for the rest of his life suffered from a number of ailments stemming from this period. They included amoebic dysentery, bacillary dysentery, hook worm, beriberi, ptomaine poisoning, ulcerated legs caused by leeches, malaria, dengue fever, jaundice, TB, and throat polyps.

Perhaps the most poignant of letters I received during my search for Angus was from Catherine Butcher, daughter of Regimental Sergeant-Major (RSM) Sandy Munnoch, photographed tramping through the mangrove swamps of Singapore island with Angus as adjutant and Ian Stewart, then the Battalion's second in command. Sergeant Munnoch survived imprisonment but at a relatively young age, while working as an instructor at Bradfield College, fractured his skull in a traffic accident. He died in 1956. After the British surrender, he was imprisoned at Kanchanabuli on the River Kwai in Thailand. In this prison camp he was ordered to cremate the bodies of men who had died of cholera. The cremations took place at night and afterwards Sergeant Munnoch would stand alone in the jungle to salute the dead men. When he returned to the camp the sergeant took the precaution of washing himself with Lysol disinfectant.

Although I was aware of the 60th anniversary in 2002 of the Fall of Singapore I had not then begun my research on Angus. But in 2003 I visited Hopie Maitland, Mum's childhood friend who used to stay at Largie for lessons in English, Arithmetic, and French with governess, Miss Harding. Hopie knew all the Macdonalds and had explored their home from top to bottom, from boot-hole to Broonie's room at the top of the castle. Before I left, I asked Hopie what had happened to Angus (at that time I knew next to nothing about him).

"Oh! It was so sad," she said elliptically.

"With all that disaster in the family," I ventured, "why didn't the Broonie take better care of them?"

"Yes," she said solemnly. "That's what he was meant to do. But he didn't, did he?"

ACKNOWLEDGEMENT AND BIBLIOGRAPHIC INFORMATION

I KNEW NEXT TO NOTHING when I began my search on Angus. All I could lay my hands on were three of his letters and some anecdotes about him from elderly individuals. After gaining material from the British Army, my uncle's schools, his university college and regiment, I discovered relevant information on internet websites and in the columns of contemporary newspapers. In my attempt, however, to mould some version of the truth from these scattered fragments, I incurred many debts. I thank my family for their enthusiasm and encouragement. My daughter Julia was at all times, supportive; so were sisters, Lis and Janet Gladstone; Hamish Macdonald Lockhart provided help and assistance in writing and producing a previously published private version of Angus's story. This volume helped supply me with material for *Largie Castle: A Rifled Nest*. Shian Maclean, the only living family member who remembers Angus, shared her memories of him with me; Sir John Maxwell Macdonald Bt., and Richard Willan gave permission to reproduce images, the former of Largie Castle, the latter, a portrait of Violet and Daisy Crabbe.

I also was very fortunate in being able to correspond with, and even meet some offspring and nephews, including a niece, of Angus's Argyll colleagues: Major James Greenfield, son of Brigadier Hector Greenfield, Angus's commanding officer in India and Malaya, generously informed me of the connection between his family and the Macdonalds and helped me gain valuable insight into his father's personal and professional association with Angus. I am particularly indebted to him for his advice on army terminology and military lore. Thanks also to David Gibbon, son of Lieutenant-Colonel Aubrey Gibbon, OBE (Order of the British Empire), Catherine Butcher, daughter of RSM (Regimental Sergeant Major) Munnoch and Margaret Gibb, niece of Drummer Hardie for their personal and original insights into the battalion and its personnel. Michael Wainwright kindly sent me a copy of his carefully researched monograph on his uncle, Captain Michael

Blackwood. In this document, I found a list of names, which was of great advantage to me in my research as I contacted several officers, men, and women on it. I also appreciated Michael's detailed account and accompanying map of our uncles' escape across Sumatra after the Fall of Singapore. The nephew of Lieutenant Colonel Angus Rose, Major Hugh Rose, tirelessly furnished me with important details for my narrative.

Perhaps the most poignant moment in my research was when I made contact with veteran Argyll officers, all in their nineties, who served with Angus. In spite of his very poor health, which he had suffered from since his captivity by the Japanese, the late Captain Kenneth McLeod made a huge effort during the final year of his life to write to me about Angus and the life they led in Singapore before the Japanese invasion of December 1941.When I wrote in 2010 to the late Colonel Peter Farquhar, I didn't expect an answer as nobody in the UK had heard from him for over a decade.However, soon after I sent him a letter, he responded with warmth and friendliness from a nursing home near Melbourne in Australia, affirming his esteem for Angus who, he deemed, was a 'very professional soldier and good friend.' Although in Singapore, the late Major Gordon Smith only knew Angus by sight, he helped by providing me with details on the battalion and its officers. I'm immensely grateful to these officers whose memories assisted me in bringing to life my uncle's story.

The most exciting synchronicity for me in my search for Angus occurred when I discovered Dr Marjorie DesRosier, nursing professor at the University of Washington. She has undertaken exhaustive research on Hopital Temporaire, the unit in France where my grandfather volunteered during World War One. As a result of our email correspondence, Dr DesRosier recommended books to read, advised on where to go for further research and even informed me, on request, as to what kind of man my grandfather was. Until that date, I did not know.

I tried to visit all the places where Angus had lived and served. Fiona MacAlister organised a visit to Kintyre where we met the late Captain Ian MacDonald, ex-President of the Kintyre Antiquarian Society and Fellow of the Society of Antiquaries (Scotland), who was a mine of information on the locality. I am also grateful to John Macdonald of Tayinloan, whose mother was the cook at Largie Castle, Winnie Byrd, daughter of Ronald Reid, the Largie gamekeeper and sister of Lance Corporal James Reid, Graham McCulloch, who conveyed Julia and me in his boat to Cara and Duncan McIsaac of the Glenbarr War Memorial. For Angus's education I owe a debt to Nick Hodson of The Old West Downs Society, Patrick Herring (house-master of Moberley's), Squadron Leader Dick Stanton, Oxford University Air Squadron, and to archivists, Suzanne Foster (Winchester College), and Dr Robin Darwall Smith (Magdalen College). In Stirling, Rod Mackenzie, Deputy Curator, and Archie Wilson, Museum Attendant, of The Argylls Museum were of enormous help, for which many thanks. Also Dr Alastair Massie of the National Army Museum in Chelsea (London). I cannot forget Henry Hopkinson's humour, hospitality and help, nor the willingness of Simon and Georgina Hawtrey Woore to assist. To all, I offer my thanks.

While visiting Malaysia, Daniel and Jus Kassim and their two young children, were extremely welcoming as our hosts, meeting us from the railway station at Kuala Lumpur, answering my innumerable questions on the Malayan Campaign and driving us to Port Dickson, past old rubber plantations and to a part of the jungle itself. When we departed, Daniel chauffeured us to the Cameron Highlands where we stayed at the Smoke House hotel. Andrew Hwang offered penetrating thoughts on Angus's role as chief-of-staff of the brigade in Malaya. He also showed us many old colonial buildings and sites in Kuala Lumpur. Back in the UK, Anthony Warin, son of William and Nora, the original owners of The Smoke House, explained over the telephone how his father set up the Smoke House and sent me an advert of the hotel shortly after it was founded in the 30s. Michael Pether from New Zealand made contact with me after I placed a notice in the journal of the Malayan Volunteers Group and shared the results of his painstaking research on the passenger lists of several ships, including the Rooseboom. I owe thanks also to Doug Taylor of Newtyle near Dundee, who let me see and sit in his beautifully renovated Fiat 500.

I CONSULTED many documents, papers and books, including official and regimental histories, memoirs and diaries. Without access to Kit (Margaret) McNeil's *MacAlister Chronicles*, I would not have been able to describe in such detail the Kintyre of Angus's early childhood. For the history of the Lockharts and Macdonalds, my uncle, Simon Macdonald Lockhart's *Seven Centuries: the History of the Lockharts of Lee and Carnwath*, which includes a chapter on the Macdonalds, was very helpful. Towards the chapters on Angus's education, I am indebted to Mark Hitchens' *West Downs: A Portrait of an English Prep School*, James Sabben-Clare's *Winchester College, After 606 Years (1382-1988)* and L.W.B. Brockliss, editor of Magdalen College, *Oxford: A History*. I owe huge thanks to my cousin, Charles Gordon Clark for his excellent, scholarly contribution to my efforts in creating this family history. Through his inspired and exhaustive research into the Crabbes, I was able to write about Angus's military forebears. Henry C. Day's *On a Troopship to India*, was an excellent source for my chapter on Angus's voyage to the sub-continent. John Masters' *Bugles and a Tiger*, helped me to communicate the vagaries of Indian buses in Angus's time. For my uncle's army career, Brigadier Ian M. Stewart's *The Thin Red Line, 2nd Argylls in Malaya* and Audrey Holmes McCormick and Jonathan Moffatt's *Moon over Malaya* were crucial. Audrey was phenomenally helpful and resourceful in her assistance, not least in contacting veteran Argylls and gaining valuable information. Two of Angus's Argyll friends wrote about the campaign and I have drawn from both: Angus Rose's *Who Dies Fighting?*, published two years after the British defeat in Malaya and David Wilson's *The Sum of Things*, which came out in 2001. For the Japanese invasion of Malaya, I relied chiefly on Major-General S. Woodburn Kirby, *The History of the Second World War,*

The War Against Japan, Vol. 1, The Loss of Singapore, Lieutenant-General A.E. Percival's *The War In Malaya* and the excellent diary of Lieutenant-Colonel C.C. Deakin. From the National Archives at Kew, I accessed eyewitness accounts (S.G. Taylor's lively description in particular) of Angus's escape from Singapore and reports on the sinking of the Rooseboom.

Finally, I'm very grateful to Elihu Blotnick for his courage and willingness to publish my book and for his clear-sighted advice on how to organise the text so that it appeals to a wide readership. His perspective on my uncle, family, and country is invaluable and is all the more inspiring because his base is from a different culture to my own.

Lightning Source UK Ltd.
Milton Keynes UK
UKOW03f0223210417
299566UK00001B/143/P